Students with Autism Spectrum Disorders

Effective Instructional Practices

L. Juane Heflin
Georgia State University

Donna Fiorino Alaimo
Private Consultant

PEARSON

Merrill
Prentice Hall

Upper Saddle River, New Jersey
Columbus, Ohio

Library of Congress Cataloging-in-Publication Data

Heflin, Juane.
    Students with autism spectrum disorders: effective instructional
practices/L. Juane Heflin, Donna Fiorino Alaimo.
       p. ; cm.
    Includes bibliographical references and index.
    ISBN 0-13-118170-X
      1. Autism—Patients—Rehabilitation. 2. Students—Mental health.
3. Autistic children—Education.   I. Alaimo, Donna Fiorino.
II. Title.
    [DNLM: 1. Autistic Disorder—psychology. 2. Education, Special—methods.
3. Teaching—methods. LC 4717 H461s 2007]
RC553.A88H44 2007
616.85′88206—dc22

2006001215

Vice President and Executive Publisher:
Jeffery W. Johnston
Senior Editor: Allyson P. Sharp
Editorial Assistant: Kathleen S. Burk
Production Editor: Sheryl Glicker Langner
Production Coordination: *TechBooks/GTS*
York, PA

Design Coordinator: Diane C. Lorenzo
Cover Design: Aaron Dixon
Cover Image: Images.com
Production Manager: Laura Messerly
Director of Marketing: Ann Castel Davis
Marketing Manager: Autumn Purdy
Marketing Coordinator: Brian Mounts

This book was set in 10/12 Garamond Book by TechBooks/GTS Companies, York, PA.
It was printed and bound by R.R. Donnelley & Sons Company. The cover was printed by
R. R. Donnelley & Sons Company.

Pearson Education Ltd.
Pearson Education Singapore Pte. Ltd.
Pearson Education Canada, Ltd.
Pearson Education–Japan

Pearson Education Australia Pty. Limited
Pearson Education North Asia Ltd.
Pearson Educación de Mexico, S.A. de C.V.
Pearson Education Malaysia Pte. Ltd.

10 9 8 7 6 5 4 3 2 1
ISBN: 0-13-118170-X

Preface

Most people who choose to dedicate their professional lives to the study of Autism Spectrum Disorders (ASD) do so because of one child. Many professionals remember the first individual with ASD they met, a meeting that initiated a lifelong journey of discovery and fascination. Because of broadened public awareness and an expansion of the confines of the spectrum disorders, more individuals are being identified as having ASD, so more people may begin the journey.

Our intent in writing this text was to provide a roadmap for the educators who spend thousands of hours each year studying, planning, collaborating, and instructing one of the most unique and challenging populations of students. Drawing upon our own experiences as teachers and teacher trainers, we have organized the text around the questions usually asked in regard to students with ASD. For educators who are just beginning their careers, this book provides a systematic approach for addressing instructional considerations in the order in which they tend to emerge as priorities. For experienced educators, this resource allows for the refinement and advancement of their professional craft. The outcome is that educators should feel confident that the programming they are providing is making a difference in the lives of the students they serve.

To engage readers and reassure them that they do not have to know everything the first time they meet students with ASD, we introduce Ms. Harris. In the opening chapter, Ms. Harris is just completing her cross-categorical special education certification program. Many states have begun offering such certifications (referred to by various names such as *cross-categorical, noncategorical, generic, interrelated,* and so forth) and tend to rely less on categorical certifications. Among the states that still provide categorical certification programs through licensing agencies and universities, few offer a specialized certification in ASD. As the population of students with ASD grows, this may change. However, there will still be many educators who, like Ms. Harris, find themselves certified to teach a variety of students without benefit of in-depth training on any one of the disabilities.

Readers will follow Ms. Harris through the text as she experiences one challenge after another in her quest to be the most effective teacher she can for a delightful group of students who have some very unusual learning profiles. Chapter 1 provides an overview of characteristics associated with ASD, discusses the challenges in diagnosis, and mentions the separate process for determining eligibility for special education services. Chapter 2 reviews the history of the recognition of ASD as unique disabilities and discusses the fascinating research that has been conducted to identify what causes the spectrum disorders. Volatile issues such as changing prevalence rates and the role of environmental toxins (e.g., vaccines) are addressed. Controversies surrounding the development of effective programming are discussed in Chapter 3 and guidelines for effective collaboration are presented.

In Chapter 4, Ms. Harris is guided through the considerations for establishing an instructional context that has the highest likelihood of supporting the unique learning needs of students with ASD. The chapter on sensory issues is presented early in the text (Chapter 5), not because sensory issues are a priority for students with ASD but because Ms. Harris, like other educators, needs to recognize that self-stimulatory and stereotypic behaviors often serve adaptive functions. Early recognition of this fact may provide an alternate perspective about which behaviors are considered problems and lead to insight regarding a source of powerful reinforcement that may be useful when providing instruction.

Chapter 6 summarizes and differentiates applied behavior analysis (ABA) and Discrete Trial Training (DTT). In Chapter 7, Ms. Harris is kicked and bitten (but admits she should have seen it coming) and learns about the powerful technology of providing positive behavioral support. A brief review of typical communication development contrasted with communication and language development in individuals with ASD is provided in Chapter 8, followed by descriptions of empirically based strategies for increasing communication and verbal behavior. Chapter 9 discusses assessment and intervention for social behavior, believed by some to be the core deficit in ASD.

Differentiated instruction for students with ASD is presented in Chapter 10, with particular emphasis on the core content areas of written expression, reading, spelling, and mathematics. Chapter 11 extends beyond curricular areas and describes strategies that can be useful in small group instruction as well as inclusive environments for promoting engagement and achievement. This chapter also discusses the perils of homework and summer school. The text concludes with an epilogue that summarizes some of the information Ms. Harris has learned.

Although the *DSM-IV-TR* uses the term "Pervasive Developmental Disorders (PDD)" to refer to the population of students described in this text, we concur with the growing body of advocates who prefer the term "Autism Spectrum Disorders (ASD)" and will use this term throughout. We recognize that there are more males with ASD than females but have alternated pronoun references between "he" and "she" in order to accentuate that many of the students with ASD are female. We realize that some of the trademarked names will change over the years, as programs used today are replaced by programs currently being developed; however, we wanted to provide concrete examples of some of the available technologies and programs. We have also cited references that are older than 10 years to provide a historical context. As a framework for learning, key terms are listed at the beginning of each chapter and defined within the chapter. At the end of each chapter there is a set of discussion questions and activities designed to reinforce and extend the material covered. Learning with Ms. Harris, readers will gain the tools needed to enhance the quality of life and promote independence for students functioning across the range and ages of Autism Spectrum Disorders.

Rather than being an 18-month project, this text is the culmination of more than 25 years of fascination, heartbreak, and triumph. We hope it will be beneficial for anyone who is striving to understand and meet the needs of students with Autism Spectrum Disorders in an instructional context.

ACKNOWLEDGMENTS

JH:

My sincere appreciation is extended to the following individuals who have played separate roles in creating the cohesive whole of who I am:

- Dr. Ina Green, professor of psychology, who introduced me to the fascinating world of ASD in her undergraduate class at Abilene Christian University.
- Dr. Ivar Lovaas, who pioneered a future for individuals with ASD and made me wonder if slapping Pammy was necessary.
- Irma Muga and Mary Palmer, two extraordinary paraprofessionals who taught me much and who were willing to try new things even if they weren't doing what Ms. Harris had always done.
- Carlene Dennis, principal and exemplary leader, who believed I was competent even when she looked puzzled.
- Evelyn Bowen, who demonstrated unparalleled commitment as a social worker and ingrained in me the importance of working closely with families.
- Dr. Lyndall M. Bullock, Regent's Professor at the University of North Texas (UNT), who convinced me that I had a future teaching teachers.
- The university students at UNT, Stephen F. Austin State University, and Georgia State University, who questioned, learned, and applied their skills to truly make a difference in the lives of children, youth, and adults on the spectrum. A special thanks goes to the members of the fall 2004 class of EXC 7320 who turned a critical eye on earlier drafts of this text. Also to Sheila Connell, who shared pieces of her own life to make "David" come to life, and Chris Cox, who provided some of the photographs.

Heartfelt thanks also to:

- Allyson Sharp, who never lost her enthusiasm for the project and secured five anonymous reviewers who provided invaluable suggestions.
- The reviewers, for their comprehensive and insightful comments: Kevin J. Callahan, University of North Texas; Laura J. Hall, San Diego State University; Thomas S. Higbee, Utah State University; Brenda C. Seal, James Madison University; and Thomas Oliver Williams, Jr., Virginia Polytechnic Institute and State University.
- Karen Heflin, who demonstrated hidden talents in verifying references.
- And most importantly to Karen McCleskey, without whose assistance, support, and encouragement this text would not have been written.

DA:

Along my journey to learn what the compelling issues were for students with ASD, I am eternally grateful to the following individuals who taught me that to truly understand one must be like Sherlock Holmes and maintain an inquiring mind:

- Brandon, the mysterious preschooler who introduced me to the world of autism, was the catalyst that shaped my life's interest in supporting families and children with ASD.

- The students with ASD, their families, and colleagues in Fayette County who welcomed me into their lives and always bestowed upon me their total trust when I dared to be unconventional.

- Carolyn Colburn (OT) and Kim Pisor (behavior specialist), whose commitment to educating others on ASD made the years we worked together my most memorable and valuable experiences as we learned to savor the small steps and appreciate their importance.

Finally, my deepest and most sincere gratitude to the following individuals for their endless support during this project, without which my participation would have remained a dream rather than a reality:

- Dr. Heflin, mentor to aspiring teachers and future researchers, educator, and advocate for families and students with ASD. I am indebted to her for her confidence and unwavering patience (regardless of how frustrated she may have been with my zeal to keep reading and adding new information). I remain in awe of her extensive knowledge, which is the inspiration for me to learn all I can about ASD, yet realize there's always so much more to learn.

- Sherri Fasci, Leslie Gresham, students in the PETaL Program, and colleagues at Landmark: Without their understanding, indulgent flexibility, and prayers I would not have been able to accomplish this feat and honor His plan for me. Sherri and Leslie's tolerance truly model the meaning of grace.

- My parents, Palma and Joseph Fiorino, have always been the "Wind Beneath My Wings." They have been unyielding in their support so that I could feel comfortable taking advantage of this wonderful opportunity.

- Tom, my husband and best friend, whose infinite patience and dedication, words of encouragement, and sense of humor have enabled me to keep going when I didn't think I could and to whom I am forever thankful.

- My children and guiding stars, Joseph, Thomas, and Victoria, whose faith in me never faltered and who fervently believe that this text can make an impact on the lives of students with ASD. More than anyone else, they have endured the most and I am very proud of their unselfishness.

Note: The names assigned to the students in this text are special to us because they remind us of students we have taught. Please note, however, that we combined the characteristics of many students to create the student profiles in this text, and any resemblance to actual people is purely coincidental.

**MERRILL
PRENTICE HALL**

Teacher Preparation Classroom

See a demo at
www.prenhall.com/teacherprep/demo

Your Class. Their Careers. Our Future. Will your students be prepared?

We invite you to explore our new, innovative and engaging website and all that it has to offer you, your course, and tomorrow's educators! Organized around the major courses pre-service teachers take, the Teacher Preparation site provides media, student/teacher artifacts, strategies, research articles, and other resources to equip your students with the quality tools needed to excel in their courses and prepare them for their first classroom.

This ultimate on-line education resource is available at no cost, when packaged with a Merrill text, and will provide you and your students access to:

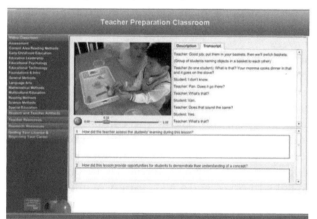

Online Video Library. More than 150 video clips—each tied to a course topic and framed by learning goals and Praxis-type questions—capture real teachers and students working in real classrooms, as well as in-depth interviews with both students and educators.

Student and Teacher Artifacts. More than 200 student and teacher classroom artifacts— each tied to a course topic and framed by learning goals and application questions— provide a wealth of materials and experiences to help make your study to become a professional teacher more concrete and hands-on.

Research Articles. Over 500 articles from ASCD's renowned journal *Educational Leadership.* The site also includes Research Navigator, a searchable database of additional educational journals.

Teaching Strategies. Over 500 strategies and lesson plans for you to use when you become a practicing professional.

Licensure and Career Tools. Resources devoted to helping you pass your licensure exam; learn standards, law, and public policies; plan a teaching portfolio; and succeed in your first year of teaching.

How to ORDER *Teacher Prep* for you and your students:

For students to receive a *Teacher Prep* Access Code with this text, instructors **must** provide a special value pack ISBN number on their textbook order form. To receive this special ISBN, please email **Merrill.marketing@pearsoned.com** and provide the following information:
- Name and Affiliation
- Author/Title/Edition of Merrill text

Upon ordering *Teacher Prep* for their students, instructors will be given a lifetime *Teacher Prep* Access Code.

Discover the Merrill Education Resources for Special Education Website

Technology is a constantly growing and changing aspect of our field that is creating a need for new content and resources. To address this emerging need, Merrill Education has developed an online learning environment for students, teachers, and professors alike to complement our products—the *Merrill Education Resources for Special Education* Website. This content-rich website provides additional resources specific to this book's topic and will help you—professors, classroom teachers, and students—augment your teaching, learning, and professional development.

Our goal with this partnership and initiative is to build on and enhance what our products already offer. For this reason, the content for our user-friendly website is organized by topic and provides teachers, professors, and students with a variety of meaningful resources all in one location. With this website, we bring together the best of what Merrill has to offer: text resources, video clips, web links, tutorials, and a wide variety of information on topics of interest to general and special educators alike. Rich content, applications, and competencies further enhance the learning process.

The *Merrill Education Resources for Special Education* Website includes:

- Video clips specific to each topic, with questions to help you evaluate the content and make crucial theory-to-practice connections.

- Thought-provoking critical analysis questions that students can answer and turn in for evaluation or that can serve as basis for class discussions and lectures.

- Access to a wide variety of resources related to classroom strategies and methods, including lesson planning and classroom management.

- Information on all the most current relevant topics related to special and general education, including CEC and Praxis standards, IEPs, portfolios, and professional development.

- Extensive web resources and overviews on each topic addressed on the website.
- A search feature to help access specific information quickly.

To take advantage of these and other resources, please visit the *Merrill Education Resources for Special Education* Website at

http://www.prenhall.com/heflin

Brief Contents

Contents

3   *Collaborating to Develop Effective Programs*   85

6 *Using Applied Behavior Analytic Instructional Strategies*   171

7 *Programming for Challenging Behavior*   199

9 *Enhancing Socialization and Social Competence*   271

10 *Promoting Academic Skill Acquisition*   301

CHAPTER 1

Identifying and Describing Individuals with Autism Spectrum Disorders

KEY TERMS

Aspergers

Autism

Childhood Disintegrative Disorder (CDD)

Delayed Echolalia

Developmental Disability

Diagnostic and Statistical Manual of Mental Disorders (DSM-IV-TR)

Differential Diagnosis

High-functioning Autism (HFA)

Immediate Echolalia

ICD-10 Classification of Mental and Behavioural Disorder

Perseverations

Pervasive Developmental Disorder (PDD)

Pervasive Developmental Disorder-Not Otherwise Specified (PDD-NOS)

Rett's Disorder

Triad of Deficits

❖ LEARNING WITH MS. HARRIS: Life After Graduation

Shawna Harris was excited about the prospect of her new career. The last semester of her cross-categorical certification program in special education was almost over. Just a few more days in student teaching and a couple of final exams and she would be finished. Student teaching had been challenging. Ms. Harris was surprised how much time her supervising teacher spent on administration and how it seemed that students were taking state-mandated tests every time she turned around. And there was that one little incident of getting locked in the supply closet by students who couldn't pass up the golden opportunity. But she was wiser now, and her student teaching evaluations had been excellent.

As Ms. Harris walked through the front doors of the school for her last day of student teaching, the principal spotted her and motioned for her to come over to him. He had wanted to hire Ms. Harris, but wasn't going to have any openings. However, a principal at another school had some vacancies for the fall and had asked him if he knew anyone who might be available. Was Ms. Harris interested? She had submitted her application to the personnel office in the district but knew that it was a popular district with very little turnover. Here was a chance! Her stomach fluttering, Ms. Harris said, "Yes!" and got directions so she could stop by after school and meet the other principal.

When she arrives at Phillips Elementary, most of the students and staff have left. The secretary is taking orders for Field Day T-shirts from a few parents, but stops to usher Ms. Harris to the principal's office. The inter-view goes well. The principal, Ms. Stokes, seems to be very organized as well as committed to her students, which impresses Ms. Harris. Ms. Stokes asks Ms. Harris questions about her approach to classroom management and what she would do if a student wadded up his work and threw it at her. Ms. Stokes seems satisfied with Ms. Harris's answers and tells her that the opening is for a teacher who will provide intensive instruction to a group of children with varying disabilities, most of whom are on the autism spectrum. In addition to having her own classroom, Ms. Harris will be expected to support the children when they participate in general education environments. Ms. Stokes indicates that the personnel office will call Ms. Harris later if she is chosen for the job.

As Ms. Harris thanks the principal for her time, she feverishly begins to make a mental list of information she needs to look up. She feels confident that her college program has prepared her to provide instruction, but because her training was cross-categorical, she needs to learn more about the characteristics of Autism Spectrum Disorders and how instruction should be differentiated. She has a vague recollection of reading about students with autism and their educational needs in some of her college classes, but it was all very hazy. How many disorders are there on the autism spectrum? What are the differences among them? What will the children be like? Will they be aggressive? Will they be easily upset? She has a quick flashback to a scene from Rain Man *in which the smoke detector goes off and Dustin Hoffman becomes very agitated, but instead of leaving, runs into a corner and covers his ears, rocking back and forth. Feeling excited and nervous at the same time, Ms. Harris makes a beeline for her apartment to get out her notes and books. "So much for a lazy summer," Ms. Harris thinks. "It's time to get busy!"*

There has been a tremendous evolution in the definitions of the disorders that comprise the autism spectrum since Leo Kanner (1943) and Hans Asperger (1944) first described the syndromes they observed (a more complete histori-cal overview is provided in Chapter 2). Commonalities among the Autism

Spectrum Disorders (ASD) are based on a "triad" of core deficits (Wing & Gould, 1979). This chapter describes the triad of deficits and discusses variations within each of these core areas. The psychiatric classification system that places ASD under the broad umbrella term of **Pervasive Developmental Disorder (PDD)** is used as a framework for describing the characteristics of the five spectrum disorders. The process for diagnosing ASD and determining eligibility for special education services are addressed. The chapter concludes with a summary of the definitive conclusions that can be drawn about ASD.

CHARACTERISTICS OF AUTISM SPECTRUM DISORDERS

Individuals with ASD demonstrate great variability in their behaviors, skills, preferences, functioning, and learning needs that change as they grow (Hollander et al., 1998; Lord, Cook, Leventhal, & Amaral, 2000). The effort to characterize ASD is fraught with the need to make generalizations that may not always adequately describe a particular individual. With this caution in mind, characteristics that are commonly associated with individuals on the spectrum fall into a **triad of deficits** in the areas of:

1. Communication
2. Socialization
3. Interests and activities

Figure 1.1 contains a Venn diagram of the three core deficits. The diagram illustrates that not everyone will have the same degree of impairment across the spectrum disorders.

Communication

Communication abilities among individuals with ASD vary from a total lack of spoken language or recognizable communication to highly sophisticated language (Lord & Paul, 1997). There may be a marked absence or delay in the use of spoken language with little attempt to use alternative forms of

FIGURE 1.1
Triad of Core Deficits in ASD

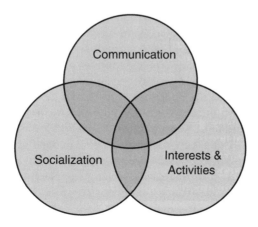

communication such as gestures (Baranek, 1999; Osterling & Dawson, 1994). Individuals on the spectrum who want something inaccessible may take another person's hand and lead the person to the object, but the overture is not communicative in nature; it is a way to accomplish an end and is referred to as using another person as a tool (Wetherby & Prizant, 2005). At least one third of all individuals with ASD fail to develop spoken language (Bryson, 1996).

Those who develop spoken language usually manifest obvious differences in their use of language (Wing, 1997). Many engage in "echolalia," which is the repetition of others' speech (Schuler, Prizant, & Wetherby, 1997). - **Immediate echolalia** is the repetition of something just heard (e.g., What's your name?—What's your name?). **Delayed echolalia** is the repetition of something heard after some amount of time has passed (e.g., repeating scripts from videos and television programs). Echolalia can lead to the commonly observed occurrence of pronoun reversals (Kanner, 1943). Since the child has heard, "Do you want a cookie? I want one!" he may refer to himself as *you* and the other person as *I*. Interestingly, some individuals with ASD who use spoken language demonstrate good use of irregular verbs, probably because they are repeating what they have heard rather than attempting to apply rules of grammar (Van Meter, Fein, Morris, Waterhouse, & Allen, 1997). Irregular verbs are those that do not change tense predictably. For example, *-ed* is usually added to indicate past tense. *Walk* becomes *walked* if it happened yesterday. However, *get* does not become *getted*, but *got* as it changes tense. Typically developing children demonstrate many errors with irregular verbs as they overgeneralize the rules of grammar being learned. Possibly because they tend to repeat what they hear rather than apply rules of grammar, some children with ASD may not demonstrate these errors.

Echolalia may be spoken with the same inflection and intonation of the original speaker. When not using echolalia, the cadence and intonation of the words spoken by persons with ASD may have unusual qualities (Lord et al., 2000; Young, Diehl, Morris, Hyman, & Bennetto, 2005). Speech may sound as if it is generated by a machine, with little inflection or animation. Or the pitch may be too high, or every statement may sound like a question (Shriberg et al., 2001). The unusual sound and cadence of speech may be the feature that most immediately creates an impression that something is different about the individual (VanBourgondien & Woods, 1992).

Individuals with ASD who acquire spoken language may have difficulties initiating or sustaining conversations with others (Ghaziuddin & Gerstein, 1996; Landa, 2000). They may use language in unusual ways. As an example, one five-year-old with autism was told that he could not have a cookie until he ate his fish sticks. The little boy said he did not want square food, he wanted round food. Subsequently, he asked for food by shape and sometimes color. Instead of asking for grapes, he requested green oval food.

In additional to unusual use of language, individuals with ASD may have difficulty with the pragmatics of language: knowing how and when social convention dictates that it is appropriate to say certain things and not others (Volkmar, Carter, Grossman, & Klin, 1997). For example, the individual may make a comment about someone being overweight without realizing that the person may be offended. Difficulty with pragmatics also includes an inability to understand nonliteral language such as idioms, figures of speech, and abstract concepts (Strandburg et al., 1993). Telling a child with an ASD to "hop to it" might result in the child literally hopping across the floor. This inability to understand the nuances and symbolism of language translates into an absence of imaginative play.

The nonverbal aspects of communication are also impaired in ASD and may be significantly associated with later language development (Charman et al., 2005). The absence of nonverbal behaviors, such as gesturing, may be early predictors of subsequent manifestation of ASD (Alexander, 1995; Vostanis et al., 1998). Individuals with ASD tend to have difficulty using eye gaze appropriately, failing to make eye contact to initiate or sustain a conversation and being unable to simultaneously attend to objects or events (Wetherby et al., 2004). Some have noted that individuals with autism may prefer to use their peripheral vision, standing beside people and items to look at them with fleeting gazes out of the corners of their eyes (Tiegerman-Farber, 2002), possibly eliminating some of the visual stimuli that could be overwhelming. Individuals with ASD may also fail to use gestures and facial expressions to communicate.

In summary, deviations in communication may include:

- Absent or delayed verbal language
- Failure to use alternative forms of communication such as gesturing
- Using others as "tools"
- Echolalia (immediate or delayed)
- Pronoun reversal
- Difficulty understanding nonliteral language
- Impairments in nonverbal communication

Socialization

Some have suggested that the social impairment in ASD is the defining component of the syndrome (Kanner, 1943; Waterhouse, Fein, & Modahl, 1996) and may be correlated highly with language function (Lord & Paul, 1997). Typically developing infants show a preference for looking at people's eyes (Haith, Bergman, & Moore, 1979) and for social stimuli over inanimate stimuli (Spelke, Phillips, & Woodward, 1995). In contrast, infants later diagnosed with ASD are retrospectively described by their parents as avoiding eye contact (Volkmar, Cohen, & Paul, 1986) and showing a strong interest in objects rather than people (Dawson, Meltzoff, Osterling, Rinaldi, & Brown, 1998; Swettenham et al., 1998). They may smile less frequently and vocalize less (Maestro, Casella, Milone, Muratori, & Palacio-Espasa, 1999). By 2 years of age, typically developing children orient reliably to another person's voice, even if the person is not calling the child's name. Young children with ASD may not show this preference for human voices (Klin, 1992; Kuhl, Coffey-Corina, Padden, & Dawson, 2005). Failure to respond when their names are called may be a fairly reliable predictor of ASD (Osterling & Dawson, 1994).

Eye gaze, a critical component of socialization, has been studied extensively among individuals with ASD. Lack of eye contact has been noted (Adrien, 1991), which makes initiating and sustaining interactions very difficult as well as severely curtailing the information received from others. Eye gaze is critical for the establishment of joint attention and has been noted as absent very early in life for individuals with ASD (Wimpory, Hobson, Williams, & Nash, 2000). The child may not follow another person's gaze and may not try to get someone to look at what she finds interesting (Wetherby, Prizant, & Hutchinson, 1998). Failure to follow another's gaze may have detrimental implications for language development (Dawson et al., 2004) because the child may not notice the object the adult is looking at and labeling (Baldwin, 1995). Unlike children with ASD, typically developing children try to get another person's attention to look at something they find fascinating (e.g., they point up to the sky as an airplane flies overhead). In addition to pointing up to the sky, the child looks back at the other person to see if she or he is also looking up. Moreover, typically developing children are usually aware of their parent's presence and will look at the parent fairly frequently, which is called *referencing*. For example, typically developing children who drop or break something quickly look at the caregiver to see if that person noticed or is upset. Children with ASD may not point to indicate interest or engage in social referencing (Cox et al., 1999). However, they may point to communicate their wants as frequently as typically developing children (Stone, Ousley, Yoder, Hogan, & Hepburn, 1997).

Individuals with ASD tend to appear oblivious to the social aspects of interpersonal relationships. They may act as though they are not interested in being around others and may not act in accordance with social conventions (Lord & Magill-Evans, 1995; Sigman & Ruskin, 1999). They do not tend to share information about themselves with others. Those who develop spoken language tend to share facts and details about favorite topics rather than about how they are feeling or what something means to them (Ghaziuddin & Gerstein, 1996). The lack of behaviors important for social reciprocity impedes the development of relationships and friendships.

In summary, deviations in socialization may include:

- Being oblivious to the presence of others
- Showing disregard for social conventions
- Failing to orient to another's voice
- Lack of joint attention and social referencing
- Preferring to share only facts about favorite topics with others
- Having few reciprocal relationships

Interests and Activities

Individuals with ASD may demonstrate a narrow range of interests that are unusual by developmental standards. Some of this may be attributed to a tendency to prefer objects over people (Dawson et al., 1998) and specifically to prefer parts of objects rather than the comprehensive whole (Rinehart, Bradshaw,

Moss, Brereton, & Tonge, 2000). For instance, a child may turn a toy car upside down and spin the wheels incessantly, rather than roll the car around. Or the child may be able to take equipment apart and put it back together. The child may prefer to list all the stats for the baseball players rather than talk about an actual game. Or the child may prefer to complete jigsaw puzzles with the pieces turned upside down so that the distracting picture is not visible.

The preference for the details of objects rather than social stimuli has been demonstrated in fascinating studies of eye gaze in which individuals with ASD are shown to focus on physical features such as light switches and lamps rather than attending to people (Klin, Jones, Schultz, Volkmar, & Cohen, 2002a). When individuals with ASD do look at people, they tend to look at mouths, shoulders, or other body parts rather than eyes (Klin, Jones, Schultz, Volkmar, & Cohen, 2002b). Older children with autism may recognize people by their lower facial features (Langdell, 1978). This tendency to focus on features other than the eyes has negative implications for the ability of individuals with ASD to take in important social information (Klin et al, 1999; Schultz et al., 2000), although facial recognition appears to be better in older and more cognitively able individuals with ASD (Boucher & Lewis, 1992). Fixation on mouths and objects instead of eyes correlates with poorer social functioning (Klin et al., 2002b).

In addition to relating better to objects, and possibly isolated parts of objects, individuals with ASD tend to behave in a restricted fashion, with little variability in their behavior (Bregman, 2005). For example, an individual might be very interested in placing objects in a row and will persist in this activity for an extended period of time. Activities that are repeated for long periods of time are called **perseverations.** Individuals with ASD may perseverate on their favorite topics or activities if left uninterrupted and may become agitated if they are interrupted.

Restrictions in interests and activities may also be seen in an insistence on sameness (Lewis & Bodfish, 1998). Individuals with autism may become upset if furniture is rearranged, the route to school is different, or their bedtime routine is altered (Volkmar et al., 1997).

Evidence of restricted interests and activities includes repetitive motor movements, often called *stereotypies* and *self-stimulatory behaviors,* which conform to a repetitive general pattern and serve no obvious purpose. Self-stimulatory behaviors can take countless forms, such as hand flapping, head weaving, rocking, making facial grimaces, and so forth. All typically developing infants engage in self-stimulation and stereotypy (Thelen, 1979, 1981), and infants between 9 and 12 months of age with developmental delays may demonstrate higher rates of self-stimulatory behavior than infants who are later diagnosed with ASD (Baranek, 1999). These repetitive behaviors usually become more pronounced in children with ASD between 2 and 5 years of age (Lord, 1995; Losche, 1990). Although young children with ASD may engage in self-stimulatory behaviors at the same rate as their peers matched on mental age, the children with ASD tend to engage in more gross motor behaviors and focus more exclusively on the behavior (Smith & Van Houten, 1996). Early in the study of ASD, it was believed that stereotypic and self-stimulatory behaviors served no purpose and should be eliminated (Rincover, 1986). However, current understanding posits self-stimulatory and stereotypic behavior as adaptive (Chapter 5 contains a more complete discussion).

Although sensory differences are not listed in the *DSM-IV-TR* criteria for the subtypes of PDD, both Kanner (1943) and Wing (1969) describe unusual sensory responses and sensory-seeking behaviors. Indeed, the commonly identified behaviors of failing to orient to name and demonstrating problems with eye gaze may be indicative of underlying sensory issues (Baranek, 1999). Retrospective video analysis and parental reports consistently document qualitative differences in sensory functioning in children with ASD (Adrien et al., 1993; Baranek, 1999; Rogers, Hepburn, & Wehner, 2003), although there is a great deal of variability in sensory responsiveness (Baranek, 2002). Descriptive studies have identified that 42–80% of individuals with ASD demonstrate unusual sensory responses, which include rubbing surfaces, finger licking, body rocking, and failing to respond to particular visual and auditory stimuli (Kientz & Dunn, 1997; Rapin, 1996; Volkmar, Cohen, Bregman, Hooks, & Stevenson, 1989). These individuals may cover their ears if they hear a noise they do not like (e.g., fire alarm, toilet flushing) or may pull away if someone else attempts to touch them (Baranek, 1999). The stereotypies commonly seen in individuals with ASD may indicate lack of responsiveness or exaggerated responsiveness to sensory input (Ornitz, 1985).

In summary, restricted activities and interests are characterized by:

- Unusual interests that are few in number
- Interest in parts of objects or isolated facts
- Perseverative engagement in favorite activities
- Insistence on sameness
- Repetitive motor movements (self-stimulatory behaviors or stereotypies)
- Unusual responses to sensory stimuli

Other differences among those with ASD can include varying levels of intellectual functioning or the presence of other medical conditions. They may demonstrate deficits in adaptive functioning that are not predicted by cognitive functioning (Liss et al., 2001). These characteristics, however, are considered less pivotal in defining most of the spectrum disorders.

PERVASIVE DEVELOPMENTAL DISORDERS IN THE *DSM-IV-TR*

In the United States, the American Psychiatric Association has provided a classification system for differences in behavior and learning since 1951. The classification system is described in the current edition of the ***Diagnostic and Statistical Manual of Mental Disorders,*** which is the text revision of the fourth edition (***DSM-IV-TR***) (APA, 2000). An international diagnostic system also exists in the form of the ***ICD-10 Classification of Mental and Behavioural Disorders,*** currently in its 10th revision (***ICD-10***) (WHO, 1993). The *ICD-10* lists eight types of Pervasive Developmental Disorders and is used by the international community and by researchers. At this time, the *ICD-10* is not used by most practitioners in the United States so it will not be discussed here.

The *DSM-IV-TR* lists five subtypes of ASD under the umbrella category of Pervasive Developmental Disorders. They are:

- Autistic disorder (term used in *DSM-IV-TR*)
- Asperger's disorder (term used in *DSM-IV-TR*)
- Rett's disorder
- Childhood disintegrative disorder
- PDD-NOS (not otherwise specified)

The following brief descriptions of each subtype provide a general idea of how the triad of deficits manifest across the subtypes—not the tools to diagnose a disorder. With these broad descriptions comes a caution. Individuals with ASD represent a heterogeneous population. An oft-quoted phrase is, "If you've seen one child with Autism Spectrum Disorders, you've seen one child with Autism Spectrum Disorders." Few generalizations can be made and none of these descriptions can adequately describe any one individual. Likewise, there are significant inconsistencies even among individuals with the same diagnostic label.

Autistic Disorder

This term describes individuals who are most similar to the children Kanner described in 1943. Synonyms for autistic disorder include *autism, early infantile autism, childhood autism,* and *Kannerian autism.*

To be identified with **autism,** an individual must show unusual behavior in the areas of communication, socialization, and interests and activities prior to the age of 3 years. Some students are not diagnosed before that age, so the examiner may have to assess the presence of the criteria retrospectively to determine whether they were present prior to age 3. As many as 35–40% of individuals with autism do not develop spoken language (Mesibov, Adams, & Klinger, 1997). In addition to the deviations in communication, socialization, and range of activities and interests, only 25–33% of individuals with ASD have measured intelligence in the average or above average ranges (Fombonne, 1999), with the majority of individuals demonstrating full-scale IQ scores and developmental quotients in the range of mental retardation (Rutter, Bailey, Bolton, & LeCouteur, 1994). Individuals with autism who do not have mental retardation are often referred to as having **"high-functioning autism" (HFA)** (Klin, Pauls, Schultz, & Volkmar, 2005). Epilepsy and unusual electrical discharges in the brain have been noted in 35% of children with autism studied (Canitano, Luchetti, & Zappella, 2005), and there appears to be an increased risk among individuals with autism for developing seizure disorders in adolescence or early adulthood (Gillberg & Steffenburg, 1987; Volkmar & Nelson, 1990), possibly reducing life expectancy (Isager, Mouridsen, & Rich, 1999).

❖ LEARNING WITH MS. HARRIS: A Trip to McDonald's

After spending several hours looking at books and articles about ASD in the university library (and she had sworn after she finished her last exam that she would never go there again!), Ms. Harris was famished. She stopped at McDonald's for a late lunch. As she looked over some of her notes while munching on her fries, Ms. Harris heard a commotion coming from two booths away. A child, whom Ms. Harris guessed to be about eight years old, was screaming and trying to get out of the booth across the body of a woman who was desperately trying to keep him in his seat. As Ms. Harris watched, the weary woman gave up and allowed the child to leave the booth. The boy immediately stopped screaming and stood at the end of the booth, reaching across to get his chicken nuggets and alternately eating one and then jumping up and down while wiggling his fingers in front of his eyes. The woman, noticing Ms. Harris's astonished look, said defensively, "He has autism. We have sat in this booth every Wednesday for the last two years. Someone has ripped the vinyl seat. He doesn't want to sit on it."

"Oh," said Ms. Harris. "This is my lucky day! I'm trying to learn everything I can about autism. Would you be willing to tell me about your son?" Quickly gauging the number of chicken nuggets remaining, the woman said, "We'll have to leave in less than five minutes. If you want to give me your phone number, I'll call you later tonight while Eric is watching a video."

Later that evening, Ms. Harris listened to a remarkable tale. Ms. Owens began, "Eric was a good baby, too good, in fact. He never cried to be picked up and never sought attention. He was the most content when left alone in his crib with a toy plastic toaster. No soft, cuddly comfort objects for our Eric! He always had to have the hard plastic toaster. When I did pick him up, Eric usually arched his back as if to get away from me. We went through early intervention services and Eric was identified as having autism. Eric does not talk to people, but repeats things he has heard. His favorite show is Wheel of Fortune *and he can emulate the opening segment of the show very realistically while saying 'Wheel . . . of . . . fortune!' He can say 'Git outta here!' so that it sounds just like his older sister (who is often overheard telling Eric, 'Get out of here!' when he is in her room). Eric has a hard time with change and frantically tried to find glasses-like objects to put on his dad's face when his father broke his own glasses and couldn't wear them. Eric doesn't like going from long pants to shorts when the seasons change (and vice versa), and has been known to insist on wearing his heavy winter coat to school well into April.*

"Of course, my life seems easy sometimes compared to my friend, Catherine. We met at a support group for parents of children with autism. She's probably about the only real friend I have anymore. It's just too hard

to explain Eric to other people, and we have found that it's just not worth it to try to take him out. And forget trying to find a babysitter! Anyway, Catherine's son, David, gets really agitated when things don't go the way he expects. For example, Catherine can't even put gas in the car unless David takes the nozzle off the pump. If she gets in a hurry and tries to do it herself, he gets so violent that she has to get back in the car, pull around the gas station, and start all over again. I honestly don't know how Catherine manages as a single mother, although quite a few of the parents I have met at the support group are divorced. The stress of raising a child with autism can be quite taxing on a marriage. Everything *revolves around the child—routines have to stay the same, we have to constantly be aware of how things smell or sound, and it is a full-time job trying to figure out what Eric wants or doesn't want."*

"What kinds of things does Eric like?" interjected Ms. Harris. She could hear the smile in Ms. Owens's voice as she answered, "Eric's favorite activity is playing with his trains. He lays elaborate track designs for his trains and then lines the trains up on the track. In fact, he gets very upset if anyone touches the tracks or the trains."

"How do you know he's upset?" Ms. Harris asked.

"That's easy," answered Ms. Owens. "When he's upset, Eric screams loudly and throws himself on the ground, taking down anything in close proximity. If someone gets close to him when he is upset, Eric tries to bite and scratch the other person."

"How does he let you know if he wants something?"

"Oh, he usually just gets what he wants himself," said Ms. Owens. "Now, if he can't reach or otherwise can't access what he wants (like when the VCR was broken because he stuffed train tracks in the opening), he takes one of our hands—it doesn't matter whose, just whoever is closer—and leads us over to what he wants. He puts our hand on the object and then watches our hand to see if we will make it work. If we fail to come through for him, he gets upset."

"What do you like most about Eric?" asked Ms. Harris. Ms. Owens replied warmly, "Eric is so innocent. He is unaware of social nuances, so if someone makes fun of him, it hurts me much more than it hurts him. He is amazed by the most trivial things and will get enamored with the sound of an insect, the inflection in someone's voice, the smell of the garbage truck . . . so many things. Eric reminds us of the little things in life that often go unnoticed. Uh-oh—it sounds as if his sister has turned off his video. I'd better go before the meltdown is too far gone."

Asperger's Disorder

More commonly referred to as Asperger syndrome or simply **Aspergers,** this condition, according to the *DSM-IV-TR,* is characterized by typical language development without any delays or communication impairments. However, parents of children with Aspergers may report delays in the emergence of language and language skills in adulthood that are not commensurate with age (Howlin, 2003), and there is debate regarding the validity of this criterion (Bregman, 2005). Some parents indicate that when their children started to talk, they talked constantly, using complete sentences to discuss their preferred topics. Although individuals with Aspergers do tend to demonstrate extensive vocabularies and can talk for long periods of time (Wing, 1981), there is a tendency for them to talk "at" rather than "to" a listener. They do not wait to see if the listener is interested in their topic and do not seem interested in giving the listener a chance to say anything (Ghaziuddin & Gerstein, 1996). For this reason, some have called individuals with Aspergers "little professors" (Safran, 2001). They tend to amass a great deal of information on a particular topic and can lecture on that topic for an extended time. The quantity of language tends to overshadow the fact that individuals with Aspergers still have language impairments related to language use and comprehension (Mayes, Calhoun, & Crites, 2001), as well as the nonverbal aspects that typically accompany spoken word.

Individuals with Aspergers have impaired use of nonverbal communication and have difficulty reading and sending nonverbal messages (Church, Alisanski & Amanullah, 2000). For example, most people recognize that someone glancing frequently at a watch is communicating imminent disengagement. Individuals with Aspergers tend not to pick up on that social cue and continue talking at the person even as he or she attempts to leave. Like individuals with autism, individuals with Aspergers may have difficulty with nonliteral language (Nikolaenko, 2004; Strandburg et al., 1993). Phrases such as "the pot calling the kettle black" are confusing to them because they know inanimate objects like pots cannot talk. This difficulty with abstract language, coupled with the inability to correctly interpret nonverbal language, can make them targets of teasing and bullying (Heerey, Capps, Keltner, & Kring, 2005; Little, 2001). Like the speech of individuals with autism, their speech quality tends to be unusual, with intonation and prosody differences.

Difficulty with the pragmatics of language only exacerbates the problems that a person with Aspergers has with socialization. Like individuals with autism, they may display problems with eye contact and facial expressiveness. They may be interested in having friends, but unwittingly tend to do things that drive friends away (Marriage, Gordon, & Brand, 1995). They are "honest to a fault" because they do not consider the impact their communication may have on another person. This, coupled with their interest in telling others about their special interests, tends to alienate others. They also tend to seek out others who can add to their knowledge about their particular interests, which, as children, often results in a lack of interest in their same-age peers (Volkmar et al., 1997). Attwood (2002) has humorously defined people with Asperger syndrome as individuals in the pursuit of knowledge and truth, with adults, books, computers, and libraries the favorite sources.

In regard to interests and activities, individuals with Aspergers tend to have a narrowly defined range of interests (Asperger, 1944). As children, their preoccupations with specific topics tend toward the precocious (Wing, 1981). For example, they may be interested in trains and be able to identify differences in engines and gauges well beyond what someone of a similar chronological age could do. Given a high interest in acquiring factual information, persons with Aspergers can make model citizens. Once they learn the rules, they are very reluctant to break those rules. For example, as a teacher steps out of a classroom, she may say, "Remember, stay in your seat and keep working while I am gone." Naturally, this translates into most of the children getting up and milling about in the teacher's absence. Not the student with Aspergers. Not only will he stay in his seat, he will note who is breaking the rules. As soon as the teacher returns, he will raise his hand to say, "Mary went over to the aquarium; Tony went and sharpened his pencil; Susan and Lisa were looking at the books," and so forth. The student with Aspergers probably does not realize the impact his revelations have on the other students. All he knows is that he is uncomfortable that the rules are being broken. He may even believe that others are equally uncomfortable so that they will applaud his attempt to right the social injustice that has just occurred. This rigid adherence to rules and routines can lead to difficulty in changing schedules or seating arrangements and even in postponing plans. The mother of a son with Aspergers is reported to have asked him what "hell" is. His reply? "Surprises" (Pyles & Attwood, 2002).

Attempts to define Asperger syndrome include not only recognition of the marked differences in communication, socialization, and interests and activities, but also cognitive development. The current criteria in the *DSM-IV-TR* suggest that individuals with Aspergers cannot show any delay in cognitive development or self-help skills. They are frequently cited as having trouble with motor skills (Volkmar et al., 1994; Walters, Barrett, & Feinstein, 1990), which are not correlated with cognitive functioning (Dawson & Watling, 2000). Their fine motor difficulties may translate into illegible handwriting (Mayes & Calhoun, 2003). They may also be challenged by spatial relationships and may not have an accurate perception of where their bodies are in relation to other objects, so they appear to be clumsy (Asperger, 1944; Wing, 1981). One of the more frustrating features for advocates for individuals with Aspergers is that their problems comprehending language, understanding the social world, and functioning independently are often obscured by their large vocabularies, vast knowledge on particular topics, and excellent memories (Frith, 2004).

❖ LEARNING WITH MS. HARRIS: An English Composition

The following is an English composition written by Sean Young during his senior year of high school when he was 16 years old. Sean was diagnosed with Aspergers when he was 7. He has since earned his high school diploma and has a scholarship to study computer engineering at a college in Ohio.

"Sometimes I wish I was a caterpillar; I could close myself off from the world and still grow into something beautiful." I made this statement to my mom one day when I just needed to have some space. People affected by Asperger

Syndrome often feel this way. Asperger Syndrome is a neurological syndrome that affects the wiring of the brain. You cannot tell if someone has Asperger Syndrome (AS) by looking, because these individuals appear normal. However, individuals with AS find social interactions baffling. They are often physiologically challenged and frequently think differently than "neurotypicals." The result is people with AS often experience exclusion. I know because I have Asperger Syndrome.

Challenged with Asperger Syndrome, I struggle most with navigating the social aspects of life. I am uncomfortable in many social situations, and I have experienced the sting of rejection. People with Asperger Syndrome do not intuitively acquire the social "rules" that most people learn on their own. For example, I have trouble reading facial expressions and body language. If someone is annoyed or angry, I may not realize it. Consequently, I may aggravate them further. I am getting better at social rules, such as looking people in the eye, reacting to heavy sighs, and varying the conversation instead of perseverating on topics I like. Empathy can be an issue for me as well. It is not that I don't care about another person's feelings, but rather I struggle with identifying that person's emotions. If someone is hurting, I want to help, but the problem is discerning when that person is in pain.

Asperger Syndrome also brings about many physiological challenges. I am hypersensitive to many sensations. Certain sounds, smells, or textures cause sensations which I abhor. The sound of a styrofoam cooler rubbing against an object, the smell of bleach, or the texture of velvet, all create distressful sensations within my system. I avoid even the thought of these experiences, just as most neurotypicals avoid "fingernails on a blackboard." Weak motor coordination is an issue that I struggle with as well. I was slow to learn and develop soccer and basketball skills. Consequently, the other people on my teams, who were very competitive, excluded me during the games. Even today, I avoid team sports, preferring individual activities, such as cycling and walking.

In addition to social and physiological trials, Asperger Syndrome brings about many cognitive and emotional challenges. These challenges are not obvious, but are important because they influence my behavior. I take medication to help with anxiety and distraction. I can be overly detailed, which causes me to focus on small, technical, and insignificant details. This frustrates others, especially when I'm working in a group.

I also think very literally, meaning I often assume that people mean exactly what they say. For example, the instructor of my composition class recently asked us to look up several terms. As instructed, I found the definitions to these terms on the Internet, but I did not write down or print out the definitions because he did not instruct us to do so. These types of literal interpretations have resulted in frequent misunderstandings. Over the years, I have gotten better about recognizing idiomatic, metaphoric, or implicit statements. However, my literal interpretations still cause confusion in my everyday life.

The social, physiological, and mental challenges of Asperger Syndrome have forced me to exert considerable effort to accomplish tasks that many neurotypical people do with ease. While I have overcome many obstacles, Asperger Syndrome will always be a part of me. Author Tony Attwood (1998) comments, "[People with AS] are a bright thread in the rich tapestry of life. Our civilization would be extremely dull and sterile if we did not have and treasure people with Asperger Syndrome." Even though I cannot completely close myself off from the world, I believe I can still grow into something beautiful.

Rett's Disorder

Rett's disorder has emerged as a syndrome distinct from the others on the autism spectrum (National Research Council, 2001), primarily because it is now identified as a genetic disorder linked to a single gene defect (Ellaway & Christodoulou, 1999). Rett's disorder has been included in the *DSM-IV-TR* as a type of PDD because of behavioral similarities with autism (Lord et al., 2000). Described first by Andreas Rett in 1966, the disorder primarily affects females, as the genetic defect proves fatal in males. A 6- to 18-month period of apparently normal development is followed by sudden loss of acquired skills such as words and mobility. There is a deceleration of head growth between 5 and 48 months and a loss of hand skills between 5 and 30 months. Instead of continuing to use their hands purposefully, the young girls bring their hands together and engage in continuous hand-wringing motions. Their gait and coordination suffer, and they may lose the ability to ambulate. Rett's disorder progresses through stages from minor involvement to no volitional movement and full dependence on others for care, with the possibility that the child may fixate at any one of the stages and not gain or lose more skills. Life expectancy is typical. Mental retardation often occurs with Rett's disorder, and the girls display communication deficits. Deficits in socialization may be transient as the girls begin to show interest in interacting with others. Rett's disorder is considered a very rare disorder, with the National Institute of Health citing the prevalence figure as 1/15,000. Given that it is now considered a rare genetic disorder with more differences than similarities to the other subtypes of PDD, little else will be discussed in this text about Rett's disorder. A thorough description and discussion of a group of girls and young women diagnosed with Rett's disorder is provided in Lindberg (1994).

Childhood Disintegrative Disorder

Childhood disintegrative disorder (CDD) was first described in 1908 by Theodor Heller, a special educator in Vienna, and is sometimes called *Heller's syndrome*. Although criteria in the *DSM-IV-TR* for identifying the qualitative differences in communication, socialization, and interests and activities in CDD are similar to those for autism, the developmental sequence and perceived etiologies differ. Because the emergence of CDD follows a period of two years of normal growth (but must be identifiable by the age of 10), it is different from autism, which must be manifest prior to 3 years of age. To receive a diagnosis of CDD, there must be evidence of normal growth and development until the age of 2 years. To be diagnosed after that time, the child must experience an immediate or insidious loss in at least two of the previously acquired skill areas, such as bowel or bladder control, adaptive behavior, expressive or receptive language, motor skills, social interaction, or play skills. Rapin (1965, p. 760) provided a bleak profile for children with CDD, in which a "well-adjusted child becomes dull and indifferent," losing the ability to recognize his parents and feeding himself with his hands.

Although the behavioral manifestations of CDD are very similar to those seen in autism, Kanner (1943) perceived the two conditions to be distinct. Whereas autism may be perceived by some to have socialization as the core deficit, the core deficit in CDD is communication (Malhotra & Gupta, 1999). Likewise, CDD appears to affect individuals more severely than autism (Volkmar & Rutter, 1995), even though the age of onset is later.

Some controversy exists as to whether CDD represents a distinct subtype of PDD or whether it reflects an artifact of our society. Those who would suggest that CDD represents a distinct type of PDD have some support from research currently being done on the limbic system (to be described more fully in the next chapter), in which lesions in neonatal animals produce a period of normal development followed by significant regression. Those who suggest that CDD represents an artifact of our society identify it as a form of PDD that occurs as a result of children being vaccinated, particularly around the age of 2. This explanation is becoming less plausible because research has failed to substantiate a link between ASD and vaccinations (DeStefano et al., 2004). Given the ambiguity that surrounds a clear understanding of CDD, few professionals give a diagnosis of CDD, and little is written regarding the disorder in the professional literature.

Pervasive Developmental Disorder— Not Otherwise Specified

The diagnostic category of **Pervasive Developmental Disorder—Not Otherwise Specified (PDD-NOS)** is used when children meet some, but not all of the criteria for the other subtypes of PDD. Several disorders in the *DSM-IV-TR* provide for close but not exact matches by using the NOS caveat. As such, there are no actual diagnostic criteria for PDD-NOS in the *DSM-IV-TR*. PDD-NOS is also referred to as *atypical autism* and is the diagnosis of choice if uncharacteristic or mild symptoms of the other subtypes are present. Characteristics of *Pervasive Developmental Disorders* must still occur in the form of disordered communication, socialization, or interests and activities. However, the entire constellation does not need to be present. According to the *DSM-IV-TR,* children may be diagnosed with PDD-NOS with qualitative differences in any one of the three areas (Volkmar, Klin, & Cohen, 1997), which may be contributing to the increased prevalence of ASD (discussed more fully in Chapter 2).

DIAGNOSING AUTISM SPECTRUM DISORDERS

The ability to detect and define the disorders that comprise the autism spectrum has improved dramatically in the last few decades. However, a number of issues continue to make diagnosis a challenging endeavor. There is currently

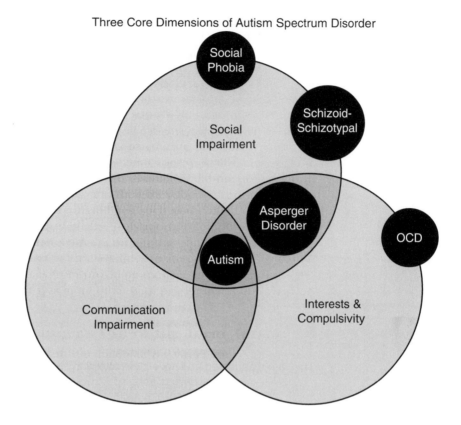

FIGURE 1.2
Core Deficits Among Those Without ASDs
Source: Hollander et al., CNS Spectrum, 1998; 3(3): 22-26, 33-39

no biological marker or medical test to diagnose ASD (Bristol-Power & Spinella, 1999). Instead, ASDs are behaviorally defined disorders that are diagnosed based on observing behavior and interviewing others about the person's behavior. But none of the behaviors seen in any of the spectrum disorders is unique to the autism spectrum. All of the behaviors associated with autism are demonstrated by people without autism at some time (e.g., many people are irritated by changes, such as when a favorite television show is preempted by coverage of a political convention or someone else is parked in "their" parking spot at work), and certainly by individuals who have other types of disabilities (e.g., individuals with obsessive-compulsive disorders tend to perseverate on activities and demonstrate stereotypic behaviors). Figure 1.2 contains a Venn diagram that superimposes disorders experienced by people without ASD on the triad of core deficits seen in ASD.

Admittedly, this diagram doesn't list all the possible associations and combinations. For example, someone who is electively or selectively mute may

THE LANGUAGE OF 'US' AND 'THEY'
by Mayer Shevin

We like things.
They fixate on objects.
We try to make friends.
They display attention-seeking behaviors.
We take a break.
They display off-task behaviors.
We stand up for ourselves.
They are noncompliant.
We have hobbies.
They self-stim.
We choose our friends wisely.
They display poor peer socialization.
We persevere.
They perseverate.
We love people.
They have dependencies on people.
We go for a walk.
They run away.
We insist.
They tantrum.
We change our minds.
They are disoriented and have short attention spans.
We have talents.
They have splinter skills.
We are human.
They are ???????

FIGURE 1.3
The Language of Us and They

Source: *Advocate,* 1991. Reprinted with permission of the Autism Society of America.

have communication impairment, as would someone with a speech delay. "Restricted interests and compulsivity" could describe students cramming for an exam or trying to finish a major project. The important thing to remember is that an autism spectrum diagnosis is difficult to make because of the similarities between behaviors associated with ASD and behaviors demonstrated by all people. Figure 1.3 is a poem published in 1991 by the Autism Society of America, which highlights similarities and differences between those with ASD and those without. The poem conveys the tendency to put a negative skew on behavior in the presence of a disability.

In addition to the lack of hallmark or distinguishing characteristics, the range of differences among individuals on the spectrum often complicates diagnosis. As mentioned earlier, no two children with ASD behave exactly alike. For any individual, some of the characteristics associated with the spectrum disorder will be more pronounced whereas others are virtually nonexistent.

In the *DSM-IV-TR,* each of the types of PDD (except PDD-NOS) has a list of criteria that are used to diagnose the disorders. Qualified professionals interview caregivers and observe the child to determine which criteria the child may be demonstrating. (The list of who is considered qualified to give *DSM* diagnoses varies from state to state.) In addition to evaluating the child by the *DSM-IV-TR* criteria, the qualified professional collects a thorough developmental history of the child to determine the timing of the onset of symptoms. This may influence the diagnosis. For example, according to the *DSM-IV-TR* criteria, autism is evident early in life, whereas CDD manifests after a period of normal development. Milder manifestations of the spectrum disorders may be even more difficult to detect, and cautious professionals may use the least drastic of the diagnoses (PDD-NOS) until symptoms become more obvious or disappear. Diagnosticians may also choose to give a diagnosis of PDD-NOS to young children in order to retain the option of later assigning a diagnosis of Aspergers. This is because *DSM-IV-TR* (and *ICD-10*) criteria dictate that if an individual has ever had a diagnosis of autism, he or she cannot be identified as having Aspergers (Volkmar, Lord, Bailey, Schultz, & Klin, 2004). The more severe the disability, the easier it is to make a confident diagnosis, although there are some syndromes, such as reactive attachment disorder, Cornelia de Lange syndrome, Landau-Kleffner syndrome, and William's syndrome (Dykens & Volkmar, 1997; Hall & Geher, 2003; Minshew, Sweeney, & Bauman, 1997; Mukaddes, Kaynak, Kinali, Besikci, & Issever, 2004), that closely emulate autism and may confound an accurate diagnosis.

Diagnoses must be based on the complete triad of core deficits—not just one area. As Freeman (1997) states, there must be a constellation of behaviors present that form a pattern consistent with an ASD, not merely isolated indicators. Documentation of unusual behaviors as well as the absence of typical behaviors are needed to make a diagnosis (Baranek, 2002; Wetherby et al., 2004). Diagnosis requires collecting a complete record of the child's history, including mother's pregnancy, birth, developmental history, general health, sleeping and eating habits, and so forth. Information is needed about previous functioning as well as current functioning (Tidmarsh & Volkmar, 2003).

EARLY INDICATORS OF POSSIBLE ASD

As attention has turned to the importance of early intervention, there has been an increased push to identify children with ASD as early as possible. Historically, many parents of children with disabilities have been frustrated in their attempts to obtain an accurate diagnosis. In a large-scale study, Howlin and Moore (1997) documented that fewer than 10% of the parents were given a diagnosis when they discussed their concerns about their children with a doctor. Twenty-five percent of the parents were told "not to worry" and 10% were told to come back later but that their child would probably "grow out of it." This has been reported as a common scenario among families of children with ASD, although more than 50% state that they knew something was different about their child within the first year of life (Howlin & Moore, 1997), citing concerns about their children's lack of shared enjoyment and poor eye contact (Young, Brewer, & Pattison, 2003). Ninety percent of parents report they were clearly worried by the time the child was 2 years old (De Giacomo & Fombonne, 1998). The parents interviewed in the study by Young et al. (2003) indicate that it took an average of 34 months (almost 3 years) for them to secure a diagnosis after their initial concerns were reported.

Unfortunately, the diagnostic criteria contained in the *DSM-IV-TR* are not as useful for identifying young children with ASD, because they describe characteristics that do not show up until later in life (Woods & Wetherby, 2003). The characteristics in the categories of social and communication impairments probably are not measurable until about 24 months of age, and the characteristics in the category of restricted patterns of behavior may not manifest until 36 months of age. For example, echolalia is commonly seen among typical toddlers because they learn language by repeating what they hear, and it would not be considered unusual in young children. The self-stimulatory and inflexible behaviors listed in the category of restricted and stereotyped patterns of behavior are more common among toddlers with developmental disabilities than in those with ASD (Wetherby et al., 2004) and may not become more pronounced in children with ASD until the children are 3 or 4 years old (Lord, 1995).

Although it may be difficult to distinguish a deficit from a delay in very young children (Sigman, Dijamco, Gratier, & Rozga, 2004), an emerging body of research suggests that indications occurring early in life may be useful for identifying ASD at younger ages. Infants are profoundly social creatures, and the absence of social relatedness should indicate some cause for concern. Osterling, Dawson, and Munson (2002) suggest that the frequency with which infants look at others and orient to their names may allow for the identification of ASD as early as 12 months of age. Disturbances in sensory processing may likewise be noticeable during the first year of life (Dawson et al., 2000). For infants, failure to demonstrate joint attention and to orient to social stimuli may predict later ASD diagnoses (Dawson et al., 2004; Lewy & Dawson, 1992). Research on accurate identification of ASD in very young children will continue.

In 2000, a subcommittee of the American Academy of Neurology published practice parameters to encourage medical professionals to avoid adopting the "wait and see" attitude and to accurately identify the presence of a spectrum disorder at the earliest age possible (Filipek et al., 2000). These guidelines appear on the American Academy of Neurology's Web site (*www.aan.com*) along with brief printable summaries: one for parents and caregivers and one for clinicians. The practice parameters contain the following indicators that should be considered early markers and lead to more comprehensive evaluation:

- Absence of babbling, pointing, or other gestures by 12 months (pointing or gestures to request something may be present but pointing or gestures to share something are absent)

- Absence of single words by 16 months
- Absence of two-word spontaneous (not echolalic) phrases by 24 months
- Loss of any language or social skill at any age

These early markers do not necessarily indicate that the child has an ASD, but do indicate that further evaluation and close monitoring are necessary.

❖ LEARNING WITH MS. HARRIS: Returning the Call

"It seems like it is difficult to get an accurate diagnosis for an autism spectrum disorder," thinks Ms. Harris. During their brief phone call, Ms. Owens didn't say much about the process of securing Eric's diagnosis. Ms. Harris waits until she thinks it's video time, and calls Ms. Owens. Fortunately, all is calm at the Owens' home, and Ms. Owens is happy to share her family's experiences.

She says, "Eric met most of his motor milestones rather early (sitting up and taking his first steps much earlier than his sister), and seemed so thoughtful (lying contentedly in his crib for long stretches) that we told ourselves that he was going to be a genius! We were a little concerned because he wouldn't wave 'bye-bye' but seemed much more interested in smelling things (my arm, his food, the dog). When Eric wasn't talking by the age of two, I took him to his pediatrician. The pediatrician examined Eric and said there was nothing wrong with him physically and, since he had us and an older sister to anticipate his every wish, Eric had no reason to talk. The pediatrician told us to stop babying Eric and he would grow out of the phase he was in. Not too long after that, I realized that Eric never looked at me when I called his name. I took Eric in for a hearing screening when he was three years old and it was a traumatic experience! Eric didn't want the headphones on his head and had one tantrum after another. Although the audiologist was unable to measure Eric's hearing, when Eric turned around to orient to the sound of the man opening a candy wrapper, the audiologist said his hearing was probably fine.

"The thing that really started bothering us was that Eric never showed us anything. You know how a child picks up something he thinks is interesting and takes it over to someone to show it off? Eric never did that. In fact, when he picked up toys, he'd do the strangest things with them. He really liked to take things apart. His sister used to get upset because Eric dismantled her Barbie dolls. She'd come into the room screaming and waving a Barbie doll body, and we'd be off on the search for the head, arms, and legs. I finally saw a show about autism on one of those television news programs and thought how much those kids sounded like Eric. I called Eric's pediatrician back, and he gave me the number for the Early Intervention Services office that was in our area.

"They did a screening and then directed us to a developmental psychologist who knew about autism. She asked me a lot of questions and then tried to play with Eric. It didn't take long for her to say he had autism! It was such

a relief to finally know the name of what Eric has—but it was also devas-
tating. We all cried and cried because we didn't want Eric to have autism.
My husband's father still refuses to believe that anything is different about
Eric. He keeps talking about what Eric is going to do when he grows up and
it is pretty heartbreaking. For me, having the diagnosis means that I can
educate myself about Eric's condition and do more to help him. Speaking of
whom, there is a little guy in the kitchen trying to get something out of the
refrigerator. I'd better go see what he wants."

ASSESSMENTS FOR ASD

Although few readers of this text will be responsible for assessing and
diagnosing students with ASD, familiarity with the ever-expanding number
of available assessments may be beneficial. Table 1.1 is a brief summary of
some of the common assessments currently being used to screen for or
diagnose the presence and severity of ASD. In addition to the assessments
summarized here, assessments that are relevant to topics in subsequent
chapters will be described for the purpose of planning and evaluating
educational programming.

Administering any of the individual assessments profiled in Table 1.1
would be insufficient for conducting a comprehensive evaluation (Campbell,
2005). However, these assessments may be used in conjunction with other
psychological, behavioral, and developmental evaluations to derive a diagnosis and determine a student's strengths and weaknesses. Be cautious when
interpreting scores from scales that use arbitrary cutoffs to distinguish those
with ASD from those without ASD, because the social traits associated
with ASD are continuously distributed throughout the general population
(Constantino & Todd, 2003).

ADDITIONAL TESTS AND EVALUATIONS

For children who appear to meet the behavioral diagnostic criteria for an
autism spectrum disorder, additional testing may be beneficial. The purpose
of the testing is not to confirm a spectrum diagnosis but to rule out the presence of mitigating factors (Bauman, 2003). Chromosomal/DNA analysis can
be useful for determining whether the child suffers from a genetic disorder
such as Rett's or Fragile X. Such information may not make a great deal of difference to the children themselves but could be useful to the families (e.g.,
Fragile X is inherited through the maternal side, and the mother may want
her female siblings and daughters to know the possibility that they may carry
the gene). Electroencephalograms (EEGs) are not usually very helpful because
about 15% of the typical population have abnormal EEGs, and a significant
number of children with an ASD have inconsistent EEG results (Canitano
et al., 2005). However, if a seizure disorder is suspected, an EEG could provide
definitive documentation. It may be equally useless to undertake imaging
studies, such as MRIs or CTs, unless a tumor is suspected.

Likewise, metabolic studies (blood and urine analysis) are not warranted unless an underlying metabolic disorder is suspected (Rutter, Bailey, Bolton, & Le Couteur, 1994). If the student is not making progress in a good program, is easily fatigued, looks "different," or experiences unusual illnesses, then a metabolic screen may be indicated (Bauman, 2003). The benefit of testing a high-functioning child with normal appearance and IQ is minimal (Skjeldal, Sponheim, Ganes, Jellum & Bakke, 1998). Again, the purpose is not to confirm an autism spectrum diagnosis, but to see if other factors that may suggest different treatments may be present. Other assessments such as hair analysis, celiac antibodies testing, allergy testing, testing for immunological or neurochemical abnormalities, testing micronutrient (vitamin) levels or intestinal permeability, stool analysis, urinary peptides analysis, testing for mitochondrial disorders, and thyroid functioning tests probably will not provide enough useful information to be worth the expense and effort (Filipek et al., 1999).

DIFFERENTIAL DIAGNOSES

To provide a **differential diagnosis** is to determine that the student fits one set of criteria better than all others and, therefore, that there is a strong likelihood of a correct diagnosis. Because there are no unique behaviors that characterize ASD and because students under the same diagnostic category can appear dissimilar, it can be challenging to recognize ASD from other differences in behavior and learning. Although differentiating students with ASD from those without ASD has become more reliable, differentiating the spectrum disorders from each other continues to be very difficult (Mahoney et al., 1998). Identifying students who may have ASD is further complicated by the fact that a number of conditions result in individuals demonstrating "autistic-like" behaviors without having an ASD. Conditions that result in autistic-like behaviors include sensory impairments (blindness and deafness), Fragile X, Rett's syndrome, mental retardation, Landau-Kleffner syndrome, Cornelia de Lange syndrome, William's syndrome, tuberous sclerosis, schizophrenia, Kluver-Bucy syndrome, sensory integrative dysfunction, nonverbal learning disabilities, and obsessive-compulsive disorders (OCD) (Klin & Volkmar, 1997; Walters, Barrett, & Feinstein, 1990).

The process of identifying young children as having an ASD is made more difficult because they have behaviors in common with typically developing infants, such as echolalia (McLaughlin, 1998) and stereotypic behavior (Thelen, 1981) as well as behavioral differences that match those of children with other developmental disabilities. For example, infants between 9 and 12 months of age with developmental delays may demonstrate higher rates of self-stimulatory behavior than infants who are later diagnosed with ASD (Baranek, 1999). Young children later diagnosed as having ASD have been noted to spend as much time engaged in object play as their typically developing peers, but the quality of play is different (Baranek et al., 2005). And young children later diagnosed as having ASD may point as frequently as their

TABLE 1.1
Summary of ASD Assessments

Acronym	Assessment	Authors	Description	Requirements
ABC	Autism Behavior Checklist	Krug, Arick, & Almond, 1980	Intended to be completed by teachers as initial step in educational planning; emphasizes observable features associated with ASD	No special training is required; completed by teachers with parental input
AAPEP	Adult-Adolescent Psychoeducational Profile	Mesibov, Schopler, Schaffer, & Landrus, 1988	Provides an evaluation of current and potential skills in individuals with autism who have moderately to severely impaired intellectual functioning, to identify instructional priorities	Direct observation scored while interacting/observing, can be administered with minimal language, takes about $1\frac{1}{2}$ hours; Home Scale and School/Work scale are completed through interviewing relevant individuals and take about 1 hour each
ADI-R	Autism Diagnostic Interview-Revised	Rutter, LeCouteur, & Lord, 2003	Diagnostic tool; semistructured parent interview to identify autism and PDD; focuses on current behavior and queries if behaviors were ever observed	Evaluator must be trained in conducting the interview; administration and scoring take 1.5–2.5 hours; usually takes 90 minutes

Subscales	Ages	Scoring	Support
57 items, scored present or absent, in 5 areas: sensory, relating, body & object use, language, social interaction & self-help	School-age children, 3 years of age and older	Items are weighted and summed for total score; scores $>= 67$ indicate high probability of autism; scores $<= 53$ indicate low probability of autism	May not be useful as independent diagnostic instrument; parents' scores are usually higher than teachers'; may miss higher functioning and under-estimate severity in nonverbal; may be useful in documenting response to interventions
Direct observation of skills with evaluations of performance in residential setting and vocation (school/work); each scale divided into 6 areas: vocational skills, independent functioning, leisure skills, vocational behavior, functional communication, interpersonal behavior	Older than 12 years	Items are marked "pass," "fail," "emerge"; scoring allows for verbal and nonverbal responses	Adequate reliability and validity reported on most items by developers
93 items in domains of language and communication; reciprocal social interactions; and restricted, repetitive, and stereotyped behaviors and interests; separate scores generated for socialization, communication (nonverbal and verbal), and	Children and adults with mental ages above 2 years 0 months	Scoring and coding procedures result in three broad patterns of scores with diagnostic algorithms for interpretation	Often referred to as the "gold standard" for research studies; valid and reliable for diagnosing autism in preschool children; may be overinclusive of children under 18 months with develop-mental delays and fail to identify a small percentage of high-functioning and PDD-NOS

Acronym	Assessment	Authors	Description	Requirements
ADOS	Autism Diagnostic Observation Schedule	Lord, Rutter, DiLavore, & Risi, 1999	Diagnostic tool; standardized protocol for observation of social and communicative behavior	Evaluator must be trained in administering assessment; directs evaluator to give range of demands and social "presses"; trained evaluator can conduct each module in 30–45 minutes
ASDS	Asperger Syndrome Diagnostic Scale	Myles, Bock, & Simpson, 2001	Norm-referenced rating scale to identify students with AS, develop goals, document progress; can be used for research	Rater can be anyone who has at least 2 weeks of sustained contact with student and knows him/her well; takes 10–15 minutes to complete
ASSQ	Autism Spectrum Screening Questionnaire	Ehlers, Gillberg, & Wing, 1999	Screening instrument to determine if more comprehensive assessment needed; created for use in epidemiological study; not normed; designed for individuals without MR	10 minutes to complete; parent and teacher forms

Subscales	Ages	Scoring	Support
restricted repetitive behaviors; shortened version has 40 items			
Four modules available but use only one relative to student based on expressive language level and age; each module has four domains: communication, reciprocal social interaction, (module 1 = play; modules 2–4 = imagination/ creativity), stereotyped behaviors, and restricted interests	Toddlers to adults; no speech to fluent	Items coded based on scores available, which vary by item; cutoff scores indicating autism and ASD provided for communication and social domains with a combined communication + social score cutoff as well	Often referred to as the "gold standard" for research studies; not useful for nonverbal adolescents and adults
50 items marked as present or absent, in five subscales: language, social, maladaptive, cognitive, sensorimotor	5–18 years	Items summed to provide Asperger syndrome quotient (ASQ) (M = 100, SD = 15); cannot interpret subscales	Concern regarding standardization sample and ability of test to differentiate students within spectrum; not intended to be used for diagnostic purposes
27 behavioral descriptions rated on 3-point scale, in five areas: social interaction, communication, restricted & repetitive behavior, motor clumsiness, associated symptoms	6–17 years	Raw score total ranges 0–54; recommended cutoff score = 13	Acceptable reliability and adequate specificity as a screening tool

Acronym	Assessment	Authors	Description	Requirements
ASQ	Autism Screening Questionnaire	Replaced by Social Communication Questionnaire (see below)		
CARS	Childhood Autism Rating Scales	Schopler, Reichler, & Renner, 1988	One of the earliest screening tools specifically for autism; distinguished children with autism from those without and provides indication of severity	Evaluator must be trained (video available); evaluator scores items based on interview and after or while observing/interacting with child; takes 30 to 45 minutes to administer
CAST	Childhood Asperger Syndrome Test	Scott, Baron-Cohen, Bolton & Brayne, 2002	Designed to screen children and youth for AS	Parents complete
GADS	Gilliam Asperger's Disorder Scale	Gilliam, 2001	Norm-referenced rating scale to identify students with AS, develop goals, document progress; can be used for research	Raters must have two weeks of contact with student and can include teachers, paras, parents, psychologists or psych associates; includes Parent Interview Form, which is not scored; takes 10 minutes to complete
GARS	Gilliam Autism Rating Scale	Gilliam, 1995	Checklist for use by parents, teachers, and other professionals to identify and estimate severity of symptoms of autism	No special requirements for adminstering

Subscales	Ages	Scoring	Support
15 items rated numerically 1 to 4 with $\frac{1}{2}$ point increments	Not specified	Items summed and scores $> = 30$ indicate autism (30–36.5 = mild to moderate autism; 37–60 = severe autism); cutoff may be adjusted up for young children and down for high-functioning adolescents & adults	Useful for screening but not diagnostics or research; imprecise in descriptive ability but has good reliability; may overidentify 2-year-olds; minimal verbal skills and/or moderate to severe mental retardation more likely to score >30
37 items scored as present or absent	4–11 years	31 items summed for overall score (6 items relate to general development and are not added in); score $=> 15$ indicates need for further evaluation	Reliability not documented; seems sensitive and specific for differentiating AS and non-AS; poor predictive validity
32 items for indicating frequency of behaviors in four subscales: social interaction, restricted patterns of behavior, cognitive patterns, pragmatic skills	3–22 years	Raw scores summed for scaled scores (M = 10; SD = 3); summed for Asperger's disorder quotient (ADQ) (M = 100; SD = 15)	Large standardization group with adequate representation, although diagnoses not verified and cognitive abilities not known
56 items in four scales: social interaction, communication, and stereotyped behaviors scales rate current behaviors;	3–22 years	Items summed and converted to standard scores (M = 10, SD = 3); provides global rating of autism (autism quotient) (M = 100,	May fail to identify individuals with autism; author has proposed lowering cutoff score to 80

Acronym	Assessment	Authors	Description	Requirements
KADI	Krug Asperger Disorder Index	Krug & Arick, 2003	Norm-referenced rating scale to identify students with AS and develop goals; can be used for research	Ability to read at sixth grade level and had regular and daily contact for a few weeks; takes 5–10 minutes to complete
M-CHAT	Modified-Checklist for Autism in Toddlers	Robins, Fein, Barton, & Green, 2001	Modified the CHAT by adding items for children 18–24 months and to adapt for use in US	Parent completes
PEP-R	Psychoeducational Profile-Revised	Schopler, Reichler, Bashford, Lansing, & Marcus, 1990	Developmental assessment to identify instructional priorities for IEPs; can be used to record progress	Items may be delivered in any order and directions eliminated or simplified
SCQ	Social Communication Questionnaire	Rutter, Bailey, & Lord, 2003	Screening questionnaire based on the original ADI; provides	Parent completes questionnaire; usually takes less than 10 minutes with

Subscales	Ages	Scoring	Support
developmental disturbances scale rates past severe behavior; items rated on 4-point scale from "never observed" to "frequently observed"		SD = 15); score of 90 or above indicates probable autism	
11 items to screen if should continue (if > 18 points, complete rest of 32 items)	Elementary form for ages 6–11 and secondary form for ages 12–21	Raw scores weighted and summed for total score (M = 100, SD = 15); higher scores = more likely to have AS	Strong reliability; diagnoses not verified in sample and cognitive abilities not known
23 items to rate "yes" or "no" for behaviors such as pointing to express interest, responsiveness to name, interest in peers, showing behavior, response to joint attention, social imitation	18–30 months of age identified at risk for developmental disorders	Yes/no answers convert to pass/fail; key provided; if child "fails" two or more "critical" items or "fails" three items, further assessment is indicated	Preliminary studies support adequate discriminent validity, interrater reliability, and sensitivity
Seven domains: imitation, perception, eye-hand integration, fine motor, gross motor, cognitive verbal, cognitive performance; also contains behavior rating scale in four domains: relating, materials, sensory, language	6 months–7 years functioning at or below preschool range; for children 7–12 years of age, can provide useful information if some skills are below first-grade level	Items are marked "pass," "fail," "emerge"; provides scores and age equivalents for each domain and overall and development scores	Normative data collected in development of test; adequate interrater reliability and validity; correlates well with Merrill-Palmer and Vineland Social Maturity scales
40 items rated "yes" or "no"; two forms: one rating entire developmental history for	Child needs to be above 4 years of age with mental age > 2 years	Provides single overall score; score of >= 15 on lifetime form indicates need for	Cannot provide diagnosis but can assist with screening; lower threshold score is recommended for

Acronym	Assessment	Authors	Description	Requirements
			indication of ASD symptoms	another 5 minutes to score
SRS	Social Responsive-ness Scale	Constantino, 2005	Designed to measure the severity of ASDs as they occur in natural social settings; used to screen, aid with diagnosis, or measure response to intervention	Parent or teacher completes in 15–20 minutes

Note: AS = Asperger syndrome

Sources: Synthesized from Bregman, 2005; Campbell, 2005; Filipek et al., 1999; Handleman & Delmolino, 2005; Lord, 1997; Lord & Bailey, 2002; South et al., 2002; Tidmarsh & Volkmar, 2003, Volkmar, Lord, Bailey, Schultz, & Klin, 2004.

typically developing peers, but may do so only to indicate when they want things, not to show something to another person (Stone, Ousley et al., 1997).

Differentiating individuals with ASD from those with other disabilities continues to be challenging as they grow older. Particularly challenging is the population of students with Aspergers and PDD-NOS. These usually very verbal students with normal or above-average intelligence are often diagnosed at age 11 years or older (Howlin & Asgharian, 1999), after having gone through various other diagnoses such as ADHD, nonverbal learning disabilities (NLD), or semantic-pragmatic language disorders (Filipek et al., 1999; Gagnon, Mottron, & Joanette, 1997; Ghaziuddin, Weidmer-Mikhail, & Ghaziuddin, 1998; Klin & Volkmar, 1997; Molina, Ruata, & Soler, 1986; Rourke, 1989; Stein, Klin, & Miller, 2004). Lord and Bailey (2002) suggest that it is easier to differentiate individuals with ASD from those with OCD. The rituals and compulsions demonstrated by some individuals with ASD tend not to upset them nor are these rituals linked to the prevention of unwanted events. In contrast, individuals with OCD often wish they could stop the rituals, which include washing, checking, and counting in order to protect themselves from potential harm.

Within the spectrum, it can be problematic to secure a differential diagnosis. One of the most difficult issues is distinguishing among Aspergers, high-functioning autism, and PDD-NOS. Historically, Aspergers was defined as a mild form of autism (Gillberg & Gillberg, 1989) and the term was used

Subscales	Ages	Scoring	Support
purpose of referral (lifetime) and one rating previous three-month period for evaluating treatment		further assessment	individuals with other risk factors (e.g., marked language impairment or sibling with autism)
65 items regarding social deficits, language difficulties, and repetitive behaviors; items rated on quantitative scale	4–18 years of age	Provides total score as well as subscale scores; separate norms for parents and teachers	Cannot provide diagnosis but can assist with screening; used in research studies

synonymously with PDD-NOS (Szatmari, Bremner, & Nagy, 1989). Some of the difficulty resides in the fact that there are five widely circulating definitions of Aspergers (Volkmar et al., 2004) and much controversy regarding the accuracy of the classifications contained in the *DSM-IV-TR* and *ICD-10*. Mayes et al., (2001) suggested that it would be impossible to diagnose anyone with Aspergers using the *DSM-IV-TR* criteria. Miller and Ozonoff (1997) added that even the young men Hans Asperger described would not be identified with Aspergers using the *DSM-IV-TR* criteria. In a reanalysis of the cases used to validate the *DSM-IV* criteria, Woodbury-Smith, Klin, and Volkmar (2005) noted that 68% of the participants with Aspergers would be identified as having Aspergers based on the criteria. The authors conclude, therefore, that it is not impossible to identify someone as having Aspergers using the *DSM-IV* criteria but conceded that there are problems with the diagnostic system.

In attempting to differentiate, it has been suggested that individuals with PDD-NOS demonstrate fewer stereotyped behaviors than those with Aspergers and autism (Walker et al., 2004). These authors also propose three types of PDD-NOS: (1) one that resembles Aspergers but with transient language delays and some mild cognitive deficits; (2) one that resembles autism but manifests at a later age or for which the child is too young to meet the full diagnostic criteria for autism; and (3) one that differs from autism due to fewer stereotyped and repetitive behaviors. Others have attempted to differentiate between Aspergers and high-functioning autism on the basis of intelligence testing, with verbal IQ scores greater than performance IQ scores reflecting Aspergers and performance IQ scores greater than verbal IQ scores being indicative of autism (Klin, Volkmar, Sparrow, Cicchetti & Rourke, 1995); however, these findings are inconsistent (Ghaziuddin & Mountain-Kimchi, 2004). The uneven profiles may be typical of all forms of ASD (Reitzel & Szatmari, 2003), and differences noted in young children that distinguish them into different subtypes disappear as they age (Gilchrist et al., 2001). Allegations that high-functioning autism is distinguished from Aspergers by poorer verbal scores appear to be an artifact of the diagnostic criteria (Frith, 2004).

Differentiated diagnoses are sought because of the desire for differentiated interventions. For example, a diagnosis of obsessive-compulsive disorder makes available a number of medications that can be effective with the population. Given the proposed similarity between individuals with Aspergers and those with nonverbal learning disabilities, and the obvious dissimilarities with individuals with autism functioning on the lower end of the spectrum, perhaps the interventions deemed effective for individuals with NLD could be useful for those with Aspergers (Klin et al., 1995).

Misdiagnosing a student who has ASD may result in overlooking the need to address social deficits as a priority issue (Gagnon et al., 1997; Wing, 1981). The danger in misdiagnosing students with Aspergers, PDD-NOS, and high-functioning autism is the denial of educational services because the students appear to be bright and doing well academically (Klin & Volkmar, 2000). Indeed, the label of Aspergers has made it possible to identify individuals who have suffered poor outcomes because of a lack of intervention for their socially odd and perseverative behaviors (Frith, 2004). Individuals with Aspergers and individuals with high-functioning autism appear to experience similar outcomes. As adults, both groups lack close friends, depend on their families for support, and experience low employment status (Howlin, 2003). The only difference Howlin found between the two groups was their level of educational attainment. Unfortunately, the higher levels of education enjoyed by the individuals with Aspergers did not translate into better employment outcomes. The question "Is Aspergers different from autism and PDD-NOS?" has yet to be answered (Rinehart, Bradshaw, Brereton & Tonge, 2002; Volkmar et al., 2004).

DETERMINING ELIGIBILITY FOR SPECIAL EDUCATION

Diagnosis of an ASD made by a qualified professional according to the criteria listed in the *DSM-IV-TR* does not automatically qualify students for special education services in their local school system. Such a diagnosis can contribute to an understanding of the student, but by law (currently the Individuals with Disabilities Education Improvement Act of 2004, P.L. 108–446), the school system has to undertake its own evaluation process to determine if the student has one of the qualifying, eligible conditions that adversely affects educational performance. In 1990, autism was added to the law as a distinct category of eligibility. According to IDEA:

> Autism means a developmental disability significantly affecting verbal and non-verbal communication and social interaction, generally evident before age three that adversely affects a child's educational performance. Other characteristics

often associated with autism are engagement in repetitive activities and stereo-typed movements, resistance to environmental change or change in daily routines, and unusual responses to sensory experiences. The term does not apply if a child's education performance is adversely affected primarily because the child has an emotional disturbance. [34 CFR § 300.7 (c) (1)]

Each state must develop its own definition and determine the eligibility criteria for ASD, with the definition at least recognizing the minimum constructs as provided in the federal regulations. Most states have created definitions that encompass the range of ASD by specifically including Aspergers, CDD, Rett's disorder, and PDD-NOS.

To determine eligibility, school system personnel across a number of disciplines conduct a variety of evaluations. Parents may provide the results of independent assessments, including *DSM-IV-TR* diagnoses, if available. Many of the younger students may arrive at school with diagnoses of autism, CDD, Rett's disorder, or PDD-NOS. A diagnosis of Aspergers is usually not given until around age 11 (Howlin, 2003), so school systems may be integrally involved in providing documentation that may lead to that diagnosis. If an independent diagnosis has not been provided, someone within the school system should collect data using one or several of the assessments summarized in Table 1.1.

In addition to collecting data using instruments designed to identify the presence or absence of ASD, school psychologists or other diagnosticians will attempt to measure IQ/cognitive functioning/developmental level, academic level, and adaptive behavior. For students with ASD, an adequate evaluation requires the use of multiple assessments, particularly in the IQ/cognitive functioning/developmental domains (Lord & Bailey, 2002). The importance of adhering to the standardization procedures of these assessments should be balanced with the need for results that adequately reflect the student's functioning (Handleman & Delmolino, 2005). The validity of the results will be influenced by the evaluator's skill and experience in working with students with ASD (Lord, 1997). Speech-language pathologists (SLPs) will conduct assessments of language and communication, including articulation, oral-motor coordination, language comprehension, expressive language, and conventional and nonconventional nonverbal behavior (Wetherby & Prizant, 2000). Knowledge of ASD should enable SLPs to look past the quantity of language in students functioning on the higher end of the spectrum in order to evaluate the quality of language, including pragmatics and social use of language. Occupational therapists may be needed to assess the students' functional adaptations and evaluate their sensory performance. Physical therapists, education specialists, and others may also conduct evaluations as necessary. Many districts have personnel who are specialists in ASD and they may supervise specialized assessments. Each of the professionals is trained to know which assessments are necessary and most likely to provide valid and reliable information for eligibility determination and identification of present levels of performance. The choice of which evaluations to conduct depends on the unique needs of the student. The school system's purpose for conducting the evaluations is to get as accurate a picture as possible of the child's current level of functioning and areas of need to determine eligibility and develop an appropriate program.

SUMMARY OF ASD FACTS

Figure 1.4 summarizes the few facts currently known about ASD. Most of the facts have been identified in the chapter. However, a few warrant more explanation. ASD are **developmental disabilities,** meaning that the disorders must become noticeable during the developmental period of an individual's life, usually between birth and age 18. Therefore, behavioral manifestations change over time. A student who is fascinated by toilets today, for example, may have different interests in the future. A student will not always become upset by the same stimuli. In addition, the presence of an ASD affects the student's progress. ASD is no longer a low-incidence disability, and autism is now reported to occur as often as 1 in every 600 individuals, while the full spectrum is reported to occur as often as 1 in every 200 individuals (Chakrabarti & Fombonne, 2001).

ASD occur more often in males than in females (Gillberg & Coleman, 1992; Lord et al., 2002). Although Kanner (1943) first suggested that autism occurs in wealthy families, ASD occur in families of all socioeconomic and ethnic backgrounds (Fombonne, Simmons, Ford, Meltzer, & Goodman, 2001), and a better understanding of how a family's culture influences adjustment to a family member with ASD is needed (Dyches, Wilder, Sudweeks, Obiakor, & Algozzine, 2004). ASD are not emotional disturbances. Unfortunately, certain behaviors have become inextricably associated with ASD in some people's minds. However, none of the behaviors associated with ASD are unique to the population. It is possible to demonstrate the behaviors associated with ASD and not have one of the syndromes. Finally,

---

- Developmental disability
- Occurs in 1/500 individuals
- Third most common developmental disability
- 4:1 male:female ratio
- No ethnic or socioeconomic preferences
- Not an emotional disturbance
- Represents a spectrum of disorders
- Possible to have some of the characteristics of ASD and not have an ASD
- No cure

FIGURE 1.4
Facts About Autism Spectrum Disorders

until scientists develop the ability to fix aberrant neurology or alter genes, there is no cure for ASD.

CONCLUSION

Individuals with ASD demonstrate a triad of deficits in the core areas of communication, socialization, and range of interests and activities. The differences in behavior in these three areas are not only quantitative in nature but also qualitative. Individuals with ASD do not simply display fewer competencies in the three areas, but the quality and nature of their abilities are also different. The *DSM-IV-TR* describes five subtypes of pervasive developmental disorders with characteristics that differ slightly, primarily in terms of rate and sequence of manifestation. Historically, medical professionals have been reluctant to identify ASD in young children, but with growing evidence supporting the importance of early intervention, diagnoses are being provided at earlier ages. Diagnostic procedures rely on information collected from developmental histories as well as interactions with the student. Information is collected to secure an accurate picture of the student's functioning so that appropriate programming can be developed.

DISCUSSION QUESTIONS AND ACTIVITIES

1. Examine Figure 1.1 containing the triad of core deficits in ASD. Read the descriptions of the characteristics of the five *DSM-IV-TR* subtypes of PDD and determine which core deficit is involved with each subtype. Discuss how interactions among the core deficits would influence an individual's functioning.

2. Create a blank Venn diagram. Locate two individuals with ASD functioning on opposite ends of the spectrum. (Use the main characters in *Rain Man* and *Mercury Rising* if desired.) Record the observed behaviors in the appropriate circles on the diagram. Compare and contrast the behaviors demonstrated by individuals representing the opposite ends of the spectrum.

3. Compare and contrast the three core deficits for individuals with autism, Aspergers and PDD-NOS.

4. Interview a family member of a student with an ASD. Ask about the process of getting a diagnosis and about the joys and challenges of daily life.

5. The federal law provides a definition for determining if a student is eligible to receive special education services under the category of autism. Each state can provide more detail for identifying students with autism. Locate several states' criteria for determining eligibility for autism and identify how they are different and how they are similar.

REFERENCES

Adrien, J. (1991). Autism and family home movies: Preliminary finds. *Journal of Autism and Developmental Disorders, 21,* 43–49.

Adrien, J. L., Lenoir, P., Martineau, J., Perrot, A., Haneury, L., Larmande, C., et al. (1993). Blind ratings of early symptoms of autism based upon family home movies. *Journal of the American Academy of Child and Adolescent Psychiatry, 33,* 617–626.

Alexander, D. (1995). *The emergence of repair strategies in chronologically and developmentally young children.* Unpublished doctoral dissertation, Florida State University, Tallahassee.

American Psychiatric Association. (2000). *Diagnostic and statistical manual of mental disorders* (4th ed., text revision). Washington, DC: Author.

Asperger, H. (1944/1991). Autistic psychopathy in childhood (Trans). In U. Frith (Ed.), *Autism and Asperger syndrome* (pp. 37–92). Cambridge, UK: Cambridge University Press.

Attwood, T. (1998). *Asperger's syndrome: A guide for parents and professionals.* London: Jessica Kingsley.

Attwood, T. (2000). Strategies for improving the social integration of children with Asperger syndrome. *Autism: The International Journal of Research and Practice, 4,* 85–100.

Baldwin, D. A. (1995). Understanding the link between joint attention and language. In C. Moore & P. J. Dunham (Eds.), *Joint attention: Its origins and role in development* (pp. 131–158). Hillsdale, NJ: Erlbaum.

Baranek, G. T. (1999). Autism during infancy: A retrospective video analysis of sensory-motor and social behaviors at 9–12 months of age. *Journal of Autism and Developmental Disorders, 29,* 213–224.

Baranek, G. T. (2002). Efficacy of sensory and motor interventions for children with autism. *Journal of Autism and Developmental Disorders, 32,* 397–422.

Baranek, G. T., Barnett, C. R., Adams, E. M., Wolcott, N. A., Watson, L. R., & Crais, E. R. (2005). Object play in infants with autism: Methodological issues in retrospective video analysis. *American Journal of Occupational Therapy, 59,* 20–30.

Bauman, M. L. (2003, December). The role of the physician: Diagnosis, management, and treatment. In *Innovative interventions in autism/NVLD: Practical outcomes in home and school.* Symposium conducted at the meeting of the Continuing Education Programs of America, Atlanta, GA.

Boucher, J., & Lewis, V. (1992). Unfamiliar face recognition in relatively able autistic children. *Journal of Child Psychology and Psychiatry, 33,* 843–859.

Bregman, J. D. (2005). Definitions and characteristics of the spectrum. In D. Zager (Ed.), *Austism spectrum disorders* (3rd ed., pp. 3–46). Mahwah, NJ: Erlbaum.

Bristol-Power, M. M., & Spinella, G. (1999). Research on screening and diagnosis in autism: A work in progress. *Journal of Autism and Developmental Disorders, 29,* 435–438.

Bryson, S. D. (1996). Brief reports: Epidemiology of autism. *Journal of Autism and Developmental Disorders, 26,* 165–167.

Campbell, J. (2005). Diagnostic assessment of Asperger's disorder: A review of five third-party rating scales. *Journal of Autism and Developmental Disorders, 35,* 25–35.

Canitano, R., Luchetti, A., & Zappella, M. (2005). Epilepsy, electroencephalographic abnormalities, and regression in children with autism. *Journal of Child Neurology, 20,* 27–31.

Chakrabarti, S., & Fombonne, E. (2001). Pervasive developmental disorders in preschool children. *Journal of the American Medical Association, 285,* 3093–3099.

Charman, T., Taylor, E., Drew, A., Cockerill, H., Brown, J., & Baird, G. (2005). *Journal of Child Psychology & Psychiatry & Allied Disciplines, 46,* 500–513.

Church, C., Alisanski, S., & Amanullah, S. (2000). The social, behavioral, and academic experiences of children with Asperger syndrome. *Focus on Autism and Other Developmental Disabilities, 15,* 12–20.

Constantino, J. N. (2005). *Social responsiveness scale (SRS).* Los Angeles: Western Psychol-ogical Services.

Constantino, J. N. & Todd, R. D. (2003). Autistic traits in the general population: A twin study. *Archives of General Psychiatry, 60,* 524–530.

Cox, A., Klein, K., Chaman, T., Baird, G., & Baron-Cohen, S. (1999). Autism spectrum disorders at 20 and 42 months of age: Stability of clinical and ADI-R diagnosis. *Journal of Child Psychology and Psychiatry, 40,* 719-732.

Dawson, G., Meltzoff, A. N., Osterling, J., Rinaldi, J., & Brown, E. (1998). Children with autism fail to orient to naturally occurring social stimuli. *Journal of Autism and Developmental Disorders, 28,* 479-485.

Dawson, G., Osterling, J., Meltzoff, A., & Kuhl, P. (2000). Case study of the development of an infant with autism from birth to 2 years of age. *Journal of Applied Developmental Psychology, 21,* 299-313.

Dawson, G., Toth, K., Abbott, R., Osterling, J., Munson, J., Estes, A., et al. (2004). Early social attention impairments in autism: Social orienting, joint attention, and attention to distress. *Developmental Psychology, 40,* 271-283.

Dawson, G., & Watling, R. (2000). Interventions to facilitate auditory, visual, and motor integration in autism: A review of the evidence. *Journal of Autism and Developmental Disorders, 30,* 415-421.

De Giacomo, A., & Fombonne, E. (1998). Parental recognition of developmental abnormalities in autism. *European Child and Adolescent Psychiatry, 7,* 131-136.

DeStefano, F., Bhasin, T. K., Thompson, W. W., Yeargin-Allsopp, M., & Boyle, C. (2004). Age at first measles-mumps-rubella vaccination in children with autism and school-matched control subjects: A population-based study in metropolitan Atlanta. *Pediatrics, 113,* 259-266.

Dyches, T. T., Wilder, L. K., Sudweeks, R. R., Obiaker, F. E., & Algozzine, B. (2004). Multicultural issues in autism. *Journal of Autism and Developmental Disorders, 34,* 211-222.

Dykens, E. M., & Volkmar, F. R. (1997). Medical conditions associated with autism. In D. Cohen & F. Volkmar (Eds.), *Autism and pervasive developmental disorders* (2nd ed, pp. 388-407). New York: Wiley.

Ehlers, S., Gillberg, C., & Wing, L. (1999). A screening questionnaire for Asperger syndrome and other high-functioning autism spectrum disorders in school age children. *Journal of Autism and Developmental Disorders, 29,* 129-141.

Ellaway, C., & Christodoulou, J. (1999). Rett syndrome: Clinical update and review of recent genetic advances. *Journal of Paediatrics & Child Health, 35,* 419-426.

Filipek, P. A., Accardo, P. J., Ashwal, S., Baranek, G. T., Cook, Jr., E. H., Dawson, G., et al. (2000). Practice parameter: Screening and diagnosis of autism: Report of the Quality Standards Subcommittee of the American Academy of Neurology and the Child Neurology Society. *Neurology, 55,* 468-479.

Filipek, P. A., Pasquale, J. A., Baranek, G. T., Cook, E. H., Jr., Dawson, G., Gordon, B., et al. (1999). The screening and diagnosis of autistic spectrum disorders. *Journal of Autism and Developmental Disorders, 29,* 439-484.

Fombonne, E. (1999). The epidemiology of autism: A review. *Psychological Medicine, 29,* 769-786.

Fombonne, E., Simmons, H., Ford, T., Meltzer, H., & Goodman, R. (2001). Prevalence of developmental disorders in the British nationwide survey of child mental health. *Journal of the American Academy of Child and Adolescent Psychiatry, 40,* 820-827.

Freeman, B. J. (1997). Guidelines for evaluating intervention programs for children with autism. *Journal of Autism and Developmental Disorders, 27,* 641-651.

Frith, U. (2004). Emanuel Miller lecture: Confusions and controversies about Asperger syndrome. *Journal of Child Psychology and Psychiatry, 4,* 672-686.

Gagnon, L., Mottron, L., & Joanette, Y. (1997). Questioning the validity of the semantic-pragmatic syndrome diagnosis. *Autism, 1,* 37-55.

Ghaziuddin, M., & Gerstein, L. (1996). Pedantic speaking style differentiates Asperger syndrome from high-functioning autism. *Journal of Autism and Developmental Disorders, 26,* 585-595.

Ghaziuddin, M., & Mountain-Kimchi, K. (2004). Defining the intellectual profile of Asperger syndrome: Comparison with high-functioning autism. *Journal of Autism and Developmental Disorders, 34,* 279-285.

Ghaziuddin, M., Weidmer-Mikhail, E., & Ghaziuddin, N. (1998). Comorbidity of Asperger syndrome: A preliminary report. *Journal of Intellectual Disability Research, 42,* 279-283.

Gilchrist, A., Green, J., Cox, A., Rutter, M., & Le Couteur, A. (2001). Development and current functioning in adolescents with Asperger syndrome: A comparative study. *Journal of Child Psychology and Psychiatry, 42,* 227-240.

Gillberg, C. & Coleman, M. (1992). *The biology of the autistic syndromes* (2nd ed.). London: MacKeith Press.

Gillberg, I. C., & Gillberg, C. (1989). Asperger syndrome: Some epidemiological considerations: A research note. *Journal of Child Psychology and Psychiatry and Allied Disciplines, 30,* 631–638.

Gillberg, C., & Steffenburg, S. (1987). Outcome and prognostic factors in autism and similar conditions: A population-based study of 46 cases followed through puberty. *Journal of Autism and Developmental Disorders, 17,* 273–287.

Gilliam, J. E. (1995). *Gilliam autism rating scale (GARS).* Austin, TX: Pro-Ed.

Gilliam, J. E. (2001). *Gilliam Asperger's disorder scale (GARS).* Austin, TX: Pro-Ed.

Haith, M. M., Bergman, T., & Moore, M. J. (1979). Eye contact and face scanning in early infancy. *Science, 198,* 853–855.

Hall, S. E. K. & Geher, G. (2003). Behavioral personality characteristics of children with reactive attachment disorder. *Journal of Psychology, 137,* 145–162.

Handleman, J. S., & Delmolino, L. M. (2005). Assessment of children with autism. In D. Zager (Ed.), *Autism spectrum disorders* (3rd ed., pp. 269–293). Mahwah, NJ: Erlbaum.

Heerey, E. A., Capps, L. M., Keltner, D., & Kring, A. M. (2005). Understanding teasing: Lessons from children with autism. *Journal of Abnormal Child Psychology, 33,* 55–68.

Hollander, E., Cartwright, C., Wong, C. M., DeCaria, C. M., DelGiudice-Asch, F., Buchsbaum, M. S., et al. (1998). A dimensional approach to the autism spectrum. *CNS Spectrums, 3,* 22–26, 33–39.

Howlin, P. (2003). Outcome in high-functioning adults with autism with and without early language delays: Implications for the differentiation between autism and Asperger syndrome. *Journal of Autism & Developmental Disorders, 33,* 3–13.

Howlin, P., & Asgharian, A. (1999). The diagnosis of autism and Asperger syndrome: Findings from a survey of 770 families. *Developmental Medicine and Child Neurology, 41,* 834–839.

Howlin, P., & Moore, A. (1997). Diagnosis of autism. A survey of over 1200 patients in the UK. *Autism, 1,* 135–162.

Isager, T., Mouridsen, S. E., & Rich, B. (1999). Mortality and causes of death in pervasive developmental disorders. *Autism, 3,* 7–16.

Kanner, L. (1943). Autistic disturbances of affective contact. *The Nervous Child, 2,* 217–250.

Kientz, M. A., & Dunn, W. (1997). A comparison of the performance of children with and without autism on the sensory profile. *American Journal of Occupational Therapy, 51,* 530–537.

Klin, A. (1992). Listening preference in regard to speech: A possible characterization of the symptom of social withdrawal. *Journal of Autism and Developmental Disorders, 21,* 29–42.

Klin, A., Jones, W., Schultz, R., Volkmar, F., & Cohen, D. (2002a). Defining and quantifying the social phenotype in autism. *American Journal of Psychiatry, 159,* 895–908.

Klin, A., Jones, W., Schultz, R., Volkmar, F., & Cohen, D. (2002b). Visual fixation patterns during viewing of naturalistic social situations as predictors of social competence in individuals with autism. *Archives of General Psychiatry, 59,* 809–816.

Klin, A., Pauls, D., Schultz, R., & Volkmar, F. (2005). Three diagnostic approaches to Asperger syndrome: Implications for research. *Journal of Autism & Developmental Disorders, 35,* 221–234.

Klin, A., Sparrow, S. S., de Bildt, A., Cicchetti, D.V., Cohen, D. J., & Volkmar, F. R. (1999). A normed study of face recognition in autism and related disorders. *Journal of Autism and Developmental Disorders, 29,* 497–507.

Klin, A. & Volkmar, F. R. (1997). Asperger's syndrome. In D. Cohen & F. Volkmar (Eds.), *Handbook of autism and pervasive developmental disorders* (2nd ed., pp. 94–122). New York: Wiley.

Klin, A., & Volkmar, F. R. (2000). Treatment and intervention guidelines for individuals with Asperger syndrome. In A. Klin, F. R.Volkmar, & S. S. Sparrow (Eds.), *Asperger syndrome* (pp. 340–366). New York: Guilford Press.

Klin, A.,Volkmar, F. R., Sparrow, S. S., Cicchetti, D. V., & Rourke, B. P. (1995). Validity and neuropsychological characterization of Asperger syndrome: Convergence with nonverbal learning disabilities syndrome. *Journal of Child Psychology and Psychiatry, 36,* 1127–1140.

Krug, D. A., & Arick, J. R. (2003). *Krug Asperger's disorder index.* Austin, TX: Pro-Ed.

Krug, D. A., Arick, J., & Almond, P. (1980). Behavior checklist for identifying severely handicapped individuals with high levels of autistic behavior. *Journal of child Psychology & Psychiatry & Allied Disciplines, 21,* 221-229.

Kuhl, P. K., Coffey-Corina, S., Padden, D., & Dawson, G. (2005). Links between social and linguistic processing of speech in preschool children with autism: Behavioral and electrophysiological measures. *Developmental Science, 8,* F1-F12.

Landa, R. (2000). Social language use in Asperger syndrome and high-functioning autism. In A. Klin, F. Volkmar, & S. Sparrow (Eds.), *Asperger syndrome* (pp. 125-158). New York: Guilford Press.

Langdell, T. (1978). Recognition of faces: An approach to the study of autism. *Journal of Child Psychology and Psychiatry, 19,* 225-238.

Lewis, M. H. & Bodfish, J. W. (1998). Repetitive behavior disorders in autism. *Mental Retardation and Developmental Disabilities Research Reviews, 4,* 80-89.

Lewy, A. L., & Dawson, G. (1992). Social stimulation and joint attention in young autistic children. *Journal of Abnormal Child Psychology, 20,* 555-566.

Lindberg, B. (1994). *Understanding Rett syndrome: A practical guide for parents, teachers, and therapists.* Kirkland, WA: Hogrefe & Huber.

Liss, M., Harel, B., Fein, D., Allen, D., Dunn, M., Feinstein, C., et al. (2001). Predictors and correlates of adaptive functioning in children with developmental disorders. *Journal of Autism and Developmental Disorders, 31,* 210-230.

Losche, G. (1990). Sensorimotor and action development in autistic children from infancy to early childhood. *Journal of Child Psychology and Psychiatry, 31,* 749-761.

Lord, C. (1995). Follow-up of two-year-olds referred for possible autism. *Journal of Child Psychology and Psychiatry, 36,* 1365-1382.

Lord, C. (1997). Diagnostic instruments in autism spectrum disorders. In D. Cohen & F. Volkmar (Eds.), *Handbook of autism and pervasive developmental disorders* (2nd ed., pp. 460-483). New York: Wiley.

Lord, C., & Bailey, A. (2002). Autism spectrum disorders. In M. Rutter and E. Taylor (Eds.), *Child and adolescent psychiatry* (4th ed., pp. 636-663). Malden, MA: Blackwell.

Lord, C., Cook, E. H., Leventhal, B., & Amaral, D. G. (2000). Autism spectrum disorders. *Neuron, 28,* 355-363.

Lord, C., & Magill-Evans, J. (1995). Peer interactions of autistic children and adolescents. *Development & Psychopathology, 7,* 611-626.

Lord, C., & Paul, R. (1997). Language and communication in autism. In D. Cohen & F. Volkmar (Eds.), *Handbook of autism and pervasive developmental disorders* (2nd ed., pp. 195-225). New York: Wiley.

Lord, C., Risi, S., Lambrecht, L., Cook, E. H., Leventhal, B. L., DiLavore, P. C., et al. (2000). The autism diagnostic observation schedule—generic: A standard measure of social and communication deficits associated with the spectrum of autism. *Journal of Autism and Developmental Disorders, 30,* 205-223.

Lord, C., Rutter, M., DiLavore, P., & Risi, S. (1999). *Autism diagnostic observation schedule (ADOS).* Los Angeles, CA: Western Psychological Services.

Maestro, S., Casella, C., Milone, A., Muratori, F., & Palacio-Espasa, F. (1999). Study of the onset of autism through home movies. - *Psychopathology, 32,* 292-300.

Mahoney, W. J., Szatmari, P., MacLean, J. E., Bryson, S. E., Bartolucci, G., Walter, S. D., et al. (1998). Reliability and accuracy of differentiating pervasive developmental disorder subtypes. *Journal of the American Academy of Child & Adolescent Psychiatry, 37,* 278-285.

Malhotra, S., & Gupta, N. (1999). Childhood disintegrative disorder. *Journal of Autism and Developmental Disorders, 29,* 491-498.

Marriage, K. J., Gordon, V., & Brand, L. (1995). A social skills group for boys with Asperger syndrome. *Australian and New Zealand Journal of Psychiatry, 29,* 58-62.

Mayes, S. D. & Calhoun, S. L. (2003). Ability profiles in children with autism: Influence of age and IQ. *Autism, 6,* 65-80.

Mayes, S. D., Calhoun, S. L., & Crites, D. L. (2001). Does *DSM-IV* Asperger's disorder exist? *Journal of Abnormal Child Psychology, 29,* 263-271.

McLaughlin, S. (1998). *Introduction to Language Development.* San Diego, CA: Singular.

Mesibov, G. B., Adams, L. W., & Klinger, L. G. (1997). *Autism: Understanding the disorder.* New York: Plenum.

Mesibov, G., Schopler, E., Schaffer, B., & Landrus, R. (1988). *Adolescent and adult psychoeducational profile (AAPEP).* Austin, TX: Pro-Ed.

Miller, J. N., & Ozonoff, S. (1997). Did Asperger's cases have Asperger disorder? A research note. *Journal of Child Psychology and Psychiatry, 38,* 247–251.

Minshew, N. J., Sweeney, J. A., & Bauman, M. L. (1997). Neurological aspects of autism. In Donald J. Cohen and Fred R. Volkmar (Eds.), *Handbook of autism and pervasive developmental disorders* (2nd ed., pp. 344–369). New York: Wiley.

Molina, J. L., Ruata, J. M., & Soler, E. P. (1986). Is there a right-hemisphere dysfunction in Asperger's syndrome? *British Journal of Psychiatry, 148,* 745–746.

Mukaddes, N. M., Kaynak, F. N., Kinali, G., Besikci, H., & Issever, H. (2004). Psychoeducational treatment of children with autism and reactive attachment disorder. *Autism: The International Journal of Research & Practice, 8,* 101–109.

Myles, B. S., Bock, S. J., & Simpson, R. L. (2001). *Asperger syndrome diagnostic scale (ASDS).* Los Angeles, CA: Western Psychological Services.

National Research Council. (2001). *Educating children with autism.* Committee on Educational Interventions for Children with Autism. Division of Behavioral and Social Sciences and Education. Washington, DC: National Academy Press.

Nikolaenko, N. N. (2004). Metaphorical and associative thinking in healthy children and in children with Asperger syndrome at different ages. *Human Physiology, 30,* 532–536.

Ornitz, E. M. (1985). Neurophysiology of infantile autism. *Journal of American Academy of Child Psychiatry, 24,* 251–262.

Osterling, J., & Dawson, G. (1994). Early recognition of children with autism: A study of first birthday home videotapes. *Journal of Autism and Developmental Disabilities, 24,* 247–257.

Osterling, J. A., Dawson, G., & Munson, J. A. (2002). Early recognition of 1-year-old infants with autism spectrum disorder versus mental retardation. *Development and Psychopathology, 14,* 239–251.

Pyles, L. & Attwood, T. (2002). *Hitchhiking through Asperger syndrome.* London: Jessica Kingsley.

Rapin, I. (1965). Dementia infantilism. In C. H. Carter (Ed.), *Medical aspects of mental retardation* (pp. 760–767). Springfield, IL: Charles C Thomas.

Rapin, I. (Ed.). (1996). Preschool children with inadequate communication: Developmental language disorder, autism, low IQ. *Clinics in Developmental Medicine, No. 139.* London: Mac Keith Press.

Reitzel, J., & Szatmari, P. (2003). Learning difficulties in Asperger syndrome. In M. Prior (Ed.), *Asperger syndrome, behavioral and educational aspects* (pp. 35–54). New York: Guilford Press.

Rincover, A. (1986). Behavioral research in self-injury and self-stimulation. *Psychiatric Clinics of North America, 9,* 755–766.

Rinehart, N. J., Bradshaw, J. L., Brereton, A. V., & Tonge, B. J. (2002). A clinical and neurobehavioural review of high-functioning autism and Asperger disorder. *Australian and New Zealand Journal of Psychiatry, 36,* 762–770.

Rinehart, N. J., Bradshaw, J. L., Moss, S. A., Brereton, A. V., & Tonge, B. J. (2000). Atypical interference of local detail on global processing in high functioning autism and Asperger disorder. *Journal of Child Psychology and Psychiatry, 41,* 769–778.

Robins, D. K., Fein, D., Barton, M. L., & Green, J. A. (2001). The modified checklist for autism in toddlers: An initial study investigating the early detection of autism and pervasive developmental disorders. *Journal of Autism & Developmental Disorders, 31,* 131–144.

Rogers, S. J., Hepburn, S., & Wehner, E. (2003). Parent reports of sensory symptoms in toddlers with autism and those with other developmental disorders. *Journal of Autism and Developmental Disorders, 33,* 631–642.

Rourke, B. (1989). *Nonverbal learning disabilities: The syndrome and the model.* New York: Guilford Press.

Rutter, M., Bailey, A., Bolton, P., & Le Couteur, A. (1994). Autism and known medical conditions: Myth and substance. *Journal of Child Psychology and Psychiatry, 35,* 311–322.

Rutter, M., Bailey, A., & Lord, C. (2003). *SCQ: The social communication questionnaire.* Los Angeles: Western Psychological Services.

Rutter, M., LeCouteur, A., & Lord, C. (2003). *ADI-R: Autism diagnostic interview-revised.* Los Angeles: Western Psychological Services.

Safran, S. P. (2001). Asperger syndrome: The emerging challenge to special education. *Exceptional Children, 67,* 151–160.

Schopler, E., Reichler, R. J., Bashford, A., Lansing, M. D., & Marcus, L. M. (1990). *Psychoeducational profile revised (PEP-R)*. Austin, TX: Pro-Ed.

Schopler, E., Reichler, R. J., & Renner, B. R. (1988). *The childhood autism rating scale (CARS)*. Los Angeles: Western Psychological Services.

Schuler, A. L., Prizant, B. M., & Wetherby, A. M. (1997). Enhancing language and communication development: Prelinguistic approaches. In D. J. Cohen & F. R. Volkmar (Eds.), *Handbook of autism and pervasive developmental disorders* (2nd ed., pp. 539-571). New York: Wiley.

Schultz, R. T., Gauthier, I., Klin, A., Fulbright, R., Anderson, A., Volkmar, F. R., et al. (2000). Abnormal ventral temporal cortical activity among individuals with autism and Asperger syndrome during face discrimination. *Archives of General Psychiatry, 57,* 331-340.

Scott, F., Baron-Cohen, S., Bolton, P., & Brayne, C. E. G. (2002). The CAST (childhood Asperger syndrome test): Preliminary development of a UK screen for mainstream primary-school-age children. *Autism: The International Journal of Research & Practice, 6,* 9-31.

Shriberg, L. D., Paul, R., McSweeney, J. L., Klin, A., Cohen, D. J., & Volkmar, F. R. (2001). Speech and prosody characteristics of adolescents and adults with high-functioning autism and Asperger syndrome. *Journal of Speech, Language, and Hearing Research, 44,* 1097-1115.

Sigman, M., Dijamco, A., Gratier, M., & Rozga, A. (2004). Early detection of core deficits in autism. *Mental Retardation and Developmental Disabilities Research Reviews, 10,* 221-233.

Sigman, M., & Ruskin, E. (1999). Continuity and change in the social competence of children with autism, Down syndrome, and developmental delays. *Monographs of the Society in Research in Child Development, 64,* 1-114.

Skjeldal, O. H., Sponheim, E., Ganes, T., Jellum, E., & Bakke, S. (1998). Childhood autism: The need for physical investigations. *Brain Development, 20,* 227-233.

Smith, E. A., & Van Houten, R. (1996). A comparison of the characteristics of self-stimulatory behaviors in "normal" children and children with developmental delays. *Research in Developmental Disabilities, 17,* 253-268.

South, M., Williams, B. J., McMahon, W. M., Owley, T., Filipek, P. A., Shernoff, E., et al. (2002). Utility of the Gilliam autism rating scale in research and clinical populations. *Journal of Autism and Developmental Disorders, 32,* 593-599.

Spelke, E. S., Phillips, A., & Woodward, A. L. (1995). Infants' knowledge of object motion and human action. In D. Sperber, D. Premack, & A. J. Premack (Eds.), *Causal cognition: A multidisciplinary debate* (pp. 44-78). Oxford, UK: Oxford University Press.

Stein, M. T., Klin, A., & Miller, K. (2004). When Asperger syndrome and a nonverbal learning disability look alike. *Journal of Developmental & Behavioral Pediatrics, 25,* 190-193.

Stone, W. L., Ousley, O. Y., & Littleford, C. (1997). Motor imitation in young children with autism: What's the object? *Journal of Abnormal Child Psychology, 25,* 475-485.

Stone, W. L., Ousley, O. Y., Yoder, P. J., Hogan, K. L., & Hepburn, S. L. (1997). Nonverbal communication in two- and three-year-old children with autism. *Journal of Autism and Developmental Disorders, 27,* 677-696.

Strandburg, R. J., Marsh, J. T., Brown, W. S., Asarnow, R. F., Guthrie, D., & Higa, J. (1993). Event-related potentials in high-functioning adult autistics: Linguistic and nonlinguistic visual information processing tasks. *Neuropsychologia, 31,* 413-434.

Swettenham, J., Baron-Cohen, S., Charman, T., Cox, A., Baird, G., Drew, A., et al. (1998). The frequency and distribution of spontaneous attention shifts between social and nonsocial stimuli in autistic, typically developing and nonautistic developmentally delayed infants. *Journal of Child Psychology and Psychiatry, 39,* 747-753.

Szatmari, P., Bremner, R., & Nagy, J. (1989). Asperger syndrome: A review of clinical features. *Canadian Journal of Psychiatry, 34,* 554-560.

Thelen, E. (1979). Rhythmical stereotypies in normal human infants. *Animal Behavior, 27,* 699-715.

Thelen, E. (1981). Kicking, rocking, and waving: Contextual analysis of rhythmical stereotypies in normal human infants. *Animal Behavior, 29,* 3-11.

Tidmarsh, L. & Volkmar, F. R. (2003). Diagnosis and epidemiology of autism spectrum disorders. *Canadian Journal of Psychiatry, 48,* 517-525.

Tiegerman-Farber, E. (2002). Autism spectrum disorders: Learning to communicate. In D. K. Bernstein & E. Tiegerman-Faber (Eds.), *Language and communication disorders in children* (5th ed., pp. 510-564). Boston: Allyn & Bacon.

Van Bourgondien, M., & Woods, A. (1992). Vocational possibilities for high-functioning adults with autism. In E. Schopler & G. Mesibov (Eds.), *High-functioning individuals with autism* (pp. 227-242). New York: Plenum.

Van Meter, L., Fein, D., Morris, R., Waterhouse, L., & Allen, D. (1997). Delay versus deviance in autistic social behavior. *Journal of Autism and Developmental Disorders, 27,* 557-569.

Volkmar, F. R., Carter, A., Grossman, J., & Klin, A. (1997). Social development in autism. In D. Cohen & F. Volkmar (Eds.), *Handbook of autism and pervasive developmental disorders* (2nd ed., pp. 173-194). New York: Wiley.

Volkmar, F. R., Cohen, D. J., Bregman, J. D., Hooks, M. Y., & Stevenson, J. M. (1989). An examination of the social typologies in autism. *Journal of the American Academy of Child and Adolescent Psychiatry, 28,* 82-86.

Volkmar, F. R., Cohen, D. J., & Paul, R. (1986). An evaluation of *DSM-III* criteria for infantile autism. *Journal of the American Academy of Child Psychiatry, 25,* 190-197.

Volkmar, F. R., Klin, A., & Cohen, D. J. (1997). Diagnosis and classification of autism and related conditions: Consensus and issues. In D. Cohen & F. Volkmar (Eds.), *Handbook of autism and pervasive developmental disorders* (2nd ed., pp. 5-40). New York: Wiley.

Volkmar, F. R., Klin, A., Siegel, B., Szatmari, P., Lord, C., Campbell, M., et al. (1994). Field trial for autistic disorder in DSM-IV. *American Journal of Psychiatry, 151,* 1361-1367.

Volkmar, F. R., Lord, C., Bailey, A., Schultz, R. T., & Klin, A. (2004). Autism and pervasive developmental disorders. *Journal of Child Psychology and Psychiatry, 45,* 135-170.

Volkmar, F. R., & Nelson, D. S. (1990). Seizure disorders in autism. *Journal of the American Academy of Child and Adolescent Psychiatry, 29,* 127-129.

Volkmar, F. R., & Rutter, M. (1995). Childhood disintegrative disorder: Results of the *DSM-IV* autism field trial. *Journal of the American Academy of Child and Adolescent Psychiatry, 34,* 1092-1095.

Vostanis, P., Smithe, B., Corbett, J., Sungum-Paliwal, R., Edwards, A., Gingell, K., et al. (1998). Parental concerns of early development in children with autism and related disorders. *Autism, 2,* 229-242.

Walker, D. R., Thompson, A., Zwaigenbaum, L., Goldberg, J., Bryson, S. E., Mahoney, W. J., et al. (2004). Specifying PDD-NOS: A comparison of PDD-NOS, Asperger syndrome, and autism. *Journal of the American Academy of Child & Adolescent Psychiatry, 43,* 172-180.

Walters, A., Barrett, R. P., & Feinstein, C. (1990). Social relatedness and autism: Current research, issues, directions. *Research in Developmental Disabilities, 11,* 303-326.

Waterhouse, L., Fein, D., & Modahl, C. (1996). Neurofunctional mechanisms in autism. *Psychological Review, 103,* 457-489.

Wetherby, A. M., & Prizant, B. M. (2000). *Autism spectrum disorders: A developmental, transactional perspective.* Baltimore, MD: Paul Brookes.

Wetherby, A. M., & Prizant, B. M. (2005). Enhancing language and communication development in autism spectrum disorders: Assessment and intervention guidelines. In D. Zager (Ed.), *Autism spectrum disorders* (3rd ed., pp. 327-365). Mahwah, NJ: Erlbaum.

Wetherby, A. M., Prizant, B. M., & Hutchinson, T. A. (1998). Communicative, social/affective and symbolic profiles of young children with autism and pervasive developmental disorders. *American Journal of Speech-Language Pathology, 7,* 77-91.

Wetherby, A. M., Woods, J., Allen, L., Cleary, J., Dickinson, H., & Lord, C. (2004). Early indicators of autism spectrum disorders in the second year of life. *Journal of Autism and Developmental Disorders, 34,* 473-493.

Wimpory, D. C., Hobson, R. P., Williams, J. M., & Nash, S. (2000). Are infants with autism socially engaged? A study of recent retrospective parental reports. *Journal of Autism and Developmental Disorders, 30,* 525-536.

Wing, L. (1969). The handicaps of autistic children: A comparative study. *Journal of Child Psychology and Psychiatry, 10,* 1–40.

Wing, L. (1981). Asperger syndrome: A clinical account. *Psychological Medicine, 11,* 115–129.

Wing, L. (1997). Syndromes of autism and atypical development. In D. J. Cohen & F. R. Volkmar (Eds.), *Handbook of autism and pervasive developmental disorders* (2nd ed., pp. 148–170). New York: Wiley.

Wing, L., & Gould, J. (1979). Severe impairments of social interaction and associated abnormalities in children: Epidemiology and classification. *Journal of Autism and Developmental Disorders, 9,* 11–29.

Woodbury-Smith, M., Klin, A., & Volkmar, F. (2005). Asperger's syndrome: A comparison of clinical diagnoses and those made according to the *ICD-10* and *DSM-IV. Journal of Autism & Developmental Disorders, 35,* 235–240.

Woods, J. J., & Wetherby, A. M. (2003). Early identification of and intervention for infants and toddlers who are at risk for autism spectrum disorder. *Language, Speech, & Hearing Services in Schools, 34,* 180–194.

World Health Organization (WHO). (1993). *The ICD-10 classification of mental and behavioural disorders: Diagnostic criteria for research.* Geneva: Author.

Young, R. L., Brewer, N., & Pattison, C. (2003). Parental identification of early behavioral abnormalities in children with autistic disorder. *Autism: The International Journal of Research and Practice, 7,* 125–144.

Young, E. C., Diehl, J. J., Morris, D., Hyman, S. L., & Bennetto, L. (2005). The use of two language tests to identify pragmatic language problems in children with autism spectrum disorders. *Language, Speech, and Hearing Services in Schools, 36,* 62–72.

CHAPTER 2

Historical Perspectives and Etiology of Autism Spectrum Disorders

KEY TERMS

Autistic Psychopathy

Cross-modal Associative Memory

Etiology

Feral Children

Habit Memory

Lesion

Low-incidence Disability

Multiplex Family

Neural Plasticity

Neurotransmitters

Neurotypical

Organic Disorder

Prevalence

Psychopharmacological

Representational Memory

❖ **LEARNING WITH MS. HARRIS: The Need to Learn More**

Ms. Harris is amassing a great deal of information about ASD. She treasures the insight into family life provided by Ms. Owens and accompanied her to a parent support meeting where Ms. Harris continued to be amazed at the parents' resilience in facing the daily challenges their children present. Although Ms. Harris laughed about becoming as pedantic as some individuals on the spectrum, she talked about ASD to anyone who would sit still. At dinner with a group of her friends one evening, however, Ms. Harris's sense of superior knowledge vanished as her friends started asking questions.

"OK, so some kids have autism and some kids have Asbergers," stated Leia.

"AsPERgers," corrected Ms. Harris.

"Yeah, right," replied Leia, "Anyway, so why do they call them that?"

"Oh, I know," said Franklin. "They got the name autism from that kid on St. Elsewhere *on TV."*

"No way," shouted Twyla. "Dustin Hoffman did Rain Man *before that. The name came from him."*

"That's right," responded Franklin. "And I remember when Dustin Hoffman said he interviewed some guy named Joseph Sullivan in order to prepare for the part. Wonder where Joseph came up with the name?"

"I think 'AsPERgers'", said Leia, pronouncing carefully, "sounds like some kind of detergent."

"Oh, and I heard that kids get autism from their parents," interjected Twyla.

Ms. Harris, dizzy from all the banter, realizes she has no idea where the terms came from or when they were first applied. She vaguely recalls one of her professors saying the term had something to do with the Greeks, which would certainly predate the kid on St. Elsewhere *as well as Dustin Hoffman. Could there be any truth to the idea that parents cause autism? For the first time in weeks, Ms. Harris changes the subject to something other than ASD and eats the rest of her meal very quietly.*

AUTISM THROUGH HISTORY

Autism is not a new disability. Individuals have demonstrated the characteristics associated with Autism Spectrum Disorders (ASD) for thousands of years. Long ago, children born with autism probably suffered the same fate experienced by babies born with any disability. Infants and children seen as defective were abandoned in remote areas and left to die (Kirk, Gallagher, & Anastasiow, 1993). Indeed, in 1799, Jean Marc Gaspard Itard made history in special education when a child named Victor, who had been found living in the woods among wolves, was brought to him. Itard determined to demonstrate that he could socialize the boy (Itard, 1806/1962; Lane, 1976). Victor's ability to survive alone in the wilderness indicates that he was not an infant when abandoned but older, yet his behavior was viewed as uncontrollable. This would be consistent with the presence of autism. Although most instances of autism are present at birth, many children, particularly those born centuries ago, might not have been perceived as markedly different until they were 3 or 4 years old or even older. Itard wanted to prove that appropriate instructional techniques could teach a boy as wild as Victor. Unfortunately, Victor proved to be resistant to Itard's efforts, and Itard deemed his experiment a failure. Given his abandonment and his resistance to Itard's efforts, it is highly likely that Victor had autism.

Victor is not an isolated example of the historical presence of ASD. A number of **feral children** (children growing up isolated from humans, said to be raised by animals) have been described in the literature, including Kaspar Hauser and the "wolf-girls" of India (Candland, 1993; MacLean, 1977; Newton, 2003). Frith (2003) marvelously recounts the story of Peter, the Wild Boy of Hanover, who was discovered in Germany when he was about 12 years of age. Peter, who captured the interest of King George I and Queen Caroline, never learned to speak even though he was given every advantage. However, Peter loved music and would hum tunes he heard.

Although ASD, like many other disabilities, has been present in humans for centuries, efforts to educate individuals with disabilities have been a relatively recent phenomenon. Specialized instructional techniques and schools for students with disabilities did not appear in the United States until after the 1820s, and then they focused primarily on individuals with peripheral sensory disabilities, such as the blind or deaf (Hallahan & Kauffman, 2003). Even with the legislation of compulsory education toward the end of the nineteenth century in the United States, it was still not compulsory for children with disabilities to attend school. This did not keep interested individuals from providing training and education to persons with disabilities, but it was more often with private than public services.

Kanner's Use of the Term *Autism*

Toward the middle of the twentieth century, a psychiatrist at Johns Hopkins University named Leo Kanner began to notice similarities among a group of children who had been brought to him for diagnoses and treatment. Kanner published an article in which he described these 11 children (Kanner, 1943) as having marked differences in their ability to socialize with others and extreme rigidity in their behaviors. Although the term had been used in the early 1900s by Bleuler to describe socialization deficits and a singular focus on personal interests in persons with schizophrenia (Bleuler as cited in Frith, 1991), Kanner was the first to apply the term *autism* to a group of children who were demonstrating remarkably similar behavioral features.

The Greek root of the term *autism* is *autos* which roughly translates as *self*. *Autos* is also the root for the word *automatic* which is equated with independent functioning without the need for external input (like an automatic transmission or an automatic dishwasher). Kanner viewed the children as demonstrating little need for interaction with others and viewed them as being self-absorbed and self-satisfied. Therefore, he used the term *autism* to characterize the children's behaviors (Volkmar, Carter, Grossman, & Klin, 1997).

Much of what Kanner described about those children's characteristics form the basic description of individuals who have what is now termed *classic* or *Kannerian* autism. However, Kanner made a few assertions that have proved inaccurate. First, Kanner noted that the children lacked any obvious physical differences, so the condition could not have been organic (i.e., not a congenital condition or some type of birth defect) and therefore would have no associated medical conditions. Today it is recognized that autism is an **organic disorder** (present at birth) and may be associated with other medical conditions such as seizure disorders, Cornelia de Lange syndrome, Fragile X, William's syndrome, tuberous sclerosis, and Landau-Kleffner syndrome (Canitano, Luchetti, & Zappella, 2005; Rutter, Bailey, Bolton & Le Couteur, 1994).

Second, Kanner noted that the children he examined all had intelligence quotients (IQs) in the normal range, and stated that children with autism would have normal intelligence. Researchers today document that the majority of individuals with autism demonstrate some level of mental retardation (i.e., IQ < 70; Fombonne, 1999; Rutter et al., 1994). Kanner used the term *functionally retarded* to refer to the children's dysfunction in the presence of what he thought was normal intelligence. Kanner's position that the children with autism had a normal or brilliant innate capacity which was not being exhibited continues to be believed by many people today, even in the face of evidence to the contrary.

Finally, Kanner certainly saw a skewed population. In the 1940s, the parents who brought their children to his office at Johns Hopkins University were university professors and other professionals who probably earned enviable salaries. This led Kanner to conclude that autism would occur only in families of higher socioeconomic status. Today it is recognized that autism occurs in families at any and all income levels and is not unique to the wealthy. Because of a presumed focus on their career rather than their children, Kanner also postulated that the parents played a role in the development of autism. Today it is recognized that the only role parents play might be via genetics (Szatmari, Jones, Zwaigenbaum, & MacLean, 1998).

In 1908, even before Kanner began to study this group of children, a special educator in Vienna, Theodor Heller, was describing children who apparently had typical early development but then regressed severely as exhibited by their lack of language, interest in others, and relatedness. In addition to social withdrawal, children with "Heller's dementia infantilis" engaged in bizarre and perseverative, or repetitious, motor behaviors as well as sensory avoidance (Yakovlev, Weinberger, & Chipman, 1948). Today, Heller's syndrome is synonymous with what some view as a type of autism called childhood disintegrative disorder (CDD) (Malhotra & Gupta, 1999), described in Chapter 1.

Asperger Describes a Similar Profile

About the same time that Leo Kanner was studying the similarities in children who had been brought to his clinic, Hans Asperger, a doctor in Vienna during World War II, wrote about four young boys (6 to 11 years old) who were seen at the University Paediatric Clinic at which he worked. In what would become his second doctoral thesis, Asperger wrote that the boys all seemed to have "clever-sounding language" (Frith, 1991, p. 10) with obvious differences in nonverbal communication, including unusual eye gaze, prosody, voice tone, and gestures. Asperger described the boys as having typical intellectual abilities but inept social skills. He reported being concerned about how frequently the boys were bullied and teased by their peers at school. They also experienced motor problems and were clumsy, and they had severely restricted interests, including obsessively collecting unusual objects. Asperger described the boys' egocentrism and pursuit of circumscribed interests as leading to aggression, noncompliance, and negativism (Asperger, 1944/1991). These differences in behavior seemed to emerge in the second year of the children's lives, and the boys had family histories of such differences. **Autistic psychopathy** is the term Asperger used to designate the boys' condition. Although this term is unusual by today's standards, it simply reflects that Asperger believed the boys' condition to be stable as opposed to progressive (Frith, 2004).

Asperger's work was relatively unknown in English-speaking countries until Wing (1981) wrote a series of case studies profiling the syndrome. It is from Wing's writing that the term **Asperger syndrome** (and more recently, simply Aspergers) began to be used rather than autistic psychopathy. With the translation of Asperger's work into English (Frith, 1991), more people became aware of the syndrome that was eventually associated with similar pervasive developmental disorders in the *DSM-IV*. Currently there is great disagreement regarding the similarities and differences between high-functioning autism and Aspergers, with some arguing a lack of distinction (Howlin, 2003) and others claiming the presence of clinical and neurobiological uniqueness (Rinehart, Bradshaw, Brereton, & Tonge, 2002). Asperger (1977) believed the syndrome he defined was different from Kanner's autism.

As with Kanner's observations, many of the characteristics described by Asperger and associated with Asperger syndrome continue to be accurate today. And like Kanner, Asperger made several assertions that have now been proved incorrect (Frith, 2004). First, since he had met only males with the characteristics, Asperger indicated that this condition would occur only in males. In reality, although at a smaller percentage, Asperger syndrome is also observed in females. Second, in the late 1940s, Asperger suggested that individuals with this syndrome would demonstrate unusual intellectual abilities. The *DSM-IV-TR* contains normal intelligence as a criterion for Asperger syndrome, although some individuals with Asperger syndrome may test in the range of mild intellectual disabilities. Finally, Asperger described the males he studied as having good language skills. Today, it is recognized that individuals with Asperger syndrome may have excellent vocabularies and possess the ability to talk incessantly (Ghaziuddin & Gerstein, 1996), but there may be delays in the emergence of language, difficulties with the pragmatics (use) of language, and an inability to understand nonliteral language (Ghaziuddin & Gerstein, 1996; Mayes, Calhoun, & Crites, 2001; Minshew, Goldstein, Muenz, & Payton, 1992; Young, Diehl, Morris, Hyman, & Bennetto, 2005).

ETIOLOGY OF AUTISM SPECTRUM DISORDERS

The **etiology** is the assignment of cause or source for a disorder. As researchers began to describe and define the conditions that now fall under the broader category of ASD, there was speculation about what causes such dramatic differences in behavior and learning. From the 1940s until the late 1960s, the predominant theory was that psychological factors caused autism. According to this theory, a healthy child was born into an environment where she or he did not feel loved and accepted (Rank, 1955). Because of the extreme psychological stress related to this absence of affection, the child would turn inward and become isolated from, and unresponsive to, the outside world. This theory held the parents responsible for the child's condition, placing specific blame on the mother for being cold and unloving and for not being more emotionally available to the child. Indeed, Bruno Bettelheim (1967) used the term "Refrigerator Mother" to refer to the root cause of a child's autism. Treatment for children with autism during this time was solely directed at the parents, with mothers being subjected to hours of psychoanalysis to determine why they failed to love their children enough. Blame was extended to the fathers, who were also made to endure psycho-analysis to identify their shortcomings and their contribution to their child's condition.

As it became apparent that the parents were operating from love and for the best interests of their children, the perception that autism was caused by "Refrigerator Parents" gradually lost favor. The etiology of autism continued to exist in the psychological realm, however. The emphasis shifted from the actions and inactions of the parents to the children's environments. The "deprived" environment theory gained in popularity and suggested that the children had to turn inward to escape from external environments that they found deplorable. Children with autism were still believed to be born healthy and capable of typical development, but were then forced to retreat into their own worlds due to inadequate home environments. Because of glaring contradictions based on the presence of stimulating and favorable environ-ments, the deprived environment theory was soon replaced by a more rea-sonable theory for the etiology of autism. However, it would be years before the originally held etiological misconceptions that psychological factors caused autism would be totally discredited. Although there have always been those who maintain that autism is present at birth and caused by something intrinsic to the child, an impressive body of research now demonstrates that ASDs are related to neurological dysfunctions of unknown origins.

NEUROLOGICAL DIFFERENCES

There is consensus that ASD are neurodevelopmental disorders of prenatal origin (Bailey, Phillips, & Rutter, 1996). This fact is received as both good and bad news. The good news is that attributing the etiology to the individual's neurological system eliminates useless exploration of psychological deter-minants. The news is also good because of the brain's ability to compensate for some defects or **lesions** (injuries). The bad news is that science knows relatively little about the brain in typically developing populations, much less in populations where the brain is known to be different (Lord & Bailey, 2002). For individuals with ASD, the heterogeneity of the population further complicates the study of neurological development and functioning (Lord, Cook, Leventhal, & Amaral, 2000).

The majority of what is known about the brains of individuals with ASD comes from three branches of investigation (Lord et al., 2000; Pickett, 2001). Researchers evaluate the brains of individuals with ASD by examining them after death or through neuroimaging procedures while the person is alive (the most common procedures being EEG, CT, PET, MRI, and fMRI). Researchers also study brains of typically developing people and make inferences regarding differences. Finally, researchers create animal models, in which the neural systems of the animals are altered to see how behavior is affected (e.g., removing part of the animal's brain). The use of animal models can be suggestive but caution is warranted because it is likely that differences exist between species (Lane, 2002). What becomes confusing across these types of analyses is that there is great variety in the neurological differences exhibited by individuals with ASD.

Although the brain is labeled with separate and distinct terms, it functions only because of the interdependence of the components. For example, the amygdala can be labeled on the diagram of the brain. Serotonin, a neurochemical, can be measured. Neuroimaging can reveal brain structures and activity. However, the brain functions as a result of the structural, chemical, and functional components working together; they would be useless in isolation. This is an important consideration to keep in mind when reading the results of research conducted on individual components in order to guard against simplistic conclusions drawn from limited data on isolated neurological aspects (Goodman, 2002). For example, finding chemical differences may indicate that there are also structural and functional differences that have not been detected (Santangelo & Tsatsanis, 2005).

Even with the caution against overgeneralizing research results, research is critical for enhancing an understanding of the neurological differences in individuals with ASD for the purposes of developing genetic, pharmacological, and behavioral interventions (Pickett, 2001). The summary of research provided here of the structural, chemical, and functional aspects of the neurological system are intended to lay a foundation for understanding why individuals with ASD might behave the way they do and how their neurological systems may predispose them to interact with the world differently.

STRUCTURAL DIFFERENCES

The inconvenience, expense, and reluctance on the part of participants who are involved in studying the brain results in only small samples of a population being studied. Historically, the studies of the human brain in persons with autism were limited to those conducted during autopsy or done using unwieldy and expensive equipment. Kanner (1943) noted that the heads of his 11 subjects were larger than normal, suggesting differences in brain size. Kanner's suspicions were confirmed when it was found that the brains of autistic children who were younger than 12 years of age were found to be slightly heavier and with more volume than those of their matched controls (Bailey, Palferman, Heavey, & Le Couteur, 1998), whereas conclusions about the brain structure of autistic adults were inconsistent (Dekaban & Sadowsky, 1978; Rakic, 1971; Rakic & Sidman, 1970). These differences could be attributed to one or a combination of factors including an interruption of normal maturation in the limbic system, a change in prenatal neural development in the first 30 weeks of gestation, or initial swelling of the brain followed by atrophy and cell loss (Kemper & Bauman, 1998).

Courchesne, Redcay, and Kennedy, (2004) found evidence to support the third of the possible factors influencing the size difference. He noted that children with autism have small head circumferences at birth but experience a period of rapid head growth between 6 and 14 months of age. The rapid period of growth appears to affect a disproportionate increase in the volume of the white matter relative to the gray matter, which connects the cerebral cortex to other areas of the brain (Filipek et al., 1992). The theory is that this rapid period of growth that selectively affects only certain parts of the brain may impede interhemispheric connectivity, making it difficult for the infant to interact with the environment. The overgrowth could result from inflammation of the brain based on innate immunologic problems (Vargas, Nascimbene, Krishnan, Zimmerman, & Pardo, 2004) influenced by genetics or exposure to neurotoxins. Whatever the cause, these defects in neural maturation affect cortical organization and the brain's capacity for learning. The overgrowth could lead to fewer neural connections and decreased brain size (Akshoomoff, Pierce, & Courchesne, 2002). Dementieva et al. (2005) reported that 35% of their 364 participants experienced accelerated head growth during the first 2 months of life. However, they correlated this finding to higher levels of adaptive functioning and less social impairment.

In addition to considering the brain as a whole, various substructures of the brain have been examined to determine whether differences exist in individuals with ASD. A number of structures in the brain have been examined with the majority of the research being conducted on the brainstem, limbic system, cerebrum, and cerebellum. As mentioned, these findings are merely suggestive since they attempt to isolate individual parts of a complex whole. However, even rudimentary knowledge of a simplified approach to understanding the brain provides educators with excellent insight regarding the implications of neurological differences found in some individuals with ASD. Figure 2.1 contains a diagram of the major brain structures that will be discussed.

Brainstem

The brainstem controls basic functions such as breathing, eating, balance, reflexes, and motor coordination. The brainstem also influences waking, sleeping, arousal, and focus of attention, and it helps regulate sensory input and motor output. In individuals with ASD, a fondness for twirling and other self-stimulatory behavior was seen as indicative that the brainstem needed more stimulation (Wong & Wong, 1991). Researchers noted that children

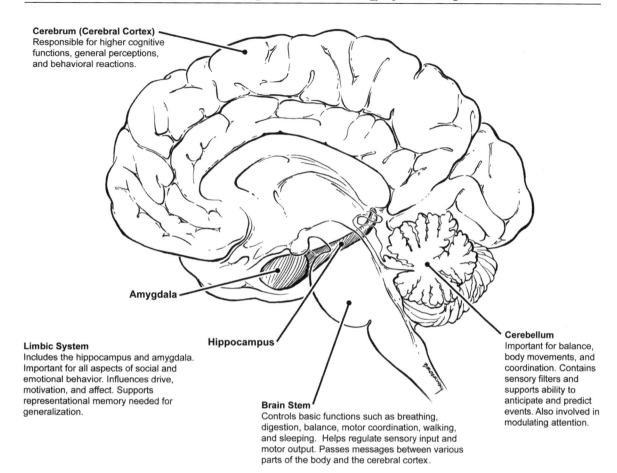

Cerebrum (Cerebral Cortex)
Responsible for higher cognitive functions, general perceptions, and behavioral reactions.

Amygdala

Limbic System
Includes the hippocampus and amygdala. Important for all aspects of social and emotional behavior. Influences drive, motivation, and affect. Supports representational memory needed for generalization.

Hippocampus

Brain Stem
Controls basic functions such as breathing, digestion, balance, motor coordination, walking, and sleeping. Helps regulate sensory input and motor output. Passes messages between various parts of the body and the cerebral cortex.

Cerebellum
Important for balance, body movements, and coordination. Contains sensory filters and supports ability to anticipate and predict events. Also involved in modulating attention.

FIGURE 2.1
Major Brain Structures Researched in ASDs
Source: Provided by Brian Brockway, Brockway Biomedical Studios.

with ASD moved differently. Attempts to turn the head resulted in the whole body turning. Additionally, researchers noted that children with ASD retained their primitive reflexes longer than typically developing children and experienced more sleep disturbances (Limoges, Mottron, Bolduc, Berthiaume, & Godbout, 2005; Schreck, Mulick, & Smith, 2004; Tani et al., 2004). Likewise, individuals with ASD react differently to sensory stimuli, with some being overly responsive to sounds or touch and others being noticeably less responsive (Rogers, Hepburn, & Wehner, 2003).

Early nystagmus studies suggested differences in the brainstem. These studies evaluated the eyes of individuals who were subjected to rapid spinning and then stopped suddenly. In most typical individuals, the rapid spinning produced side-to-side bouncing of the eyes. But this was not so for subjects with autism; their eyes did not bounce in response to the spinning.

Differences have also been shown in tissue samples from the brainstem of a woman with autism (Rodier, 2000). In the analysis, the scientists discovered that the brainstem was shorter, had a smaller facial nucleus (400 v. 9,000 cells), and was missing the superior olive. The facial nucleus is responsible for controlling the muscles for facial expressions, and the superior olive acts as a relay station for auditory information. This preliminary study demonstrated that the brainstem of this woman with autism was different, and the mechanisms for controlling facial expressions and processing auditory information were missing or diminished. Rodier's research corroborated the work by Tanguay and Edwards (1982), who suggested that brainstem differences could distort auditory input, negatively affecting language and cognitive development. Individuals functioning on the lower end of the spectrum may experience more of an auditory delay (Wong & Wong, 1991) than individuals functioning on the higher end of the spectrum (Courchesne, Courchesne, Hicks, & Lincoln, 1985). However, for those individuals functioning on the higher end of the spectrum, problems comprehending spoken language may be as detrimental as the problems perceiving auditory input (Mayes et al., 2001).

Limbic System

The limbic system has received considerably more attention than the brainstem, primarily due to the demonstration of autistic-like behaviors in animals that have had their limbic systems altered. The limbic system, which includes the hippocampus and amygdala, provides the foundation for all aspects of social and emotional behavior. It allows people to gather psychological meaning from events and influences drive, motivation, and affect. The limbic system is also credited with creating a desire for social and emotional contact (Joseph, 1999). In research on adult rats, those who are inflicted with lesions to the hippocampus complex become hyperactive, demonstrate stereotypic motor behaviors, and respond unusually to novel stimuli (Kimble, 1963; Roberts, Dember, & Brodwick, 1962). Some animals with limbic system lesions become overresponsive to touch, temperature changes, lights, and sounds (Green & Schwartzbaum, 1968). When lesions are made to the amygdala in adult monkeys, they demonstrate a loss of fear, withdrawal, compulsive indiscriminate examination of objects, and a reduced ability to attach meaning to events (Mishkin & Aggleton, 1981; Vergnes, 1981). In addition to these outcomes, the animals experience severely impaired **cross-modal associative memory** (Murray & Mishkin, 1985), which means they have problems recognizing by sight something previously touched or tasted and therefore demonstrate an impaired ability to generalize.

The inability to generalize affects the development of representational memory (Mishkin & Appenzeller, 1987; Murray, 1990; Squire & Zola-Morgan, 1991). **Representational memory** involves all sensory modalities and mediates the processing of facts, experiences, and events. Representational memory develops over time as neuronal circuitry matures, but appears to be abnormal in persons with ASD (Bauman, 1997). What appears to be deterioration in some young children identified as having ASD may just be the emergence of the abnormality in representational memory (Kemper & Bauman, 1998). Another type of memory, habit memory, which resides in systems within the cerebral hemisphere, does not appear to be abnormal in individuals with ASD.

Habit memory occurs with the repeated presentation of the same stimulus and allows for automatic connections between those stimuli and the expected responses. Because of repeated pairings, habit memory is not a conscious process. For example, when the phone rings, the automatic response is to answer it. When driving, it is automatic to slam on the brakes if the car in front stops suddenly. Habit memory appears to be intact in individuals with ASD and repetitive pairings of stimulus-response, such as what occurs in discrete trial training, capitalizes on that fact. Unfortunately, as an unconscious process and specific to the repeated trials, habit memory does not usually lead to the reliable or functional use of the skills learned in this method; however, habit memory can allow individuals to memorize facts or acquire specialized skills in areas of their fixation (e.g., playing the piano and drawing). In addition to good rote memorization, reliance on habit memory without representational memory can lead to preoccupations with a narrow range of activities and interests as well as a need for sameness (Kemper & Bauman, 1998).

The limbic system matures across time, requiring social, emotional, and environmental stimulation during the first years of life to function properly (Joseph, 1999). For example, the limbic system supports the preference young infants have for any human face. Infants later identified as having ASD do not show a preference for faces (Pascalis, de Schonen, Morton, Deruelle, & Fabre-Grent, 1995), instead orienting more frequently to objects (Dawson, Meltzoff, Osterling, Rinaldi, & Brown, 1998). By about 8 months of age, typically developing infants show a preference for their mother's face over other faces, and shortly after that will discriminate between faces of people they know and faces of strangers. Some young children with ASD fail to show a differentiated response to their mother's face over a stranger's (Dawson et al., 2002), which may diminish the subsequent development of emotion and attachment. Although typically developing infants form attachments early in life, some children with ASD have been found to show preference for and attachment to their caregivers between 3 to 5 years of age (Sigman, Dijamco, Gratier, & Rozga, 2004). The development of attachment, which appears to be influenced by the limbic system, may be affected by mental age (Rutgers, Bakermans-Kranenburg, van Uzendoorn, & van Berckelaer-Onnes, 2004). Individuals with ASD may demonstrate unusual attachments (Rogers, Ozonoff, & Maslin-Cole, 1993), with strong attachments to objects (Volkmar et al., 1994).

Given that the limbic system matures over time, researchers wondered if early damage to the limbic system would produce the same effects as damage inflicted to the limbic systems of adult animals. Researchers found that when the amygdala is altered or removed in very young animals, differences in behavior do not occur immediately as they had with the adult animals, but emerge over time (Bachevalier & Vargha-Khadem, 2005). After about 8 months, the animals withdrew socially and did not interact well with other animals. At 3 years of age, the animals were not only socially deficit, but also hyperactive (Thompson, 1981). When both the hippocampus and amygdala were altered in neonatal nonhuman primates, a period of typical development was followed by the emergence of behavioral abnormalities that included stereotypies (rocking, crouching, doing somersaults); tantrums in novel situations; blank, expressionless faces; unusual posturing; and poor eye contact (Bachevalier, 1991, 1994). Unlike the adult animals, the animals with early insults did not demonstrate a loss of fear (Bachevalier, Málková, & Mishkin, 2001). The behavioral manifestations were slightly different among animals even though lesions were inflicted on the same areas of the brain. The implications of this research suggest that limbic system problems, present at birth, may not manifest noticeably until about 2 or 3 years of age. Some postmortem studies on the brain have found structural abnormalities within the limbic system (Kemper & Bauman, 1998).

Cerebrum

Unusual findings on computerized tomography suggest the presence of left hemisphere processing deficits that interfere with integration of various systems of the brain. Behaviorally, researchers have noted that some individuals with ASD fail to develop a right ear advantage, as is commonly seen in the population of persons without autism. While not conclusive (Rinehart, Bradshaw, Brereton, & Tonge, 2002), some behavioral observations would suggest that individuals with autism (as opposed to Asperger syndrome) have left hemisphere deficits because of their greater problems with spoken language (Dawson, 1983; Rumsey, 1992), whereas individuals with Asperger syndrome may have more right hemisphere difficulties because their language is relatively intact (when compared to individuals with autism). Additionally, the differences in the white matter of the brain among individuals with Asperger syndrome may be similar to differences seen in those with nonverbal learning disabilities (Rourke, 1989; Tsai, 1992).

Cerebellum

Researchers have found differences in the size of the cerebellum in individuals with ASD (Courchesne, Yeung-Courchesne, Press, Hesselink, & Jernigan, 1988; Miles & Hillman, 2000; Saitoh & Courchesne, 1998). In addition to assisting in the regulation of emotion and higher level thinking (Kemper & Bauman, 1998), the cerebellum plays an important role in learning associations that allow individuals to anticipate and prepare for upcoming events (Grafman et al., 1992; Leiner, Leiner, & Dow, 1987). Individuals with ASD do not lack associative learning, but often their associations are considered unusual. For example, the teacher of a child with autism introduced a daily puppet activity by gently bopping the child on the head with the puppet and saying "hello." During an assessment in a clinic, the child picked up an available puppet and bopped himself on the head, much to the dismay of the evaluators, who thought he was being self-abusive. Fortunately, the teacher was watching from behind a one-way mirror and was able to explain the association the child had acquired.

Without the development of appropriate associations, it is difficult to predict what will happen next. That makes it hard to prepare for upcoming events because a majority of cerebellar activity goes toward figuring out what is happening. As an individual develops associations and increases predictability, he can focus attention elsewhere. If, however, his routines are disrupted, it may be difficult for him to predict what will happen next and he must concentrate on trying to determine that. For example, most people drive the same route to go home from school or work. Since the trip is predictable, the driver can think of many other things while driving and even engage in nondriving activities like eating and talking on a phone. However, if there is a wreck and traffic is being diverted, the driver must pay attention and devise an alternate route to get to the destination. She may discontinue the call, stop eating, and even turn off the radio. As predictability decreases, the need to concentrate increases. Imagine what it must be like for students whose cerebellar differences make associations and predictions difficult. They must spend a great deal of energy trying to figure out what is going on. This goal will be much easier if everything stays the same and there is little variability in schedules, routines, or even furniture arrangements (Volkmar, Carter, Grossman, & Klin, 1997; Steingard, Zimnitzky, DeMaso, Bauman, & Bucci, 1997). Indeed, students functioning on the higher end of the spectrum have been found to have typical motor execution but were unable to anticipate which motor movements were needed for an activity (Rinehart, Bradshaw, Brereton, & Tonge, 2001), interfering with their ability to participate in sports.

In addition to the important role the cerebellum plays in prediction and preparation (Courchesne & Allen, 1997), the cerebellum also contains the brain's filtering system by way of the Purkinje cells. The cerebellum in some individuals with autism is 20–30% smaller than in those without autism, and they have fewer Purkinje cells (Arin, Bauman, & Kemper, 1991; Bailey et al., 1998; Kemper & Bauman, 1998; Ritvo et al., 1986). Without a filtering system, all sensory information assaults the brain with the same intensity and importance. Irrelevant noises such as fans, airplanes, and distant noises are perceived by the brain to be as important as the voice of a teacher (Teder-Sälejärvi, Pierce, Courchesne, & Hillyard, 2005). The lack of adequate sensory filtering can also make certain fabrics or tags in clothing feel very uncomfortable. The impact of a deficient filtering system is described more completely in Chapter 5. Purkinje cell loss has also been found among individuals with seizure disorders (Dam, 1992) raising an interesting question about the correlation between Purkinje cell loss and seizure disorders, which can affect a substantial minority of individuals with ASD (Canitano et al., 2005; Volkmar & Nelson, 1990).

The cerebellum also plays a critical role in the capture, maintenance, and shift of attention between visual and auditory stimuli (Courchesne, Akshoomoff & Townsend, 1992). Some individuals with ASD have been noted to have difficulty disengaging from one stimuli in order to attend to a new stimuli (Townsend, Courchesne, & Egaas, 1996), much like the behavior seen in a typically developing 2-month-old (Landry & Bryson, 2004). In studies using alternating stimuli, individuals with autism and without autism show that they can shift attention from one stimulus to another, but it takes longer for the shift to occur (Wainwright-Sharp & Bryson, 1993). Shifting attention is easier if there is a cue (e.g., adult pointing) that stays in place (Bryson & Landry, 1994; Townsend, Harris, & Courchesne, 1996) and sufficient time for the shift to occur (Townsend & Courchesne, 1994). Klin, Jones, Schultz, Volkmar, and Cohen, (2002a) noted that individuals with ASD who are watching a movie tend to focus on nonsocial stimuli, like a picture on the wall or a lamp, instead of the human characters' faces. Likewise, individuals with autism may be more interested in details or the component parts, rather than the comprehensive entity (Boucher & Lewis, 1992; Hobson, Ouston, & Lee, 1988; Langdell, 1978; Tantam, Monaghan, Nicholson, & Stirling, 1989). This awareness of details is documented by the finding that some individuals with ASD are able to locate figures hidden in pictures better than individuals without ASD (Mottron, Burack, Iarocci, Belleville, & Enns, 2003). Indeed, the tendency to focus on component parts may lead to differences in processing facial information because they look at others' mouths rather than eyes to try to understand communicative content (Klin, Jones, Schultz, Volkmar, & Cohen, 2002b; Langdell, 1978).

Abnormal development of the cerebellum interferes with the development of other neurological systems. Indeed, differences in any area of neuroanatomical development affect development of other areas of the brain (Kemper & Bauman, 1998). Although some of the more researched neural systems were described separately, the subsystems of the brain are highly interrelated, and it is important to consider the intricate functioning of the brain as a whole with many unexplained variances (Bailey, Phillips, & Rutter, 1996).

NEURAL PLASTICITY

The brain changes due to maturation and experience, modifying existing neural circuitry and creating novel circuitry. The functions of an area of the brain that is deficient or damaged may be taken over by another area of the brain, particularly in terms of one hemisphere taking over responsibility for specialized functions usually associated with the other damaged hemisphere (e.g., language; Rutter, 2002). The term **neural plasticity** describes this compensatory ability in the brain (Lenn, 1991; Nass, 2002). For people who have had strokes or head injuries, rehabilitation techniques begun as soon as possible following the trauma take advantage of the brain's plasticity by compensating for areas of the brain that have been damaged. Neural plasticity may provide some of the explanation for why individuals with the same initial neurological pathology can have different functional outcomes. Much of the emphasis on early intervention for children with ASD is based on the hope that the strategies can facilitate the development of compensatory brain activity and mitigate the effects of the neurological differences. However, researchers are beginning to realize that the behavioral manifestations in ASD are the result of systems failures or lesions in both hemispheres of the brain, not just pinpointed lesions to one hemisphere (Rutter, 2002), overwhelming the capacity of neural plasticity. Intervention may certainly promote skill acquisition and improved performance, but may not result in neural changes sufficient to compensate for deficits.

There is also emerging speculation that neural plasticity may actually contribute to the development of ASD (Courchesne et al., 1992). The brain develops through an individual's experiences. For individuals with ASD, their neurological differences tend to interfere with their experiences. For example, differences in the limbic system may result in infants being more interested in objects than people (Dawson et al., 1998), which then does not support the neural development of a preference for faces (Pascalis et al., 1995; Werner, Dawson, Osterling, & Dinno, 2000). The neurological differences that are probably present at the time of birth (although they may not manifest until later) set the stage for experiencing the world differently, which then causes further changes in the brain (Kemper & Bauman, 1998). Therefore, the neural reorganization that occurs because of the brain's plasticity may be more harmful than beneficial because of the extension of disrupted functioning to other neural systems (Bachevalier et al., 2001). Although there is a clear genetic and biologic component for some neuroanatomical differences, an interesting question is whether subsequent neurological differences that are evident in postmortem and neuroimaging studies cause ASD or are the result of the individual having an ASD (Akshoomoff et al., 2002; Bauman & Kemper, 2005).

CHEMICAL DIFFERENCES AND PSYCHOPHARMACOLOGICAL TREATMENTS

In addition to structural differences that have been suspected or detected among individuals with ASD, researchers have found chemical differences in the neurology. Indeed, all of the major **neurotransmitters** (chemicals that transport signals and messages in the brain) have been implicated in ASD, but many of the research conclusions lack replication (Lord & Bailey, 2002). As with the study of the structure of the brain, research on neurotransmitters relies on the use of animal models and comparisons between individuals with ASD and those with other clinical conditions, as well as inferences made about neurochemistry by monitoring **psychopharmacological** (use of medications to cause an effect on the mind) interventions. Medications cannot be used to cure ASD; however, they can be used to address some of the behavioral symptoms (Palermo & Curatolo, 2004). For example, a number of stimulant medications have been used to treat overactivity in individuals with ASD (Nicolson & Castellanos, 2000).

Many individuals with ASD may be prescribed medications as a primary form of intervention (Aman, Van Bourgondien, Wolford, & Sarphare, 1995). The challenge in using medications is to balance the benefit against the risk, since all medications have side effects. For example, some medications carry the risk of causing seizures. Those may not be the first choice for use with a population already at high risk for experiencing seizures (Canitano et al., 2005). Some of the stimulant medications may increase anxiety and stereotypies (Aman et al., 1995), which already exist at high levels in a number of individuals with ASD (Bellini, 2004; Tani et al., 2004). Many of the medications used with individuals on the spectrum have a sedative side effect. Although the sedation may reduce problem behaviors, it may also decrease social interaction and reduce the student's attention to learning tasks (Lord & Bailey, 2002). However, without a medication, the student's behavior may preclude the opportunity for instruction. Additional medication may be given to counteract the side effects of the primary medication, resulting in the need for the student to take several medications each day. Medications should be used in combination with other interventions that teach students important skills.

Given the copious amount of research conducted on the neurochemistry of individuals with ASD, it is disappointing that there are so few conclusive answers. The lack of conclusive answers relates both to methodological issues with some of the studies as well as to the unique responses of individuals to various medications. Serotonin has been the most consistently implicated neurotransmitter in ASD and is of interest because of its role in language production (Chandana et al., 2005) and sensory responses. A number of researchers have verified that about one-third of individuals with ASD have elevated levels of serotonin (Anderson et al., 1987; Cook, 1990, 1996; Hollander et al., 1998), as do their close relatives. Chugani, Muzik, and Rothermel (1997) found elevated serotonin synthesis in seven boys with autism but not the one girl.

The elevated levels of serotonin in some individuals but not others suggest unusual brain synthesis of serotonin in the brain, but the reasons are not clear (Palermo & Curatolo, 2004). Elevation in serotonin is evident in typically developing children, but the levels slowly decline by 5 years of age. This decline does not appear to occur in some individuals with ASD (Chugani et al., 1999). About half of individuals with mental retardation also have increased levels of serotonin (Martineu, Barthelemy & LeLord, 1992). Elevated serotonin levels have been suggested as a possible familial marker signaling a genetic risk for ASD (Piven et al., 1991).

Fenfluramine (Pondimin) was one of the first medications to be systematically studied for reducing elevated levels of serotonin. After initially promising results, researchers and families became frustrated by the negative side effects, which included increased irritability and aggression (Ekman, Miranda-Linné, Gillberg, Garle, & Wetterberg, 1989). Subsequently, fenfluramine (a common ingredient in some medications for losing weight) was found to be associated with heart problems (Connolly & Crary, 1997) and is no longer recommended for use in modifying serotonin levels.

Other researchers have used selective serotonin reuptake inhibitors (SSRIs) to modify serotonin levels in individuals with ASD. The SSRIs (fluoxetine [Prozac], sertraline [Zoloft], fluvoxamine [Luvox], and paroxetine [Paxil]) may reduce anxiety, obsessive and repetitive behaviors, and self-injury (McDougle et al., 1996). Hollander et al. (2005) found that liquid fluoxetine was more effective than a placebo in reducing repetitious behavior in 45 children and adolescents with ASD. A review of studies using SSRIs as well as a nonselective serotonin reuptake inhibitor (Potenza & McDougle, 1997) concluded that the medications promoted improvement in some symptoms (including reductions in repetitive and aggressive behavior and increased eye contact) in some participants, but was also associated with behavioral deterioration and unwanted side effects (e.g., seizures) in other participants. The SSRIs may hold more potential for individuals with family members who have histories of anxiety and depression (DeLong, Teague, & McSwain-Kamran, 1998; Lord & Bailey, 2002), and the presence of compulsive behaviors may also predict a positive response (Hollander et al., 1998).

In addition to elevated levels of serotonin, some individuals with ASD have been found to have a higher production and turnover of dopamine, which is associated with hyperactivity, stereotypies, attention differences, and cognitive deficits (Campbell, Small, Anderson, Malone, & Locascio, 1992). Others have suggested that dopamine deficiency is common in children with ASD because of similarities in performance with children with poorly controlled phenylketonuria (PKU) (Dennis et al., 1999). Dopamine may also be important for modulating the brain's ability to plan behavior. Treatment with medications that serve as dopamine antagonists (e.g., haloperidol, risperidone) have shown some promise for use with individuals with ASD but present some cautions. Research regarding the effectiveness of haloperidol [Haldol] has shown some benefit for decreasing hyperactivity while increasing verbal production and attention. However, haloperidol has also been shown to increase aggressive behaviors and exacerbate stereotypies. Early suggestions that haloperidol could be useful in conjunction with structured teaching have not been verified (Anderson et al., 1989). The long-term use of haloperidol is associated with the development of involuntary movements that continue after withdrawal, resulting in the need for caution with the use of this medication (Lord & Bailey, 2002; Palermo & Curatolo, 2004).

Risperidone [Risperdal], classified as an atypical neuroleptic, also inhibits dopamine production and turnover. Risperidone has been used effectively to treat the symptoms of schizophrenia. A small number of controlled studies with individuals with ASD demonstrate its effectiveness in reducing interfering behaviors (repetitive movements, self-injury, aggression) while improving social awareness, with few side effects (McDougle et al., 1998).

Some individuals with autism have also been found to have elevated levels of endogenous opioids (Panksepp & Sahley, 1987) that not only influence attachment and motor activity, but also leave the individual in a high state of self-satisfaction with an increased pain threshold. High levels of opioids appear to diminish responsiveness to social stimuli and may lead to social withdrawal. As with serotonin, typically developing infants have an excess of opioids that become weaker and shorter acting in the months after birth (Panksepp, 1979). Some children with ASD continue to experience an excess of opioids, interfering with their responsiveness to social stimuli. Self-injurious behaviors may actually increase the opioid levels in the brain (Barrett, Feinstein, & Hole, 1989). Treatment using opioid antagonists (e.g., naltrexone, naloxone) is typically provided only in cases of severe self-injurious behavior. Contradictory findings (Gillberg, 1995) have interfered with the ability to draw definitive conclusions regarding the positive impact of the medication on reductions in self-injury and overactivity (Campbell et al., 1993).

Oxytocin is a neuropeptide critical for the development of attachment, bonding, and social behavior. In animal models, mice without oxytocin exhibit severe deficits in socialization (Lim, Bielsky, & Young, 2005). The similarities in social deficits between the mice without oxytocin and individuals with ASD have led to an exploration of this chemical. Waterhouse, Fein, and Modahl (1996) found that the social impairments in 30 children with ASD correlated significantly with their levels of oxytocin. Because of concerns that the oxytocin levels of individuals with ASD might be precipitated by the use of pitocin (containing oxytocin) during labor and delivery (Wahl, 2004), Gale, Ozonoff, and Lainhart (2003) studied 41 boys with ASD compared to a matched control group containing typically developing boys and boys with mental retardation. They found no link between the use of pitocin during labor and the subsequent development of ASD. At this point, direct manipulation of oxytocin is occurring only in animal models (Welch et al., 2005).

A considerable amount of research has been and continues to be conducted to identify the neurochemical differences that may influence the development and maintenance of ASD. Again, the interconnectivity of the brain requires that the chemical differences found in some individuals with ASD, although described and studied separately, suggest structural and functional differences (Santangelo & Tsatsanis, 2005).

FUNCTIONAL DIFFERENCES

Study of the functional differences in the brains of individuals with ASD brings together the structural and chemical components. Advances in the technology used to analyze living brains have led to remarkable discoveries about the neurological functioning of individuals with ASD. The earliest studies involved electroencephalogram (EEG) technology. Using EEGs, abnormalities were noted in 50% of the participants with ASD (Minshew, 1991). Although the findings have not been verified, some suggested that the abnormalities shown on EEGs may have been the reason why typically developing children appeared to regress into ASD (Lewine et al., 1999). Event-related potentials (ERPs) have been used to demonstrate that some children with autism show an absence of electrophysiological activity when looking at pictures of their mothers and increased activity when looking at pictures of their favorite toys (Dawson, Osterling, Meltzoff, & Kuhl, 2000). For many years, event-related potentials were the only method for examining the functioning of the brain during active engagement. Problems with the technology made it difficult to interpret readings and may have contributed to contradictory findings (Lord & Bailey, 2002).

The functioning of the brain was also inferred through observations taken during the performance of activities commonly associated with intelligence and achievement tests. For example, individuals with ASD have been compared to individuals who are typically developing or who have other disabilities on tasks that required recall, imitation, visual-spatial processing, problem solving, and so forth. Using this approach, Minshew et al. (1992) found that individuals with ASD appeared to lack organizing strategies, such as categorization, and flexibility of thinking that would enable them to perform better on tasks involving higher order processing. Other individuals with ASD were found to have problems with immediate and delayed recall of faces and family scenes (Williams, Goldstein, & Minshew, 2005). A large number of studies have documented deficits in higher order thinking (executive functioning) in individuals with ASD of various ages and different cognitive levels (Ozonoff, 1997) using the observation of performance. However, evidence for the use of compensatory strategies among individuals with ASD has been well documented in empirical literature (Klin et al., 2002a), and the question that couldn't be answered through behavioral observation was: Which of the neurological systems were being used in the performance of tasks?

The advent of functional magnetic resonance imaging (fMRI) technology opened a window for direct observation of how the brain functions during activities. An impressive quantity of research is being conducted that identifies differences in brain functioning in individuals with ASD. A number of studies have demonstrated that the areas of the brain used by individuals without ASD to recognize and process faces as well as identify emotions (areas in the amygdala) are not used by individuals with ASD (Ashwin, Wheelwright, Baron-Cohen, 2005; Baron-Cohen et al., 2000; Pierce, Muller, Ambrose, Allen, & Courchesne, 2001). Those with ASD tend to use a part of the brain that is usually reserved for nonface object recognition (Schultz et al., 2000; Schultz, 2005). However, when one boy with an ASD was shown a picture of his favorite cartoon character (Digimon), he used the same parts of the brain that others use to recognize human faces (Grelotti et al., 2005).

Using fMRIs, researchers can also see how various parts of the brain work together. For some individuals with ASD, the parts of the brain that should be working together to process photographs of fearful faces were not working together (Welchew et al., 2005). Luna et al. (2002) compared the brain functioning of 11 individuals with ASD and 6 typically developing controls to determine which parts of the brain were connected for accomplishing specific mental tasks. They found that both groups performed the tasks, but that the individuals with ASD relied on lower regions of the brain while the individuals without ASD used higher functioning regions of the brain. Probably due to structural and chemical differences affected by maturation, the higher order neural systems had not developed in the participants with ASD. A similar finding was reported for sentence comprehension tasks (Just, Cherkassky, Keller, & Minshew, 2004). In contrast to a typically developing control group, 17 participants with ASD showed less integrated brain patterns, less activity in the area of the brain that processes connected speech, and more activity in the part of the brain that processes individual words.

Further evidence of differences in brain functioning among individuals with ASD is the unusually high percentage that develop seizure disorders (Canitano et al., 2005), particularly in adolescence and young adulthood (Volkmar & Nelson, 1990). Abnormal brain activity, such as seizures, can further inhibit brain functioning (Vargha-Khadem, Issacs, van der Werf, Robb, & Wilson, 1992).

Evidence clearly links behavioral differences among individuals with ASD to differences in the functioning of the brain, which is influenced by the interconnected structural and chemical aspects. Ironically, individuals functioning on the high end of the spectrum have actually used the term **neurotypical** (having a normally functioning brain) to describe people who do not have ASD, even developing a Web site with an assessment for diagnosing and suggestions for treating "neurotypical syndrome" (*www.autistics.org/isnt/*).

Although new knowledge is continuously being discovered, a basic understanding of how neuralgic differences could manifest in behavior can be helpful for putting the behaviors and needs of students with ASD in perspective. Clearly, some of the neurological differences found in individuals with ASD are shared by individuals who are neurotypical as well as by those with other disabilities. To summarize, some of the neurological differences associated with ASD can lead to behavioral differences. These may include:

- Sensory input and motor output regulation problems
- Need for greater levels of sensory stimulation
- Sleep disturbances
- Retention of primitive reflexes
- Stereotypic behaviors
- Compulsive behaviors
- Inability to recognize with one sense something experienced by another sense (failure to watch and then do)
- Difficulty with novel situations
- Poor eye contact
- Inability to predict upcoming events; preference for status quo
- Equal and potent response to sensory stimuli (magnified sensation); may compensate by shutting out and becoming intensely preoccupied with something else
- Attention to irrelevant details
- Difficulty shifting attention quickly
- Good fact memorization (habit memory)
- Good rote motor acquisition
- Poor generalization
- Difficulty with higher level information processing

ROLE OF GENETICS

The behavioral and learning differences that are demonstrated by individuals with ASD are clearly a result of differences in neurology. The next logical question is to ask: What causes those differences? Palermo and Curatolo (2004, p. 155) sum up the prevailing belief succinctly when they state that ASD are a "genetically heterogeneous polygenic neurodevelopmental disorder." ASD are "genetically heterogeneous" because there is no simple dominant/recessive or X-linked pattern of transmission (Szatmari et al., 1998). The spectrum is "polygenic" because there appear to be 10 or more genes interacting to produce ASD (Pickles et al., 1995; Piven & Folstein, 1994; Wassink, Brzustowicz, Bartlett, & Szatmari, 2004; Risch et al., 1999). "Neurodevelopmental" refers back to the fact that the genetic foundation leads to changes in the brain and the way it develops.

Several factors together provide fairly conclusive evidence that ASD are genetically based. Some of the structural and chemical differences in the brain support the idea that ASD evolve from genetic or biologic causes that affect the fetus early in development. Research suggests that neural development is different as early as 20–24 days after conception (Rodier, Ingram, Tisdale, Nelson, & Romano, 1996). Differences in the cerebellum can be traced to fetal development during the fifth week of gestation (Courchesne, 1997). Other critical neurological differences occur prior to 12 weeks of gestation (Bailey et al., 1998; Rodier et al., 1996) and still others before 28–30 weeks' gestation (Bauman, 1997). Behavioral manifestations that occur during the first several years of life, such as the emergence of "regressive" autism (occurring at about 2 years of age), may reflect a latent effect of genetic inheritance (Lawler, Croen, Grether, & Van de Water, 2004). Clearly, the potential exists that neurological differences are based on events that occur prior to birth, which suggests that genetics play a crucial role.

Analyses of multiplex families provide the most compelling evidence that ASDs are genetically based. A **multiplex family** is one in which more than one family member has an ASD. Two percent to 8% of the siblings of individuals with ASD also have an ASD, a percentage that is significantly greater than what is found in the general population (Chudley, Gutierrez, Jocelyn, & Chodirker, 1998). The genetic predisposition is further supported by research done with twins. With identical (monozygotic) twins, if one child has autism, there is a 60% chance that the twin will also have autism (Bailey et al., 1995). However, there is a 92% chance that if one of them has autism, the other will have associated communication and social disorders. In contrast, if the twins are fraternal (dizygotic) and one is diagnosed with autism, there is a 0–10% chance that the other will have associated communication disorders. The genetic similarities between identical twins provide strong substantiation for the genetic basis of ASD. Since the chance of both identical twins demonstrating autism is not 100%, other factors must have some influence over the genetic predisposition.

In addition to the higher rates of associated conditions in siblings and twins, immediate and extended biological families of children with ASD often report histories of language, learning, or social problems (Bolton et al., 1994; Dawson et al., 2002; Folstein & Rutter, 1977; Piven et al., 1994), including psychiatric issues such as obsessive compulsive disorders, depression, schizophrenia, social phobia, and bipolar disorder (DeLong, 1999; Ghaziuddin, 2005; Hollander, King, & Delaney, 2003). Asperger (1944) wrote that he was concerned about the parents of the boys he studied because of their social isolation and problems with un- and underemployment. Extended family members also report increased rates of other health issues such as rheumatoid arthritis, lupus, otitis media (ear infections), and other autoimmune disorders. The presence of numerous health issues in families of children on the spectrum suggests that susceptibility to common infections may indicate unusual immune responses based in genetic makeup. Szatmari et al. (1998) concluded that 90% of the cases of autism are related to the genetic contributions of heredity.

The question then becomes: How does genetics precipitate or influence the development of ASD? A number of options are possible. Recent speculation suggests that individuals with some of the characteristics of ASD are mating and producing children who then demonstrate enough of the characteristics to be diagnosed, a phenomenon known as *assortative mating* (Constantino & Todd, 2005). Holden (2005) cites as evidence for this concept that the fathers and grandfathers of a number of individuals with ASD tend to work in very technical professions such as engineering and demonstrate weak social skills. Another option is that genetic inheritance may result in disabilities with known genetic causes. A very small percentage of individuals with single gene defects, such as those that lead to phenylketonuria (PKU), Cornelia de Lange syndrome, tuberous sclerosis, Angelman syndrome, and Fragile X syndrome, are also diagnosed as having an ASD (Gillberg, Gillberg, & Ahlsen, 1994; Hunt & Shepherd, 1993; Muhle, Trentacoste, & Rapin, 2004; Rapin, 1999). Rett syndrome, currently considered akin to autism, is linked to a single gene (Ellaway & Christodoulou, 1999). Another option is that multiple genes may contribute to the situation in which the individual is more susceptible to experiencing neurological damage or disruption because the system has lost protective factors, as in the case of a weakened immune system.

IMMUNE SYSTEM INVOLVEMENT

Genetic predispositions may lead to compromises in the immune system that make the individual susceptible to autoimmune disorders and a dysfunctional immune system, a predisposition that may occur in populations in addition to those with ASD (Lawler et al., 2004). These may anatomically change the brain or result in behavioral changes. The genetic predisposition toward a suppressed immune system can also make an individual more sensitive to toxins in the environment, affecting the neurology of the developing fetus or even of the developing child (Arndt, Stodgell, & Rodier, 2005). The link between certain toxins and development of ASD has been speculated for years. In-utero exposure to rubella was shown to increase the chance that a child would develop autism (Chess, Korn, & Fernandez, 1971). Maternal use of antiseizure medication (valporic acid (VPA) as in Depakote) during pregnancy has been linked to the development of ASD (Moore et al., 2000). Vaccines, and more specifically some of the compounds in the vaccines (i.e., ethylmercury, thimerosal), have been linked to the emergence of ASD. For some, the link has been refuted (Barbaresi, Katusic, Colligan, Weaver, & Jacobsen, 2005; DeStefano, Bhasin, Thompson, Yeargin-Allsopp, & Boyle, 2004; Hviid, Stellfeld, Wohlfahrt, & Melbye, 2003; Kaye, del Mar Melero-Montes, & Jick, 2001), but for others the possibility still exists (c.f., Rimland, 2004). Although rare complications from a vaccine cannot be ruled out (Chen, Landau, Sham, & Fombonne, 2004), scientists suggest that the likelihood of a child contracting a fatal childhood disease if not vaccinated is much greater than the likelihood that the child will develop autism if given vaccinations.

Some have speculated that the genetic predisposition that underlies the immune system suppression or even alteration might lead to heightened sensitivity to food products. Advocates of this theory suggest that the main culprits for individuals with ASD are gluten (wheat products) and casein (amino acid found in milk products). Some believe that eliminating these ingredients from the diet may result in improvements in communication, socialization, and independent functioning (Knivsberg, Reichelt, Noland, & Hoien, 1995). Although there is a great deal of popular support for these claims, research does not demonstrate that eliminating specific foods can help a child recover from an ASD.

IMPACT OF ENVIRONMENTAL TOXINS

If the genetic predisposition leads to suppression of the immune system, an individual may be more susceptible to environmental toxins. Intuitive logic supports this view, because it is recognized that individuals with ASD are not distributed evenly across geographic areas (Rutter et al., 1994). There are two plausible reasons for this phenomenon. The most simple is that families tend to relocate to areas where services are available for their children, resulting in higher concentrations of children with ASD in some geographic locales than others. The second reason goes back to the possibility that environmental toxins negatively affect developing neurology, leading to the manifestation of ASD. However, it would be unusual for an environmental toxin to be the only precipitating agent for the development of ASD. The more likely scenario is that an environmental toxin would only negatively impact children who have an increased genetic susceptibility (Lawler et al., 2004). Although there is no conclusive support in published literature for environmental links to ASD via agents that are toxic to the developing brain, the possibility is intriguing and additional scrutiny is probably justified.

❖ LEARNING WITH MS. HARRIS: Sunday Night in Front of the Television

Ms. Harris, as is her habit, is glued to the television set on a Sunday evening, watching her favorite news exposé program. Tonight, following a discussion on how to protect oneself from identity theft, the program profiles children with ASD and how they are unable to take another person's perspective. The program fascinates Ms. Harris, particularly since she has just read a similar article in one of the news magazines and also because one of her cousin's sons has been diagnosed with autism. "Wow," thinks Ms. Harris, "we were taught in college that autism is a low-incidence disability. Why is it that everywhere I turn, someone is talking about knowing someone who has autism?"

HOW MANY PEOPLE HAVE AN ASD?

Prevalence is an accounting of how often something occurs. For example, the prevalence rate of left-handedness in a classroom depends on the number of people who are left-handed divided by the total number of people in the class. If there are 12 left-handed people in a class of 50 students, the prevalence rate of left-handedness is .24 (12/50) or 24%. Until the end of the twentieth century, prevalence rates for autism (not ASD) were 5–15 out of every 10,000 (Wing & Gould, 1979). This low prevalence rate resulted in autism being referred to as a **low-incidence disability,** meaning that it was relatively rare.

The prevalence rates documented in international studies published between 1966 and 1997 show an increase in the prevalence of autism (not the full spectrum) (Gillberg, 1999). Figure 2.2 provides the results of this analysis.

Fombonne (2003) indicated that a reasonable prevalence rate for autism is 10 of every 10,000 individuals or 1 in 1,000. The full spectrum has a higher prevalence at 27.5 per 10,000 or 1 in 364. To answer Ms. Harris's question, ASD are no longer a low-incidence disability. ASD are the third most commonly diagnosed developmental disability. Only mental retardation and cerebral palsy are more common among children than ASD. ASD occur more often than Down syndrome, childhood cancer, cystic fibrosis, multiple sclerosis, or juvenile diabetes.

Late 1960s/early 1970s	4.4/10,000
Late 1970s	4.9/10,000
1980s (*DSM-III* criteria)	7.7/10,000
1990s	9.6/10,000 (approx. 1/1,000)

FIGURE 2.2
Prevalence Rates for Autism
Source: Gillberg (1999).

Several explanations exist as to why the prevalence of ASD has increased so dramatically. It has been suggested that previously published prevalence rates were too low. Some of the increase is attributable to the increase in knowledge about ASD and the ability to correctly identify the syndromes (Lord et al., 2001). However, this knowledge can also be responsible for over-diagnosis of the disability, and this may be what is actually occurring. As Temple Grandin (2002), a woman with high-functioning autism, has so aptly wondered, at what point does a computer nerd become someone with Asperger syndrome?

Some of the increase in the number of individuals identified with ASD relates to changes in the way autism is defined (Fombonne, 1999). Whereas autism was previously thought of only in the classic or Kannerian sense, the recognition of Asperger syndrome and PDD-NOS have greatly expanded perceptions of what constitutes autism. Indeed, the vernacular used in this chapter supports the idea that autism has expanded to include a spectrum of disorders with some common characteristics. Figure 2.3 gives a side-by-side comparison of definitions provided by the Autism Society of America (ASA) at the end of the 1990s, which clearly illustrates changes in the perspectives of ASD.

At the end of 1996, the definition of autism describes it as a "severely incapacitating" disability that occurred at a prevalence rate of 15/10,000. The criteria used to describe the symptoms are clinical in nature and similar to those used in the *DSM*. The definition concludes that autism is treatable, particularly if identified early.

The next newsletter published by ASA (Jan./Feb. 1997) defines autism differently. It is now a "developmental disability" that is not identified as "severely incapacitating." The prevalence rate continues to be listed as 15/10,000. However, the criteria used to characterize the symptoms are less clinical and more broadly defined. The definition reports that 400,000 individuals in the United States have autism. Gone is the optimistic view of autism as being treatable. This has been replaced by the allegation that few people know how to effectively work with individuals with autism.

The definition published by ASA then changed again. In the Sept./Oct. 1998 issue of their newsletter, ASA adds the qualifier "complex" to the description that autism is a developmental disability. The prevalence rates are reported to be 1 in every 500 individuals with a half-million people in the United States having autism (an increase of 100,000 people in approximately 18 months). The description further softens behavioral symptoms, and aggression and self-injurious behaviors have been removed. The allegation remains that few know how to effectively work with individuals with this complex developmental disability. As is shown in this illustration, prevalence changes are partially attributable to expanded definitions of what constitutes autism, since the spectrum has been broadened to include milder forms of the disorder.

In addition to being influenced by expanded definitions of ASD, better di-agnostics, and overidentification, prevalence rates may be influenced by

Definition of Autism

AUTISM is a severely incapacitating lifelong developmental disability that typically appears during the first three years of life. The result of a neurological disorder that affects functioning of the brain, autism and its behavioral symptoms occur in approximately fifteen out of every 10,000 births. Autism is four times more common in boys than girls. It has been found throughout the world in families of all racial, ethnic, and social backgrounds. No known factors in the psychological environment of a child have been shown to cause autism.

Some behavioral symptoms of autism include:

1. Disturbances in the rate of appearance of physical, social, and language skills.
2. Abnormal responses to sensations. Any one or a combination of senses or responses are affected: sight, hearing, touch, balance, smell, taste, reaction to pain, and the way a child holds his or her body.
3. Speech and language are absent or delayed, while specific thinking capabilities may be present.
4. Abnormal ways of relating to people, objects, and events.

Autism occurs by itself or in association with other disorders that affect the function of the brain, such as viral infections, metabolic disturbances, and epilepsy. It is important to distinguish autism from retardation or mental disorders since diagnostic confusion may result in referral to inappropriate and ineffective treatment techniques. The severe form of the syndrome may include extreme self-injurious, repetitive, highly unusual and aggressive behavior. Special educational programs using behavioral methods have proved to be the most helpful treatment for persons with autism.

AUTISM IS TREATABLE—Early diagnosis and intervention are vital to the future development of the child. (Nov./Dec. 1996)

What Is Autism?

Autism is a developmental disability that typically appears during the first three years of life. The result of a neurological disorder that affects functioning of the brain, autism and its associated behaviors occur in approximately 15 of every 10,000 individuals.

Autism is four times more prevalent in boys than girls and knows no racial, ethnic, or social boundaries. Family income, life-style and educational levels do not affect the chance of autism's occurrence.

Autism interferes with the normal development of the brain in the areas of reasoning, social interaction and communication skills. Children and adults with autism typically have deficiencies in verbal and non-verbal communication, social interactions, and leisure or play activities. The disorder makes it hard for them to communicate with others and relate to the outside world. They may exhibit repeated body movements (hand flapping, rocking), unusual responses to people or attachments to objects and resist any changes in routines. In some cases, aggressive and/or self-injurious behavior may be present.

It is conservatively estimated that nearly 400,000 people in the U.S. today have some form of autism. Its prevalence rate now places it as the *third* most common developmental disability—more common than Down's syndrome. Yet the majority of the public, including many professionals in the medical, educational, and vocational fields are still unaware of how autism affects people and how to effectively work with individuals with autism. (Jan./Feb. 1997)

What Is Autism?

Autism is a complex developmental disability that typically appears during the first three years of life. The result of a neurological disorder that affects the functioning of the brain, autism and its associated behaviors have been estimated to occur in as many as 1 in 500 individuals. Autism is four times more prevalent in boys than girls and knows no racial, ethnic, or social boundaries. Family income, lifestyle, and educational levels do not affect the chance of autism's occurrence.

Autism interferes with the normal development of the brain in the areas of social interaction and communication skills. Children and adults with autism typically have difficulties in verbal and nonverbal communication, social interactions, and leisure or play activities. The disorder makes it hard for them to communicate with others and relate to the outside world. They may exhibit repeated body movements (hand flapping, rocking), unusual responses to people or attachments to objects, and they may resist changes in routines.

Over one half million people in the U.S. today have some form of autism. Its prevalence rate now places it as the *third* most common developmental disability—more common than Down syndrome. Yet most of the public, including many professionals in the medical, educational, and vocational fields, are still unaware of how autism affects people and how to effectively work with individuals with autism. (Sept./Oct. 1998)

FIGURE 2.3

Changing Definitions Published by the Autism Society of America

Source: Advocate. Reprinted with permission of the Autism Society of America.

diagnostic substitution (Volkmar, Lord, Bailey, Schultz, & Klin, 2004). Although the need for additional data and further analyses exists, diagnostic substitution was suggested as a factor in changing prevalence rates for autism in California (Croen, Grether, Hoogstrate, & Selvin, 2002). In this study, the researchers noted an inverse relationship between the number of children with autism presenting for services in the Department of Developmental Services' regional centers system versus the number of children with mental retardation. As the number of children with autism increased, the number of children with mental retardation decreased. Of interest is the fact that the California State Department of Developmental Services reported the first decrease in the number of diagnoses of new cases with autism in 2004.

As another example, during the 1992–1993 school year, which is the first year that schools were able to use autism as a distinct eligibility category, the total number of students under that label in the 50 states, District of Columbia, and Puerto Rico was 12,222 (U.S. DOE, 1995). Almost a decade later, the total number of students with autism was 78,717 (U.S. DOE, 2004), reflecting a 544% increase in the number of children identified as eligible for special education because they have an ASD. Although some of this increase has to do with better diagnostics using broader definitions as well as the growing population in the United States, some of this increase probably has to do with the transition from other eligibilities on the spectrum (i.e., Other Health Impaired) to the eligibility of autism. That is, many of those students were already receiving services through the public education system, but not under the label of autism, so the increase in prevalence is attributable to the availability of the more accurate eligibility.

Other conditions affecting children have shown remarkable growth. Prevalence rates for asthma, allergies, Type 1 diabetes, autoimmune disorders, and ADHA have also increased precipitously (Lawler et al., 2004). Prevalence rates are one metric to consider with a disability such as ASD. In contrast to prevalence, which simply describes the current number of people identified with the syndrome, incidence rates can be critical for planning future needs for services. Incidence rates project how many individuals will be born in a given time frame (usually a year) with certain conditions. An accurate figure of the incidence of autism has been elusive, and it is not possible to determine if incidence for ASD is changing (Tidmarsh & Volkmar, 2003).

CONCLUSION

Evidence from the reports of "feral" children suggests that individuals with ASD have a long historical presence. Leo Kanner and Hans Asperger provided systematic descriptions of behavioral characteristics in the respective populations they studied that, with few exceptions, have withstood the test of time and continue to ring relevant. Controversy exists as to whether or not the populations they described are truly distinct or represent opposite ends on a continuous spectrum.

Autism Spectrum Disorders are the result of neurological differences that lead to the unusual constellation of behaviors characteristic of individuals on the spectrum. The etiologies of neurological differences are still being examined. There is compelling evidence that neurological differences emerge from a genetic predisposition. Genetics set in motion a sequence of prenatal development of neurological differences that continue to evolve throughout life. Genetics may provoke brain differences through inherited disorders, new mutations, or chromosomal aberrations, which may result in early manifestation or latent emergence of the spectrum disorders. Research has yet to determine if any one of the neurological differences is primary for the development of the spectrum disorders or if the fundamental problem resides in the connectivity within and between different systems in the brain. Side effects of medications that may be useful for addressing some of the symptoms will need to be evaluated and managed. Improvements in social, communication, and cognitive skills may reflect responsiveness to interventions as well as neurological maturation. ASDs are currently diagnosed based on behavioral manifestations. In the future, it may be possible to use medical technology, such as that used for neuroimaging and genetic screening, to diagnose the presence of the spectrum disorders.

The discrete manner in which the chemical and structural differences of the brain were described fails to adequately portray the complex and interconnected functioning of the brain. However, awareness of the possible neurological differences can lead to the development of appropriate accommodations and interventions. Classroom manifestations of the neurological differences and general suggestions for supporting associated behaviors in students with ASD, as well as those with other disabilities, are provided in Table 2.1. The instructional strategies suggested in the right column will be described more fully in the following chapters. Readers may find the figure useful for helping colleagues understand some of the probable reasons for a few of the behavioral differences seen in students with ASD.

DISCUSSION QUESTIONS AND ACTIVITIES

1. ASD may be based in similar neurological pathologies. However, functional outcomes can be quite varied across individuals because of the impact of experience and learning on the plasticity of the developing brain. Identify two individuals who have the same diagnosis (e.g., both have been diagnosed with autism, Aspergers, or cerebral palsy) but different behaviors and characteristics. Solicit information from them about their lives to identify variations in their experiences that might account for the difference in their outcomes.

2. Generate a list of as many behavioral characteristics as possible that would result from the differences described in the brainstem, limbic system, cerebrum, and cerebellum for individuals with autism.

3. Watch *Rainman* or *Mercury Rising* and speculate which neurological differences might be affecting the lead characters.

TABLE 2.1
Basic Strategies to Support Neurologic Differences

Neurology	Behavior Related to Differences	Instructional Strategies
rainstem eticular activatin s stem e ulates sensor in ut out ut im ic s stem otivation an a ect eanin attac e to events	nusual reactions to sensations Stims to increase vesti ular in ut nmotivate t ical incentives nusual a ect i icult un erstan in cause e ect	nvironmental anal sis Sanctione movement se re erences to motivate eac rea in o social cues an social s ills Su icient re etition
Cere rum Au itor rocessin an inte ration	Slo to ails to res on to irections ails to orient to ver alizations	ive in ormation visuall se tele ra ic s eec en ivin irections
Cere ellum ur in e cells ilterin s stem	ersensitive to sensor in ut Si t Soun Smell aste ouc Co in mec anisms to loc sensor in ut verselective attention Sel stimulator e avior e avioral avoi ance	nvironmental en ineerin e uce eliminate stimuli Clari oun aries eac com ensator strate ies ovin to a uieter ar er area sin lo tec evices olite re usals i li t im ortant in ormation Color size ol mar e as in tem late i
Cere ellum o ulate attention ca ture maintain s it	i icult to et attention asil istracte S i tin is er o ten s i te to ron lace ta es lon er to s i t attention	nvironmental en ineerin e uce istractions eac clear si nals se visual cues to ca ture an irect attention Allo a e e tra secon s or res onse
Cere ellum re arator s stem	ants a set routine esists c an es erseverations Sel stimulator e aviors to co e	isual sc e ules activit lo s recorrect arn o u comin transitions re uent revie an reassurance

75

4. Using Table 2.1, think of a student with an ASD and design environmental modifications that could be helpful in supporting his or her participation in school environments. Identify the neurotypical students in the school environment who would benefit from the same modifications.

5. Create a timeline that depicts the evolution of the understanding of ASD. Trace the changes in identification, etiology, and prevalence for the spectrum disorders.

REFERENCES

Akshoomoff, N., Pierce, K., & Courchesne, E. (2002). The neurobiological basis of autism from a developmental perspective. *Development and Psychopathology, 14,* 613-634.

Aman, M. G., Van Bourgondien, M. E., Wolford, P. L., & Sarphare, G. (1995). Psychotropic and anticonvulsant drugs in subjects with autism: Prevalence and patterns of use. *Journal of the American Academy of Child and Adolescent Psychiatry, 34,* 1672-1681.

Anderson, G. M., Freedman, D. X., Cohen, D. J., Volkmar, F. R., Hoder, E. L., McPhedran, P., et al. (1987). Whole blood serotonin in autistic and normal subjects. *Journal of Child Psychology & Psychiatry & Allied Disciplines, 28,* 885-900.

Anderson, L. T., Campbell, M., Adams, P., Small, A. M., Perry, R., & Shell, J. (1989). The effects of haloperidol on discrimination learning and behavioral symptoms in autistic children. *Journal of Autism and Developmental Disorders, 19,* 227-239.

Arin, D. M., Bauman, M. L., & Kemper, T. L. (1991). The distribution of Purkinje cell loss in the cerebellum in autism. *Neurology, 41,* 307.

Arndt, T. L., Stodgell, C. J., & Rodier, P. M. (2005). The teratology of autism. *International Journal of Developmental Neuroscience, 23,* 189-199.

Ashwin, C., Wheelwright, S., & Baron-Cohen, S. (2005). Laterality biases to chimeric faces in Asperger syndrome: What is right about face-processing? *Journal of Autism and Developmental Disorders, 35,* 183-196.

Asperger, H. (1944/1991). Autistic psychopathy in childhood (Trans). In U. Frith (Ed.), *Autism and Asperger syndrome* (pp. 37-92). Cambridge, UK: Cambridge University Press.

Asperger, H. (1977). Problems of infantile autism. *Communication, 13,* 45-52.

Bachevalier, J. (1991). An animal model for childhood autism: Memory loss and socioemotional disturbances following neonatal damage to the limbic system in monkeys. In C. A. Tamminga & S. C. Schultz (Eds.), *Advances in neuropsychiatry and psychopharmacology: Schizophrenia research* (pp. 129-140). New York: Raven Press.

Bachevalier, J. (1994). The contribution of medial temporal lobe structures in infantile autism: A neurobehavioral study in primates. In M. L. Bauman & T. L. Kemper (Eds.), *The neurobiology of autism* (pp. 146-169). Baltimore: Johns Hopkins University Press.

Bachevalier, J., Malkova, L., & Mishkin, M. (2001). Effects of selective neonatal temporal lobe lesions on socioemotional behavior in infant rhesus monkeys. *Behavioral Neuroscience, 115,* 545-559.

Bachevalier, J., & Vargha-Khadem, F. (2005). The primate hippocampus: Ontogeny, early insult and memory. *Current Opinion in Neurobiology, 15,* 168-174.

Bailey, A., Le Couteur, A., Gottesman, I., Bolton, P., Simonoff, E., Yuzda, E., et al. (1995). Autism as a strongly genetic disorder: Evidence from a British twin study. *Psychological Medicine, 25,* 63-78.

Bailey, A., Luthert, P., Dean, A., Harding, B., Janota, I., Montgomery, M., et al. (1998). A clinicopathological study of autism. *Brain, 121,* 889-905.

Bailey, A., Palferman, S., Heavey, L., & Le Couteur, A. (1998). Autism: The phenotype in relatives. *Journal of Autism and Developmental Disorders, 28,* 369-392.

Bailey, A., Phillips, W., & Rutter, M. (1996). Autism: Towards an integration of clinical, genetic, neuropsychological, and neurobiological perspectives. *Journal of Child Psychology and Psychiatry, 37,* 89-126.

Barbaresi, W. J., Katusic, S. K., Colligan, R. C., Weaver, A. L., & Jacobsen, S. J. (2005). The incidence of autism in Olmsted County, Minnesota, 1976-1997. *Archives of Pediatrics and Adolescent Medicine, 159,* 37-44.

Baron-Cohen, S., Ring, H. A., Bullmore, E. T., Wheelwright, S., Ashwin, C., & Williams, S. C. (2000). The amygdala theory of autism. *Neuroscience and Biobehavioral Reviews, 24,* 355-364.

Barrett, R. P., Feinstein, C. B., & Hole, W. (1989). Effects of naloxone and naltrexone on self-injury: A double-blind, placebo-controlled analysis. *American Journal of Mental Retardation, 93,* 644-651.

Bauman, M. L. (1997). The neuroanatomy of autism: Clinical implications. In P. J. Accardo, B. K. Shapiro, & A. J. Capute (Eds.), *Behavior belongs in the brain: Neurobehavioral syndromes* (pp. 69-95). Baltimore: York Press.

Bauman, M. L., & Kemper, T. L. (2005). Neuroanatomic observations of the brain in autism: A review and future directions. *International Journal of Developmental Neuroscience, 23,* 183-187.

Bellini, S. (2004). Social skill deficits and anxiety in high-functioning adolescents with autism spectrum disorders. *Focus on Autism and Other Developmental Disabilities, 19,* 78-86.

Bettelheim, B. (1967). *The empty fortress: Infantile autism and the birth of the self.* New York: Free Press.

Bolton, P., Macdonald, H., Pickles, A., Rios, P., Goode, S., Crowson, M., et al. (1994). A case-control family history study of autism. *Journal of Child Psychology and Psychiatry, 35,* 877-900.

Boucher, J., & Lewis, V. (1992). Unfamiliar face recognition in relatively able autistic children. *Journal of Child Psychology and Psychiatry, 33,* 843-859.

Bryson, S., & Landry, R. (1994). Brief report: A case study of literacy and socioemotional development in a mute autistic female. *Journal of Autism and Developmental Disorders, 24,* 225-232.

Campbell, M., Anderson, L. T., Small, A. M., Adams, P., Gonzalez, N. M., & Ernst, M. (1993). Naltrexone in autistic children: Behavioral symptoms and attentional learning. *Journal of the Academy of Child and Adolescent Psychiatry, 32,* 1283-1291.

Campbell, M., Small, A. M., Anderson, L. T., Malone, R. P., & Locascio, J. J. (1992). Pharmacotherapy in autism. In H. Naruse & E. M. Ornitz (Eds.), *Neurobiology of Infantile Autism* (pp. 235-243). Amsterdam: Excerpta Medica.

Candland, D. K. (1993). *Feral children and clever animals: Reflections on human nature.* New York: Oxford University Press.

Canitano, R., Luchetti, A., & Zappella, M. (2005). Epilepsy, electroencephalographic abnormalities, and regression in children with autism. *Journal of Child Neurology, 20,* 27-31.

Chandana, S. R., Behen, M. E., Juhasz, C., Muzik, O., Rothermel, R. D., Mangner, T. J., et al. (2005). Significance of abnormalities in developmental trajectory and asymmetry of cortical serotonin synthesis in autism. *International Journal of Developmental Neuroscience, 23,* 171-182.

Chen, W., Landau, S., Sham, P., & Fombonne, E. (2004). No evidence for links between autism, MMR, and measles virus. *Psychological Medicine, 34,* 543-553.

Chess, S., Korn, S. J., & Fernandez, P. B. (1971). *Psychiatric disorders of children with congenital rubella.* New York: Brunner/Mazel.

Chudley, A. E., Gutierrez, E., Jocelyn, L. J., & Chodirker, B. N. (1998). Outcomes of genetic evaluation in children with pervasive developmental disorder. *Journal of Developmental and Behavioral Pediatrics, 19,* 321-325.

Chugani, D. C., Muzik, O., Behen, M., Rothermel, R., Janisse, J. J., Lee, J., et al. (1999). Developmental changes in brain serotonin synthesis capacity in autistic and nonautistic children. *Annals of Neurology, 45,* 287-295.

Chugani, D. C., Muzik, O., & Rothermel, R. (1997). Altered serotonin synthesis in the dentatothalamocortical pathway in autistic boys. *Annals of Neurology, 42,* 666-669.

Connolly, H. M., & Crary, J. L. (1997). Valvular heart disease associated with fenfluramine-phentermine. *New England Journal of Medicine, 337,* 581-588.

Constantino, J. N., & Todd, R. D. (2005). Intergenerational transmission of subthreshold autistic traits in the general population. *Biological Psychiatry, 57,* 655-660.

Cook, E. H. (1990). Autism: Review of neurochemical investigation. *Synapse, 6,* 292-308.

Cook, E. H. (1996). Pathophysiology of autism: Neurochemistry. *Journal of Autism and Developmental Disorders, 26,* 221-225.

Courchesne, E. (1997). Brainstem, cerebellar, and limbic neuroanatomical abnormalities in autism. *Current Opinion in Neurobiology, 7,* 269–278.

Courchesne, E., Akshoomoff, N. A., & Townsend, J. (1992). Recent advances in autism. In H. Naruse & E. M. Ornitz (Eds.), *Neurobiology of infantile autism* (pp. 111–128). Amsterdam: Elsevier Science.

Courchesne, E., & Allen, G. (1997). Prediction and preparation: Fundamental functions of the cerebellum. *Learning & Memory, 4,* 1–35.

Courchesne, E., Courchesne, R. Y., Hicks, G., & Lincoln, A. J. (1985). Functioning of the brainstem auditory pathway in non-retarded autistic individuals. *Electroencephalography and Clinical Neurophysiology, 61,* 491–501.

Courchesne, E., Redcay, E., & Kennedy, D. P. (2004). The autistic brain: Birth through adulthood. *Current Opinion in Neurology, 17,* 489–496.

Courchesne, E., Yeung-Courchesne, R., Press, G. A., Hesselink, J. R., & Jernigan, T. L. (1988). Hypoplasia of cerebellar vermal lobules VI and VII in autism. *New England Journal of Medicine, 26,* 1349–1354.

Croen, L. A., Grether, J. K., Hoogstrate, J., & Selvin, S. (2002). The changing prevalence of autism in California. *Journal of Autism and Developmental Disorders, 32,* 207–215.

Dam, M. (1992). Quantitative neuropathology in epilepsy. *Acta Neurology Scandinavia, 137,* 51–54.

Dawson, G. (1983). Lateralized brain dysfunction in autism: Evidence from the Halstead-Reitan Neuropsychological Battery. *Journal of Autism and Developmental Disorders, 13,* 269–286.

Dawson, G., Carver, L., Meltzoff, A. N., Panagiotides, H., McPartland, J., & Webb, S. J. (2002). Neural correlates of face and object recognition in young children with autism spectrum disorder, developmental delay, and typical development. *Child Development, 73,* 700–717.

Dawson, G., Meltzoff, A. N., Osterling, J., Rinaldi, J., & Brown, E. (1998). Children with autism fail to orient to naturally occurring social stimuli. *Journal of Autism and Developmental Disorders, 28,* 479–485.

Dawson, G., Osterling, J., Meltzoff, A., & Kuhl, P. (2000). Case study of the development of an infant with autism from birth to 2 years of age. *Journal of Applied Developmental Psychology, 21,* 299–313.

Dekaban, A. S., & Sadowsky, D. (1978). Changes in brain weights during the span of human life: Relation of brain weights to body heights and body weights. *Annals of Neurology, 4,* 345–356.

DeLong, G. R. (1999). Autism: New data suggest a new hypothesis. *Neurology, 52,* 911–916.

DeLong, G. R., Teague, L. A., & McSwain-Kamran, M. (1998). Effects of fluoxetine treatment in young children with idiopathic autism. *Developmental Medicine Child Neurology, 40,* 551–562.

Dementieva, Y. A., Vance, D. D., Donnelly, S. L., Elston, L. A., Wolpert, C. M., Ravan, S. A., et al. (2005). Accelerated head growth in early development of individuals with autism. *Pediatric Neurology, 32,* 102–108.

Dennis, M., Lockyer, L., Lazenby, A. L., Donnelly, R. E., Wilkinson, M. & Schoonheyt, W. (1999). Intelligence patterns among children with high-functioning autism, phenylketonuria, and childhood head injury. *Journal of Autism and Developmental Disorders, 29,* 5–17.

DeStefano, F., Bhasin, T. K., Thompson, W. W., Yeargin-Allsopp, M., & Boyle, C. (2004). Age at first measles-mumps-rubella vaccination in children with autism and school-matched control subjects: A population-based study in metropolitan Atlanta. *Pediatrics, 113,* 259–266.

Ekman, G., Miranda-Linné, F., Gillberg, C., Garle, M., & Wetterberg, L. (1989). Fenfluramine treatment of twenty children with autism. *Journal of Autism and Developmental Disorders, 19,* 511–532.

Ellaway, C., & Christodoulou, J. (1999). Rett syndrome: Clinical update and review of recent genetic advances. *Journal of Paediatrics & Child Health, 35,* 419–426.

Filipek, P. A., Richelme, C., Kennedy, D. N., Rademacher, J., Pitcher, D. A., Zidel, S., et al. (1992). Morphometric analysis of the brain in developmental language disorders and autism. *Annals of Neurology, 32,* 475.

Folstein, S., & Rutter, M. (1977). Infantile autism: A genetic study of 21 twin pairs. *Journal of Child Psychology and Psychiatry, 18,* 297–321.

Fombonne, E. (1999). The epidemiology of autism: A review. *Psychological Medicine, 29,* 769–786.

Fombonne, E. (2003). Epidemiology of pervasive developmental disorders. *Trends in Evidence-Based Neuropsychiatry, 5,* 29–36.

Frith, U. (Ed.). (1991). *Autism and Asperger Syndrome.* Cambridge, UK: Cambridge University Press.

Frith, U. (2003). *Autism: Explaining the enigma* (2nd ed.). Malden, MA: Blackwell.

Frith, U. (2004). Emanuel Miller lecture; Confusions and controversies about Asperger syndrome. *Journal of Child Psychology and Psychiatry, 4,* 672-686.

Gale, S., Ozonoff, S., & Lainhart, J. (2003) Brief report: Pitocin induction in autistic and nonautistic individuals. *Journal of Autism and Developmental Disorders, 33,* 204-208.

Ghaziuddin, M., & Gerstein, L. (1996). Pedantic speaking style differentiates Asperger syndrome from high-functioning autism. *Journal of Autism and Developmental Disorders, 26,* 585-595.

Gillberg, C. (1995). Endogenous opioids and opiate antagonists in autism: Brief review of empirical finds and implications for clinicians. *Developmental Medicine and Child Neurology, 37,* 239-245.

Gillberg, C. (1999). Prevalence of disorders in the autism spectrum. *Infants and Young Children, 12,* 64-74.

Gillberg, I. C., Gillberg, C., & Ahlsen, G. (1994). Autistic behaviour and attention deficits in tuberous sclerosis: A population-based study. *Developmental Medicine and Child Neurology, 36,* 50-56.

Goodman, R. (2002). Brain disorders. In M. Rutter & E. Taylor (Eds.), *Child and Adolescent Psychiatry* (4th ed., pp. 241-260). Malden, MA: Blackwell.

Grafman, J., Litvan, I., Massaquoi, S., Stewart, M., Sivigu, A., & Hallet, M. (1992). Cognitive planning deficit in patients with cerebellar atrophy. *Neurology, 42,* 1493-1496.

Green, R. H., & Schwartzbaum, J. S. (1968). Effects of unilateral septal lesions on avoidance behavior, discrimination reversal, and hippocampal EEG. *Journal of Comparative and Physiological Psychology, 65,* 388-396.

Grelotti, D. J., Klin, A. J., Gauthier, I., Skudlarksi, P., Cohen, D. J., Gore, J. C., et al. (2005). FMRI activation of the fusiform gyrus and amygdala to cartoon characters but not to faces in a boy with autism. *Neuropsychologia, 43,* 373-385.

Hallahan, D. P., & Kauffman, J. M. (2003). *Exceptional learners: An introduction to special education* (9th ed.). Boston, MA: Allyn & Bacon.

Hobson, R. P., Ouston, J., & Lee, A. (1988). What's in a face? The case of autism. *British Journal of Developmental Psychology, 79,* 441-453.

Holden, C. (2005). Mating for autism? *Science, 308,* 948.

Hollander, E., Cartwright, C., Wong, C. M., DeCaria, C. M., DelGiudice-Asch, F., Buchsbaum, M. S., et al. (1998). A dimensional approach to the autism spectrum. *CNS Spectrums, 3,* 22-26, 33-39.

Hollander, E., King, A., Delaney, K., et al. (2003). Obsessive-compulsive behaviors in parents of multiplex autism families. *Psychiatry Research, 117,* 11-16.

Hollander, E., Phillips, A., Chaplin, W., Zagursky, K., Novotny, S., Wasserman, S., et al. (2005). A placebo controlled crossover trial of liquid fluoxetine on repetitive behaviors in childhood and adolescent autism. *Neuropsychopharmacology, 30,* 582-589.

Howlin, P. (2003). Outcome in high-functioning adults with autism with and without early language delays: Implications for the differentiation between autism and Asperger syndrome. *Journal of Autism & Developmental Disorders, 33,* 3-13.

Hunt, A., & Shepherd, C. (1993). A prevalence study of autism in tuberous sclerosis. *Journal of Autism and Developmental Disorders, 23,* 329-339.

Hviid, A., Stellfeld, M., Wohlfahrt, J., & Melbye, M. (2003). Association between thimerosal-containing vaccine and autism. *Journal of the American Medical Association, 290,* 1763-1766.

Itard, J. M. G. (1806/1962). *The wild boy of Aveyron* (G. Humphrey & M. Humphrey, Trans.). Upper Saddle River, NJ: Prentice Hall.

Joseph, R. (1999). Environmental influences on neural plasticity, the limbic system, emotional development, and attachment: A review. *Child Psychiatry and Human Development, 29,* 189-208.

Just, M. A., Cherkassky, V. L., Keller, T. A., & Minshew, N. J. (2004). Cortical activation and synchronization during sentence comprehension in high-functioning autism: Evidence of underconnectivity. *Brain, 127,* 1811-1821.

Kanner, L. (1943). Autistic disturbances of affective contact. *The Nervous Child, 2,* 217-250.

Kaye, J. A., del Mar Melero-Montes, M., & Jick, H. (2001). Measles, mumps, and rubella vaccine and the incidence of autism recorded by general practitioners: A time trend analysis. *British Medical Journal, 322,* 460–463.

Kemper, T. L., & Bauman, M. (1998). Neuropathology of infantile autism. *Journal of Neuropathology and Experimental Neurology, 57,* 645–652.

Kimble, D. P. (1963). The effects of bilateral hippocampal lesions in rats. *Journal of Physiological Psychology, 56,* 273–283.

Kirk, S. A., Gallagher, J. J., & Anastasiow, N. J. (1993). *Educating exceptional children* (7th ed.). Boston, MA: Houghton Mifflin.

Klin, A., Jones, W., Schultz, R., Volkmar, F., & Cohen, D. (2002a). Defining and quantifying the social phenotype in autism. *The American Journal of Psychiatry, 159,* 895–908.

Klin, A., Jones, W., Schultz, R., Volkmar, F., & Cohen, D. (2002b). Visual fixation patterns during viewing of naturalistic social situations as predictors of social competence in individuals with autism. *Archives of General Psychiatry, 59,* 809–816.

Knivsberg, A., Reichelt, K., Noland, M., & Hoien, T. (1995). Autistic syndrome and diet: A follow-up study. *Scandinavian Journal of Education Research, 39,* 223–236.

Lane, H. (1976). *The wild boy of Aveyron.* Cambridge, MA: Harvard University Press.

Lane, S. J. (2002). Structure and function of the sensory systems (pp. 35–70) & Sensory modulation (pp. 101–122). In A. C. Bundy, S. J. Lane, & E. A. Murray (Eds.), *Sensory integration: Theory and practice* (2nd ed.). Philadelphia: F. A. Davis.

Landry, R., & Bryson, S. E. (2004). Impaired disengagement of attention in young children with autism. *Journal of Child Psychology and Psychiatry, 45,* 1115–1122.

Langdell, T. (1978). Recognition of faces: An approach to the study of autism. *Journal of Child Psychology and Psychiatry, 19,* 225–238.

Lawler, C. P., Croen, L. A., Grether, J. K., & Van de Water, J. (2004). Identifying environmental contributions to autism: Provocative clues and false leads. *Mental Retardation and Developmental Disabilities Research Reviews, 10,* 292–302.

Leiner, H. C., Leiner, A. L., & Dow, R. S. (1987). Cerebrocerebellar learning loops in apes and humans. *Italian Journal of Neurological Science, 8,* 425–436.

Lenn, N. J. (1991). Neuroplasticity: The basis for brain development, learning and recovery from injury. *Infants and Young Children, 3,* 39–48.

Lewine, J. D., Andrews, R., Chez, M., Arun-Angelo, P., Devinsky, O., Smith, M., et al. (1999). Magnetoencephalographic patterns of epileptiform activity in children with regressive autism spectrum disorders. *Pediatrics, 104,* 405–418.

Lim, M. M., Bielsky, I. F., & Young, L. J. (2005). Neuropeptides and the social brain: Potential rodent models of autism. *International Journal of Developmental Neuroscience, 23,* 235–243.

Limoges, E., Mottron, L., Bolduc, C., Berthiaume, C., & Godbout, R. (2005). Atypical sleep architecture and the autism phenotype. *Brain: A Journal of Neurology, 128,* 1049–1061.

Lord, C., & Bailey, A. (2002). Autism spectrum disorders. In M. Rutter & E. Taylor (Eds.), *Child and Adolescent Psychiatry* (4th ed., pp. 636–663). Malden, MA: Blackwell.

Lord, C., Cook, E. H., Leventhal, B., & Amaral, D. G. (2000). Autism spectrum disorders. *Neuron, 28,* 355–363.

Luna, B., Minshew, N. J., Garver, K. E., Lazar, N. A., Thulborn, K. R., Eddy, W. F., et al. (2002). Neocortical system abnormalities in autism: An fMRI study of spatial working memory. *Neurology, 59,* 834–840.

MacLean, C. (1977). *The wolf children.* New York: Hill and Wang.

Malhotra, S., & Gupta, N. (1999). Childhood disintegrative disorder. *Journal of Autism and Developmental Disorders, 29,* 491–498.

Martineau, J., Barthelemy, C., Muh, J. P., & Lelord, G. (1992). Dopamine, serotonin and their derivatives: Biochemical markers in childhood autism? In H. Naruse & E. M. Ornitz (Eds.), *Neurobiology of Infantile autism* (pp. 251–268). Amsterdam: Excerpta Medica.

Mayes, S. D., Calhoun, S. L., & Crites, D. L. (2001). Does *DSM-IV* Asperger's disorder exist? *Journal of Abnormal Child Psychology, 29,* 263–271.

McDougle, C. J., Holmes, J. P., Carlson, D. C., Pelton, G. H., Cohen, D. J., & Price, L. H. (1998). A double-blind, placebo-controlled study of risperidone in adults with autistic disorder and other pervasive developmental disorders. *Archives of General Psychiatry, 55,* 633–641.

McDougle, C. J., Naylor, S. T., Cohen, D. J., Volkmar, F. R., Heninger, G. R., & Price, L. H.

(1996). A double-blind placebo-controlled study of fluvoxamine in adults with autistic disorder. *Archives of General Psychiatry, 53,* 1001-1008.

Miles, J. H., & Hillman, R. E. (2000). Value of a clinical morphology examination in autism. *American Journal of Medical Genetics, 91,* 245-253.

Minshew, N. (1991). Indices of neural function in autism: Clinical and biological implications. *Pediatrics, 87,* 774-780.

Minshew, N., Goldstein, G., Muenz, L., & Payton, J. (1992). Neuropsychological functioning of non-mentally retarded autistic individuals. *Journal of Clinical and Experimental Neuropsychology, 14,* 749-761.

Mishkin, M., & Aggleton, J. P. (1981). Multiple functional contributors of the amygdala in the monkey from the amygdaloid complex. In Y. Ben-Ari (Ed.), *INSERM Symposium, No. 20.* Amsterdam: Elsevier/North Holland Biomedical Press.

Mishkin, M., & Appenzeller, T. (1987). The anatomy of memory. *Scientific American, 256,* 80-89.

Moore, S. J., Turnpenny, P., Quinn, A., Glover, S., Lloyd, D. J., Montgomery, T., et al. (2000). A clinical study of 57 children with fetal anticonvulsant syndrome. *Journal of Medical Genetics, 37,* 489-497.

Mottron, L., Burack, J. A., Iarocci, G., Belleville, S., & Enns, J. T. (2003). Locally oriented perception with intact global processing among adolescents with high-functioning autism: Evidence from multiple paradigms. *Journal of Child Psychology and Psychiatry and Allied Disciplines, 44,* 904-913.

Muhle, R., Trentacoste, S. V., & Rapin, I. (2004). The genetics of autism. *Pediatrics, 113,* e472-e486.

Murray, E. A. (1990). Representational memory in non-human primates. In R. P. Kesner & D. S. Olton (Eds.), *Neurobiology of comparative cognition* (pp. 127-155). Hillsdale, NJ: Lawrence Erlbaum.

Murray, E. A., & Mishkin, M. (1985). Amygdaloidectomy impairs crossmodal association in monkeys. *Science, 228,* 604-606.

Nass, R. (2002). Plasticity: Mechanisms, extent and limits. In S. J. Segalowitz & I. Rapin (Eds.), *Handbook of neuropsychology* (2nd ed., pp. 29-68). Amsterdam: Elsevier Science.

Newton, M. (2002). *Savage girls and wild boys: A history of feral children.* New York: St. Martin's Press.

Nicolson, R., & Castellanos, F. X. (2000). Considerations on the pharmacotherapy of attention deficits and hyperactivity in children with autism and other pervasive developmental disorders. *Journal of Autism and Developmental Disorders, 30,* 461-462.

Ozonoff, S. (1997). Components of executive function deficits in autism and other disorders. In J. Russell (Ed.), *Autism as an executive disorder* (pp. 179-211). Oxford, UK: Oxford University Press.

Palermo, M. T., & Curatolo, P. (2004). Pharmacologic treatment of autism. *Journal of Child Neurology, 19,* 155-164.

Panksepp, J. (1979). A neurochemical theory of autism. *Trends in Neuroscience, 2,* 174-177.

Panksepp, J., & Sahley, T. L. (1987). Possible brain opioid involvement in disrupted social intent and language development of autism. In E. Schopler & G. B. Mesibov (Eds.), *Neurobiological issues in autism* (pp. 357-372). New York: Plenum.

Pascalis, O., de Schonen, S., Morton, J., Deruelle, C., & Fabre-Grent, M. (1995). Mother's face recognition by neonates: A replication and extension. *Infant Behavior and Development, 18,* 79-95.

Pickett, J. (2001). Current investigations in autism brain tissue research. *Journal of Autism and Developmental Disorders, 31,* 521-527.

Pickles, A., Bolton, P., Macdonald, H., Bailey, A., Le Couteru, A., Sim, C. H., et al. (1995). Latent class analysis of recurrence risks for complex phenotypes with selection and measurement error: A twin and family history study of autism. *American Journal of Human Genetics, 57,* 717-726.

Pierce, K., Muller, R. A., Ambrose, J., Allen, G., & Courchesne, E. (2001). Face processing occurs outside the fusiform "face area" in autism: Evidence from functional MRI. *Brain, 124,* 2059-2073.

Piven, J., & Folstein, S. (1994). The genetics of autism. In M. L. Bauman & T. L. Kemper (Eds.), *The Neurobiology of Autism* (pp. 18-44). Baltimore: Johns Hopkins University Press.

Piven, J., Tsai, G. C., Nehme, E., Coyle, J. T., Chase, G. A., & Folstein, S. E. (1991). Platelet serotonin: A possible marker for familial autism. *Journal of Autism and Developmental Disorders, 21,* 51-59.

Piven, J., Wzorek, M., Landa, R., Lainhart, J., Bolton, P., Chase, G. A., et al. (1994). Personality characteristics of the parents of autistic individuals (preliminary communication). *Psychological Medicine, 24,* 783–795.

Potenza, M. N., & McDougle, C. J. (1997). The role of serotonin in autism spectrum disorders. *CNS Spectrums, 2,* 25–42.

Rakic, P. (1971). Neuron-gila relationship during granule cell migration in developing cerebellar cortex: A Golgi and electron microscopic study in macacus rhesus. *Journal of Comparative Neurology, 141,* 282–312.

Rakic, P., & Sidman, R. L. (1970). Histogenesis of the cortical layers in human cerebellum particularly the lamina dissecans. *Journal of Comparative Neurology, 139,* 473–500.

Rank, B. (1955). Intensive study and treatment of preschool children who show marked personality deviations, or "atypical development" and their parents. In G. Caplan (Ed.,), *Emotional problems of early childhood* (pp. 491–501). New York: Basic Books.

Rapin, I. (1999). Autism in search of a home in the brain. *Neurology, 52,* 902–904.

Rimland, B. (2004). Association between thimerosal-containing vaccine and autism. *Journal of the American Medical Association, 291,* 180.

Rinehart, N. J., Bradshaw, J. L., Brereton, A. V., & Tonge, B. J. (2001). Movement preparation in high-functioning autism and Asperger disorder: A serial choice reaction time task involving motor reprogramming. *Journal of Autism and Developmental Disorders, 31,* 79–88.

Rinehart, N. J., Bradshaw, J. L., Brereton, A. V., & Tonge, B. J. (2002). A clinical and neurobehavioural review of high-functioning autism and Asperger's disorder. *Australian and New Zealand Journal of Psychiatry, 36,* 762–770.

Risch, N., Spiker, D., Lotspeich, L., Nouri, N., Hinds, D., Hallmayer, J., et al. (1999). A genomic screen of autism: Evidence for a multilocus etiology. *American Journal of Human Genetics, 65,* 493–507.

Ritvo, E. R., Freeman, B. J., Scheibel, A. B., Duong, T., Robinson, H., & Guthrie, D. (1986). Lower Purkinje cell counts in the cerebella of four autistic subjects: Initial findings of the UCLA-NSAC autopsy research report. *American Journal of Psychiatry, 143,* 862–866.

Roberts, W. W., Dember, W. N., & Brodwick, H. (1962). Alteration and exploration in rats with hippocampal lesions. *Journal of Comparative Psychiatry, 55,* 695–700.

Rodier, P. M. (2000). The early origins of autism. *Scientific American, 282,* 56–63.

Rodier, P. M., Ingram, J. L., Tisdale, B., Nelson, S., Romano, J. (1996). Embryological origin for autism: Developmental anomalies of the cranial nerve motor nuclei. *Journal of Comparative Neurology, 370,* 247–261.

Rogers, S. J., Hepburn, S., & Wehner, E. (2003). Parent reports of sensory symptoms in toddlers with autism and those with other developmental disorders. *Journal of Autism and Developmental Disorders, 33,* 631–642.

Rogers, S. J., Ozonoff, S., & Maslin-Cole, C. (1993). Developmental aspects of attachment behavior in young children with pervasive developmental disorders. *Journal of the American Academy of Child and Adolescent Psychiatry, 32,* 1274–1282.

Rourke, B. (1989). *Nonverbal learning disabilities: The syndrome and the model.* New York: Guilford Press.

Rumsey, J. M. (1992). Neuropsychological studies of high-level autism. In E. Schopler & G. B. Mesibov (Eds.), *High-functioning individuals with autism* (pp. 41–64). New York: Plenum.

Rutgers, A. H., Bakermans-Kranenburg, M. J., van Uzendoorn, M. H., & van Berckelaer-Onnes, I. A. (2004). Autism and attachment: A meta-analytic review. *Journal of Child Psychology and Psychiatry and Allied Disciplines, 45,* 1123–1134.

Rutter, M. (2002). Development and psychopathology. In M. Rutter & E. Taylor (Eds.), *Child and Adolescent Psychiatry* (4th ed., pp. 309–324). Malden, MA: Blackwell.

Rutter, M., Bailey, A., Bolton, P., & Le Couteur, A. (1994). Autism and known medical conditions: Myth and substance. *Journal of Child Psychology and Psychiatry, 35,* 311–322.

Saitoh, O., & Courchesne, E. (1998). Magnetic resonance imaging study of the brain in autism. *Psychiatry and Clinical Neuroscience, 52,* S219–S222.

Santangelo, S. L., & Tsatsanis, K. (2005). What is known about autism: Genes, brain, and behavior. *American Journal of Pharmacogenomics, 5,* 71–92.

Schreck, K. A., Mulick, J. A., & Smith, A. F. (2004). Sleep problems as possible predictors of intensified symptoms of autism. *Research in Developmental Disabilities, 25,* 57–66.

Schultz, R. T. (2005). Developmental deficits in social perception in autism: The role of the amygdala and fusiform face area. *International Journal of Developmental Neuroscience, 23,* 125-141.

Schultz, R. T., Gauthier, I., Klin, A., Fulbright, R., Anderson, A., Volkmar, F. R., et al. (2000). Abnormal ventral temporal cortical activity among individuals with autism and Asperger syndrome during face discrimination. *Archives of General Psychiatry, 57,* 331-340.

Sigman, M., Dijamco, A., Gratier, M., & Rozga, A. (2004). Early detection of core deficits in autism. *Mental Retardation and Developmental Disabilities Research Reviews, 10,* 221-233.

Squire, L. R., & Zola-Morgan, S. (1991). The medial temporal lobe memory system. *Science, 253,* 1380-1386.

Steingard, R. J., Zimnitzky, B., DeMaso, D. R., Bauman, M. L., & Bucci, J. P. (1997) Sertraline treatment of transition-associated anxiety and agitation in children with autistic disorder. *Journal of Child and Adolescent Psychopharmacology, 7,* 9-15.

Szatmari, P., Jones, M. B., Zwaigenbaum, L., & MacLean, J. E. (1998). Genetics of autism: Overview and new directions. *Journal of Autism and Developmental Disorders, 28,* 351-368.

Tanguay, P. E., & Edwards, R. (1982). Electrophysiological studies of autism: The whisper of the bang. *Journal of Autism and Developmental Disorders, 12,* 177-184.

Tani, P., Lindberg, N., Nieminen-von Wendt, T., von Wendt, L., Virkkala, J., Appelberg, B., et al. (2004). Sleep in young adults with Asperger syndrome. *Neuropsychobiology, 50,* 147-152.

Tantam, D., Monaghan, L., Nicholson, H., & Stirling, J. (1989). Autistic children's ability to interpret faces: A research note. *Journal of Child Psychology and Psychiatry, 30,* 623-630.

Teder-Salejarvi, W. A., Pierce, K. L., Courchesne, E., & Hillyard, S. A. (2005). Auditory spatial localization and attention deficits in autistic adults. *Brain Research, 23,* 221-234.

Tidmarsh, L. & Volkmar, F. R. (2003). Diagnosis and epidemiology of autism spectrum disorders. *Canadian Journal of Psychiatry, 48,* 517-525.

Townsend, J., & Courchesne, E. (1994). Parietal damage and narrow "spotlight" spatial attention. *Journal of Cognitive Neuroscience, 6,* 220-232.

Townsend, J., Courchesne, E., & Egaas, B. (1996). Slowed orienting of covert visual-spatial attention in autism: Specific deficits associated with cerebellar and parietal abnormality. *Development and Psychopathology, 8,* 563-584.

Townsend, J., Harris, N. S., & Courchesne, E. (1996). Visual attention abnormalities in autism: Delayed orienting to location. *Journal of the International Neuropsychological Society, 2,* 541-550.

Tsai, L. Y. (1992). Diagnostic issues in high-functioning autism. In E. Schopler & G. B. Mesibov (Eds.), High-functioning individuals with autism (pp. 11–40). New York: Plenum Press.

U.S. Department of Education. (1995). *Seventeenth annual report to Congress on the implementation of the Individuals with Disabilities Education Act.* Washington, DC: Author.

U.S. Department of Education. (2004). *Twenty-sixth annual report to Congress on the implementation of the Individuals with Disabilities Education Act.* Washington, DC: Author.

Vargas, D. L., Nascimbene, C., Krishnan, C., Zimmerman, A. W., & Pardo, C. A. (2004). Neurological activation and neuroinflammation in the brain of patients with autism. *Annals of Neurology, 57,* 67-81.

Vargha-Khadem, F., Isaacs, E., van der Werf, S., Robb, S., & Wilson, J. (1992). Development of intelligence and memory in children with hemiplegic cerebral palsy: The deleterious consequences of early seizures. *Brain, 115,* 315-329.

Vergnes, M. (1981). Effect of prior familiarization with mice on elicitation of mouse killings in rats: Role of the amygdala. In Y. Ben-Ari (Ed.), *The amygdaloid complex.* INSERM Symposium, No. 20. Amsterdam: Elsevier/North Holland Biomedical Press.

Volkmar, F. R., Carter, A., Grossman, J., & Klin, A. (1997). Social development in autism. In D. Cohen & F. Volkmar (Eds.), *Handbook of autism and pervasive developmental disorders* (2nd ed., pp. 173-194). New York: Wiley.

Volkmar, F. R., Klin, A., Siegel, B., Szatmari, P., Lord, C., Campbell, M., et al. (1994). Field trial for autistic disorder in *DSM-IV. The American Journal of Psychiatry, 151,* 1361-1367.

Volkmar, F. R., Lord, C., Bailey, A., Schultz, R. T., & Klin, A. (2004). Autism and pervasive developmental disorders. *Journal of Child Psychology and Psychiatry, 45,* 135–170.

Volkmar, F. R., & Nelson, D. S. (1990). Seizure disorders in autism. *Journal of the American Academy of Child and Adolescent Psychiatry, 29,* 127–129.

Wahl, R. U. (2004). Could oxytocin administration during labor contribute to autism and related behavioral disorders? A look at the future. *Medical Hypotheses, 63,* 456–460.

Wainwright-Sharp, J. A., & Bryson, S. E. (1993). Visual orienting deficits in high-functioning people with autism. *Journal of Autism and Developmental Disorders, 23,* 1–13.

Wassink, T. H., Brzustowicz, L. M., Bartlett, C. W., & Szatmari, P. (2004). The search for autism disease genes. *Mental Retardation and Developmental Disabilities Research Reviews, 10,* 272–283.

Waterhouse, L., Fein, D., & Modahl, C. (1996). Neurofunctional mechanisms in autism. *Psychological Review, 103,* 457–489.

Welch, M. G., Welch-Horan, T. B., Anwar, M., Anwar, N., Ludwig, R. J., & Ruggiero, D. A. (2005). Brain effects of chronic IBD in areas abnormal in autism and treatment by single neuropeptides secretin and oxytocin. *Journal of Molecular Neuroscience, 25,* 259–274.

Welchew, D. E., Ashwin, C., Berkouk, K., Salvador, R., Suckling, J., Baron-Cohen, S., et al. (2005). Functional disconnectivity of the medial temporal lobe in Asperger syndrome. *Biological Psychiatry, 57,* 991–998.

Werner, E., Dawson, G., Osterling, J., & Dinno, N. (2000). Brief report: Recognition of autism spectrum disorder before one year of age: A retrospective study based on home videotapes. *Journal of Autism and Other Developmental Disorders, 30,* 157–167.

Williams, D. L., Goldstein, G., & Minshew, N. J. (2005). Impaired memory for faces and social scenes in autism: Clinical implications of memory dysfunction. *Archives of Clinical Neuropsychology, 20,* 1–15.

Wing, L. (1981). Asperger's syndrome: A clinical account. *Psychological Medicine, 11,* 115–129.

Wing, L., & Gould, J. (1979). Severe impairments of social interaction and associated abnormalities in children: Epidemiology and classification. *Journal of Autism and Developmental Disorders, 9,* 11–29.

Wong, V., & Wong, S. N. (1991). Brainstem auditory evoked potential study in children with autistic disorder. *Journal of Autism and Developmental Disorders, 21,* 329–340.

Yakovlev, P. I., Weinberger, M., & Chipman, C. E. (1948). Heller's Syndrome as a pattern of schizophrenic behavior disturbance in early childhood. *American Journal of Mental Deficiency, 53,* 318–337.

Young, E. C., Diehl, J. J., Morris, D., Hyman, S. L., & Bennetto, L. (2005). The use of two language tests to identify pragmatic language problems in children with autism spectrum disorders. *Language, Speech, and Hearing Services in Schools, 36,* 62–72.

CHAPTER 3

Collaborating to Develop Effective Programs

KEY TERMS

Active Listening

Clarification of Intent

Effective Collaboration

Heterogeneous Population

Individually Tailored Programs

Paraphrasing

Physiologically Based Approach

Placebo Effect

Positive Trajectory

Reflecting Feelings

Relationship-Based Approach

Responding with Empathy

Skills-Based Approach

SOLER

❖ LEARNING WITH MS. HARRIS: One School System's Experience

Ms. Harris was excited! The first day of school was still weeks away and Ms. Stokes had given her the opportunity to attend a conference on autism spectrum disorders. Several well-known ASD experts were presenting papers at the conference, and many of the strategies and ideas Ms. Harris had been reading about were coming to life in her mind. At the end of an interesting session promoting a particular methodology, an argument broke out between the presenter and some of the participants. Ms. Harris listened in amazement as a special education director talked about a due process case that her school system had just won. Funny thing was, it didn't sound as if there were any winners. The administrator who was talking was clearly bitter *about all the time and energy that her personnel had put into defending the school's program. The case had lasted for almost two years and had cost the district over $1,000,000. An excellent teacher had quit as a result of the stress and harassment she endured when she was questioned during the proceedings. The family that had requested the due process was unhappy with the decision and had instigated an appeal. "How did it turn so ugly?" wondered Ms. Harris. "Isn't it obvious how students with ASD should be taught?"*

UNDERSTANDING THE CONTROVERSY

Everyone involved in developing programs for students with ASD is committed to promoting benefits for the student and avoiding harm, including that due to lost instructional opportunities. Some of the conflict that occurs in the process of collaborating to develop programs is related to differing perspectives, confusing interventions with outcomes, and the dramatic influence of marketing on perceptions of effectiveness.

Differing Perspectives

Unfortunately, determining how and what students with autism spectrum disorders should be taught is not obvious but very controversial (Heflin & Simpson, 1998a). Some of the controversy revolves around two distinct perspectives that are brought together when it is time to develop an appropriate educational program. Families have one perspective; school systems have another.

Imagine for a moment the perspective of the family of the child with an ASD. The parents, like all parents, want what is best for their child and want the child to be happy and self-sufficient. But their child has a neurological disorder that creates incredible challenges and makes even the simplest tasks daunting. The family is probably under stress and worn out from trying to keep a consistent routine. It is highly likely that the family has not taken a vacation in years and probably cannot find a sitter, so the parents have not been out on a "date" for a long time. And then there is the constant quest for a "cure." Of all disabilities, ASDs are the ones with the greatest proliferation of "miraculous" cures (Rogers, 1998). Parents find themselves caught between optimism and skepticism as almost weekly media features and Internet postings broadcast some child's recovery. They may even be pressured by family and friends to try treatments that are expensive, time consuming, and potentially detrimental to the family as a whole. Yet, if they do not try the treatment, they will always wonder if it might have been the one that would have restored their child's functioning. The parents' focus is, and should be, on the welfare of their child.

Now imagine the perspective of school personnel. Schools are charged with promoting the achievement and welfare of all students, not attempting to maximize the potential of one student (*Board of Education of the Hendrick Hudson Central School District v. Rowley,* 1982). Whether publicly or privately funded, schools are held accountable for demonstrating that all students make progress in acquiring important and critical skills, and for using curricula and methodology that have demonstrated effectiveness for teaching skills. Schools are not directed to provide access to programs that treat the symptoms of a disability. To help students who are eligible for specialized services, a team comprised of school personnel and family members develop an Individualized Educational Plan (IEP) that is calculated to provide benefit for the student. All involved want the student to succeed, and each member brings a slightly different perspective to what success means for the individual child.

Interventions vs. Outcomes

Also controversial are discussions that confuse interventions and outcomes. To consider a treatment by name (e.g., "Fast ForWord," "Sensory Integration Therapy") may conceal the fact that multiple programs promote similar outcomes. Indeed, alternative programs promoting similar outcomes may even have a higher likelihood of being successful for a particular student than the program being requested. When a particular treatment or intervention is requested by name, the IEP team should first consider the potential outcomes and then determine whether the outcomes are meaningful for the student and, if so, whether there are more effective programs for accomplishing those outcomes. The effectiveness of a program is verified by objective data that link the behavioral changes and the intervention.

Marketing Hype

Treatments and interventions are frequently requested by name because of the marketing blitz surrounding many of the programs for students with ASD. From computers to herbal supplements, advertisements appear in national magazines, media programs, Internet sites, and even magazines on airplanes that endorse treatments promising amazing results. People are sensitive to such marketing hype (as demonstrated by the number of unused pieces of exercise equipment that inhabit most homes). Additionally, those who market interventions can make many claims and promises, no matter how grandiose, because there is no oversight process for evaluating such claims. In contrast, schools are held accountable for any claims they make because their constituents demand proof. Indeed, schools are evaluated annually to determine if students are making adequate yearly progress (NCLB, 2001). Most schools provide effective instruction but lack expertise in marketing (Hart, 1995). Even when schools try to publicize student success, a glance at any newspaper reflects that the media is interested in schools only in instances of violence or scandal.

Given the differing perspectives, the confusion between interventions and outcomes, and the inequitable marketing hype that exists, it is not surprising that controversies occur when attempting to develop appropriate programming for students with ASD. Unfortunately, an analysis of published literature does not provide definitive answers either.

CRITICAL ANALYSIS OF PUBLISHED LITERATURE

In addition to the tendencies for people to operate from their own perspectives, view outcomes and interventions as the same, and fall prey to the persuasive effects of marketing, other sources of controversy emerge that render agreement difficult. Issues regarding published literature, which should offer guidance, can inhibit potential contributions toward consensus. A critical analysis of published literature reveals that researchers do not always agree on the essential components of effective programming. The nature of ASD as a heterogeneous population and the fact that individuals with ASD develop dynamically further complicate attempts to draw conclusions from professional literature.

Contradictory Conclusions

The professional literature is replete with thousands of studies that demonstrate the effectiveness of a wide variety of approaches for enhancing skill acquisition and making a positive impact on the behavior of children, youth, and adults. Obviously, many methods are available that are effective for students with ASD (NRC, 2001). Controversy occurs when it is realized that some of the methodologies contradict each other. Some researchers suggest that maximum progress occurs when a student participates in a program consisting of many hours of intensive, massed Discrete Trial Training (DTT) (Lovaas, 1987). Others suggest that maximum benefit occurs when students are educated in inclusive environments using methods of teaching that take advantage of naturally occurring events (McGee, Morrier, & Daly, 1999). Others focus on carefully engineering environments to support independent task completion (Mesibov, 1997). Still others suggest that students will not benefit from school-based activities until they have related to a caregiver and have attained specific levels of emotional maturity (Greenspan & Weider, 1997). Citing research, proponents can establish arguments for supporting a variety of methodologies that are impossible to use simultaneously.

Heterogeneous Population

Although some of the contradictory evidence is based on differences in how studies are designed, some of the conflicting results are produced because students with ASD present a heterogeneous mix of abilities and needs (Lord, Cook, Leventhal, & Amaral, 2000). Individuals with ASD constitute a **heterogeneous population** because there is almost as much variability within the population of students with ASD as there is between individuals with and without ASD (VanMeter, Fein, Morris, Waterhouse, & Allen, 1997). The push to identify subtypes among the population of individuals with ASD reflects a need to know why some students benefit from certain interventions and others do not (Rutter & Schopler, 1992).

Even with the high publicity given to intensive behavioral therapy (i.e., "Lovaas"), it is clear the intervention is not equally effective for all children and there is a need to determine why some individuals benefit more than others (Kazdin, 1993). Pretreatment developmental IQ scores as well as family stress levels have been found to influence posttreatment outcomes more than the number of hours or type of intervention provided (Gabriels, Hill, Pierce, Rogers, & Wehner, 2001). Cole, Dale, and Mills (1991) noted that students with higher scores on language pretests benefit from didactic language training, while those with lower pretest scores benefit more from a naturalistic training approach. Harris and Handleman (2000) provided the same treatment to a group of students with autism and found that those who were younger with higher IQs when treatment began graduated from the program into general education classes; students who were older with lower IQs graduated into self-contained special education classes. Lovaas (1987) indicated that individuals with measured IQs of less than 50 would not respond as well to intensive behavioral therapy.

The mystery of why some students benefit from a particular treatment and others do not has led to the demand for exact descriptions of those individuals participating in research, not only in terms of scores on multiple assessments, but also in regard to their communication abilities, functional skills, and interaction styles. In addition to the comprehensive demographic information about the participants, it will be beneficial for researchers to provide careful descriptions of variables that appear to affect treatment outcomes. These include the facility, teacher, and parent characteristics (NRC, 2001), because parent characteristics have been shown to influence outcomes for children (Siller & Sigman, 2002).

There is no doubt that intervention outcomes are affected by the variability within the heterogeneous population. More attention needs to be given to identifying subgroups within the autism spectrum (Lord et al., 2000; Rapin, 1987) as well as to the social and environmental variables surrounding the participant.

Developmental Disability

The fact that ASDs are developmental disabilities also influences interpretations of the research literature. By definition, developmental disabilities manifest during the developmental period, which extends between birth and 18 years of age. As a developmental disability, an ASD has a profound effect on the individual's development. For example, an infant's interest in objects (Dawson, Meltzoff, Osterling, Rinaldi, & Brown, 1998) can interfere with social development, which negatively affects the development of communication. Some of the unusual behaviors evident in early infancy become more unusual because the brain does not develop through typical patterns of interacting with the world (Kemper & Bauman, 1998). Also like a developmental disability, the behaviors demonstrated by an individual with an ASD naturally change over time (Campbell, Schopler, Cueva, & Hallin, 1996). A child with severe sensory defensiveness at 4 years of age may have fewer problems with certain sensory information as her neurological system develops. A student who is fascinated by trains at age 7 may be much more interested in cryptozoology when he is 9. Symptoms such as echolalia, withdrawal, and stereotypies abate with age (Szatmari, Bartolucci, Bremner, Bond, & Rich, 1989).

Since ASD are developmental disabilities, caution is warranted in evaluating treatments that require a significant time commitment before determining effectiveness. Improvements in socialization, language, and cognition may result from the treatment or may occur simply as a result of the maturation of the neurological system (Courchesne, Akshoomoff, & Townsend, 1992). As an example, dietary modifications are promoted as requiring six months to a year before their effectiveness is shown. The question then arises: What else could have happened within that time frame that could have advanced behavioral changes? Because ASD affect and are affected by development, the role of coincidence and maturation must be considered in interventions that require lengthy amounts of time to demonstrate effectiveness.

ADDITIONAL CONSIDERATIONS WHEN INTERPRETING RESEARCH LITERATURE

In addition to the role of contradictory conclusions and the implications of developmental disabilities among a heterogeneous population, other factors affect interpretations of research and influence discussions concerning effective programs. These factors include the tendency for individuals to improve over time regardless of intervention **(positive trajectory),** research design issues such as nonrandom selection and the delineation of questionable indicators for determining effectiveness, recognition of the placebo effect, and the necessity of considering the needs of the entire family in discussions about appropriate programming.

Positive Trajectories

Individuals with ASD mature physiologically just like those without ASD. As the individual experiences more events and as the neurological system changes over time, improvements in behavior may become evident (Kanner, Rodriguez, & Ashenden, 1972). Although typical functioning may not emerge, many individuals with ASD will demonstrate improvement over time with or without interventions (Gabriels et al., 2001), especially if they do not have mental retardation (Mayes & Calhoun, 1999). In a long-term follow-up study of individuals with autism who had IQ scores between 68 and 110, Szatmari et al. (1989) found that, regardless of treatment, 50% had attended or were attending college, were employed, and lived independently, and that 25% would not be identifiable as having an ASD. Participants' characteristics, specifically in regard to cognitive functioning, are emerging as the strongest predictor for responsiveness to treatment, any treatment, regardless of type and intensity (Eaves & Ho, 2004; Gabriels et al., 2001).

Even with this information, educators cannot withhold intervention from students functioning on the higher end of the spectrum in the hopes that they may spontaneously improve. However, research studies that include only participants functioning at the high end of the range should be scrutinized carefully, because the outcomes may be based more on the positive trajectories of the participants and less on the treatments or interventions employed (Mayes & Calhoun, 2003).

Nonrandom Selection and Outcome Measures

Almost all research conducted to date with individuals with ASD have used necessity or convenience as the means of identifying participants. Studies are conducted on individuals who are available and whose behaviors necessitate intervention. Or researchers recruit participants using available resources such as mailing lists. Using nonrandom samples produces an inherent bias that may mitigate outcomes (Rogers, 1996; Schloss & Smith, 1999). Such a bias must be considered when interpreting outcomes. Additionally, researchers select their own indicators of success for evaluating the outcomes of their interventions. Research that uses IQ scores and postintervention placement as indicators of effectiveness are suspect.

Changes in IQ scores during an intervention are of limited use as an indicator of effectiveness for two reasons. First, positive changes in IQ scores do not necessarily indicate meaningful gains because the nonverbal portions tap into a relative strength for individuals with ASD (Rogers, 1998). However, IQ scores may not provide a measure of overall functioning. Second, research suggesting that a change in IQ scores between preschool age and school entry is due to intervention fails to recognize that most children show, on average, a 23-point increase when tested at those two times (Lord & Schopler, 1989a; Lord & Schopler, 1989b; Sigman, Dissanayake, Arbelle, & Ruskin, 1997). In a study that monitored 49 two-year-olds for two years, Eaves and Ho (2004) found that 35% of the children with ASD gained 25–26 points on IQ measures, regardless of the type of treatment or the number of hours it was being provided. Gabriels et al. (2001) noted that 52% of their participants demonstrated large IQ gains without specific or intensive treatment. Others have found average increases of 15 points in IQ when testing individuals with IQs greater than 70 (Freeman, Ritvo, Needleman, & Yokota, 1985; Mayes & Calhoun, 1999). In addition, examiners may artificially increase IQ scores based on how tests are administered (Koegel, Koegel, & Smith, 1997). Although researchers should provide IQ scores (if available) as demographic data for participants, the use of IQ scores as an outcome measure for interventions is discouraged (NRC, 2001).

Similarly, the use of postintervention placement as a measure of outcome reflects less on the abilities of the participants and more on variables unrelated to the student, such as administrative preferences, availability of services, and trends toward full inclusion. To say that a student receives services in general education classrooms as a result of receiving an intervention says nothing about the intervention.

Placebo Effect

Any intervention that uses the opinion or rating of someone who has expectations about the benefit of an intervention is subject to the **placebo effect** (Schopler, 1987; Shapiro, 1978). A twist on a familiar saying best illustrates this point: "If I hadn't believed it, I wouldn't have seen it." People see differences in behavior because they know an intervention is being provided and they *want* to see differences (Kaplan, Polatajko, Wilson, & Faris, 1993). Parents have reported being very satisfied with in-home discrete trial training despite a lack of measurable improvement (Boyd & Corley, 2001). When committing investments of time, energy, and resources to an intervention, individuals have a vested interest in experiencing results.

The use of secretin as an intervention provides a dramatic example of the placebo effect, specifically with students with ASD. Many families took their children with ASD to receive injections of secretin, an amino acid hormone typically used in diagnostic procedures for digestive problems, which was promoted in the late 1990s on television, the Internet, and in trade magazines as a miraculous cure for autism. Initially, considerable effort and expense were required to secure secretin treatments, leading some to attribute the positive outcomes that were reported to the fact that "parents see what they want to see" (Pollack, 2004, A12). Masked clinical trials of secretin have found that the drug is no more effective than a placebo in changing the symptoms of ASD (Chez et al., 2000; Molloy et al., 2002; Owley et al., 2001). Indeed, when parents and other observers did not know which children were receiving secretin vs. placebo, the outcome was that *all* children appeared to improve (Sandler et al., 1999). The placebo effect can have a strong influence on determining effectiveness, underscoring the need for objective measures for documenting change and the use of evaluators who are unaware of the intervention (Rogers, 1996).

Consideration of Entire Family

The utility of an intervention should consider the impact of the intervention on the family as a whole. Family involvement is consistently listed as a critical feature in appropriate programming (Iovannone, Dunlap, Huber, & Kincaid, 2003), and a good predictor of positive long-term outcomes for children with ASD is a functional and balanced family. Children with ASD unintentionally may place great stress on the family unit, challenging its functioning and balance (Harris, 1994). Major transitions (e.g., adolescence, 21st birthday) exacerbate stress as families are reminded again of the possibly sharp distinctions between the functioning of their family member compared with others who do not have ASD (Winkler, Wasow, & Hatfield, 1981). Parents of children with ASD experience considerable stress that changes across their children's development (Domingue, Cutler, & McTarnaghan, 2000), and possibly more stress than parents of children with other disabilities (Dumas, Wolf, Fisman, & Culligan, 1991). Parental stress is predicted by lower levels of adaptive functioning in their children (Weiss, Sullivan, &

Diamond, 2003). One study suggested that parents of children with ASD were more depressed than the parents of children who were dying (Johnson, 2000).

Bromley, Hare, Davison, and Emerson (2004) concluded that over half of the 68 mothers in their study who had children with ASD experienced significant psychological distress. This raises the interesting question: Which came first? Can having a child with an ASD lead to psychological distress, or does the presence of mental health issues contribute to the possibility that a child will have an ASD? Members of some immediate and extended families of individuals with ASD report experiencing their own psychiatric issues such as obsessive-compulsive disorders, depression, schizophrenia, social phobia, and bipolar disorder (DeLong, 1999; Ghaziuddin, 2005; Hollander et al., 2003). The genetics involved in producing ASD may also affect family members to a lesser degree. For this reason, medical professionals working with some of the families of children with ASD may discuss the effective management of associated symptoms in the family (Santangelo & Tsatsanis, 2005).

In addition to the parents, the siblings of students with ASD may need to be considered in the development of effective programming. Siblings of individuals with ASD may experience more behavioral problems and fewer prosocial behaviors than their peers who do not have a sibling with a disability (Hastings, 2003). Siblings may be called upon to provide care for their brother or sister with a disability or may feel unimportant because of the need for a high level of parental attention to the sibling with an ASD.

Finally, the shift away from viewing the family member with an ASD as someone who is "defective and needing to be fixed" (Dyches, Wilder, Sudweeks, Obiakor, & Algozzine, 2004) can eliminate the pressure to find a cure. Indeed, some individuals functioning on the high end of the spectrum are lobbying for acceptance rather than intervention (Harmon, 2004).

Providing support for families can be critical for the prognosis of the student with an ASD (NRC, 2001) and must be considered when evaluating different options, because some interventions appear to be more empowering to families than others (Bristol, Gallagher, & Holt, 1993; Koegel, Bimbela, & Schreibman, 1996).

Given all of the factors mentioned, it is remarkable that the members of an IEP team can reach any agreement when collaborating to design an approach to promote positive outcomes for the student and his or her family. However, there is another source of controversy that exerts considerable influence. Logical, illogical, intuitive, and calculated consideration generate particular perspectives that provide a framework for understanding and addressing the needs of students with ASD. These perspectives exert a powerful influence in the collaborative process.

DIFFERING APPROACHES FOR THE SAME POPULATION

In addition to different personal perspectives, advocates have differing perspectives regarding the core deficit in ASD and desired goals of intervention. Intervention approaches for students with ASD have been divided into three broad categories: relationship-based, skills-based, and physiologically based (Heflin & Simpson, 1998a). Some treatment and intervention programs combine aspects of each approach, and most advocates incorporate strategies from multiple approaches. Each will be discussed briefly to illustrate how readily disagreements can arise.

Relationship-Based Approaches

Relationship-based approaches view the core deficit in ASD as the failure to develop an attachment for and relationship with other people. This absence of relatedness then underlies the associated difficulties with socialization, communication, and range of interests. It is important to remember that individuals with ASD fail to develop secure attachments because of their neurological differences, not because of the characteristics or activities of their caregivers. Relationship-based approaches strive to promote the formation of secure attachments and relationships. Advocates for relationship-based approaches propose that once relatedness is established, skills develop and ASD symptomology vanishes.

Toward this end, relationship-based approaches emphasize the development of attachment, emotional regulation, and relatedness without regard for skill attainment or physiologic change (Ricks & Wing, 1976; Sigman & Ungerer, 1984). The relationship-based approaches are characterized by:

- Unconditional acceptance
- Almost constant contact
- Following the lead of the child

In order to create a foundation for attachment, the child's behavior is unconditionally accepted. Within a relationship-based approach, the child is never told that she may be doing something unacceptable; to negate the child's behavior is to negate the child. Relationship development is fostered if adults stay in close proximity to the child and attempt to engage him in activities that he prefers. The four most frequently discussed relationship-based programs are: Holding Therapy, Gentle Teaching, Options, and the Developmental Individual Relationship Based approach (Floortime). They are popularly promoted on the Internet and via anecdotal reports, but none has a sufficient empirical basis at this time to substantiate effectiveness. Research is beginning to appear in the professional literature that may provide support for effectiveness (Mahoney & Perales, 2005), but researchers will be challenged to clearly articulate the components of the interventions and link them specifically to changes in students' behaviors.

Skills-Based Approaches

The **skills-based** perspective suggests that individuals with ASD have deficits that can be minimized through explicit instruction. According to this approach, students must acquire the necessary skills for interacting, communicating, and participating before relationships will form. Skill-based interventions emphasize the attainment of skills and, as such, are characterized by the necessity to:

- Assess skill deficits
- Systematically teach skills
- Collect data

Given schools' accountability for teaching skills, skills-based approaches are those most often used by educators. Skills-based approaches that demonstrate effectiveness are those that employ the principles of applied behavior analysis (ABA) (Chapter 6), using a behavioral model to examine environmental events that determine behavior and learning. Not all applied behavior analytic interventions have been articulated into programs with recognizable names. However, Functional Communication Training (FCT), Discrete Trial Training (DTT), Natural Language Paradigm (NLP), Incidental Teaching, Picture Exchange Communication System (PECS), Rapid Toilet Training (RTT), and Pivotal Response Training (PRT) are all based on the principles of applied behavior analysis. The skills-based approaches have varying amounts of research to support their effectiveness for students with ASD, and all of the ones mentioned would be considered at least promising practices (Simpson et al., 2005), with interventions using the principles of ABA (as described in Chapter 6), DTT, and PRT considered scientifically based practices for promoting positive outcomes for students with ASD (Simpson et. al., 2005).

Physiologically Based Approaches

The **physiologically based approach** promotes the correction of sensory and neurological functioning for improved behavior and relatedness. Some advocates suggest the use of physiologically based approaches to treat the symptoms of ASD in hopes of moderating how the neurological system receives and processes information. According to this perspective, by correcting intrinsic biologic and neurological deficits, ASD symptomology will abate and the individual will develop relationships and learn skills. Physiologically based approaches are characterized by an emphasis on:

- Assessment by a specialist
- Development of a treatment plan

Specialists conducting assessments include medical doctors, dieticians, occupational therapists, and self-professed experts. Parents and educators are told to carefully follow the treatment plan developed by the specialist. Treatment plans may vary dramatically between individuals, even those receiving the same type of treatment. The vast majority of treatments proliferated in the media and on the Internet have a physiological base and promise amazing results.

A sample of physiologically based approaches include psychopharmacology, dietary supplements, dietary restrictions, Sensory Integration (SI), auditory therapies (AIT à la Tomatis; AIT à la Edelson, Samonas), vision therapies (orthoptics, Irlen lenses), cranial-sacral therapy, music therapy, and hippotherapy. Even exorcism and Epsom salt baths can be found on the Internet as treatments for individuals with ASD. With the exception of the use of medications to alter neurochemistry and promote behavioral changes (which has empirical validation but its own controversy), none of the physiologically based approaches are substantiated empirically. Effectiveness either is not shown or is based entirely on testimonials that cannot validate changes in behavior nor link reported changes to the treatment provided. Caution is warranted if considering the use of physiologically based approaches.

Combination Approaches

Some programs combine aspects of relationship-based, skills-based, and physiologically based approaches to create programs that promote growth and development from multiple angles. Programs provided by public schools, although primarily skill oriented, incorporate aspects from each of the other approaches to address the comprehensive needs of students. Table 3.1 provides a summary of the three approaches and a nonexhaustive synopsis of how schools incorporate aspects of each.

GUIDELINES FOR USE IN DEVELOPING EFFECTIVE PROGRAMS

The most effective programs for students with ASD are those that are structured, educational, and individually tailored (Hung, Rotman, Cosentino, & MacMillan, 1983). To be structured, the program must include clearly articulated, theoretically sound components for supporting the development of skills that are maintained across time and generalized across contexts. Components for providing environmental support are described in Chapter 4. Various chapters in this text describe systematic instruction across domains. As will be profiled in this text, educational programs for students with ASD specify priority objectives, employ effective teaching strategies, and collect data to link outcomes to strategies and to inform instructional decision making. **Individually tailored programs** are based on the student's strengths and help identify areas of need.

Individually tailored programs are not necessarily individually delivered. Indeed, as described in Chapter 11, a variety of instructional groupings prove beneficial for supporting different facets of learning (Kamps, Walker, Locke, Delquadri, & Hall, 1990). The structured, educational, and individually tailored program should result in personal independence and social responsibility (Kavale & Forness, 1999).

No doubt, cures and miraculous treatments will continue to be discovered and advertised. For this reason, individual advocates and IEP teams need a framework to analyze whether or not a particular treatment should be incorporated into a student's program. A collaborating group of professionals can establish any set of guidelines that seems reasonable but should, at a

TABLE 3.1
Differing Approaches Applied in Schools

Relationship Priorities

Common Features	Application in Schools
• Focus is on the development of attachment and relationships rather than on teaching skills. • Child is unconditionally accepted in warm and nurturing environments. • Activities are initiated or discontinued as the child directs. • Interactions do not attempt to "change" the child or his/her behavior.	• School environments are designed to convey a student-centered focus that highlights student products and accomplishments. • School personnel develop relationships of rapport with students and create a sense of community. • School personnel encourage students to participate in learning and use strategies suggested by research to increase active involvement.

Skill Priorities

Common Features	Application in Schools
• Assessments are conducted to determine skill needs. • Skills are taught using applied behavior analytic strategies such as prompting, chaining, reinforcement, and fading. • Data are collected on the acquisition of the skills and subsequent changes in functioning.	• School personnel conduct formal and informal assessments to determine student achievement and instructional needs. • School personnel use a variety of systematic instructional strategies to present skills. • Massed practice may include the use of worksheets and text assignments. • Skills practice is distributed to promote retention and generalization. • Schools use predictable routines and symbols to guide students through the school day. • Reading is taught as an essential skill, using a variety of methods. • Computers are used to teach skills and reinforce learning, and as tools to prepare products.

Physiologic Priorities

Common Features	Application in Schools
• Emphasis is on remediation of factors internal to the child that result in behaviors associated with the spectrum. • A specialist assesses the child to determine the best plan of treatment. • Parents and school personnel follow the guidelines provided by the specialist.	• Environmental factors, such as sounds, smells, and other distractors that may hinder learning, are identified and modified. • School personnel allow students opportunities to take breaks from academic work and move around. • School programs typically include directed movement activities, such as physical education. • Dieticians and/or nutritionists plan healthy school meals.

1. What are the anticipated outcomes of the treatment?
   ☑ Do these match the child's goals?
   ☑ Are they meaningful?
   ☑ Does the treatment consider the unique needs of individuals with an ASD?
   ☑ How similar is the child to others who have benefited from the approach?
   ☒ Be cautious of treatments described as having the same outcome for all individuals who use it.
2. How will the treatment be evaluated?
   ☑ How will progress be demonstrated?
   ☑ Who will do the evaluating?
   ☑ How often will evaluation occur?
   ☑ What criteria will be used to determine if the treatment should be continued?
3. What are the potential risks?
   ☑ Immediate risks for student?
   ☑ Risks for staff/parents?
   ☑ Effect on quality of life?
   ☑ Implications if the treatment fails?
4. What proof is available?
   ☑ Is the treatment theoretically sound, well defined, objective, and replicable?
   ☑ Are results published in peer-reviewed journals?
   ☑ Are the studies of high quality?
   ☑ Is there information on effectiveness from a variety of sources?
   ☑ Is there empirical validation or just testimonials?
5. What would we be excluding by choosing this approach?
   ☑ Less restrictive alternatives?
   ☑ Better researched alternatives?

FIGURE 3.1
Guidelines to Develop Effective Programs

minimum, consider the outcomes, evaluation, and empirical basis of a given treatment. Figure 3.1 presents a suggested set of questions collected from research to guide discussion (Campbell et al., 1996; Freeman, 1997; Gresham, Beebe-Frankenberger, & MacMillan, 1999; Hart, 1995; Heflin & Simpson, 1998b; Klin & Cohen, 1997; Lehr & Lehr, 1997; NRC, 2001; Nickel, 1996; Rogers, 1999).

As mentioned in this chapter, a number of factors should be considered when discussing the merit of an intervention or treatment. In addition to being keenly aware of the general variables that affect the potential value of a treatment, the needs of the individual student must be compared against the purported benefit of using the program. Decisions must be made on the merit of criteria that will be used to gauge the effectiveness of the program for the individual student, with specific consideration given to protecting against the influence of the placebo effect.

With the exception of some of the interventions employing the principles of applied behavior analysis, much of what has been promoted as effective for students with ASD comes from a small sample of data supported by anecdotal reports that are selected to confirm existing beliefs (Huebner & Emery, 1998), rather than actual scientific evidence. More research using scientific methods needs to be conducted to identify interventions or aspects of interventions that are responsible for positive effects (Rogers, 1996).

COLLABORATIVE DEVELOPMENT OF PROGRAMS

Students with ASD represent a heterogeneous population that is remarkable in its diversity of abilities and needs. An effective program requires input from a team of people representing a variety of disciplines. The characteristics of the individual student will dictate who should be involved in the decision-making process. When the team works well together, the resulting program promotes the student's skill acquisition, increased independence, and enhanced quality of life. When the team does not work well together, lawyers and judges make the critical decisions at considerable expense. The vignette that opened this chapter presents an extreme example of the implications of discord among an IEP team.

The challenge facing individuals who need to work together is that collaboration is a skill to be learned like all others. It would be a mistake to believe that collaboration will occur naturally without effort. The skills necessary for effective collaboration must be recognized and practiced. According to Bondy and Brownell (1997), essential skills for collaboration include:

- Active listening
- Soliciting everyone's ideas
- Understanding and respecting others' perspectives
- Communicating clearly
- Emphasizing the common goal

Active Listening

Effective communication has been identified as the most important skill in collaboration (Pugach & Johnson, 1995). Communication comprises both the transmission and receipt of information. The goal of receiving messages is to make the other person feel heard. When people feel that they have been heard, they will be more inclined to listen (Dettmer, Dyck, & Thurston, 1999). **Active listening** involves both nonverbal and verbal aspects of communication. Nonverbal aspects include posture, expressions, gestures, and gaze. Nonverbal messages can influence the speaker's perceptions of being heard. If the listener is looking at a watch, yawning, gazing off, or scowling, the speaker may become defensive or withdraw. Nonverbal behaviors that encourage a speaker to continue to share information include eye contact, nods, and facial expressions that register sympathy, surprise, puzzlement, and appreciation. A common acronym for nonverbal behavior that will make a speaker feel heard is **SOLER** (Egan, 1986). SOLER indicates the listener is *S*quarely facing the speaker, has an *O*pen posture (arms and legs uncrossed), is *L*eaning toward the speaker slightly, is making appropriate *E*ye contact (as dictated by culture and socialization), and is *R*elaxed.

Listening with the intent to truly understand the other person's point of view is critical for effective collaboration. Specific verbal skills are useful in understanding the message being sent. These include:

- *Clarification:* Ask the speaker to provide **clarification of intent** rather than make assumptions. Requests for clarification often come in the form of questions (e.g., "I'm not sure I understood what you said. Can you say that again?" "Did you say___?"). Avoid asking "Why?" which tends to put speakers in a defensive position because they feel they have to justify their perspective.
- *Paraphrasing:* In **paraphrasing**, the listener restates the main ideas of what has been said without making any interpretations. Paraphrasing is not parroting what was said but a brief restatement of the content of the message.
- *Reflecting feelings:* Unlike paraphrasing, which emphasizes the content of the message, the listening skill of **reflecting feelings** provides a reflection of the emotion contained in the message.
- *Responding with empathy:* The skill of **responding with empathy** combines both paraphrasing and reflecting feelings. The listener determines the most important thing being said and adds how it appears the speaker is feeling. A framework for responding with empathy is to say, "You feel _____ because _____."

Individuals must listen carefully to ask clarifying questions, paraphrase, reflect feelings, and respond with empathy. Avoid preplanning a response that inhibits active listening.

Soliciting Everyone's Ideas

A collaborative discussion should be a conversation, not a diatribe by one or a few individuals. Using active listening, it is important to make sure that each participant's concerns and ideas are heard and understood (Dettmer et al., 1999). A helpful practice for encouraging reticent team members to share ideas is to recognize contributions (Turnbull & Turnbull, 2001) through the process of active listening. Paraphrasing, reflecting feelings, and responding with empathy validate comments and encourage further participation.

Understanding and Respecting Others' Perspectives

As discussed earlier in the chapter, each individual brings a unique perspective to any discussion. When the discussion centers on developing a program for a child with an ASD, parents tend to bring a desperate perspective to the table. These parents have found themselves responsible for a child who may present great daily challenges and who may have the potential to need life-long care. These parents have probably been told that their child will be "cured" or that a "recovery" is possible if certain interventions are used. In their perspective, the school system's unwillingness to provide the necessary intervention is the only barrier to their child's cure. On the other hand, the school system is under legislative mandate to use scientifically based research (NCLB, 2001) and is held accountable for demonstrating that the students are acquiring skills.

In addition, each member of the team deals with issues unrelated to the IEP process that the others may not know about (Dettmer et al., 1999), but which may influence their ability to participate fully. Each member has beliefs and assumptions in addition to perspectives that may interfere with effective collaboration (Bondy & Brownell, 1997). Each also brings a personal communication style that may or may not be appreciated by others. Interpersonal skills, beliefs, and personal attributes have the greatest impact on the outcomes of collaboration (West & Cannon, 1988). For successful collaboration, effort must be made to understand and respect different perspectives, while withholding judgment and suspending bias.

Communicating Clearly

Even when not speaking, it is impossible not to communicate. Nonverbal behaviors send many messages. Crossing the arms or looking away communicates an unwillingness to consider another person's ideas. Using SOLER communicates interest in considering other views. Clear communication is characterized by the use of short responses and the avoidance of jargon and acronyms. A useful strategy for promoting clear communication is to write down what is being said (Kroth, 1985). In team meetings, use an overhead projector or whiteboard so that everyone can see the discussion thread.

There are additional strategies for promoting clear communication. Behaviors should be described objectively and specifically, not in general or judgmental terms. Avoid the use of the word "but" because it always negates what comes before it (e.g., "Stanley is a good student, but he does not complete his work."). Instead, connect phrases with "and" (e.g., "Stanley is a good student and he does not complete his work."). A very different, less condemning message is communicated by eliminating the word "but."

Frequent communication promotes the sharing of perspectives and reduces the need for lengthy conferences. Most teachers use strategies to promote on-going communication, such as "communication logs" sent between school and home on a daily basis or e-mails sent several times a week.

Emphasizing the Common Goal

All team members have a shared interest: the success of a particular student. Fortunately, the key to successful collaboration is the sharing of a common goal (Bondy & Brownell, 1997). If discussions become contentious or bog down, the team needs to stop and reestablish its focus on the goal: What is in the best interests of the student? Within that focus, look for areas of agreement (DeBoer, 1995). School personnel should avoid saying "no" to any of the parents' requests. Rather than negating the parents' perspectives or ideas, use the discussion guidelines (Figure 3.1) to tailor the discussion

- Keep in mind that the family usually has concerns and issues that have nothing to do with you personally and that you may not know about.
- Be sensitive to the language levels, vocabularies, and background of the family and adjust your language, but be yourself.
- Get enough information, but not more than you need. You don't want to appear "nosy."
- Focus discussions on factors you can control.
- Find out what has been tried before—ask advice.
- Listen so that you are completely clear about the family's concerns.
- Honor confidentiality.
- Remain open to new approaches and suggestions. Each family is different.
- Set concrete, measurable goals. Communication is clearer and measures of success are built in and promote collaboration.
- Wait until the family asks for help or until a good relationship is established before making suggestions.
- Help families solve their own problems and allow them to become, or develop the skills to become, their child's own case manager.

FIGURE 3.2
Suggestions for Successful Collaboration
Source: From P. Dettmer, N. Dyck, & L. P. Thurston, *Consultation, Collaboration, and Teamwork for Students with Special Needs,* 3e. Published by Allyn and Bacon, Boston, MA. Copyright © 1999 by Pearson Education. Reprinted by permission of the publisher.

toward decisions that are acceptable to everyone (even if on a trial basis) and beneficial to the child. Collaboration will cease if members begin to take things personally or start mixing in their own issues. When a discussion becomes a power struggle between team members, the student is no longer the focus and there is little hope of a productive outcome. When tempers flare or time constraints impinge, it is better to disengage and postpone the meeting. Figure 3.2 provides suggestions that can promote successful collaborative efforts.

Developing effective programs requires collaboration. This is especially true for programs developed for students with ASD. To promote independent functioning in multiple environments for a child with ASD, a variety of individuals from diverse disciplines need to be involved in planning a program that is structured, educational, and individually tailored to meet the student's needs. Unfortunately, collaboration is not something that just happens. **Effective collaboration** occurs when individuals who are skillful communicators work together to understand and respect each other's perspectives and maintain a focus on the needs of the student.

❖ LEARNING WITH MS. HARRIS: Her First IEP Meeting

Ms. Harris wakes up and immediately adds a trip to the education store near the mall to her list of "Things to Do." After attending yesterday's conference on strategies for teaching students with ASD, she is determined to structure the school day using those visual schedules the presenter showed and to be prepared to encourage social interactions between her students and other students throughout the school. As she reviews her notes, her mind keeps wandering to the adorable and rambunctious seven-year-old boy, Eric, she met last week at McDonald's. Ms. Harris gathers her things and decides that she is even more eager to start her new job at Phillips Elementary. She decides to stop by to see if the principal, Ms. Stokes, has her class roster and room assignment yet.

As she waits for Ms. Stokes, Ms. Harris hears the front-office secretaries talking about her classroom and how none of the other teachers should be envious of her eight students, two paraprofessionals, and two parent volunteers because anyone who teaches that *class deserves all the help she can get. As Ms. Harris gets up to tell them not to worry and that she'll be fine, Ms. Stokes walks in and invites her into the office. Ms. Stokes begins the conversation with, "Well, I have good news and bad news. Which do you want first?"*

Ms. Harris chooses the good news. "Good," says Ms. Stokes, "Your long-awaited class roster is available and you only have eight students."

Ms. Harris can't stop smiling, "This is great. When will I be able to get the students' folders and begin reviewing them?" As Ms. Stokes pulls out a folder, she lets Ms. Harris know that she will need to make an appointment with her special education supervisor to see the folders, except for this one.

"You'll get to review one of them right away, and here it is. I know that this may be a bit premature, but I'm confident you'll handle this situation in a professional and knowledgeable manner. Unfortunately, there are always some families that either postpone IEP meetings repeatedly, or their meetings are so high maintenance that they often have to be adjourned for another day, which brings us to the Averys. They are Steven's parents, who like to come to IEP meetings with advocates and were not able to co-ordinate everyone's schedules before the school year ended." Ms. Harris takes a minute and then says, "No problem! I can schedule the meeting. Do you prefer a specific process? I'll need to send the notifications out through the post office, and I probably will need to have the letters sent 'Return Receipt Requested' since it's summer."

Ms. Stokes gives Ms. Harris a great big smile and is sure that she made the right decision in hiring her. She tells Ms. Harris that the social worker has already set the date and sent out the notifications. Standing up to leave, Ms. Harris takes the folder and her copy of the notification and says, "This will just give me the opportunity to meet one of my families sooner than later."

When she gets home, she plops down on the couch, takes a deep sigh, and starts going through the paperwork. IEPs need to involve multiple disciplines, an administrator, and at least one of the student's parents. She notices on the notification form that both parents will be there. As she reviews the meeting notification, she is amazed by who was invited and wonders how much time she will have with Steven if all of these individuals pull him out to work with him. The list included a speech-language pathologist (SLP), occupational therapist (OT), art teacher, behavior specialist, parent advocate, and two names with "attorney" written after them. As Ms. Harris opens Steven's folder, she thinks, "This isn't his file, it's his autobiography."

Ms. Harris decides that it would help if she took out blank IEP forms and jotted down some notes from Steven's file while she reviews the latest psychological testing, grades from the general education classes, previous IEP, goals and objectives, and notes from the preceding teacher. "Let's see," she thinks. "First, I'll need to make sure everyone knows each other, signs in, and that a copy and an explanation of the parental rights be given to Mr. and Ms. Avery. Then I'll state the purpose of the meeting—which is to review Steven's IEP from the school year that just ended and develop a new one for the upcoming year." Ms. Harris spends the rest of that evening reviewing his file.

The day of the IEP arrives and Ms. Harris anxiously reshuffles her paperwork over and over again as she waits for the committee members to arrive. After the proper introductions and formality of signing in and providing the parental rights, she gains everyone's attention. "OK, we'll begin by reviewing Steven's present level of performance, and I'll look toward each of you to offer as much as input as possible."

Mr. Avery interrupts. "Ms. Harris, I realize you're in an awkward position, but do you really think you can develop an appropriate IEP for Steven, considering you don't know him?"

Ms. Harris is surprised that before they've even really gotten to the guts of IEPs, Mr. Avery is questioning her. She replies, "I can definitely understand your concern, Mr. Avery, but let me make you and everyone else more comfortable by reassuring you that I know I'm new and not as knowledgeable about Steven. I have carefully reviewed his file and will have to depend on all of you to help me understand Steven. This is a group effort and we all have his best interests at heart. Besides, his previous teacher, Mr. Grant, left a draft of some objectives that he felt would be appropriate for Steven to work on next year." Ms. Avery intercedes and suggests that they move along and see what the other teachers and Mr. Grant have recommended, since he always seemed to zero in on Steven's issues. Ms. Harris agrees. "Please remember that if you have any questions, just ask them. That's the only way I know what you have in mind for Steven."

Ms. Harris begins by summarizing that Steven just turned 8 years old, has a diagnosis of moderate autism, and receives most of his services in the self-contained classroom, but that he does join his first-grade general education class for art, music, PE, calendar, lunch, recess, computer, library time, and all other activities that are more social and seasonal (such as class parties and field trips). She adds that he receives related-services support from the SLP four times weekly, the OT once weekly for direct therapy and then once monthly to consult with Steven's teachers, and the behavior specialist, who is contracted to work with Steven and his family at least twice weekly and across all settings (including in the home and the community).

Ms. Avery interjects and asks if she can state something for the record. Ms. Harris thinks to herself, "What can I possibly say?" but answers, "Of course." Ms. Avery shares with the committee that although Steven is supposed to be accompanying his general education class on outside activities, they have deliberately left him out of things like the Mother's Day Tea and Earth Day.

Ms. Harris thinks carefully about how she'll respond to this, because she doesn't want to appear to be on the school's side nor does she want to sound partial to the parents. Realizing that the homeroom teacher is not there, she decides to respond. "Ms. Avery, since that teacher wasn't able to make the meeting and he probably won't be in her class again, why don't I record that you have expressed your concern that Steven may be missing some opportunities to participate in outside activities and you would like to see that improved. Is that correct?"

All of a sudden, one of the attorneys, who had been sitting quietly next to Mr. Avery and taking notes, spoke up. "That would be fine, but let me clarify one thing. Am I correct in assuming that you have already decided upon a placement for Steven?"

Immediately Ms. Harris realized her error and replied, "Of course not. I was just going on the assumption that since Ms. Avery already had some concerns, we would consider moving him to another homeroom." The attorney nodded his head in apparent satisfaction, and Ms. Harris was able to complete the current level of performance. She summarized that Steven's strengths include his ability to sort into categories (color, animals, and shapes), name those items (but only if they are grouped accordingly), hum tunes of familiar songs matching the original pitch, and complete familiar songs, poems, and routines by interjecting the word during a break. He can also follow his visual schedule, but he needs prompting for the first task; however, after that, he can complete a task, bring the icon back and put it in his "All Done" basket, pull the next icon in sequence, get the materials, and begin to work.

Ms. Harris stops at this point. "I'd like to make a note of his need to be prompted for the first task because this is something we may want to address next year. Does anyone have any input on this or any other information to share?" The art teacher comments, "I just can't believe how orderly Steven is. I wish more of my students would concern themselves about putting things away in their correct places. But . . ." Mr. Avery mumbles, "Here we go," and the art teacher shifts her posture. Ms. Harris notices this and says, "Could you tell me what he does that is inappropriate for your classroom?" The art teacher shifts her attention back toward Ms. Harris and continues to explain that often Steven will just stop what he's doing and start wiggling whatever he's using in front of his eyes (e.g., colored pencils, markers, or crayons). Ms. Harris questions if anyone else observes this behavior and if it is interfering with his ability to learn or is disruptive to the other students. Ms. Avery immediately jumps in and shares that, regardless of where they are, he will wiggle anything in front of his eyes as long as it has writing going across it. Ms. Harris wonders if this has anything to do with his sensory system and asks the OT for some input. The OT adds to the discussion and suggests that not only is it common for students with ASD to self-stim, but since Steven stims with things that are imprinted with writing, he may require even more visual (and/or possibly vestibular) input into his sensory system.

Ms. Harris gets them back on track and continues discussing his weaknesses, which include limited use of words, inability to match lowercase letters to capital letters, lack of sustained attention to task, inconsistent imitation of simple geometric figures, not requesting help or a favorite object/activity, frequent tantrums to express displeasure, and inability to transition from one broad activity period to another (such as when he finishes his work boxes and it's time for centers). "Before we move on to reviewing Steven's progress on his current IEP objectives," Ms. Harris asks, "does anyone have any updated information that they would like to share, such as medications and food preferences?" Both parents agree that nothing new has occurred.

Ms. Harris feels her stomach growling and glances down at her watch, only to see that $1\frac{1}{2}$ hours have passed and there's a lot more to cover; she hopes that she can hold out! She explains that there are five additional factors that need to be reviewed. She begins, "The first additional factor on the IEP form relates to Extended School Year Services (ESY), and I would like to address that after we review his progress on the current objectives. I believe that only then will we know whether he needs ESY or not. How does everyone feel about that?"

Mr. Avery responds, "I hope this isn't the county's way of avoiding the subject, because this is the area that we argue about every year, and I don't understand why. It's a fact that children with ASD are served better if they receive continuous intervention and go to school year round. This way they don't forget and can work on generalizing what they've learned during the year."

Ms. Harris' facial expression must have been one of surprise or dismay, because the behavior specialist intercedes on her behalf. "I'm sure that's not Ms. Harris' intent at all. But I do agree with her reasoning. She'll just make a note of it so that none of us forgets to return to that subject." Ms. Harris gives the consultant an appreciative smile and moves on to transition plans, which she explains is something they will address when Steven turns 14.

Behavioral interventions are the next factor, and as a group they discuss whether Steven exhibited behavior that impeded his learning or the learning of others. The behavior consultant feels that although Steven did not display overly aggressive tendencies, he still felt it imperative that the documentation show that Steven does not have the capacity to understand and follow all the school rules. Therefore, certain accommodations will need to be put into place, as well as developing measurable objectives so that his teachers are aware that Steven needs to be taught new behavior and the behavioral changes need to be documented systematically.

Ms. Harris was surprised that everyone agreed. "Now we're rolling," she thinks. She asks if anyone had considered the use of assistive technology. At this time, everyone was also in agreement that it was not necessary.

Ms. Harris reminds the committee, "The IEP is only a work in progress, and a meeting can be arranged any time someone has a concern." They are winding down the list of additional factors, and Ms. Harris concludes that although Steven demonstrates only limited verbal ability, he does not have limited English proficiency, nor is he blind, visually impaired, deaf, or hard of hearing. Ms. Avery adds, "But only when he wants to be." Of course, they all agree that Steven's communication is a definite factor affecting his overall success.

The objectives Steven had been working on for the last year covered the major domains of cognitive/academic, social, communication, self-help/adaptive, recreation/leisure, and motor. Each of the primary service providers reviews their goal page and states whether Steven had achieved the criterion for mastery for each objective listed. As Ms. Harris listens to each of them report, it becomes obvious to her that the services could only be described as departmentalized.

Ms. Harris repeatedly asks Mr. and Ms. Avery if they have any questions, and they insist, "No, I don't think so." She also watches the attorney carefully because he is busy writing down everything each person says underneath the objective(s).

At the end of the review, Ms. Harris states, "It seems that Steven had a successful year, but that he still struggles in expressing his frustration—especially when he has to transition. Yet, when he's involved in the activity, he will continue and do multitasks. I'm really excited about getting to work with you all next year, but I guess I should tell you now that I really want us all to work on all of his goals throughout his day—not just at specified times of the day and with specific people."

Ms. Avery starts smiling. "That is exactly what I've wanted for the longest time. Thank you." The attorney, though, looks a little skeptical. "Do you think that these percentages are a little inflated in order to show Steven making progress? Can one of you show me data of Steven working toward one objective, having a short or long vacation, and then returning to work on the same objective? I'm interested in if he regressed, and if he did, how long it took him to recoup those skills?"

The primary service providers look at one another and shuffle through papers; the behavior consultant, however, pulls a hand-drawn line graph that shows each date data were collected and the results. It also indicates where breaks occurred, and he connects the data points to display a trend in Steven's behavior. As he shows this to the parents, attorney, and advocate, Ms. Harris makes a mental note to pull out her blank data sheets from her behavior class, refresh her memory with ABA strategies and data collection methods, and prepare a template for each of Steven's new objectives before school begins.

Ms. Harris begins to address ESY. "Well, I guess this is good news that Steven's done well so it doesn't look—" Mr. Avery interrupts immediately.

"Let's not go through this again. It may not look like Steven needs ESY on paper, but we all know that the research supports providing continuous intervention for students with autism, and I will accept nothing less than that!"

Ms. Harris looks toward the veterans. The behavior consultant says that he agrees with the parents and would suggest that those objectives most meaningful for independence and leisure activities (since it's summer) be addressed. The SLP and OT nod their heads in agreement. The team decides that OT services would remain the same and add that transportation would be provided to and from school.

It seemed that once the parents realized that she wasn't trying to evade providing any services that Steven really needed, they relaxed. They had just passed the $3\frac{1}{2}$-hour mark, and the attorney gets up and excuses himself. Ms. Harris takes this opportunity to suggest that they all take a short break.

After 15 minutes, they reconvene and begin reviewing the draft objectives each of the team members had brought for the upcoming year (including Steven's parents). They decide to cover skills in each of the domains, but address them using a collaborative, team approach. Ms. Harris explains, "Of course there will always be some objectives that require direct, individualized or small-group instruction for the acquisition of skills" and indicated such on the goal sheets.

Mr. Avery says that he has two final issues he wants to discuss: more time with the SLP and a desire for Steven's cognitive/academic objectives to be addressed by someone trained in DTT for 20 hours weekly of one to one DTT. The SLP expresses her opinion that more time wasn't what Steven needed; rather, he needs to learn to use language and find the means to augment his present mode of communication so that his behavior would also improve. As Mr. Avery begins to debate the issue, Ms. Harris interrupts, "Excuse me for just a minute. Although I do agree with you, Mr. Avery, that Steven's communication program should include more time to focus on communicating with a greater variety of people and in different settings, I think that it might be more beneficial if the SLP schedules an additional time with Steven, but with at least two other peers and use a peer-mediated strategy to increase communication. What do you think?" Mr. Avery looks back and forth between his wife and Ms. Harris and finally agrees! Ms. Harris thought, "Wow, what a coup! As long as I base my decisions on what's best for Steven, the rationale speaks for itself and they agree. Why don't all teachers just follow that principle? It sure would make their life easier!" As a cohesive team, they choose to include transitioning between broad activities using a timer to signal that the time is approaching, and increasing Steven's play repertoire of objects and engaging in short (e.g., 2 minutes), reciprocal play routines prompted by a typical peer to imitate his or her play.

Ms. Harris glances at the next page of the IEP and mentally prepares herself for what she's heard is the most difficult part of the process, determining placement. She brings to mind what she learned about collaborating and supporting families that have children with disabilities. She is going to try to focus the discussion on only those factors that she can control; she's going to rely on her active listening skills so that there's no ambiguity in what their perspective is or anyone else's; and she's going to remain open to suggestions and consider options that may lie "outside of the box," as long as it is in the best interest of Steven.

Ms. Harris reminds the committee that it's time to consider Steven's placement, and they need to consider the full continuum of services before deciding which option will provide him with the least restricted access to his peers in the general education classroom and the general education curriculum. "I realize that not all these options are appropriate for Steven, but I believe we need to at least mention them and assure ourselves that we haven't overlooked anything," Ms. Harris explains. "Let's begin with considerating those options that are most restrictive, the residential facilities or a nearby but separate psychoeducational facility." Judging by their verbal and nonverbal signals, Ms. Harris quickly notes that those options are not appropriate because they do not provide Steven with the access to the general population that would provide the best models. She then introduces self-contained or resource settings, with her recommendation that Steven receive most of his instruction in the self-contained classroom. It's here that Ms. Harris can address Steven's individual needs with a curriculum that is different from the general education classroom using specialized instructional techniques. However, she quickly notes that she believes that Steven would continue to benefit from spending time in the general education class. Ms. Avery, the OT, behavior consultant, art teacher, and SLP also agree and they begin adding the hours up for each placement so that it can be identified on the form. "Wait a minute," Mr. Avery demands, "I think Steven can handle more than 5 hours weekly in the general education classroom. I want to see it increased."

Ms. Harris gets up with the goal pages and walks over to the whiteboard. "Let me explain how placement is determined. Steven's hours, in any setting, need to be governed by the objectives identified. I'm going to go through each one and let's decide where Steven can receive the best instruction." As Ms. Harris charts the objectives between general and special education, it becomes obvious that the majority of goals need to be addressed in the self-contained classroom.

Just when Ms. Harris thinks that they can move on and conclude this meeting, she hears a faint voice. "I have just one question," says the art teacher. The IEP committee listens as the art teacher expresses concern about who will be responsible for collecting data and who will decide whether Steven has met the criterion or not. Ms. Harris reassures her that the criterion was established when they wrote the goals in behaviorally objective and measurable terms, and that she will initially collect data but has intentions of training all her students' teachers how to collect data efficiently and innocuously. After completing the hours, place of service, and person providing the service, Ms. Harris guides the group through the modification/ accommodation summary that will be distributed to every teacher and staff (e.g., after-school personnel) who are responsible for Steven.

Throughout the meeting, Ms. Harris kept an ongoing list of ideas that were mentioned, and so she reviews them with the committee and asks if anyone knew of any others that would be beneficial or if there were any that they might be opposed to providing. "Boy, was I lucky that Ms. Stokes sent me to that conference!" she thinks. "They went over all the possible modifications that help students with ASD and told us to remember that just because it's down on the summary sheet doesn't necessarily mean that it applies to every single subject nor does it have to be present every day. But they do need to be available when necessary." Ms. Harris concludes by suggesting that they discuss testing, grading, and miscellaneous modifications at a later point when she's had the opportunity to find out specific information about what's administered by this county. All the committee members emphatically agree.

"I have one last thing. Mr. and Ms. Avery, I need your signature on this last page indicating that you were in attendance and had an opportunity to participate in the development of Steven's IEP." While signing, Mr. Avery looks up and says, "Ms. Harris, for someone brand-new you chaired this IEP meeting like a seasoned professional, but didn't seem removed from our or the teachers' concerns. Never once did I get the impression that you thought of us as unreasonable. Instead, we both got the feeling that you truly respected our perspectives and understood we only want what's best for Steven. Thank you, and we look forward to a great year!"

As Ms. Harris gathers the paperwork and stacks it neatly on top of the envelope, she sits in the peaceful conference room, reflects over the day, and smiles quietly as she thinks, "It may take a lot of time and energy, but I believe I'm really going to enjoy being a teacher!"

CONCLUSION

Just as each student with an ASD is a unique individual, so are the advocates who come together to develop a program that will be effective in promoting the student's development and functioning. Confounding the discussions about effective programs are the perspectives of the advocates and the contradictory information that is available for making informed decisions. School personal are required to use interventions that have an empirical basis to be at least a promising practice (Simpson et al., 2005). This emphasis will become more pronounced as the NCLB mandates for "scientifically based research" are fully implemented. Lack of evidence may not indicate that an intervention is ineffective, only that the effectiveness has not been demonstrated (Rogers, 1998). Unsubstantiated interventions need to be scrutinized within an agreed upon framework such as that suggested in Figure 3.1. The process of conducting and disseminating research to inform practice is ongoing and professionals need to stay cognizant of advances.

The team of advocates must work together to choose from among reasonable and appropriate alternatives for promoting desirable student outcomes. The bottom line is the student and the documented progress that is being made. Although collaborating to develop an effective program is not always easy, it is always worthwhile. As research unravels the mysteries of the spectrum disorder and individuals with ASD share their unique talents and gifts, a mutual respect is emerging, which contributes to the quality of life for all.

DISCUSSION QUESTIONS AND ACTIVITIES

1. Autism cures proliferate wildly on the Internet. Go online and evaluate some of the options to see which you think are the most unusual. Putting in the search terms "cure autism" will pull up many sites.

2. What would you say to someone who asks, "What is autism and what causes it?" (Do not copy any of the standard definitions; write out a narrative as if you were talking to a person.)

3. If you were the parent of a child with Autism Spectrum Disorders, what would you look for in a teacher for your child?

4. At an IEP meeting for a student with Autism Spectrum Disorders, an advocate begins demanding that the district provide a program called "Lindamood-Bell." What do you say? (Hint: Rather than criticize LMB, guide the discussion toward a general analysis of what needs to be considered when developing an effective program.)

5. After examining the three approaches that underlie many of the interventions for students with ASD, identify the one that most closely describes your beliefs. Identify which elements from across the approaches you would promote in the development of an effective program for a student with autism. (Note: You will need to have a specific student in mind because there are no generic programs for individuals with ASD.)

REFERENCES

Board of Education of the Hendrick Hudson Central School District v. Rowley. (1982). 458 U.S. 176, 102 S.Ct. 3034, 73 L. Ed. 2d 690, 5 Ed. Law Rep. 34.

Bondy, E., & Brownell, M.T. (1997). Overcoming barriers to collaboration among partners-in-teaching. *Intervention in School and Clinic, 33,* 112-115.

Boyd, R., & Corley, M. (2001). Outcome of early intensive behavioral intervention for young children with autism in a community setting. *Autism, 5,* 430-441.

Bristol, M. M., Gallagher, J. J., & Holt, K. D. (1993). Maternal depressive symptoms in autism: Response to psychoeducational intervention. *Rehabilitation Psychology, 38,* 3-9.

Bromley, J., Hare, D. J., Davison, K., & Emerson, E. (2004). Mothers supporting children with autistic spectrum disorders. *Autism: The International Journal of Research & Practice, 8,* 409-413.

Campbell, M., Schopler, E., Cueva, J., & Hallin, A. (1996). Treatment of autistic disorder. *Journal of the American Academy of Child and Adolescent Psychiatry, 35,* 134-143.

Chez, M. G., Buchanan, C. P., Bagan, B. T., Hammer, M. S., McCarthy, K. S., Ovrutskaya, I., et al. (2000). Secretin and autism: A two-part clinical investigation. *Journal of Autism and Developmental Disorders, 30,* 87-94.

Cole, K. N., Dale, P. S., & Mills, P. E. (1991). Individual differences in language delayed children's responses to direct and interactive preschool instruction. *Topics in Early Childhood Special Education, 11,* 99-124.

Courchesne, E., Akshoomoff, N. A., & Townsend, J. (1992). Recent advances in autism. In H. Naruse & E. M. Ornitz (Eds.), *Neurobiology of infantile autism* (pp. 111-128). Amsterdam: Elsevier Science.

Dawson, G., Meltzoff, A. N., Osterling, J., Rinaldi, J., & Brown, E. (1998). Children with autism fail to orient to naturally occurring social stimuli. *Journal of Autism and Developmental Disorders, 28,* 479-485.

DeBoer, A. (1995). *Working together: The art of consulting and communicating.* Longmont, CO: Sopris West.

DeLong, G. R. (1999). Autism: New data suggest a new hypothesis. *Neurology, 52,* 911-916.

Dettmer, P., Dyck, N., & Thurston, L. P. (1999). *Consultation, collaboration, and teamwork for students with special needs* (3rd ed.). Needham Heights, MA: Allyn & Bacon.

Domingue, B., Cutler, B., & McTarnaghan, J. (2000). The experience of autism in the lives of families. In A. M. Wetherby & B. M. Prizant (Eds.), *Autism spectrum disorders: A transactional developmental perspective* (pp. 369-393). Baltimore: Paul H. Brookes.

Dumas, J. E., Wolf, L. C., Fisman, S. N., & Culligan, A. (1991). Parenting stress, child behavior problems, and dysphoria in parents of children with autism, Down's syndrome, behavior disorders, and normal development. *Exceptionality, 2,* 97-110.

Dyches, T. T., Wilder, L. K., Sudweeks, R. R., Obiakor, F. E., & Algozzine, B. (2004). Multicultural issues in autism. *Journal of Autism and Developmental Disorders, 34,* 211-222.

Eaves, L. C., & Ho, H. H. (2004). The very early identification of autism: Outcome to age 4-5. *Journal of Autism and Developmental Disorders, 34,* 367-378.

Egan, G. (1986). *The skilled helper: A systematic approach to effective helping.* Monterey, CA: Brooks/Cole.

Freeman, B. J. (1997). Guidelines for evaluating intervention programs for children with autism. *Journal of Autism and Developmental Disorders, 27,* 641-651.

Freeman, B. J., Ritvo, E. R., Needleman, R., & Yokota, A. (1985). The stability of cognitive and linguistic parameters in autism: A five-year prospective study. *Journal of the American Academy of Child & Adolescent Psychiatry, 24,* 459-464.

Gabriels, R. L., Hill, D. E., Pierce, R. A., Rogers, S. J., & Wehner, B. (2001). Predictors of treatment outcome in young children with autism. *Autism, 5,* 407-429.

Ghaziuddin, M. (2005). A family history of Asperger syndrome. *Journal of Autism and Developmental Disorders, 35,* 177-182.

Greenspan, S. I., & Weider, S. (1997). *The child with special needs: Encouraging intellectual and emotional growth.* Reading, MA: Addison-Wesley.

Gresham, F. M., Beebe-Frankenberger, M. E., & MacMillan, D. L. (1999). A selective review of treatments for children with autism: Description and methodological considerations. *School Psychology Review, 28,* 559-575.

Harmon, A. (2004, December 20). How about not "curing" us, some autistics are pleading. *New York Times,* p. A1.

Harris, S. L. (1994). Treatment of family problems in autism. In E. Schopler & G. B. Mesibov (Eds.). *Behavioral issues in autism* (pp. 161-175). New York: Plenum.

Harris, S. L., & Handleman, J. S. (2000). Age and IQ at intake as predictors of placement for young children with autism: A four-to six-year follow-up. *Journal of Autism and Developmental Disorders, 30,* 137-142.

Hart, C. (1995). Teaching children with autism: What parents want. In K. A. Quill (Ed.), *Teaching children with autism: Strategies to enhance communication and socialization* (pp. 53-69). Albany, NY: Delmar.

Hastings, R. P. (2003). Brief report: Behavioral adjustment of siblings of children with autism. *Journal of Autism & Developmental Disorders, 33,* 99-104.

Heflin, L. J., & Simpson, R. L. (1998a). Interventions for children and youth with autism: Prudent choices in a world of exaggerated claims and empty promises. Part I: Intervention and treatment option review. *Focus on Autism and Other Developmental Disabilities, 13,* 194-211.

Hollander, E., King, A., Delaney, K., et al. (2003). Obsessive-compulsive behaviors in parents of multiplex autism families. *Psychiatry Research, 117,* 11-16.

Huebner, R. A., & Emery, L. J. (1998). Social psychological analysis of facilitated communication: Implications for education. *Mental Retardation, 36,* 259-268.

Hung, D. W., Rotman, Z., Cosentino, A., & MacMillan, M. (1983). Cost and effectiveness of an educational program for autistic children using a systems approach. *Education and Treatment of Children, 6,* 47–68.

Iovannone, R., Dunlap, G., Huber, H., & Kincaid, D. (2003). Effective educational practices for students with autism spectrum disorders. *Focus on Autism and Other Developmental Disabilities, 18,* 150–165.

Johnson, C. (2000, July 31). The happy family we set out to be. *Newsweek, 136,* 54.

Kamps, D., Walker, D., Locke, P., Delquadri, J., & Hall, R. V. (1990). A comparison of instructional arrangements for children with autism served in a public school setting. *Education and Treatment of Children, 13,* 197–215.

Kanner, L., Rodrigues, A., & Ashenden, B. (1972). How far can autistic children go in matters of social adaptation? *Journal of Autism and Childhood Schizophrenia, 2,* 9–33.

Kaplan, B. J., Polatajko, H. J., Wilson, B. N., & Faris, P. D. (1993). Reexamination of sensory integration treatment: A comparison of two efficacy studies. *Journal of Learning Disabilities, 26,* 342–347.

Kavale, K. A., & Forness, S. R. (1999). Effective intervention practices and special education. In Gary N. Siperstein (Ed.), *Efficacy of Special Education and Related Services* (pp. 1–9). Washington, DC: American Association on Mental Retardation.

Kazdin, A. (1993). Replication and extension of behavioral treatment of autistic disorder. *American Journal on Mental Retardation, 97,* 377–379.

Kemper, T. L. & Bauman, M. (1998). Neuropathology of infantile autism. *Journal of Neuropathology and Experimental Neurology, 57,* 645–652.

Klin, A., & Cohen, D. J. (1997). Ethical issues in research and treatment. In D. J. Cohen & F. R. Volkmar (Eds.), *Handbook of autism and pervasive developmental disorders* (2nd ed., pp. 828–841). New York: Wiley.

Koegel, R. L., Bimbela, A., & Schreibman, L. (1996). Collateral effects of parent training on family interactions. *Journal of Autism and Developmental Disorders, 26,* 347–359.

Koegel, L. K., Kogel, R. L., & Smith, A. (1997). Variables related to differences in standardized test outcomes for children with autism. *Journal of Autism and Developmental Disorders, 27,* 233–244.

Kroth, R. L. (1985). *Communication with parents of exceptional children: Improving parent-teacher relationships.* Denver, CO: Love.

Lehr, S., & Lehr, B. (1997, November). *Scientists and parents of children with autism: What do we know? How do we judge what is right?* Paper presented at the Autism National Committee and Greater Georgia ASA Conference, Decatur, GA.

Lord, C., Cook, E. H., Leventhal, B., & Amaral, D. G. (2000). Autism spectrum disorders. *Neuron, 28,* 355–363.

Lord, C., Risi, S., Lambrecht, L., Cook, E. H., Leventhal, B. L., DiLavore, P. C., et al. (2000). The autism diagnostic observation schedule-generic: A standard measure of social and communication deficits associated with the spectrum of autism. *Journal of Autism and Developmental Disorders, 30,* 205–223.

Lord, C., & Schopler, E. (1989a). The role of age at assessment, developmental level, and test in the stability of intelligence scores in young autistic children. *Journal of Autism and Developmental Disorders, 19,* 483–499.

Lord, C. & Schopler, E. (1989b). Stability of assessment results of autistic and non-autistic language-impaired children from preschool years to early school age. *Journal of Child Psychology and Psychiatry, 30,* 575–590.

Lovaas, O. I. (1987). Behavioral treatment and normal education and intellectual functioning in young autistic children. *Journal of Consulting and Clinical Psychology, 55,* 3–9.

Mahoney, G., & Perales, F. (2005). Relationship-focused early intervention with children with pervasive developmental disorders and other disabilities: A comparative study. *Developmental and Behavioral Pediatrics, 26,* 77–85.

Mayes, S. D., & Calhoun, S. L. (1999). Symptoms of autism in young children and correspondence with the DSM. *Infants and Young Children, 12,* 90–97.

Mayes, S. D., & Calhoun, S. L. (2003). Ability profiles in children with autism: Influence of age and IQ. *Autism, 6,* 65–80.

McGee, G. G., Morrier, M. J., & Daly, T. (1999). An incidental teaching approach to early intervention for toddlers with autism. *Journal of the Association for Persons with Severe Handicaps, 24,* 133–146.

Mesibov, G. (1997). Formal and informal measures on the effectiveness of the TEACCH program. *Autism, 1,* 25–35.

Molloy, C. A., Manning-Courtney, P., Swayne, S., Bean, J., Brown, J. M., Murray, D. S., et al.

(2002). Lack of benefit of intravenous synthetic human secretin in the treatment of autism. *Journal of Autism and Developmental Disorders, 32,* 545-551.

National Research Council (NRC) (2001). *Educating children with autism.* Committee on Educational Interventions for Children with Autism. Division of Behavioral and Social Sciences and Education. Washington, DC: National Academy Press.

Nickel, R. E., (1996). Controversial therapies for young children with developmental disabilities. *Infants and Young Children, 8,* 29-40.

No Child Left Behind (NCLB) Act, 20 U.S.C. § 6301 et seq. (2001).

Owley, T., McMahon, W., Cook, E. H., Laulhere, T., South, M., & Mays, L. Z. (2001). Multisite, double-blind, placebo-controlled trial of porcine secretin in autism. *Journal of the American Academy of Child and Adolescent Psychiatry, 40,* 1293-1299.

Pollack, A. (2004, January 6). Trials end parents' hopes for autism drug. *The New York Times,* A12.

Pugach, M. C., & Johnson, L. J. (1995). *Collaborative practitioners, collaborative schools.* Denver, CO: Love.

Rapin, I. (1987). Searching for the cause of autism: A neurologic perspective. In D. J. Cohn, A. M. Donnellan, & R. Paul (Eds.), *Handbook of autism and pervasive developmental disorders* (pp. 710-717). New York: Wiley.

Ricks, D. M., & Wing, L. (1976). Language, communication, and the use of symbols in normal and autistic children. In J. K. Wing (Ed.), *Early childhood autism: Clinical, social, and educational aspects.* Oxford: Pergamon.

Rogers, S. J. (1996). Brief report: Early intervention in autism. *Journal of Autism and Developmental Disorders, 26,* 243-246.

Rogers, S. J. (1998). Empirically supported comprehensive treatments for young children with autism. *Journal of Clinical Child Psychology, 27,* 138-145.

Rogers, S. J. (1999). Intervention for young children with autism: From research to practice. *Infants and Young Children, 12,* 1-16.

Rutter, M. & Schopler, E. (1992). Classification of pervasive developmental disorders: Concepts and practical considerations. *Journal of Autism and Developmental Disorders, 22,* 459-482.

Sandler, A. D., Sutton, K. A., DeWeese, J., Girardi, M., Sheppard, V., & Bodfish, J. W. (1999). Lack of benefit of a single dose of synthetic human secretin in the treatment of autism and pervasive developmental disorder. *New England Journal of Medicine, 341,* 1801-1806.

Santangelo, S. L., & Tsatsanis, K. (2005). What is known about autism: Genes, brain, and behavior. *American Journal of Pharmacogenomics, 5,* 71-92.

Schloss, P. J., & Smith, M. A. (1999). *Conducting research.* Upper Saddle River, NJ: Merrill.

Schopler, E. (1987). Specific and nonspecific factors in the effectiveness of a treatment system. *American Psychologist, 42,* 376-83.

Shapiro, A. K. (1978). Placebo effect. In W. G. Clark & J. del Giudice (Eds.), *Principles of psychopharmacology* (2nd ed., pp. 441-528). New York: Academic Press.

Sigman, M., Dissanayake, C., Arbelle, S., & Ruskin, E. (1997). Cognition and emotion in children and adolescents with autism. In D. J. Cohen & F. R. Volkmar (Eds.), *Handbook of autism and pervasive developmental disorders* (pp. 248-265). New York: Wiley.

Sigman, M., & Ungerer, J. A. (1984). Cognitive and language skills in autistic mentally retarded and normal children. *Developmental Psychology, 20,* 293-302.

Siller, M., & Sigman, M. (2002). The behaviors of parents of children with autism predict the subsequent development of their children's communication. *Journal of Autism and Developmental Disorders, 32,* 77-89.

Simpson, R. L., de Boer-Ott, S. R., Griswold, D. E., Myles, B. S., Byrd, S. E., Ganz, J. B., et al. (2005). *Autism spectrum disorders: Interventions and treatments for children and youth.* Thousand Oaks, CA: Corwin Press.

Szatmari, P., Bartolucci, G., Bremner, R., Bond, S., & Rich, S. (1989). A follow-up study of high-functioning autistic children. *Journal of Autism and Developmental Disorders, 19,* 213-225.

Turnbull, A., & Turnbull, R. (2001). *Families, professionals, and exceptionality: Collaborating for empowerment* (4th ed.). Upper Saddle River, NJ: Merrill/Prentice Hall.

Van Meter, L., Fein, D., Morris, R., Waterhouse, L., & Allen, D. (1997). Delay versus deviance in autistic social behavior. *Journal of Autism and Developmental Disorders, 27,* 557-569.

Weiss, J. A., Sullivan, A., & Diamond, T. (2003). Parent stress and adaptive functioning of individuals with developmental disabilities. *Journal on Developmental Disabilities, 10,* 129–135.

West, J. F., & Cannon, G. S. (1988). Essential collaborative consultation competencies for regular and special educators. *Journal of Learning Disabilities, 21,* 56–63.

Winkler, L., Wasow, M., & Hatfield, E. (1981). Chronic sorrow revisited: Parent vs. professional depiction of the adjustment of parents of mentally retarded children. *American Journal of Orthopsychiatry, 51,* 63–70.

CHAPTER 4

Creating Contexts for Instruction

KEY TERMS

Animated Visuals

Behavioral Expectations

Behavioral Momentum

Choice-Making

Complex Stimuli

Engagement

Premack Principle

Priming

Static Visuals

Stimulus Control

Systematic Instruction

Temporal Structure

Transitions

Visual Cues

Visually Cued Instruction

❖ **LEARNING WITH MS. HARRIS: A Room of Her Own**

Ms. Harris has learned much about autism spectrum disorders over the last few weeks of summer. She met for a day with her special education supervisor and was able to read all the files for the students assigned to her class. Well, all but one. A new student was coming from out of district, and an administrator from the sending district called Ms. Harris's supervisor to talk about the student's goals. Although the student's file was still in transit, it appeared his goals were similar to the goals of Ms. Harris's students (how it thrilled her each time to think about "her" students!). Ms. Harris spent all day reading files and running into her supervisor's office to ask questions. She knew eight students would be assigned to her class and that three of them would receive some of their instruction in general education classes for part of the day. Three others would leave her class for music and PE. The IEP teams for two of the students had determined that they would need specialized instruction for the entire school day. Some of the notes regarding aggressive behavior made Ms. Harris a little nervous. Since then, her head had been swimming with ideas for arranging the day to accommodate all the separate schedules. But first she needed a room!

At the end of her first day of new-teacher orientation, Ms. Harris stops by Phillips Elementary to find out which classroom she is assigned to so she can start planning. When she arrives at the school, it is obvious some of the veteran teachers (who didn't have to attend new-teacher orientation) have already begun setting up their rooms. There are colorful "Welcome Back" decorations on doors, and Ms. Harris glimpses orderly rooms with bulletin boards in progress. The principal, Ms. Stokes, surrounded by folders, smiles at her and sends her to the secretary for her room key and directions. Ms. Harris finds her way to Room B–3 and spots the lone, undecorated door in the hallway. "Must be it!" she thinks. With great excitement, she unlocks the door and steps inside. Her room! She surveys the chairs stacked on tables, the pile of desks in the corner, and the butcher-paper-covered shelves with a sense of mounting anxiety. Where to begin?

Most great learning environments start out as rooms with unremarkable furnishings. The physical environment can make a significant impact on students' behaviors and their learning. For many teachers, the most pressing consideration in setting up the physical environment relates to which way the student desks should face—and even that decision may be dictated by which wall contains the chalkboard or whiteboard.

However, Ms. Harris knows that she will have students with Autism Spectrum Disorders (ASD) in her class, so she has to consider additional factors. Early research demonstrated that students with autism performed better in structured teaching situations as compared with unstructured environments (Schopler, Brehm, Kinsbourne, & Reichler, 1971). With a good understanding of the neurological differences underlying the disorders, Ms. Harris knows she will need to carefully consider the components suggested by research as being conducive to a supportive learning environment. This chapter will discuss considerations for:

- Arranging the physical environment
- Establishing the temporal structure
- Using visual and concrete systems
- Providing systematic instruction
- Accommodating sensory needs
- Facilitating engagement
- Establishing stimulus control
- Priming

ARRANGING THE PHYSICAL ENVIRONMENT

The physical structure of a classroom establishes the basic foundation for the learning space and can have a tremendous influence on student behavior (Duker & Rasing, 1989; Kozol, 1991). Kanner (1943) noticed that the children with autism he observed demonstrated unusual responses to the environment. For most students with ASD, the physical structure needs to be organized to communicate boundaries and facilitate engagement (Schopler, Mesibov, & Hearsey, 1995). Furniture should be placed so that the expectations of the activity are obvious. If the space is large enough, specific areas need to be set up for individual work, small group work, and whole class work. If the space is limited, furniture can be rearranged to accommodate varying instructional formats. Furniture should be placed to minimize the impact of traffic areas and distractions. For example, the areas where the students store their personal belongings (sometimes called "cubbies," "lockers," or "bins") should be situated away from the door, unless the teacher wants to deal with traffic jams. Student desks should face away from windows and doors, if possible. Communal appliances, such as trash cans and pencil sharpeners, need to be at some distance from student desks to reduce enticing opportunities for off-task behavior. If possible, computers need to be positioned so that the displays face away from other student work areas. Care in placing furniture and creating work areas will accomplish the desired goal of minimizing distractions (Rogers, 1999).

In addition to the general considerations of where to place furniture and fixtures, students with ASD, who tend to have strengths in visual processing (Minshew, Goldstein, Muenz, & Payton, 1992), could benefit from the establishment of well-defined visual boundaries. Bookshelves can be placed to outline a travel path and divide the room into distinguishable areas. Masking tape can be used to outline areas designated for specific activities and to show where students should be. For younger students, shapes can be taped to the floor to indicate where they are to stand when they get in line. Paint, carpet squares, hula hoops, and any other material that can visually define areas can be used to support the ability of students with ASD to understand how the space is divided.

In dividing the space, consider proximity preferences and needs of the students. All people must adapt to being in close proximity to others, and each person needs sufficient space to feel comfortable. Spacing needs are influenced by culture and mood. Some students will be more comfortable with greater distances between themselves and someone else, particularly when they are agitated or frustrated. When defining the boundaries in the room, the teacher should think about activities in which students may need more separation (e.g., individual work) and activities in which they will be expected to tolerate closer physical proximity to other students (e.g., group activities). Interestingly, Wilczynski, Fusilier, Dubard, and Elliott (2005) found that the on-task behavior of a 15-year-old with ASD decreased when an adult was in close proximity. Young, Simpson, Myles, and Kamps (1997) noted an increase in self-stimulatory behavior in two of three elementary students when the paraprofessional was closer.

The room should contain an area where students can retreat to regroup and maintain or regain composure. This area, variously referred to as the "cooldown area," "home base," "time away from aversives area" (Center, 1999), or "vacation spot" (among other terms), can be a place where an adult directs students to go or students can elect to go, if necessary. Students should be taught to recognize the indicators that mean they could use time away as well as the behavior expectation for using the area. Teachers may worry that students will choose to go to the retreat space to get out of doing work. If this becomes obvious, it is time to consider the demands of the work. Certainly, it would be preferable for a student to elect to go to the cool-down area to avoid work than to have a tantrum to avoid the work. Chapter 7 contains more information on exploring what students may be communicating through such behavior and strategies for addressing the behavior.

The physical structure of the room establishes boundaries that can serve as antecedents to induce certain behavior. For most neurotypical individuals, the physical structure provides almost complete guidance for behavioral expectations. For example, when entering a room in which there is one large table and 20 chairs around the table, the expectation is that a meeting there will be more interactive than if the room were set up with 20 chairs in rows. Either way, individuals attending the meeting will have preferences as to where to sit. If the room is set up with the chairs surrounding a large table, individuals entering the room will avoid sitting at the end of the table, because that seat is usually reserved for the person who called the meeting.

Teaching Behaviors Associated with Environmentally Cued Expectations

Individuals with ASD may not pick up on the subtle social nuances of expected behavior. Students must be explicitly taught the behaviors expected in each area of the classroom: the expectations for working individually at a desk, in a small group at a table, and in a large group on the floor or at desks. Teachers need to clearly articulate the behavioral expectations for each area of the classroom and teach, model, and practice the behaviors with the students as well as offer feedback on the adequacy of the behaviors.

Behavioral expectations can be broken down into a series of routines that are linked together for the student. For example, working individually at a desk involves many routines. Students must be able to check a schedule, go to a specific desk or work area, look at a work sequence, start with the first task indicated, and move through the sequence until each task is completed and put away. Working individually at a desk may also involve routines such as putting headings on papers, locating the correct assignments, asking for assistance as needed, and putting the completed work in the proper location.

Few students with ASD know what the directive "Do your work" means unless they have had prior training. The separate routines for each type of activity need to be taught directly to the students and then linked together. Some students with ASD benefit from **visual cues** (objects, icons, written labels) to assist them in understanding how to link the separate routines together (MacDuff, Krantz, & McClannahan, 1993). Figure 4.1 provides a visual depiction of the

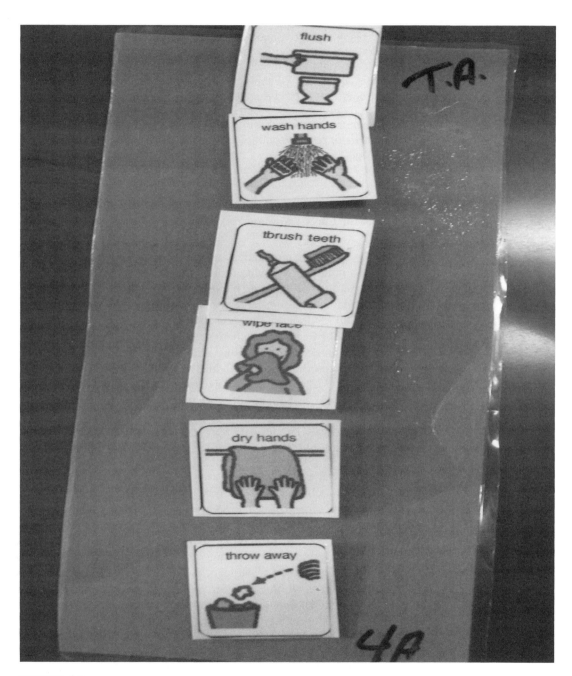

FIGURE 4.1
Expected Behavior in the Restroom
Source: Heflin and Alaimo

1. Get out blank sheet of paper.
2. Write first and last name on top left corner of paper.
3. Write today's date underneath name.
4. Write "Social Studies" on top right corner of paper.
5. Look at board and find the page numbers for today's assignment.
6. Write the page numbers underneath "Social Studies."
7. Write down the answers to the questions on those pages.
8. When finished, put the sheet of paper with the answers in the green tray on Mr. Nigel's desk.
9. Sit down and wait until Mr. Nigel gives another direction.

FIGURE 4.2
Expectations for Completing an Assignment

task-analyzed steps for demonstrating expected behaviors in the restroom that can help a student link the separate routines into a smooth sequence.

Students who are proficient at activities may still benefit from the use of visual cues that depict the steps for successfully completing a routine. Figure 4.2 provides a written reminder of the steps involved in completing an assignment that was taped to the inside of a student's social studies notebook.

Concrete boundaries (e.g., furniture, signs, tape) clearly identify the areas of the classroom according to the activities that typically occur in those areas. Students are specifically taught the behavioral routines that are expected in the various areas, and visual reminders are used to support successful linking of the steps within each routine.

ESTABLISHING THE TEMPORAL STRUCTURE

The physical structure of a classroom communicates expectations and supports appropriate behavior, and the temporal structure influences motivation and availability for learning. The **temporal structure** refers to how time is used. As described in Chapter 2, individuals with ASD may have differences in neurology that lead to difficulties in predicting sequences of events. They may become anxious if there are deviations from usual occurrences (Steingard, Zimnitzky, DeMaso, Bauman, & Bucci, 1997). The psychological discomfort that occurs when events are difficult to predict or are confusing results in the individual spending most of her cognitive energy in trying to figure out what is happening or trying to control activities to reestablish a sense of security. Establishing predictable routines can mitigate some of the psychological discomfort and result in students being more available for instruction. There will always be deviations from a set schedule, but teachers should start with predictable routines (Rogers, 1999) and gradually teach an understanding of the necessity for deviation.

Teachers can help students understand the concept of surprises in the schedule by first teaching them the pleasure of a surprise. Announcing a "surprise" and then disseminating some highly preferred object (e.g., candy, a sticker) can introduce the concept of an unexpected event very positively with little disruption of the schedule. Then, when surprises occur in the schedule, students may be primed for positive expectations and more open to hearing about the modification of the typical routine. The establishment of predictable daily routines ultimately facilitates the ability to teach flexibility. Several factors must be considered in establishing predictable daily routines for students with ASD, including the length of activities, variation of activities, how activities are indicated, when activities begin and end, and the need for smooth transitions.

Activity Length

The type of activity along with the age and abilities of the student dictate how long an activity should last. In general, relatively brief activities are more engaging for younger students (NRC, 2001). Students who are difficult to engage benefit from less time in groups and more time in more intensive instruction. Managing group times can be challenging because of the variations in ages and abilities, even within the same classroom. Some students can maintain control and attention for 20 minutes while others can be part of the group for only a few minutes. The effort that goes into considering how to include students in activities commensurate with their abilities is worthwhile, because it reduces the disruptive behavior that needs to be managed.

Some activities can be completed very quickly; others require a longer block of time. Some students with ASD do not care if an activity ends before they have completed the task, while others do not want to stop until they have finished the entire assignment. The students' abilities and idiosyncrasies as well as the requirements of the activity need to be carefully considered when determining how much time should be allotted for an activity. Judicious use of time dictates that activities should end on a successful note, meaning that some students may return to individual work while others stay to complete a group activity. Similarly, some students will need additional time to complete an activity and transition after the others.

Variation of Activities

In deciding how to sequence activities, consider the amount of effort required to complete an activity and the Premack Principle (Premack, 1959). The **Premack Principle,** translated into "Grandma's Law" as "Eat your vegetables before you get dessert," recommends careful sequencing of activities. To motivate a student to engage in a nonpreferred activity, schedule it so that completion is followed by a highly preferred activity. Thus, in some students' initial schedules, every nonpreferred task is followed by the opportunity to engage in an activity that is highly preferred. For example, every time a worksheet is completed, the student is allowed five minutes on the computer. The schedule can be modified over time so that more work is required prior to the opportunity to engage in something desirable.

Activities that require high levels of energy and effort may need to be followed by activities that require less energy and effort. Activities that involve passive participation should be interspersed with activities that demand active participation. The interspersing of easy and difficult tasks has been shown to reduce disruptive behavior and increase participation (Dunlap, 1984; Ebanks & Fischer, 2003), even in students with autism (Heckaman, Alber, Hooper, & Heward, 1998). Students should have opportunities for sanctioned movement during or between activities, particularly given the neurological research that suggests motor activity may facilitate appropriate behavior (Kern, Koegel, & Dunlap, 1984; Kern, Koegel, Dyer, Blew, & Fenton, 1982).

Motivation to complete tasks can be facilitated through the use of behavioral momentum (Nevin, Mandel, & Atak, 1983). In **behavioral momentum,** the student completes several quick and easy tasks prior to the introduction of the more difficult or less preferred task (Davis, Brady, Williams, & Hamilton, 1992). The expectation is that the student will have built up momentum by successfully completing the earlier tasks, so that there is less resistance to attempt the more difficult or less preferred task.

Delineation of Activities

The temporal schedule should be depicted in a visual manner to clearly communicate the sequence of events (Schopler et al., 1995). The visuals chosen to depict the schedule will be based on the individual student. Some students need object schedules in which objects that are a part of each activity are positioned in sequence to show what will happen first, second, third, and so forth. For example, a fork can be used to represent the activity of eating, and the schedule would continue with a toothbrush, a pencil, a piece of chain (representing a swing), and so forth. Other students are able to understand that photographs represent activities, icons represent activities, and ultimately that words represent activities. The final option is the one chosen by most adults, who have calendars or schedules in which they write down what they will be doing and when. Visual schedules have been demonstrated to be useful for increasing on-task behavior and reducing dependency on adult-delivered prompts in students with ASD (Dettmer, Simpson, Myles, & Ganz, 2000).

To promote future independence, students may benefit from having individual schedules they can check and manipulate. The schedule can be presented in a format that is appealing to the student. For example, if a student likes writing with a grease pencil and then erasing the mark, the schedule can be written out and laminated. The student uses a grease pencil to check off each activity as it is completed. After all activities have been checked, the student can erase all the marks. The first author had a student who liked to look at plastic letters on felt boards (like those used to describe the daily specials in cafeterias or listing office occupants within a building). This student's schedule was depicted using plastic letters on a felt board hanging over his desk. Each time he completed an activity, he could take the letters off the felt board and put them in an empty 35mm film canister. The opportunity to remove the letters motivated him to complete the activities.

A novel variation on schedules is to provide them via computers. Digital photos and short video clips have been imported into PowerPoint® presentations that depict sequences of events (Kimball, Kinney, Taylor, & Stromer, 2003). The computer-cued schedule can incorporate sound as well as warnings of upcoming transitions (e.g., audio of "One more minute;" beep when it is time to check the schedule). Technology on the computer can be used to fade pictures so that the student is prompted only by the word. Ultimately, the student's schedule will be in a nondescriptive format, like words written in an agenda that can be discretely checked and followed.

Teaching Starting and Stopping

The use of the grease pencil and the felt board also accomplished a key feature in the use of schedules: having a clear way to communicate the beginning and end of activities. Checking the schedule and announcing, "Now it's time for math" helps to communicate that an activity is about to begin. As much as possible, teachers need to use ancillary devices to communicate that an activity has ended (Newman et al., 1995). Rather than the teacher being the one to inform a student that it is time to stop using the computer, an ancillary device like a timer can be used to communicate the bad news. Visual timers may be more useful for students with ASD than audible timers. Some timers depict the passage of time using color on a clock face. Figure 4.3 provides an example of a visual timer that shows 15 minutes remaining in the activity.

In addition to using an ancillary device such as a visual timer, further definition of the end of an activity occurs when the student checks that the activity is finished, takes the letters off a felt board, turns over a card containing the name or picture of an activity, or moves a schedule card into a container labeled "Finished." Teachers may use repetitious routines to communicate that an activity is finished. The most common example of this in early childhood classrooms is the use of the "Clean Up" song to communicate that an activity is over.

Transitions

Transitions involve movement from one activity to the next, which can be particularly problematic for students with ASD. Teachers need to warn students of impending transitions, such as stating, "Five more minutes to work" while holding up five fingers or a card containing the words "5 more minutes," and even setting a timer for that length of time. It has been suggested that students with ASD are not bothered as much by changes in the routine as they are by the lack of prior notice that a transition is about to occur (Flannery & Horner, 1994). Students who were provided clear signals about the sequence, duration, and consequences of tasks, and warned of impending transitions,

FIGURE 4.3
Visual Timer Showing 15 Minutes of Time Remaining
Source: Used with permission. Available from Time Timer®, www.timetimer.com.

demonstrated fewer problem behaviors. These authors found that predictability (via signals for transitions) was more important than consistency for their participants.

Movement from one activity to the next can be facilitated through visually depicted schedules. When a student checks her schedule and sees that the next icon (or object, picture, or word) depicts "Work," she carries that icon to the area of the classroom designated for her to do her work. There, she puts the work icon in a preestablished place (e.g., Velcro on a matching icon on the corner of her desk). Carrying the icon can assist her in remembering what comes next and can be useful for facilitating transitions.

Establishing a clearly defined, depicted, and predictable temporal structure with activities that last the appropriate length of time for a student is important for students with ASD. Incorporating ancillary devices and providing transition assistance maximizes engaged time and minimizes instructional time lost to disruptive behavior. Visual schedules can teach change and flexibility in routines. For example, a review of the schedule in the morning may show that lunch usually occurs at 11:30, but on this day, it will be delayed until 12:00. The graphic or symbolic depiction of lunch is moved to the 12:00 slot and another activity put in place at 11:30. Even highly verbal students may benefit from explanations that occur in visual fashion.

Ultimately, the visually depicted schedule will be under the control of the student (Newman et al., 1995). The student will maintain his own schedule in the format he prefers and will have some control over the order of events. To build toward this end, schedules in schools should allow students as much choice as possible. If possible, let the student decide the order in which to complete the assignments (Dunlap et al., 1994). The importance of allowing students to make choices is more fully described later in this chapter.

VISUAL AND CONCRETE SYSTEMS

The preceding discussion highlighted the benefit of providing high levels of visual support for students with ASD (Rogers, 1999). The addition of visual elements to instruction has been termed **visually cued instruction** (Quill, 1997, p. 703). It can facilitate attention to relevant stimuli, organization of information, and an understanding of concepts and expectations. Difficulties in shifting attention (Wainwright-Sharp & Bryson, 1993) can be reduced by providing a cue (e.g., adult pointing) that stays in place (Bryson & Landry, 1994; Townsend, Harris, & Courchesne, 1996) and sufficient time for the shift to occur (Townsend & Courchesne, 1994). Rules in the classroom can be depicted graphically and accompanied by symbols or pictures. For students with limited spoken language, activities of the day can be presented on a page and the student circles the accomplished activities. The student can be taught to retrieve that page in response to the parent's or caregiver's inquiry, "What did you do at school today?" As students begin to respond to visual symbols, they can reduce their dependence on others and begin to generalize (Wacker & Berg, 1983).

The use of a "first/then" visual can show a student what must be accomplished prior to beginning a preferred activity. A piece of tagboard can be divided in half and icons or words representing the current activity placed on the left, the desired activity on the right. A visual can also be used to communicate expected behavior and feedback on performance. For example, cut a card that depicts a preferred item or activity into several pieces. Then, when the student engages in appropriate behavior for a specified amount of time (e.g., keeping her hands to herself), give her a piece. When the student earns all the pieces of the card, she can have the preferred item or activity. Figure 4.4 contains examples of two visual systems for depicting sequence and encouraging appropriate behavior.

The addition of visual cues has been found to increase the ability of students with ASD to follow spoken and modeled directions (Boucher & Lewis, 1989). In addition to being augmented by visuals, the language used in

FIGURE 4.4
Visual Systems for Depicting Sequence and Encouraging Appropriate Behavior
Source: Heflin and Alaimo

instruction needs to be as concrete as possible (Schopler et al., 1995). For example, when it is time to start an activity, rather than saying, "Let's get moving," the teacher should state, "Sit down and get out your blue notebook." When giving directions, use only the words that are necessary and avoid distracting comments. Clarify verbal directions through the use of expressions, voice tone, gestures, models, and visual prompts (Quill, 1998). Although using funny voices may be helpful for gaining attention, some students with ASD may not recognize that voice tone communicates a message (Rhea, Augustyn, Klin, & Volkmar, 2005) and may not be aware of "warning" tones that teachers sometimes try to convey through their voices. Students with ASD may not respond to instructions delivered in a monotone voice (Lamers & Hall, 2003).

The use of concrete methods for supporting instruction and communicating expectations has been found to promote the acquisition of a variety of important skills in individuals with ASD. Taylor and Levin (1998) placed a small pager-like device in the pocket of a 9-year-old boy with autism. The device, which was preset to vibrate at specific intervals, served as a concrete reminder for the boy to make a verbal comment to his peers. Shabani et al. (2002) replicated the study with three boys with autism and found similar improvements in social interactions, but noted the challenges involved in trying to fade the concrete tactile prompt. An adolescent with autism used a tape player with headphones to self-prompt on-task behavior (Tabor, Seltzer, Heflin, & Alberto, 1999). Although the message recorded on the tape originally cued the adolescent to stay on task, it was later discovered that the tape had been inadvertently erased; however, the young man continued to show improvements in on-task behavior. The headphones may have provided a concrete reminder to stay on task, even in the absence of the tape-recorded directions.

Differences Between Types of Visuals

Individuals with ASD have been found to focus and sustain attention on pictographic stimuli at levels comparable to individuals without ASD (Garretson, Fein, & Waterhouse, 1990). **Static visual** prompts (i.e., objects, pictures, icons, words) have been used to promote the acquisition of appropriate behavior (Schwartz, Garfinkle, & Bauer, 1998), decrease inappropriate behavior (Groden & LeVasseur, 1995), teach self-management of behavior (Pierce & Schreibman, 1994), and maintain on-task behavior (Bryan & Gast, 2000) among individuals with ASD. An emerging question is whether animated visuals (e.g., videotapes) would have a different effect from static visual representations.

Animated visuals use visually recorded images of other people or edited images of the individual (self-modeling) performing expected behaviors. Students view the tapes to see behaviors performed in context for vicarious learning (Bandura, 1986). Video modeling has been used to teach an array of skills to individuals ranging from ages 3 to 41 years with IQ scores ranging from profound mental retardation to average intelligence. For individuals with ASD, video modeling has been shown to teach generalization of purchasing skills (Alcantara, 1994; Haring, Kennedy, Adams, & Pitts-Conway,

1987), increase conversational skills (Charlop & Milstein, 1989; Sherer et al., 2001; Taylor, Levin, & Jasper, 1999), reduce anxiety (Luscre & Center, 1996), teach perspective taking (Charlop-Christy & Daneshvar, 2003), increase requesting (Wert & Neisworth, 2003), and teach play (D'Ateno, Mangiapanello, & Taylor, 2003). Behaviors learned during video modeling have generalized across settings and tasks. Modeling promotes generalization and response maintenance when used in conjunction with self-management (Apple, Billingsley, & Schwartz, 2005).

Attempts to determine if static or animated visual systems have differentiated effects have met with mixed results. Spencer and Heflin (under review) found static pictures to be more effective in teaching identification of body parts to three of four children with ASD, whereas the video was more effective for the fourth child. A similar disparity was discovered when comparing static and animated visual systems for teaching requesting skills (Spencer, 2002). For two children, static picture stimuli were more effective than the video model; for one child, static and animated visuals were equally effective; and the fourth child performed better during the video intervention. Further research needs to be conducted to identify student characteristics that may influence the difference in the effects of static and animated visual systems.

SYSTEMATIC INSTRUCTION

Given that individuals with ASD do not tend to acquire information incidentally, it is crucial to directly teach skills and concepts. **Systematic instruction** refers to the use of instructional technologies with demonstrated effectiveness, including those that meet the criteria as being applied behavior analytic (see Chapter 6). Students with ASD can benefit from carefully planned and predictable presentation of materials (Schreibman, 2000). One of the dimensions of applied behavior analytic teaching is that the skills and concepts are those deemed by an IFSP, IEP, or ITP team to be a priority for the student. An understanding of the core deficits across individuals with ASD, as well as consideration of the individual student's strengths, weaknesses, and plans for long-term participation, is necessary to determine priority skills.

For students with ASD, priority areas for teaching should focus on communication and socialization (Fox, Dunlap, & Philbrick, 1997; Powers, 1992), and specifically those skills that are most useful outside the school environment and in adult life (Hurth, Shaw, Izeman, Whaley, & Rogers, 1999). Toward that end, Dawson and Osterling (1997) suggest that the priority skills for young children with autism include selectively attending to stimuli in the environment, verbal and motor imitation, receptive and expressive language, appropriate toy play, and social interaction skills. The National Research Council (2001) adds functional, spontaneous communication and cognitive development. Olley (1999) expands the list to include initiation and response to social bids, recreation and leisure skills, and language comprehension. All agree that priority should be given to teaching the skills necessary for communication and socialization.

The most functional of the communication and socialization skills for the individual student should be prioritized (Iovannone, Dunlap, Huber, & Kincaid, 2003). Functionality is based on whether or not the skill will enable the student to enhance her quality of life by being more competent, more independent, and exercising more control over her environment (Dunlap & Robbins, 1991). A classic definition of functional skills, attributed to Lou Brown, defined a functional skill as one that would need to be performed for the individual by someone else if the individual did not learn the skill. For example, it would be a rare occurrence that someone would have to name the elements in the periodic table for a student if he could not do so. However, if a student did not learn to feed himself, someone would have to perform that skill for him. For students with more significant impairments, the priority functional skills may be those related to self-help. For students with less obvious impairments, the desirable functional skills may be those related to reading the affect of others and understanding social nuances. For students with high-functioning autism and Aspergers, priority goals may include developing the ability to select appropriate topics, initiating and shifting topics in an acceptable manner, and engaging in emotional regulation (NRC, 2001).

A common mistake made in teaching priority skills is that teachers inadvertently combine several skills, making it more difficult for the student to learn any of the skills. There is a huge difference between teaching a student to eliminate in a toilet and expecting that student to tell an adult when she needs to go to the restroom. Attempting to teach both skills at the same time may be confusing to the student, reducing her chance of success with either one.

Teachers commonly ask students to do things that combine multiple skills. For example, the teacher may ask the student to write his spelling words five times. Writing a spelling word one time verifies spelling accuracy. Having the student write the spelling word five times is not about spelling accuracy but about ability to comprehend and follow directions. The teacher should decide which skill needs to be targeted and modify the task accordingly. (As a note, students functioning on the higher end of the spectrum may become actively resistant if asked to perform a task multiple times.)

Systematic instruction also includes collecting data to document skill acquisition and to inform decision making about program modifications. Systematic instruction requires that programming occurs in ways that maintain skills across time as well as generalize them across settings. As discussed in Chapter 6, these practices are involved in applied behavior analytic instruction.

As summarized by Iovannone et al. (2003), systematic instruction requires careful planning to:

- Identify valid educational goals
- Identify and use effective instructional strategies to teach

- Evaluate the effectiveness of the instruction
- Modify instruction based on data

SENSORY ACCOMMODATIONS

The neurological differences underlying ASD may lead to difficulties receiving, modulating, integrating, and responding to sensory stimuli. Sensory issues can have a profound impact on the ability of students with ASD to be available for instruction. Because this is such a critical topic for understanding and addressing the needs of students with ASD, Chapter 5 covers it in detail. However, being aware of the need for sensory accommodations is a key instructional component in establishing a classroom.

Individuals vary in their need and tolerance for sensory stimulation. Even for one person, the amount of sensory stimulation needed may fluctuate throughout the day. Stress and fatigue decrease the ability to tolerate sensory stimulation. Many people have had the experience of wanting to get away from other people and noise for some relief from sensory stimulation. A person singing along with a CD and thinking about the day, while driving to an important event, needs to reduce the available sensory stimulation if she suddenly realizes she is lost. Likely, she will turn off the CD and focus on figuring out where she is and where she needs to be. In contrast, some individuals perform best under circumstances of high sensory stimulation. Some do not like the absence of sensory stimulation and can carry on a conversation and watch television while concentrating on an important task. Others have to eliminate all noise when they need to concentrate.

For some students with ASD, sensory stimulation in the classroom environment needs to be reduced to allow them to concentrate. Other students with ASD perform better if the sensory stimulation available at certain times is enhanced. The students themselves often provide the clues that sensory accommodations are necessary. For example, students who squint their eyes and cover their ears may be communicating a need for reduced sensory stimulation. Students who need less visual stimulation can wear caps or work at desks with covered carrels to reduce the amount of light they receive. They can use earplugs to reduce the audible noise level. Teachers need to analyze all sources of auditory and visual stimulation to identify stimuli that could be reduced. For example, some classroom pets make scratching and chewing noises. Most aquariums have filter systems that gurgle. Fluorescent lights and computers emit a hum.

On the other hand, students who stare into lights or stand close to a television after turning up the volume may be communicating a need for enhanced sensory stimulation. Some students who talk or make noise persistently may be indicating the need for enhanced stimulation. Putting lamps close to desks and using headphones to provide stimulation can enhance auditory stimulation. Activity levels may be higher in students who need enhanced stimulation and providing opportunities for them to move around may help. Chapter 5 offers more information about identifying and accommodating various sensory systems.

ENGAGING ACTIVITIES

Engagement is defined as active attending to and interacting with social and nonsocial environments (Dunlap, 1999). Individuals do not learn unless they are actively engaged in the learning process, and individuals who are not engaged are not available for instruction (Hurth et al., 1999). Engagement has been identified as one of the best predictors of positive student outcomes (Logan, Bakeman, & Keefe, 1997). The challenge when working with students with ASD is to develop methods of enticing them to engage in activities that are important for learning but which they may not like. Engagement can be encouraged by using techniques described in this chapter, such as establishing clear boundaries, carefully engineering schedules, using visual supports to enhance attention, and considering sensory accommodations.

Incorporating preferred materials, activities, and students' special interests can promote engagement (Grandin & Scariano, 1986; Hurth et al., 1999). For example, because it was a child's special interest, maps were incorporated into games to increase social interactions (Baker, Koegel, & Koegel, 1998). Students who enjoy playing with Legos may be more motivated to learn concepts such as color and quantity when Legos are used. Students who are fascinated by mummification may be more inclined to solve word problems involving mummies. Even adding pictures of favorite characters to worksheets may enlist student interest and enhance engagement.

In addition to incorporating special interests in order to heighten engagement, instructional presentation may be modified to encourage active participation. Gray (1996) described a student with an ASD who was more inclined to attend to materials if they were presented using vocabulary commonly found on cereal boxes. She described another student who was more engaged with information that was written in a rhyming pattern similar to rhymes found in Dr. Seuss books. Students with ASD may be more engaged with information that is provided in song or by computers (Hagiwara & Myles, 1999; Kinney, Vedora, & Stromer, 2003). Rather than expecting students with ASD to become engaged with typical learning experiences, consider incorporating their interests and modifying activities to promote maximum engagement. One effective strategy is choice-making.

Opportunities to Make Choices

Choice-making is associated with active participation and a sense of having some control over the environment (Sigafoos, 1998). Challenging behavior can result when individuals are denied the opportunity to make choices. Positive outcomes are associated with allowing students with ASD to choose from among reinforcers (Mason, McGee, Farmer-Dougan, & Risley, 1989; Newman, Needelman, Reinecke, & Robek, 2002) and tasks (Dyer, Dunlap, & Winterling, 1990; Peterson, Caniglia, & Royster, 2001). **Choice-making** can be accomplished by:

1. *Encouraging the student's expression of choice.*
   Students with ASD may use subtle or unusual modes of expressing choice. Teachers need to be sensitive to actions such as reaching,

looking, pushing away, or leaving the area (Sigafoos & Dempsey, 1992). Each of these expressions indicates a preference and needs to be shaped so that it is more readily recognized by others (Gothelf, Crimmins, Mercer, & Finocchiaro, 1994). Students who reach for objects can be taught to exchange an icon or use sign language. Many individuals can be taught to express choice verbally.

2. *Creating opportunities for the student to make choices.*
   An efficient way to teach choice-making is during naturally occurring situations. Mealtimes present many opportunities for choices. Choosing from among commonly available reinforcers presents another opportunity (Brigham & Sherman, 1973). Students can choose the order in which they want to complete their tasks (Dunlap et al., 1994) or when they would like to complete them (Brown, 1991). When students are demonstrating inappropriate behavior, the behavioral redirection can be presented as a choice (e.g., "You can't scribble on the paper, but you can type your answers on the computer or dictate them to Mr. Smelling;" Taylor, O'Reilly, & Lancioni, 1996). For students with ASD, present choices through concrete representations (e.g., pictures) rather than verbally (Vaughn & Horner, 1995).

Teaching students to make choices and giving them opportunities to exercise that skill can reduce problem behavior and increase engagement. Students also learn a skill that will be useful across time and in many contexts.

ESTABLISHING STIMULUS CONTROL

When a behavior occurs only in the presence of a particular stimulus, the behavior is said to be under **stimulus control** (Green, 2001). For example, a number of stimuli control drivers' behavior. Drivers stop when certain stimuli are present (e.g., red light, a stop sign, arrival at destination, a person in the road). Drivers continue unless those stimuli are present. Sometimes drivers attend to the incorrect stimulus, such as the car ahead of them. Drivers who attend to an incorrect stimulus may fail to notice that the traffic light has changed from yellow to red (relevant stimulus) and may be involved in a wreck.

For students with ASD, it is known that behavior may be under the control of unexpected stimuli. If the same set of materials is used to teach concepts (e.g., a set of construction paper cards to teach colors), it is not uncommon for students with ASD to suddenly lose their ability to identify colors when the materials are changed. What the teacher didn't realize was that the relevant stimuli for the student were that the red card had a bent corner, the blue card had a mark on it, the green card was wrinkled, and so on. It wasn't the colors the student "learned" but the idiosyncrasies of the cards. In a similar fashion, students with ASD may have difficulty responding to **complex stimuli,** those that contain a number of components (Burke & Cerniglia, 1990). For example, telling the student, "Go sit in the green chair that is the closest to the door and doesn't have a cushion" may not produce the desired behavior. When the stimulus becomes complex, the student may pick up on one component (closest to the door) and follow through accordingly.

To develop stimulus control, students must be taught to discriminate between stimuli (Green, 2001) and how to respond in the presence of particular stimuli. Teachers should start with simple (not complex) stimuli and rotate materials so that unexpected aspects are not the basis for the stimulus control. Teaching occurs when the stimulus is presented (e.g., verbal direction, "Line up") and the student reinforced for behaving as expected or assisted so that the student responds correctly. Repeated opportunities to practice and receive reinforcement or correction for the response promotes stimulus control.

PRIMING

Priming is a strategy for enhancing task performance by allowing the individual to practice the activity and become familiar with the materials ahead of time. Research on priming has been conducted primarily on persons without disabilities. However, emerging research indicates that priming can be effective for students with ASD because it increases predictability by allowing them to rehearse future tasks before they occur (Schreibman, Walen, & Stahmer, 2000). According to Zanolli, Daggett, and Adams (1996, p. 408):

1. Priming must be conducted prior to the activity, using the same materials.
2. The priming session contains tasks the student can easily complete.
3. High levels of reinforcement occur during the session.

Using priming, two preschoolers with autism were successfully taught to initiate social interactions prior to engaging in classroom activities (Kamps et al., 1992; Zanolli et al., 1996). Toilet training of a 3-year-old child with autism was primed by watching a video (Bainbridge & Myles, 1999). Disruptive behaviors were effectively reduced in three children with autism when they were shown videos of environments where they would be going (e.g., videos showing routes for walking through a mall; Schreibman et al., 2000). For two students, worksheets to be completed in class the next day were reviewed (Koegel, Koegel, Frea, & Green-Hopkins, 2003). The parents of one of the students reviewed the worksheets at home. The other student's parents were unavailable to assist with homework, so a school staff member reviewed the worksheets. The results of the priming were reductions in problem behavior and increases in academic responding for both students. Priming may be an effective tool for helping students with ASD know what to expect so that they participate more fully in educational and social activities.

CONCLUSION

Arranging the physical environment, establishing a schedule, using visuals, providing systematic instruction, accommodating sensory needs, and promoting engagement are considered the key instructional components of any classroom for students with ASD. Effective teachers organize the school day with interesting tasks that last an appropriate amount of time and take into account activity and sensory differences. The tasks need to be represented in a concrete manner and should be clear signals when a task is to begin and when a task is finished. Students benefit from the opportunity to make choices, and choice-making can promote engagement and motivation. Students will be more available for instruction if they are systematically taught to recognize the stimuli that cue behavioral responses. Priming can also be used to familiarize students with upcoming events and equip students with the skills needed to be successful.

DISCUSSION QUESTIONS AND ACTIVITIES

1. Generate a list of activities and learning tasks that commonly occur in classrooms at the preschool, elementary, middle, and high school levels. For each age level, categorize the activities along the parameters of typical length, difficulty, activity level, and student preference.

2. Task analyze a common routine that a student functioning on the high end of the spectrum would probably engage in at school and one that a student functioning on the low end of the spectrum would probably engage in at school. Decide how you would present each schedule visually to the respective students.

3. Pick an age group and, pretending that money is no object, draw a diagram of a classroom that contains all of the elements considered important for supporting the learning of students with ASD, tailored for the age of the group. Make a bulleted list of the elements that you cannot draw.

4. Generate a list of as many opportunities as possible for students to make choices during the school day. How can routine activities be modified so that students can make choices (e.g., use a pen instead of a pencil)?

5. Develop priming strategies for three different activities during the school day.

REFERENCES

Alcantara, P. (1994). Effects of videotape instructional package on purchasing skills of children with autism. *Exceptional Children, 61,* 40-55.

Apple, A. L., Billingsley, F., & Schwartz, I. S. (2005). Effects of video modeling alone and with self-management on compliment-giving behaviors of children with high-functioning ASD. *Journal of Positive Behavioral Interventions, 7,* 33-46.

Bainbridge, N., & Myles, B. S. (1999). The use of priming to introduce toilet training to a child with autism. *Focus on Autism and Other Developmental Disabilities, 14,* 106-109.

Baker, M. J., Koegel, R. L., & Koegel, L. K. (1998). Increasing the social behavior of young children with autism using their obsessive behaviors. *Journal of the Association for Severe Handicaps, 23,* 300-308.

Bandura, A. (1986). *Social foundations of thought and action: A social cognitive theory.* Upper Saddle River, NJ: Prentice Hall.

Boucher, J., & Lewis, V. (1989). Memory impairments and communication in relatively able autistic children. *Journal of Child Psychology and Psychiatry, 30,* 99-122.

Brigham, T. A., & Sherman, J. A. (1973). Effects of choice and immediacy of reinforcement on single response and switching behavior of children. *Journal of the Experimental Analysis of Behavior, 19,* 425-435.

Brown, F. (1991). Creative daily scheduling: A nonintrusive approach to challenging behaviors in community residences. *Journal of the Association for Persons with Severe Handicaps, 16,* 75-84.

Bryan, L. C., & Gast, D. L. (2000). Teaching on-task and on-schedule behaviors to high-functioning children with autism via picture activity schedules. *Journal of Autism and Developmental Disorders, 30,* 553-567.

Bryson, S., & Landry, R. (1994). Brief report: A case study of literacy and socioemotional development in a mute autistic female. *Journal of Autism and Developmental Disorders, 24,* 225-232.

Burke, J. C., & Cerniglia, L. (1990). Stimulus complexity and autistic children's responsivity: Assessing and training a pivotal behavior. *Journal of Autism and Developmental Disorders, 20,* 233-253.

Center, D. B. (1999). *Strategies for social and emotional behavior: A teacher's guide.* Norcross, GA: XanEdu.

Charlop, M. H., & Milstein, J. P. (1989). Teaching autistic children conversational speech using video modeling. *Journal of Applied Behavior Analysis, 22,* 275-285.

Charlop-Christy, M. H., & Daneshvar, S. (2003). Using video modeling to teach perspective taking to children with autism. *Journal of Positive Behavioral Interventions, 5,* 12-21.

D'Ateno, P., Mangiapanello, K., & Taylor, B. A. (2003). Using video modeling to teach complex play sequences to a preschooler with autism. *Journal of Positive Behavior Interventions, 5,* 5-11.

Davis, C. A., Brady, M. P., Williams, R. E., & Hamilton, R. (1992). Effects of high-probability requests on the acquisition and generalization of responses to requests in young children with behavior disorders. *Journal of Applied Behavior Analysis, 25,* 905-916.

Dawson, G., & Osterling, J. (1997). Early intervention in autism: Effectiveness and common elements of current approaches. In M. J. Guralnick (Ed.), *The effectiveness of early intervention: Second generation research* (pp. 307-326). Baltimore: Paul H. Brookes.

Dettmer, S., Simpson, R. L., Myles, B. S., & Ganz, J. B. (2000). The use of visual supports to facilitate transitions of students with autism.

Focus on Autism and Other Developmental Disabilities, 15, 163-169.

Duker, P. C., & Rasing, E. (1989). Effects of redesigning the physical environment and on-task behavior in three autistic-type developmentally disabled individuals. *Journal of Autism and Other Developmental Disorders, 19,* 449-60.

Dunlap, G. (1984). The influence of task variation and maintenance tasks on the learning and affect of autistic children. *Journal of Experimental Child Psychology, 37,* 41-64.

Dunlap, G., dePerczel, M., Clarke, S., Wilson, D., Wright, S., White, R., et al. (1994). Choice making to promote adaptive behavior for students with emotional and behavioral challenges. *Journal of Applied Behavior Analysis, 27,* 505-518.

Dunlap, G., & Robbins, F. R. (1991). Current perspectives in service delivery for young children with autism. *Comprehensive Mental Health Care, 1,* 177-194

Dyer, K., Dunlap, G., & Winterling, V. (1990). Effects of choice making on the serious problem behaviors of students with severe handicaps. *Journal of Applied Behavior Analysis, 23,* 515-524.

Ebanks, M. E., & Fischer, W. W. (2003). Altering the timing of academic prompts to treat destructive behavior maintained by escape. *Journal of Applied Behavior Analysis, 36,* 355-359.

Flannery, K. B., & Horner, R. H. (1994). The relationship between predictability and problem behavior for students with severe disabilities. *Journal of Behavioral Education, 4,* 157-176.

Fox, L., Dunlap, G., & Philbrick, L. A. (1997). Providing individual supports to young children with autism and their families. *Journal of Early Intervention, 21*(1), 1-14.

Garretson, H., Fein, D., & Waterhouse, L. (1990). Sustained attention in autistic children. *Journal of Autism and Developmental Disorders, 20,* 101-114.

Gothelf, C. R., Crimmins, D. B., Mercer, C. A., & Finocchiaro, P. A. (1994). Teaching choice-making skills to students who are deaf-blind. *Teaching Exceptional Children, 26*(4), 13-15.

Grandin, T., & Scariano, M. M. (1986). *Emergence: Labeled autistic.* New York: Warner Books.

Gray, C. (1996). *Social stories and comic strip conversations: Unique methods to improve social understanding* [video]. Arlington, TX: Future Horizons.

Green, G. (2001). Behavior analytic instruction for learners with autism: Advances in stimulus control technology. *Focus on Autism and Other Developmental Disabilities, 16,* 72–86.

Groden, J., & LeVasseur, P. (1995). Cognitive picture rehearsal: A system to teach self-control. In K. A. Quill (Ed.), *Teaching children with autism: Strategies to enhance communication and socialization* (pp. 287–306). Albany, NY: Delmar.

Hagiwara, T., & Myles, B. S. (1999). A multimedia social story intervention: Teaching skills to children with autism. *Focus on Autism and Other Developmental Disabilities, 14,* 82–95.

Haring, T., Kennedy, C., Adams, M., & Pitts-Conway, V. (1987). Teaching generalization of purchasing skills across community settings to autistic youth using videotape modeling. *Journal of Applied Behavior Analysis, 20,* 89–96.

Heckaman, K. A., Alber, S., Hooper, S., & Heward, W. L. (1998). A comparison of least-to-most prompts and progressive time delay on the disruptive behavior of students with autism. *Journal of Behavioral Education, 8,* 171–201.

Hurth, J., Shaw, E., Izeman, S. G., Whaley, K., & Rogers, S. J. (1999). Areas of agreement about effective practices among programs serving young children with autism spectrum disorders. *Infants and Young Children, 12,* 17–26.

Iovannone, R., Dunlap, G., Huber, H., & Kincaid, D. (2003). Effective educational practices for students with autism spectrum disorders. *Focus on Autism and Other Developmental Disabilities, 18,* 150–165.

Kamps, D. M., Leonard, B. R., Vernon, S., Dugan, E., Delquadri, J. C., Gershon, B., et al. (1992). Teaching social skills to students with autism to increase peer interactions in an integrated first-grade classroom. *Journal of Applied Behavior Analysis, 25,* 281–288.

Kanner, L. (1943). Autistic disturbances of affective contact. *The Nervous Child, 2,* 217–250.

Kern, L., Koegel, R. L., & Dunlap, G. (1984). The influence of vigorous versus mild exercise on autistic stereotyped behaviors. *Journal of Autism and Developmental Disorders, 14,* 57–67.

Kern, L., Koegel, R. L., Dyer, K., Blew, P. A., & Fenton, L. R. (1982). The effects of physical exercise on self-stimulation and appropriate responding on autistic children. *Journal of Autism and Developmental Disorders, 14,* 399–419.

Kimball, J. W., Kinney, E. M., Taylor, B. A., & Stromer, R. (2003). Lights, camera, action! Using engaging computer-cued activity schedules. *Teaching Exceptional Children, 36*(1), 40–45.

Kinney, E. M., Vedora, J., & Stromer, R. (2003). Computer-presented video models to teach generative spelling to a child with an autism spectrum disorder. *Journal of Positive Behavior Interventions, 5,* 22–29.

Koegel, L. K., Koegel, R. L., Frea, W., & Green-Hopkins, I. (2003). Priming as a method of coordinating educational services for students with autism. *Language, Speech, and Hearing Services in Schools, 34,* 228–235.

Kozol, J. (1991). *Savage inequalities: Children in America's schools.* New York: Crown.

Lamers, K., & Hall, L. J. (2003). The response of children with autism to preferred prosody during instruction. *Focus on Autism and Other Developmental Disabilities, 18,* 93–102.

Logan, K. R., Bakeman, R., & Keefe, E. G. (1997). Effects of instructional variables on engaged behavior of students with disabilities in general education classrooms. *Exceptional Children, 63,* 481–497.

Luscre, D. M., & Center, D. B. (1996). Procedures of reducing dental fear in children with autism. *Journal of Autism and Developmental Disorders, 26,* 547–556.

MacDuff, G., Krantz, P., & McClannahan, L. (1993). Teaching children with autism to use pictographic activity schedules: Maintenance and generalization of complex response chains. *Journal of Applied Behavior Analysis, 26,* 89–97.

Mason, S. A., McGee, G. G., Farmer-Dougan, V., & Risley, T. R. (1989). A practical strategy for ongoing reinforcer assessment. *Journal of Applied Behavior Analysis, 22,* 171–179.

Minshew, N., Goldstein, G., Muenz, L., & Payton, J. (1992). Neuropsychological functioning of non-mentally retarded autistic individuals. *Journal of Clinical and Experimental Neuropsychology, 14,* 749–761.

National Research Council. (2001). *Educating children with autism.* Committee on Educational Interventions for Children with

Autism. Division of Behavioral and Social Sciences and Education. Washington, DC: National Academy Press.

Nevin, J. A., Mandel, C., & Atak, J. (1983). The analysis of behavioral momentum. *Journal of the Experimental Analysis of Behavior, 39,* 49-59.

Newman, B., Buffington, D. M., O'Grady, M. A., McDonald, M. E., Poulson, C. L., & Hemmes, N. S. (1995). Self-management of schedule following in three teenagers with autism. *Behavioral Disorders, 20,* 190-196.

Newman, B., Needelman, M., Reinecke, D. R., & Robek, A. (2002). The effect of providing choices on skill acquisition and competing behavior of children with autism during discrete trial instruction. *Behavioral Interventions, 17,* 31-41.

Olley, J. G. (1999). Curriculum for students with autism. *School Psychology Review, 28,* 595-606.

Peterson, S. M. P., Caniglia, C., & Royster, A. J. (2001). Application of choice-making intervention for a student with multiple maintained problem behavior. *Focus on Autism and Other Developmental Disabilities, 16,* 240-246.

Pierce, K. L., & Schreibman, L. (1994). Teaching daily living skills to children with autism in unsupervised settings through pictorial self-management. *Journal of Applied Behavior Analysis, 27,* 471-481.

Powers, M. D. (1992). Early intervention for children with autism. In D. E. Berkell (Ed.), *Autism: Identification, education and treatment* (pp. 225-252). Hillsdale, NJ: Erlbaum.

Premack, D. (1959). Toward empirical behavior laws: I. Positive reinforcement. *Psychological Review, 66,* 219-233.

Quill, K. A. (1997). Instructional considerations for young children with autism: The rationale for visually cued instruction. *Journal of Autism and Developmental Disorders, 27,* 697-714.

Quill, K. A. (1998). Environmental supports to enhance social communication. *Seminars in Speech and Language, 19,* 407-422.

Rhea, P., Augustyn, A., Klin, A., & Volkmar, F. (2005). Perception and production of prosody by speakers with autism spectrum disorders. *Journal of Autism and Developmental Disorders, 35,* 205-220.

Rogers, S. J. (1999). Intervention for young children with autism: From research to practice. *Infants and Young Children, 12,* 1-16.

Schopler, E., Brehm, S., Kinsbourne, M., & Reichler, R. J. (1971). The effect of treatment structure on development of autistic children. *Archives of General Psychiatry, 24,* 415-421.

Schopler, E., Mesibov, G. B., & Hearsey, K. (1995). Structured teaching in the TEACCH system. In E. Schopler, & G. B. Mesibov (Eds.), *Learning and cognition in autism* (pp. 243-268). New York: Plenum.

Schreibman, L. (2000). Intensive behavioral/psychoeducational treatments for autism: Research needs and future directions. *Journal of Autism and Developmental Disorders, 30,* 373-378.

Schreibman, L., Whalen, C., & Stahmer, A. C. (2000). The use of video priming to reduce disruptive transition behavior in children with autism. *Journal of Positive Behavioral Interventions, 2,* 3-11.

Schwartz, I. S., Garfinkle, A. N., & Bauer, J. (1998). The Picture Exchange Communication System: Communicative outcomes for young children with disabilities. *Teaching Early Childhood Special Education, 18,* 144-159.

Shabani, D. B., Katz, R. C., Wilder, D. A., Beauchamp, K., Taylor, C. R., & Fischer, K. J. (2002). Increasing social initiations in children with autism: Effects of a tactile prompt. *Journal of Applied Behavior Analysis, 35,* 79-83.

Sherer, M., Pierce, K., Paredes, S., Kisacky, K., Ingersoll, B., & Schreibman, L. (2001). Enhancing conversation skills in children with autism via video technology: Which is better, "self" or "other" as model? *Behavior Modification, 25,* 140-158.

Sigafoos, J. (1998). Choice making and personal selection strategies. In J. K. Luiselli & M. J. Cameron (Eds.), *Antecedent control: Innovative approaches to behavioral support* (pp. 187-221). Baltimore: Paul H. Brooks.

Sigafoos, J., & Dempsey, R. (1992). Assessing choice making among children with multiple disabilities. *Journal of Applied Behavior Analysis, 25,* 747-755.

Spencer, L. G. (2002). *Comparing the effectiveness of static pictures vs. video modeling on teaching requesting skills to elementary children with autism.* Unpublished doctoral dissertation, Georgia State University, Atlanta.

Steingard, R. J., Zimnitzky, B., DeMaso, D. R., Bauman, M. L., & Bucci, J. P. (1997). Sertraline treatment of transition-associated anxiety and agitation in children with autistic disorder. *Journal of Child and Adolescent Psychopharmacology, 7,* 9–15.

Tabor, T. A., Seltzer, A., Heflin, L. J., & Alberto, P. A. (1999). Use of self-operated auditory prompts to decrease off-task behavior for a student with autism and moderate mental retardation. *Focus on Autism and Other Developmental Disabilities, 14,* 159–167.

Taylor, B. A., & Levin, L. (1998). Teaching a student with autism to make verbal initiations: Effects of a tactile prompt. *Journal of Applied Behavior Analysis, 31,* 651–654.

Taylor, B., Levin, L., & Jasper, S. (1999). Increasing play-related statements in children with autism toward their siblings: Effects of video modeling. *Journal of Developmental and Physical Disabilities, 11,* 253–264.

Taylor, I., O'Reilly, M., & Lancioni, G. (1996). An evaluation of an ongoing consultation model to train teachers to treat challenging behaviour. *International Journal of Disability, Development, and Education, 43,* 203–218.

Townsend, J., & Courchesne, E. (1994). Parietal damage and narrow "spotlight" spatial attention. *Journal of Cognitive Neuroscience, 6,* 220–232.

Townsend, J., Harris, N. S., & Courchesne, E. (1996). Visual attention abnormalities in autism: Delayed orienting to location. *Journal of the International Neuropsychological Society, 2,* 541–550.

Vaughn, B., & Horner, R. H. (1995). Effects of concrete versus verbal choice systems on problem behavior. *Augmentative and Alternative Communication, 11,* 89–93.

Wacker, D. P., & Berg, W. K. (1983). Effects of picture prompts on the acquisition of complex vocational tasks by mentally retarded adolescents. *Journal of Applied Behavior Analysis, 16,* 417–433.

Wainwright-Sharp, J. A., & Bryson, S. E. (1993). Visual orienting deficits in high-functioning people with autism. *Journal of Autism and Developmental Disorders, 23,* 1–13.

Wert, B. Y., & Neisworth, J. T. (2003). Effects of video self-modeling on spontaneous requesting in children with autism. *Journal of Positive Behavioral Interventions, 5,* 30–34.

Wilczynski, S. M., Fusilier, I., Dubard, M., & Elliott, A. (2005). Experimental analysis of proximity as a social stimulus: Increasing on-task behavior of an adolescent with autism. *Psychology in the Schools, 42,* 189–196.

Young, B., Simpson, R. L., Myles, B. S., & Kamps, D. M. (1997). An examination of paraprofessional involvement in supporting inclusion of students with autism. *Focus on Autism and Other Developmental Disabilities, 12,* 31–38.

Zanolli, K., Daggett, J., & Adams, T. (1996). Teaching preschool age autistic children to make spontaneous initiations to peers using priming. *Journal of Autism and Developmental Disorders, 24,* 407–422.

CHAPTER 5

Accommodating Sensory Issues

KEY TERMS

Auditory System

Gustatory System

Habituation

Occupational Therapist

Olfactory System

Pica

Proprioceptive System

Self-Injurious Behaviors

Self-Stimulatory Behaviors

Sensory Integration

Sensory Systems

Stereotypies

Tactile Defensiveness

Tactile System

Vestibular System

Visual System

❖ LEARNING WITH MS. HARRIS: Ms. Harris Is Puzzled

The door to Ms. Harris's classroom looks like all the other doors in the hallway: bright, colorful, and welcoming. Eight students are sitting in desks facing the calendar and group schedule. As Ms. Harris begins to work through the days of the week, she quickly recognizes that the students do not share her focus of attention. One boy has launched into what sounds like a script from a movie, another student is tensing and flexing the muscles in his arms and hands, while a third is gazing with rapt attention at her fingers. A fourth child has disappeared under his desk, a fifth is rubbing his hands across his corduroy pants, and the remaining three students appear to be looking everywhere except at the calendar. As Ms. Harris takes the card with the word "Monday" printed on it to the student rubbing his corduroy pants in order to prompt him to label the day, he begins to rub his pants faster, rocking back and forth in his seat. "What is going on?" thinks Ms. Harris. "I know I arranged the room carefully, minimized distractions, and I'm using visually cued instruction to work through the calendar activity. Why aren't the students on task?"

Ms. Harris is about to learn that one of the biggest and least understood issues she will face as a teacher will be identifying and supporting her students' sensory needs. Students with ASD are constantly challenged to grapple with the sensory information that bombards them (Grandin, 1996). Due to neurological differences that lead to behaviors associated with ASD, individuals on the spectrum are perceived as having difficulty perceiving, integrating, and using sensory information accurately. These difficulties lead to the development of compensatory strategies that extend from active avoidance to total withdrawal. To promote her students' progress, Ms. Harris will need to learn about the sensory systems and how they influence behavior as well as the roles of self-stimulatory and stereotypic behaviors. Since there is limited empirical support for sensory-based interventions (as will be discussed at the end of the chapter), Ms. Harris's task is to consider the well-documented sensory differences in individuals and consider implications for modifying her instructional environments and strategies to provide adequate support for her students' sensory differences.

SENSORY DIFFERENCES IN AUTISM SPECTRUM DISORDERS

Even in the absence of consistent empirical evidence for the effectiveness of sensory-based interventions, a rich body of descriptive literature regarding the sensory differences among individuals with ASD has been produced. Decades ago, descriptions of children with ASD mentioned sensory differences and sensory-seeking behaviors in the population (Kanner, 1943; Wing, 1969). Although sensory deficits are not mentioned in the diagnostic criteria for Pervasive Developmental Disorders (PDD) in the *DSM-IV-TR*, stereotypic and ritualistic behaviors are identified as one of the core deficits. The unusual behaviors associated with ASD may indicate difficulties in registering and processing sensory information (Baranek, 2002). Retrospective video analysis suggests sensory functioning differs qualitatively in children later diagnosed as having an ASD (Adrien et al., 1993). Analyzing videos taken of infants between 9 and 12 months of age show that children with ASD are different from children with developmental delays and those developing typically by responding slower or not at all to attention-getting strategies (e.g., responding to name) and having poor visual orientation, poor attention to sensory stimuli, and social touch aversion (Baranek, 1999). Interestingly, infants with developmental delays exhibited more stereotypies, unusual posturing, visual fixation on objects, and fewer animated expressions than did the infants with ASD. Descriptive studies have identified that 42–80% of individuals with ASD demonstrate unusual sensory responses, which include rubbing surfaces, finger licking, body rocking, and failing to respond to particular visual and auditory stimuli (Kientz & Dunn, 1997; Rapin, 1996; Volkmar & Cohen, 1989). Children with developmental delays have been found to differ from age-matched peers in displaying more gross motor stereotypies to which they orient, to the exclusion of other people and objects in their environments (Smith & Van Houten, 1996). This body of literature is sufficient to warrant consideration of the impact of sensory differences in individuals with ASD, after an overview of the research related to sensory systems and functioning.

SENSORY STIMULI

Neuroscientists describe how **sensory systems** bring information into the central nervous system (CNS) for conscious as well as unconscious processing and subsequent modulation of behavior (Freeman, 1991; Kandel, Schwartz, & Jessell, 2000). People depend on sensory systems for all information about their environments. The olfactory, gustatory, tactile, vestibular, proprioceptive, visual, and auditory systems (which will be described later in more detail) bring information to the central nervous system for processing. People do not consciously acknowledge all of the sensory stimuli they receive. For example, a person may not be consciously aware of clothing that is touching the skin, nor hear someone talking if engrossed in another activity. The ability to register sensory stimuli is influenced by the individual's biological characteristics, learned responses to sensation, and vacillating physical and psychological states (e.g., tired, hungry, angry) (Dunn, 2001).

Scientists in the fields of neurology, physiology, biology, anatomy, and so forth, as well as researchers interested in understanding the experiences of individuals with disabilities, describe how people register and use sensory information. Some people seem to have very high thresholds that require intensive sensory stimuli before the stimuli are registered. These individuals may actively seek out additional sensation (Baranek, Foster, & Berkson, 1997). Some individuals with PDD have been found to be sensation seekers (Kootz, Marinelli, & Cohen, 1981). Other people appear to have very low thresholds that allow sensations to register as they occur, and, in fact, may register more sensory stimulation than is comfortable. These individuals may avoid sensory input and, as adults, may experience more anxiety and depression than those with typical or high thresholds (Kinnealey & Fuiek, 1999). Adults who avoid sensation have reported developing coping strategies such as avoiding the stimuli, maintaining predictability, preparing mentally, talking themselves through the situation, and doing something to mitigate the discomfort associated with the stimuli (Kinnealey, Oliver, & Wilbarger, 1995). When a new stimulus is introduced to people who seek sensation, the heart rate decreases, but in those who avoid sensation, the heart rate increases (Zuckerman, 1994). Most people are somewhere in the middle and are able to register moderate levels of relevant sensory stimuli and filter out irrelevant stimuli.

Sensitivity to sensory stimuli is influenced by whether or not the person has been exposed repeatedly to the stimuli. The more a person experiences the stimuli, the more likely he becomes desensitized to them. For example, a person who lives close to a train track or busy interstate may not even register the sound of the train or vehicles, whereas a visitor may express amazement that anyone could sleep with all the noise. A learned response that diminishes the recognition of sensory stimuli is called **habituation** (Dunn, 1997). The individual becomes so accustomed to the sensory stimuli that it no longer registers. Children with Fragile X and sensory modulation disorders have been shown to be less likely to habituate to sensory stimuli (McIntosh, Miller, Shyu, & Hagerman, 1999). Being tired, hungry, angry, scared, or so forth also affects recognition of sensory stimuli. Most people tend to have lower thresholds and be less habituated to sensory stimuli when they are not physically or psychologically comfortable; this means that they are more reactive to sounds, smells, and movement.

Effective use of sensory stimuli is inferred to occur when information from different sensory systems is processed, organized, and combined to produce an adaptive motor response (Bundy & Murray, 2002). Sensory information from one receptor (e.g., eyes) coordinates with information from other receptors (e.g., nose, ears). The central nervous system uses the information to organize and execute output. In some cases, sensory information leads to a response that is protective if the central nervous system believes the stimuli to be threatening. For example, even when a person is engrossed in a television show, a loud boom may cause him to jump; the auditory stimulus elicits a startle reflex. If something brushes the legs of a person walking down a dark alley, she will automatically pull away; the tactile sensation creates a sense of alarm.

The protective response to information provided by sensory systems is an automatic response. If the stimulus is not threatening, the sensory information is integrated to produce modulated output. Take, for example, a very nonthreatening situation: writing. As a person writes, the eyes as well as the joints and muscles of the fingers take in sensory information so that output is subtly modified to produce the next letters, in correct formation, and at the correct place on the page. If the writer is suddenly startled, the hand jerks and the pen may skid across the page or the pencil lead may break. The protective response has interrupted the carefully modulated output.

In some situations, discrimination may limit a protective response from sensory information that might typically be threatening. All of the sensory systems except one, the proprioceptive system, have the capacity to discriminate, which can override the protective reaction. Complying with social conventions is often the reason why discrimination overrides the protective function. For example, being served a meal that smells bad usually results in a protective reaction. The person may make a face and may even gag. However, if it is important not to insult the host, the person may make a conscious decision to override protection and graciously accept the meal.

Students with ASD have deficits in socialization, which interfere with learning social conventions. Therefore, their responses may be unduly influenced by protective reactions elicited by sensory information they receive so that their reactions are not modified based on social expectations. In addition, for sensory information to be useful and modulated output to occur, the central nervous system must be working correctly and in an integrated fashion. Since the neurology of students with ASD has been identified as different (see Chapter 2), and social conventions have little impact, it should come as no surprise that this population would exhibit abnormal sensory stimuli responses.

Individuals vary in their need for sensory stimulation just as they vary in their responses to sensory stimuli based on biology, habituation, and physical and psychological states. Some people have lower thresholds for certain types of sensory stimuli than others. Indeed, certain sensory systems may be so sensitive that the central nervous system does not have time to integrate information from other sensory systems before a reaction occurs. For example, if a person is highly sensitive to touch, he will pull away when touched before looking to see who is touching him. In contrast, a person who has the benefit of good sensory integration and who is not overly sensitive to input from a single sensory receptor may look first to see who is touching him before making a decision whether or not to pull away.

SENSORY SYSTEMS AND BEHAVIOR

Each of the sensory systems has a primary source of input to register stimuli, which are then converted to electrochemical signals transmitted to the central nervous system via complex neural pathways for interpretation and use in multiple CNS locations (Lane, 2002). The seven sensory systems that provide information to the central nervous system are:

- Olfactory
- Gustatory
- Tactile
- Vestibular
- Proprioceptive
- Visual
- Auditory

Olfactory

The sense of smell, which is provided by the **olfactory system,** is most directly connected with arousal systems in the brain (Kimball, 1999). This is why "smelling salts" may be used with people who have become unconscious. The pungent odor from the bitter salts registers with the olfactory system, and the protective component of that system stimulates a response that arouses the person. Responses to smells are related to unique combinations of biology and experience. Biologically, some individuals are very sensitive to odors while others are not. Through associations, experience teaches that some smells are pleasant and others unpleasant.

Many students with ASD appear to have low thresholds for odors (Dunn, Myles, & Orr, 2002; Kientz & Dunn, 1997) and react in ways that would indicate they find many smells offensive (Soussignan, Schaal, Schmit, & Nadel,

1995). Some individuals may decide whether or not to participate in an activity based on how surrounding items smell. For example, a student may smell a food before deciding to eat or a student may smell an object, such as paint, before deciding to engage in the activity. When odors are offensive, students with ASD may actively attempt to get away from them. A student may throw paint that smells bad and refuse to come near the activity. Teachers need to evaluate the olfactory sensitivities of students in order to minimize disruptive responses to smells. Teachers may need to abstain from wearing perfumes/colognes or lotions. Environments need to be analyzed to identify distressing odors so that they can be eliminated, or other strategies need to be developed to enable the student to participate in the environment. Familiar odors have been shown to have a calming effect on typically developing newborns (Rattaz, Goubet, & Bullinger, 2005), and it is possible that preferred smells may be useful in creating a positive environment for students with ASD.

Gustatory

The **gustatory system** involves the sense of taste, and the receptors for this system are on the tongue. Although not as evocative as smell, the sense of taste is directly connected to arousal systems. Like smell, the gustatory system is a combination of biology and learned experiences. People acquire a sense of taste based on what they are exposed to and may consider as noxious foods and drinks that others describe as delicious. The sense of taste is strongly influenced by the sense of smell; foods and drinks taste different if they cannot be smelled. Taste comprises sensations of sweet, salty, bitter, sour, and spicy.

Children with ASD have been noted to have unusual responses to taste and smell (Rogers, Hepburn, & Wehner, 2003) that can lead to strong food preferences. This can result in the individual being described as a "picky eater," a condition that may have serious consequences for the person's health. Individuals with ASD may consume a limited variety of foods and refuse to eat anything new (Ahearn, 2003; Levin & Carr, 2001). Consumption of liquids can also be problematic for individuals with ASD (Hagopian, Farrell, & Amari, 1996; Luiselli, Ricciardi, & Gilligan, 2005). Oral medications, toothpaste, mouthwash, and products like envelopes that must be licked also have a taste. If the gustatory experience is offensive, the individual engages in behaviors to avoid it (Hoch, Babbitt, Coe, Krell, & Hackbert, 1994; Riordan, Iwata, Wohl, & Finney, 1980), and if it is pleasurable, she will seek out opportunities for engagement. The compulsive eating of nonedibles (**pica**) results from neurological differences and may involve gustatory feedback that is pleasurable (Hagopian & Adelinis, 2001; Hirsh & Myles, 1996; Piazza et al., 1998).

Tactile

The **tactile system,** also referred to as the sense of touch, discriminates between where the body ends and the rest of the world begins. Skin registers incoming tactile stimulation; however, different parts of the body have different densities of tactile receptors. Fingertips, palms, and the area around the mouth have a highly dense concentration of receptors and so are more sensitive, whereas the abdomen and back have a large field of relatively few receptors and so are less sensitive (Lane, 2002). Touch is the first sensory system to function in utero, and most infants are receptive to touch for calming and developing attachments to caregivers (Montagu, 1978). Some premature infants experience greater weight gain, fewer days in the hospital, and better developmental outcomes when they are given tactile stimulation (i.e., touched, massaged) as compared to matched controls (Schanberg & Field, 1988). Sensory information provided through touch accumulates across time, with the need for resting periods when and if the accumulated information becomes overwhelming. The tactile system allows people to find and identify items they cannot see, such as locating a light switch in a dark room. The tactile system also allows people to notice when a bug is crawling on them or when something is hot. At these times, the protective mechanism of the tactile system causes the individual to brush off the bug or move away from the heat.

Students with high thresholds of tactile recognition may not react to the sensation and may not notice if a bug is crawling on their skin, or may engage in sensory-generating behaviors like running the palm of their hand along a wooden fence. Individuals who are underreactive to tactile input may not notice when clothing is too tight, may demonstrate difficulty manipulating objects, and may touch things constantly (Arkwright, 1998). In contrast, individuals with low thresholds of tactile recognition may be overly sensitive to the feel of things, such as another person's touch or the texture of clothing on the body or tags in the back of a shirt. Those with low thresholds for tactile stimulation may be described as having **tactile defensiveness** (Ayres, 1979). They may avoid activities that require the input of tactile stimulation, like finger painting, writing, and getting dirty. Tactile defensiveness can cause individuals to avoid being in situations where others might accidentally touch them. It may also be involved in the reluctance to eat certain foods, because the individual wants to avoid the way certain foods feel in the mouth.

Vestibular

The **vestibular system** is instrumental in helping people maintain appropriate posture and a stable visual field in order to regulate current activities and guide completion of future tasks (Brooks, 1986). The vestibular system is sensitive to gravity, direction, and movement. Approximately 60% of all human activity requires vestibular input. The primary receptors for the vestibular system are located in the inner ear. Inner ear infections and disorders of the structures in the inner ear can lead to problems with balance, coordination, and movement. Individuals with a low threshold for vestibular stimulation may get carsick easily, have difficulty changing speed or direction of movement, may appear scared to jump or roll, and may lean on people or objects for support. Those who have a low threshold and are very sensitive to vestibular stimulation are referred to as being "gravitationally insecure" (Ayres, 1979) and may resist activities that involve moving the head, may appear disoriented after moving, and may demonstrate poor endurance.

Individuals who have high thresholds for vestibular stimulation may engage in activities to increase vestibular feedback such as rocking, swinging, spinning, and head weaving. These individuals do not appear to become dizzy even after extended periods of movement. These same underresponsive individuals may have difficulty tracking a moving object, engaging in activities that involve using both sides of the body, and copying from the board. In addition, they may not try to catch themselves when falling and may appear to be very clumsy.

Proprioceptive

The **proprioceptive system** allows one to sense direction and velocity of movement, and determine the amount of effort needed to grasp and lift objects (Zigmond, Bloom, Landic, Roberts, & Squire, 1999). The primary receptors for proprioceptive feedback are the muscle spindles, the degree of skin tautness, tendons, and the internal sense of effort (conscious sense of awareness that proprioception is occurring) (Schmidt, 1999). An example of the sense of effort is when a person carries something heavy that seems to get heavier the longer it is carried. Obviously, the object does not actually get heavier, but the internal sense of effort related to fatigue in the muscles makes it seem as if more effort is required to continue carrying the object. Joints also serve as receptors for the proprioceptive system at extremes of range in order to protect against overextension and overflexion (Lane, 2002).

The proprioceptive system also modulates the appropriate amount of tension in the body and works with the vestibular system to accomplish movements such as walking, sitting, holding, dressing, writing, chewing, and so forth. It is the proprioceptive system that allows people to do things without looking. Most activities that involve the use of hands are based on proprioceptive input. The most sensitive of the proprioceptive receptors is the temporal mandibular joint (TMJ), located at the hinge of the jaw, which is activated when biting or chewing. Chewing and biting provide increased proprioceptive feedback, as does walking on tiptoe.

Individuals with proprioceptive difficulties may demonstrate both fine and gross motor problems. They may have poor posture, bump into things, have to look at what is being done in order to accomplish the task, get confused when looking in mirrors, and have difficulty getting into or out of chairs, climbing stairs, or navigating climbing equipment. The proprioceptive system is refined as a result of an individual's active movement (Lane, 2002), allowing for the development of body scheme and the ability to plan movement (Kingsley, 2000). Unfortunately, passive joint compression may be less effective for providing proprioceptive stimulation (Kalaska, 1988).

Vision

For most people, vision is the sensory system that is the most relied upon for functioning (Lane, 2002). Structures within the eyes are the receptors for the **visual system,** which is used to learn about objects, maintain posture, and provide information about position in space, including the distance from others or between objects (Fox, 1999). Vision is used to verify all other sensory input. When people hear noises, they use vision to identify what made the noise. When something touches the skin, people use vision to identify what made contact.

As with most of the other sensory systems, the visual system has protective and discriminatory capacities (Lane, 2002). An example of where the protective feature of the visual system overrides the discrimination feature is when watching a 3-D movie. Although people cognitively know that a movie projected on a two-dimensional plane cannot come toward them, they may pull back or duck when it appears that a character is reaching out during a 3-D film.

Some individuals with low visual thresholds are highly sensitive to visual stimuli. Fluorescent lighting can be irritating (Colman, Frankel, Ritvo, & Freeman, 1976), as can visual clutter. Individuals with low thresholds may squint or close their eyes to reduce the amount of visual stimulation they receive. Students with ASD may prefer to use their peripheral vision, thereby self-regulating some visual stimuli (Dawson & Lewy, 1989). In contrast, individuals with high thresholds for visual input may seek out stimulation by staring at bright lights and watching objects that move.

Unusual use of the visual system in terms of eye gaze is a commonly reported feature in ASD. Some parents report that their infants and young children have an "empty gaze" (Landry & Bryson, 2004) and seem to look through them rather than at them. The tendency to use peripheral vision and look at objects sideways may be related to differences in the neurological system (Palermo & Curatolo, 2004), with some neurons being more responsive to angle of gaze (Perrett et al., 1985). Developmental level is correlated with eye contact; as children mature, they tend to make more eye contact (Mundy, Sigman, & Kasari, 1994), although eye gaze may continue to be unusual.

Eye gaze differences persist throughout life. Individuals with ASD tend to avoid looking at eyes and instead focus on the mouth or other body parts of another person (Klin, Jones, Schultz, Volkmar, & Cohen, 2002b) or on objects in the room (Klin, Jones, Schultz, Volkmar, & Cohen, 2002a). These researchers have used eye-tracking technology to determine where individuals with ASD direct their gaze. The technology substantiates that eye gaze is not used to look at others' eyes or shift back and forth between people who are interacting. Individuals with ASD tend to focus on the physical features of the setting (e.g., light switch, lamp) and fail to attend to the social features. Although most individuals with ASD are described as having strengths in visual processing (Brian, Tipper, Weaver, & Bryson, 2003), because the visual focus is not directed at others' eyes, it is therefore not necessarily adaptive for social interactions. Instead, individuals with ASD tend to focus on physical details of the materials or environment (Bayliss & Tipper, 2005), which usually are irrelevant in terms of interactive functioning (Rosenblatt, Bloom, & Koegel, 1995). Structure and task demands have been found to influence the amount of eye contact made by individuals with ASD (Volkmar, Carter, Grossman, & Klin, 1997).

Auditory

The **auditory system** is the sense of hearing. The ears are receptors for auditory stimuli. Hearing enables people to screen out irrelevant stimuli and orient themselves to relevant environmental noise. Loud noises or uncomfortably pitched sounds elicit a protective response from the auditory system. Individuals with ASD demonstrate differences in responding to auditory stimuli (Hayes & Gordon, 1977; Rogers et al., 2003) that are present during the first year of life (Dawson, Osterling, Meltzoff, & Kuhl, 2000). They may show preferences for nonhuman noises over human voices (Klin, 1992a, 1992b) and have difficulty discriminating speech from background noise (Alcántara, Weisblatt, Moore, & Bolton, 2004). Although the results of their hearing tests may be normal, there appears to be a delay in the processing of sounds (Wong & Wong, 1991). Individuals with low thresholds for sound may react very negatively to noise, becoming agitated when noise reaches an uncomfortable level or when certain noises are made. For those who are very sensitive to sound, even relatively quiet noises can be disruptive. In contrast, some individuals may have high thresholds for sound and may appear to be oblivious to noise. These individuals may seek out noise and even create their own noise to keep the room from being too quiet.

BALANCING SENSORY INFORMATION

The seven sensory systems provide information to the central nervous system—information that is necessary to function and to live. The integration of sensory information creates physiologic responses that lead to goal-directed behavior. Certain sensory information leads to a state of arousal, which generates response. Other sensory information reduces arousal and reduces response. Optimal levels of arousal occur when a person achieves a balance between the arousing and the soothing sensory information (Dunn, 2001). For example, people who get sleepy while studying may eat or chew gum to generate a higher level of arousal. Eating and chewing combine tactile, proprioceptive, gustatory, and olfactory sensory systems and create an enhanced level of arousal. In contrast, when it is time to go to sleep, a person lies still and avoids any sensory information that would be alerting.

People strive to maintain an optimum level of arousal for the activity in which they are engaged. The optimum level of arousal may be difficult for some to achieve. For individuals with low thresholds for sensory stimulation, very little input is needed to arrive at an optimum level of arousal. If there is more stimulation than necessary, the individual tries to reduce the amount of information being received (Dunn, 1997). For example, if an individual is sensitive to noise and is in a situation where there is a great deal of noise, he may try to leave, cover his ears (Tang, Kennedy, Koppekin, & Caruso, 2002), or ask others to be quiet. In some instances, individuals who are very sensitive to sensory information may develop compensatory strategies to effectively shut out all sensory stimulation. They may appear to be underreactive to sensory stimulation because they are purposely ignoring it or focusing attention elsewhere.

Individuals with high thresholds for sensory stimulation need more input to achieve an optimal level of arousal (Dunn, 1997). These individuals are underreactive and engage in sensory-generating behaviors to increase the sensory information that affects the central nervous system. For example, a person who is underreactive to olfactory input will have to find things that smell very strong before the sensory information reaches his threshold of perception. Students who need more sensory input might chew on things, make noises, handle objects, touch things, and fidget.

Achieving an optimal level of arousal can be challenging for students with ASD. Sensory information is always present, and the central nervous system is under constant demand to register, integrate, and modulate the relevant stimulation. One method through which students with ASD may attempt to achieve an optimal level of arousal is the use of stereotypies.

STEREOTYPIC AND RITUALISTIC BEHAVIOR

Stereotypies are defined as repetitive motor or posturing behaviors that have no apparent functional effects on the environment (Baumeister & Forehand, 1973; Lewis & Baumeister, 1982). All infants engage in stereotypy (Schwartz, Gallagher, & Berkson, 1986), perhaps as a precursor to motor development (Thelen, 1981). Some children, because of neurological differences and developmental delays, continue to engage in stereotypies into adolescence and adulthood, particularly if they also experience inhibited movement and ambulation (Dura, Mulick, & Rasnake, 1987; Warren & Burns, 1970). For some individuals, the stereotypies become a source of pleasure and are then referred to as **self-stimulatory behaviors** (also called "stims" or "stimming"), which involve repetitive motor and/or vocal behavior that provides personal pleasure or intense sensory feedback (Berkson & Davenport, 1962; Jensema, 1980). Interestingly, infants between 9 and 12 months of age with developmental delays may demonstrate higher rates of self-stimulatory behavior than infants who are later diagnosed with ASD (Baranek, 1999). Stereotypies typically become more pronounced in children with ASD between 2 and 5 years of age (Lord, 1995; Losche, 1990).

Ritualistic behaviors include not only stereotypic and self-stimulatory behaviors but may also involve adherence to rigid routines, such as eating the same foods, lining up objects, and insisting on holding an object in each hand. Stereotypies are seen more often in students with ASD who have cognitive impairments, whereas ritualistic behaviors are more often seen in those with normal intelligence (Tsai, 1998).

In years past, stereotypic behavior was viewed as symptomatic of ASD and something to be eliminated (Guess, Helmstetter, Turnbull, & Knowlton, 1987). However, attempts to eliminate the stereotypic behavior sometimes resulted in the emergence of another undesirable behavior (Lovaas, 1981). It is now well recognized that stereotypies, self-stimulatory behaviors, and rituals serve important functions and should not be modified without first being analyzed to determine what they indicate about an individual's environment (Meyer & Evans, 1989). This idea evolved from the knowledge that stimulation is necessary for survival. Additionally, stereotypies and stims can result in an optimal level of arousal as well as a reduction in stress.

Biologic Need for Stimulation

Without stimulation, an organism cannot survive (Joseph, 1999). In early animal studies, when select sensory systems were deprived of stimulation, those sensory systems ceased to function. For example, using a nonhuman primate as well as kittens, researchers obscured vision in one eye soon after the animal was evaluated at birth to be sighted in both eyes. After a period of time, the eye was uncovered but, due to lack of stimulation, it was found that the eye, and even the optic nerve, had atrophied to the point where they no longer functioned (Hubel & Wiesel, 1963; Joseph & Casagrande, 1980; Wiesel & Hubel, 1963). Prolonged or severe sensory deprivation leads to impaired development (Cermak & Daunhauer, 1997). For this reason, it is recommended that infants born with congenital cataracts have them removed prior to 17 months of age (Robb, Mayer, & Moore, 1987); if the cataracts are not removed until 10 years of age, permanent impairment occurs (Kandel et al., 2000). Without adequate stimulation, the brain generates hallucinations and distortions of sensory stimuli (Solomon et al., 1961). Fortunately, most people receive vast amounts of stimulation from the world around them. However, in times of low or no stimulation, people may create their own stimuli through stereotypic and self-stimulatory behaviors. Indeed, stereotypic behaviors may be internally regulated (Guess & Carr, 1991a) and neurologically based (Lewis, Baumeister, & Mailman, 1987), setting the stage for neural and motor development in children (MacLean & Baumeister, 1981; Thelen, 1979). Stereotypies and self-stimulation can provide the required amount of stimulation for survival and optimal development, as well as increase arousal or reduce stress.

Increasing Arousal

If environments are not very stimulating, stereotypies may enhance arousal to an optimal level of alertness (Cataldo & Harris, 1982; Lourie, 1949; Repp,

Karsh, Deitz, & Singh, 1992). For example, people who become drowsy when they need to stay awake engage in stereotypies to increase their level of alertness and avoid falling asleep (Jason, 1977). They may doodle, twirl their hair, flip their foot, chew gum, drink coffee, and perform a variety of other innocuous activities so that they do not embarrass themselves, call attention to themselves, or put themselves in dangerous situations by falling asleep. However, students with ASD are not aware of social conventions that suggest it is rude to fall asleep when someone is speaking, nor do they tend to evaluate their behaviors to choose those that are socially acceptable, such as doodling and foot flipping. In addition, if the sensory information received from the environment is not stimulating, individuals may engage in behaviors that are stimulating and personally satisfying (Guess, 1966; Lovaas, Newsom, & Hickman, 1987). To elevate arousal to the optimal level, individuals with ASD may flap their hands, rock back and forth, or twirl straw wrappers. Making the environment more stimulating has been shown to decrease the level of stereotypies (Brusca, Nieminen, Carter, & Repp, 1989), and modifying the feedback received from self-stimulatory behavior has been demonstrated to have an effect on the level of stereotypy (Rincover, 1978). In these cases, the stereotypies and stims elevate arousal to an optimal level, creating the desired balance (Leuba, 1955).

Reducing Stress

Stereotypies may also occur when the optimal level of arousal is disrupted because the environment is too stimulating or the individual is stressed or overaroused (Howlin, 1998; Zentall & Zentall, 1983). When the body becomes stressed, the central nervous system perceives this to be undesirable. Stereotypies may filter or block the excessive stimulation (Hutt & Hutt, 1965). Stereotypies are also thought to have a calming effect on the body by generating a physiologic reaction that helps decrease the level of stress present in the body (Hirstein, Iversen, & Ramachandran, 2001) and reduces processing demands (Fentress, 1976). For example, when a neurotypical person is given bad news that provokes stress, she usually stands up and begins to pace, and may even rub her hands across the back of her neck. Or, as Rago and Case (1978) observed, college students experiencing stress related to giving a formal presentation may engage in a number of common stereotypies such as leg rocking, finger play, foot rocking, and hair twirling, as well as some idiosyncratic ones, in order to calm themselves.

The central nervous system prompts vestibular, proprioceptive, and tactile activity to reduce the level of stress or overarousal. Activities that evoke the vestibular and proprioceptive systems together have the greatest reducing effect on the neuropeptides related to stress. Typical children around the age of two years often bite as a response to frustration, because Temporo-Mandibular Joint TMJ, one of the most sensitive of the proprioceptive receptors, is activated by biting and subsequently reduces the neuropeptides related to stress. Students with ASD who become stressed or overaroused may be prompted by the central nervous system to attempt to reduce the stress by engaging in stereotypic behaviors, particularly those involving the proprioceptive and vestibular systems. Rocking, swinging, hand flapping, jumping, and so forth serve to reduce stress. Ritualistic behaviors may also reduce stress and restore a sense of optimal arousal. For these reasons, increased stress elicits an increase in stereotypies (Hutt & Hutt, 1970) and ritualistic behavior. Medications may also be used to calm individuals who are overly aroused (Repp et al., 1992).

Stereotypies and Stims to Control the Environment

In addition to the internal, biologically based emergence of stereotypies and the use of stereotypies, stims, and ritualistic behaviors to create a state of optimal arousal, stereotypies can be used to exert control over others in the environment (Guess & Carr, 1991a). For example, students who are asked to perform a task they do not want to do may engage in stereotypies to avoid doing the task (Baumeister, MacLean, Kelly, & Kasari, 1980). Stereotypies may also indicate that the individual feels crowded (Barton & Repp, 1981) or wants to avoid interacting with certain people (Repp, Barton, & Gottlieb, 1983). Stereotypies may evolve into **self-injurious behaviors** (SIBs) that threaten or cause personal harm (e.g., hitting oneself in the face, banging the head, biting one's own arm). SIBs may represent extreme attempts to enhance or decrease levels of arousal or may serve a self-stimulatory function (Edelson, 1984). More commonly, however, SIBs are a reaction to environmental stimuli and are used to control others in the environment (Guess & Carr, 1991a). For these reasons, stereotypies and SIBs displayed to control the environment are described in terms of their communicative function and discussed in Chapter 7.

SUPPORTING SENSORY NEEDS

Students with ASD may have difficulty accurately recognizing, integrating, and processing sensory information. Because of differences in their neurological systems, students with ASD may engage in stereotypic behaviors that persist even as the person ages. They may continue to demonstrate stereotypies and stims to achieve optimal levels of arousal and pleasure (Fisher & Murray, 1991; Leuba, 1955).

The idea that stereotypies are adaptive provides insight on how students deal with experiences and gives information about their neurological and physiological functioning (Guess & Carr, 1991b), which has significant implications for intervention. For students who demonstrate stereotypies, stims, and ritualistic behavior, the teacher should conduct an environmental analysis to identify variables that may be exacerbating the behaviors and shape stereotypies and stims so that the student's sensory needs are met in a more socially acceptable manner.

Environmental Analyses

The environments in which students with ASD are expected to function must be carefully scrutinized to identify olfactory, visual, tactile, and auditory stimuli that may be offensive and therefore distracting. Unless students are able to achieve an optimal state of arousal, they will not be available to participate in instruction. Students with low thresholds tend to become overaroused by sensory stimuli, whereas those with high thresholds may engage in behaviors to create optimal levels of sensory input. Students with low thresholds may attempt to shut out all stimuli to protect themselves from the sensory stimuli that are offensive. The optimal level of sensory input varies from student to student and is affected by psychological and physiological factors such as being frustrated or being tired. Although not standardized, Figure 5.1 contains a checklist that can provide a useful starting place for evaluating a student's reactions to sensory stimulation from the environment. As noted, the checklist has not been validated as an assessment instrument but does provide a framework for considering sensory stimuli that may be influencing behavior.

Environmental analyses should lead to changes in the environment to reduce the circumstances that elicit stereotypies (Guess & Carr, 1991a). Additionally, it is important to note that an individual student's reaction to sensory information may change throughout the day depending on emotional states and task demands. However, a good understanding of the student's thresholds for sensory stimuli provides an excellent starting point for evaluating the environment when reactive, resistant, and stereotypic behaviors occur. For example, some individuals are so sensitive to tactile stimulation that the seams found on most socks are very irritating. Products that mitigate annoyances, such as seamless socks and headphones that block out noise, are available (cf. *www.sensorycomfort.com*). The Hanes Corporation has made many individuals with and without ASD more comfortable by imprinting labels for T-shirts directly on the material. Table 5.1 provides suggestions for modifying the environment to better support the sensory needs of individual students, while maintaining an environment conducive to learning for all students.

Sensory accommodations are based on an analysis of the student's reactions to sensory stimuli in the environment. Teachers should note whether students are bothered by particular smells, sights, noises, or movements. Most often, fairly simple accommodations are sufficient for modifying the environment so that sensory issues do not interfere with learning. Many of these modifications were discussed in the descriptions of the sensory systems and in Table 5.1. It may be a challenge to recognize when a student's functioning is affected by sensory stimuli. Rarely will students inform the teacher that sensory stimuli are offensive. Rather, they will express their discomfort or aversion through behaviors such as withdrawing and acting out. Unexpected sensory stimuli may be problematic, such as the sound of certain people's voices or the smell of particular cleaning products.

Impact of Sensory Input on Student Behavior & Performance

Name: _____ Age: _____ Date: _____

Completed by: _____

*The following student behavior **may** indicate a problem using sensory and motor input for successful school performance. Check those behaviors you frequently observe.*

Sensory Channel	Observed Behaviors	
	Over-responsive ⇦ ⇨ (Needs ⇩ input)	Under-responsive (Needs ⇧ input)
Hearing *Uses sounds or speech (loudness, frequency, rhythm, pitch) to respond to environment & personal requests*	☐ Upset with fire drills, class bells, sudden noises; may cover ears or become agitated ☐ Distracted by other sounds in classroom or outside (talking, heater, light fixtures, ambulance) ☐ Can't read silently unless it is quiet	☐ Oblivious to loud or sudden sounds; can't locate source of sound ☐ Doesn't respond when name called or understand teacher's directions ☐ May talk to self or make sounds with mouth, hands, or feet
Visual *Responds to color, shape size, contrast, and intensity of surroundings as well as two-dimensional space (paper & books)*	☐ Likes to read in dim light (in corners of room or under tables/desks); sharp contrasts in light are unpleasant; likes to wear sunglasses inside ☐ Distracted by sights, especially movement of others; can't focus on one part of bulletin board, blackboard, or paper	☐ Can't find materials & supplies on shelf, desk, drawer, closet ☐ Doesn't notice detail (colors, shapes) of pictures and objects; stories, speech, drawing may lack descriptors
Taste & smell *Uses scents and taste to respond to environment*	☐ Rigid about what to eat; doesn't like to try new foods; eats same lunch every day ☐ Finds many scents offensive particularly in lunchroom and science experiments	☐ Craves sharp tastes (acid, sweet) and pungent scents (vanilla, vinegar, cinnamon); says all food tastes the same ☐ Explores environment by smelling everything

FIGURE 5.1
Impact of Sensory Input on Student Behavior and Performance

Note: The checklist has not been validated as an assessment tool but may be useful for considering students' reactions to environmental stimuli.

Source: Used with permission. © Barbara Hanft, MA, OTR, FAOTA, Silver Spring, MD 20910.

Sensory Channel	Observed Behaviors	
	Over-responsive ⇦ ⇨ (Needs ⬇ input)	Under-responsive (Needs ⬆ input)
Touch, pressure, and temperature *Uses sensory info to identify texture, shape, & density of objects especially with hands and mouth; responds to environmental demands and personal requests*	☐ Overreacts to tap on shoulder, or light touch by rubbing skin, pushing person away; fidgets in groups or in line (may fight) ☐ Doesn't like water/sand play, sitting/walking in grass; avoids glue, paint, chalk, or tape on skin ☐ Covers skin with clothes (always wears hat) or wears few clothes, even in cold or heat; choosy about fabric ☐ Dislikes eating certain texture food; wants food same temperature	☐ Touches people & objects constantly; not sure where body was touched (needs heavy tap to localize) ☐ Twirls/mouths hair, bites nails, pencils, erasers, shirt cuffs ☐ Clothes in disarray (shirt out or misbuttoned, pants falling down); unaware of room temperature ☐ Unaware food is on mouth when eating; may not register pain or bruises; drops carried objects and doesn't know it
Movement and body position *Enjoys PE and recess; knows where body is in space, direction of movement and speed change; assumes and changes body position appropriate for activity*	☐ Slow to initiate action and move; avoids movement; may get carsick on bus ☐ Misperceives/fearful of height; runs hand along wall; hangs on to banister or person on stairs; dislikes playground; easily overexcited during PE/recess ☐ Holds head stiffly; doesn't like to change position quickly (retrieves object on floor by kneeling with head up); dislikes tumbling, rolling, etc. ☐ Sits rigidly at desk; very tense overall; may break pencil from tight grip	☐ Craves fast movement, likes swings & merry-go-round; never gets dizzy ☐ Poor balance; falls easily; fatigues fast; may bump into objects/furniture in classroom; avoids running & fast-paced games; likes sedentary activities ☐ Constantly moving or fidgeting; can't sit still; likes to be upside down; may stamp feet or tap hands for additional input; presses pencil hard ☐ Slumps at desk; props self up with arms; may miss chair when sitting down

FIGURE 5.1

SHAPING BEHAVIOR

In addition to carefully analyzing the environment to make changes that are sensitive to the sensory needs of the students, teachers can develop programs to shape stereotypies and stims so that they become more socially acceptable and reinforce other adaptive behaviors. In doing so, teachers

TABLE 5.1
Suggestions for Environmental Modifications

	If Student Is Overaroused	If Student Is Underaroused
Visual	Reduce number of room decorations, cover shelves with paper the same color as walls, use carrels around desk, sunshades, dim lights, allow student time to close eyes, wear cap to block amount of light, display board around desk with shield on top	Increase visual stimulation in room, use bright colors, high contrasts, pens that write in color, bright lights, flashlight beam directed to focus point, computer games, pinwheels, kaleidoscopes, wind-up and battery-operated figures, lava lamps, perpetual motion toys
Auditory	White noise or quiet music with steady beat, plastic utensils when eating, ear plugs, move away from noisy areas, turn off fluorescent lights	Headphones with music, auditory trainer/FM system, noisy activities, exaggerate voice tone and inflection, games that make noise
Olfactory	Avoid cologne/perfume, eat lunch in classroom, soothing smells in room or available to student, position away from trash cans, use unscented cleaning products	Strong smells available to student, scented lotions, strong air fresheners, scented lip balm, scented markers, peppermint or other strong-smelling candies
Gustatory	Tastes preferred by student incorporated into a variety of dishes	Strong flavorings added to food, hard candy
Tactile	Cut tags from clothing, avoid sudden touch, gloves, warm drinks	Access to variety of textures, koosh balls, slime, Playdough, sqeeze toys, vibrating pens and toys, finger painting, cold drinks
Proprioceptive	Slow stretches, deep pressure, tight clothing, body sock, weighted vest/lap snake, progressive muscle relaxation, carry heavy objects	Chewy foods, chewing gum, deep pressure, weighted vest/lap snake, tight clothing, body sock, carry heavy objects, running games, mini-trampoline, gymnastics, karate
Vestibular	Slow rocking or swinging, same direction	Fast rocking or swinging, scooter boards, Sit-n-Spin, upside down on gym equipment, change directions, tumbling

must first examine the stereotypy from the student's perspective (Guess & Carr, 1991b). What type of feedback is being provided through the behavior? Teachers should try the stereotypy for themselves to analyze which sensory systems are being activated. Consider Ms. Harris's experience.

❖ LEARNING WITH MS. HARRIS: Ms. Harris Rubs Corduroy

Still thinking about her observations that morning, Ms. Harris wanders through the department store looking for some corduroy pants to purchase. She pauses in front of a rack and rubs her fingers across a pair of pants. "Well, it feels soft," she muses, "but I just don't get it." The next day, Ms. Harris decides to wear her new pants to school. She smiles as she puts them on, thinking how they will make her immediately popular with Craig.

Sitting in her car, she rubs the pants legs and notices the enhanced feeling of the corduroy now that she is wearing them. Her palms tingle a little as she rubs her hands across the ridges. She also enjoys the deep pressure on her thighs. She notices that she is feeling a little more relaxed and sits quietly at a stoplight, still sensing the tingling in her palms. She is startled when the car behind her honks for her to go. "I can see now why Craig likes to rub corduroy," thinks Ms. Harris. "I am going to have to meet with the OT to discuss alternatives for satisfying Craig's tactile-seeking behaviors."

Looking at the other cars at the next stoplight, Ms. Harris sees evidence of other sensory-based behaviors. One man is popping his finger on his lips, a woman is twisting her hair into little knots, and another man is picking his nose. "Perhaps rubbing corduroy isn't the worst of the options," she thinks as she drives away.

Once teachers identify the relevant sensory systems involved in a stereotypy, they can identify alternatives for accomplishing the same feedback through activities that are considered more socially acceptable (Epstein, Taubman, & Lovaas, 1985; Smith & Van Houten, 1996). Students who enjoy visual stimulation can work at computers with graphics or watch a lava lamp. Students who like high levels of auditory stimulation can wear headphones to listen to music. Students who like the sensation provided by rolling small rocks between their fingers can be taught to position their hands behind their backs so that the behavior can occur unobtrusively.

One individual who engaged in rectal digging in order to smell her finger was provided with alternative scents to smell, initially every fifteen minutes, effectively replacing a behavior that was limiting her ability to participate in certain activities and environments (Smith, 1986). Alternative methods for accomplishing the desired sensory input can shape behaviors so that the students are less likely to be perceived as unusual by others (Lovaas, 2003). Teaching students the appropriate use of materials and toys can also provide alternatives for stereotypic behavior that appears unusual (Smith & Van Houten, 1996).

In addition to developing alternative means of acquiring sensory input, students can be taught that stereotypies and stims are available only at certain times and in certain places (Lovaas, 2003). This is what most people experience. Most people do not have the opportunity to engage in nonfunctional behaviors, like staring at the ocean surf or television, until they have completed other required tasks. Most students must finish homework before being allowed to play video games. Adults must work for a certain amount of time before being allowed a two-week break. Students with ASD can be taught that they may engage in stereotypies and stims as a reward for completing other requisite tasks (Hung, 1978). Stims then become the reinforcers for appropriate behavior (Lovaas, 1981). In essence, the students earn their stims. The use of self-stimulation as a reinforcer has been demonstrated to be effective for increasing participation in required tasks (Sugai & White, 1986) without resulting in increased levels of stims in other environments. Charlop-Christy and Haymes (1998) allowed children access to preferred stims such as map books, toothpaste caps, coffee swizzle sticks, and balloons as a consequence for task completion and noted that the level of stimming in other settings actually decreased for the majority of the children.

A CAUTIONARY NOTE

In 1972, an occupational therapist named Jean Ayres theorized the presence of a "neurological process that organizes sensation from one's own body and from the environment and makes it possible to use the body effectively within the environment" (p. 11), which she termed **sensory integration**. Since that time, the term "sensory integration" has evolved from describing a theoretical construct to describing an individual's functioning (e.g., "That child has good sensory integration") and describing activities that individuals experience as active or passive participants (e.g., "We're going to do some sensory integration with him"). The challenge is that neurological processes described by Ayres are not directly observable and must be inferred. Originally applied to students with learning disabilities, the neurological theory Ayres described has been criticized (Bundy & Murray, 2002). However, the conclusion that sensory experiences affect learning is widely accepted (Baranek, 2002).

The challenge in discussing sensory issues among individuals with autism is to differentiate between promoting environmental modifications and interpretations of behavior based on sensory differences and avoiding implied approval of the many unsubstantiated treatments associated with sensory integration theory (e.g., Sensory Integration Therapy, brushing, deep pressure), as well as those that address sensory systems and sensory functioning (e.g., Auditory Integration Training, Doman-Delacato). Decades of research employing various sensory integration techniques have led to the conclusion that sensory integration therapies are either not effective or no more effective than other types of interventions (Baranek, 2002; Bundy & Murray, 2002; Hoehn & Baumeister, 1994; Polatajko, Kaplan, & Wilson, 1992; Vargas & Camilli, 1999; Wilson, Kaplan, Fellowes, Gruchy, & Faris, 1992), although there is some suggestion that interventions based on sensory integration theory may be useful for young children who are overresponsive to sensory stimuli (Mulligan, 2002). Table 5.2 provides brief descriptions of various approaches to addressing sensory issues as well as a summary of empirical support.

The lack of empirical validation of sensory integration and sensory integration–based interventions left Kaplan, Polatajko, Wilson, and Faris (1993, p. 346) wondering "why so many therapists and the families of their clients are still so strongly devoted to sensory integration treatment [SIT]." Kaplan et al. (1993) suggested that sensory integration continues to be popular because of the relationships that are formed between therapists and children, a willingness to attribute changes to sensory-based interventions, and the comfort derived from a framework that attributes behavioral issues to neurological differences that are not under the parents' or children's control. Although

TABLE 5.2
Summary of Sensory Interventions

Sensory Interventions	Description	Empirical Support
Sensory Integration	Uses controlled sensory experiences to encourage child to respond with adaptive motor actions to integrate vestibular, proprioceptive, and tactile sensations. A child-centered and active approach, interventions focus on play (as opposed to cognitive behavioral strategies or repetitive drills) with experiences that become progressively more sophisticated. The hallmark is reliance on "suspended equipment."	Contradictory empirical support suggests that the interventions are either ineffective or equal in effectiveness to other interventions.
Sensory Integration–Based	Based on the foundations of Sensory Integration theory but does not incorporate suspended equipment, uses adult-directed and often passively applied experiences, and is more cognitively focused. Examples of interventions based on Sensory Integration theory include: perceptual motor training, sensory diet (systematically applied stimulation such as "brushing" and joint compression followed by specific set of activities), and the Alert program (providing cognitive strategies to enable the child to modulate arousal).	Insufficient body of well-designed, well-executed studies to support effectiveness.
Sensory Stimulation	Child is passively exposed to sensory stimulation based on the assumption that it will influence the nervous system. Examples include: deep pressure, massage, joint compression, Wilbarger Approach, Hug Machine, pressure garments, and weighted vests.	Small body of primarily anecdotal reports does not provide adequate methodological rigor to substantiate effects. Some preliminary studies using touch pressure with control groups suggest that younger children with hyperresponsive patterns may benefit more from the sensory stimulation than those who are underresponsive.
Auditory Therapies	Auditory Integration Training (AIT) uses devices that modulate and filter recorded messages and music in an attempt to remediate hypersensitivities and auditory processing. Some interventions use specialized equipment to facilitate sound through bone conduction. A number of variations exist including Porges and Samonas.	A number of well-controlled studies have resulted in the conclusion that there are no positive findings specific to AIT that maintain over time. In some studies, auditory therapies were associated with negative side effects.

(continued)

TABLE 5.2   (*continued*)

Sensory Interventions	Description	Empirical Support
Vision Therapies	Visual therapies include oculomotor exercise, ambient prism lenses, and colored filters (i.e., Irlen Lenses), which are intended to improve visual perception or processing.	Vision therapies have not been substantiated through independent experimental research.
Sensorimotor Handling Techniques	Sensorimotor handling techniques attempt to normalize movement and reprogram the central nervous system. They include Neurodevelopmental Therapy (NDT) and Doman-Delacato patterning techniques. Cranio-sacral therapy is similar to sensorimotor handling techniques in that it involves the physical manipulation of the head.	No empirical studies specific to individuals with autism have been reported in peer-reviewed journals.
Physical Exercise	Researchers have studied the effects of physical exercise on maladaptive and self-stimulatory behaviors, with the assumption that exercise would reduce stress.	A small number of well-designed studies have found some short-term benefit of physical exercise for children with autism. Although self-stimulatory behaviors temporarily decreased, no concomitant improvements in cognitive, motor, or social skills were noticed.

Source: Adapted from Baranek (2002); Bundy & Murray (2002); Mudford & Cullen (2005); Mulligan (2002); Parham & Mailloux (2000); and Simpson et al. (2005).

there is little evidence to support the effectiveness of sensory interventions, with the exception of Auditory Integration Training (AIT), no negative outcomes have been reported related to interventions using a sensory approach (Baranek, 2002), and anecdotal reports suggest that participants may find the sensory integration activities enjoyable (Dempsey & Foreman, 2001).

Occupational therapists receive training in identifying, understanding, and supporting sensory differences. Indeed, the term **sensory integrative dysfunction** (SID) has become part of their vernacular (Mulligan, 2002). The term refers to the presence of a variety of sensory-based problems such as those related to poor sensory discrimination, perception, modulation, processing, and motor planning (Parham & Mailloux, 2001). SID is not listed as a disorder in the *DMS-IV-TR,* but occupational therapists have developed assessments and informal observational measures for identifying this heterogeneous group of sensory-based disorders (Missiuna & Polatajko, 1995).

Clearly, the scientific legitimacy of sensory interventions has not been established (Kaplan et al., 1993; Mulligan, 2002). Indeed, the lack of empirical evidence for sensory integration therapies have led to the call for occupational therapists to return to the use of child-centered and playful interactions to accomplish desirable or necessary tasks within natural contexts (Bundy & Murray, 2002; Mathiowetz & Haugen, 1995). Occupational therapists are being encouraged to integrate sensory-based activities into classroom routines rather than using valuable instructional time to engage in a specialized intervention of questionable value (Baranek, 2002). Rather than assuming that sensorimotor changes are a sufficient outcome, the measure of a successful intervention should be enhanced engagement and functioning (Case-Smith, 1995; Coster, 1998). Supporting functional sensory adaptations in typical routines will ultimately prove more beneficial than providing isolated sensory stimulation (Parham & Mailloux, 2001).

CONCLUSION

Although interventions based on sensory integration theory as well as other sensory-based treatments have not been empirically validated as effective, individuals with ASD respond differently to sensory stimuli (Rogers et al., 2003). Volkmar, Cohen, and Paul (1986) reported that 81% of their participants with ASD failed to respond to sounds, 53% had heightened sensitivity to loud noises, 62% watched their hands or fingers move, and 52% engaged in arm flapping. Students with ASD have been noted to become overaroused in the presence of novel stimuli (Kootz, Marinelli, & Cohen, 1982), and lack of predictability can exacerbate difficulties modulating arousal (Dawson & Lewy, 1989). High tactile sensitivity can lead to defensive behaviors as the student tries to get away from the stimulation (Baranek et al., 1997). Sensory sensitivity can also lead to fear (Matson & Love, 1990) and behaviors associated with anxiety (Edelson, Edelson, Kerr, & Grandin, 1999; Muris, Steerneman, Merckelbach, Holdrinet, & Meesters, 1998).

Stereotypic and self-stimulatory behaviors may be useful for regulating sensory input (Koegel & Covert, 1972; Zentall & Zentall, 1983), and are demonstrated by everyone, not just those with ASD (Lovaas, et al., 1987; Rago & Case, 1978). Although stimming can interfere with learning (Koegel & Covert, 1972), suppression of such stereotypic behavior does not promote enhanced functioning. Stereotypic behaviors provide important feedback about the student's experiences in the environment and should be analyzed for their potential benefit in modulating arousal. After modifying the environment, teachers can evaluate stereotypic behaviors for their potential benefit and then can teach students socially acceptable alternatives for obtaining the same benefit. Students can also be taught the appropriate time and place to engage in stereotypic behavior, and stims can be used as powerful motivators. Awareness and identification of sensory reactions and behavior provides critical information for creating contexts conducive to attention, exploration, and learning (Dunn, 2001).

DISCUSSION QUESTIONS AND ACTIVITIES

1. Conduct an environmental analysis of a classroom. Identify elements that could be problematic for students who are overresponsive to olfactory, visual, and auditory stimuli. Discuss how you would modify the environment and implement strategies to accommodate those sensory issues.

2. Identify self-stimulatory behavior among your neurotypical peers. List five behaviors that increase arousal and five behaviors that reduce stress.

3. For each of the sensory systems, identify compensatory activities for the self-stimulatory behaviors demonstrated by students with ASD that would be appropriate at the preschool, elementary, middle school, and high school levels.

4. Observe a student with ASD and identify a self-stimulatory behavior that sets him/her apart from others. Determine all the possible sensory systems that might be involved in the stim and develop a program to shape the behavior so that it appears less unusual. Also describe how the stimming behavior could be used in interventions for skill acquisition.

5. Consider the seven sensory systems and develop environmental modifications for reducing stimulation for students who are overresponsive and increasing stimulation for students who are underresponsive (demonstrate sensory-generating behaviors). Create three strategies in each category for reducing sensory stimulation and three strategies in each category for increasing sensory stimulation that will help maintain an environment conducive to learning.

REFERENCES

Adrien, J. L., Lenoir, P., Martineau, J., Perrot, A., Haneury, L., Larmande, C., et al. (1993). Blind ratings of early symptoms of autism based upon family home movies. *Journal of the American Academy of Child and Adolescent Psychiatry, 33,* 617–626.

Ahearn, W. H. (2003). Using simultaneous presentation to increase vegetables consumption in a mildly selective child with autism. *Journal of Applied Behavior Analysis, 36,* 361–365.

Alcantara, J. I., Weisblatt, E. J. L., Moore, B. C. J., & Bolton, P. F. (2004). Speech-in-noise perception in high-functioning individuals with autism or Asperger's syndrome. *Journal of Child Psychology & Psychiatry, 45,* 1107–1114.

Arkwright, N. (1998). *An introduction to sensory integration.* San Antonio, TX: Therapy Skill Builders.

Ayres, A. J. (1979). *Sensory integration and the child.* Los Angeles: Western Psychological Services.

Baranek, G. T. (1999). Autism during infancy: A retrospective video analysis of sensory-motor and social behaviors at 9–12 months of age. *Journal of Autism and Developmental Disorders, 29,* 213–224.

Baranek, G. T. (2002). Efficacy of sensory and motor interventions for children with autism. *Journal of Autism and Developmental Disorders, 32,* 397–422.

Baranek, G. T., Foster, L. G., & Berkson, G. (1997). Tactile defensiveness and stereotyped behaviors. *American Journal of Occupational Therapy, 51,* 91–95.

Barton, L. E., & Repp, A. C. (1981). Naturalistic studies of institutionalized retarded persons: Relationship between stereotypic responding, secondary handicaps, and population density. *Journal of Mental Deficiency Research, 25,* 257–264.

Baumeister, A., & Forehand, R. (1973). Stereotyped acts. In N. R. Ellis (Ed.), *International review of research in mental retardation, 6,* 1–329.

Baumeister, A. A., MacLean, W. E., Kelly, J., & Kasari, C. (1980). Observational studies of retarded children with multiple stereotyped movements. *Journal of Abnormal Child Psychology, 8,* 501–521.

Bayliss, A. P., & Tipper, S. P. (2005). Gaze and arrow cueing of attention reveals individual differences along the autism spectrum as a function of target context. *British Journal of Psychology, 96,* 95–114.

Berkson, G., & Davenport, R. K., Jr. (1962). Stereotyped movements of mental defectives: Initial survey. *American Journal of Mental Deficiency, 66,* 849-852.

Brian, J. A., Tipper, S. P., Weaver, B., & Bryson, S. E. (2003). Inhibitory mechanisms in autism spectrum disorders: Typical selective inhibition of location versus facilitated perceptual processing. *Journal of Child Psychology and Psychiatry and Allied Disciplines, 44,* 552-56.

Brooks, V. B. (1986). How does the limbic system assist motor learning? A limbic comparator hypothesis. *Brain Behavior Evolution, 29,* 29-53.

Brusca, R. M., Nieminen, G. S., Carter, R., & Repp, A. C. (1989). The relationship of staff contact and activity to the stereotypy of children with multiple disabilities. *Journal of the Association for Persons with Severe Handicaps, 14,* 127-136.

Bundy, A. C., & Murray, E. A. (2002). Sensory integration: A. Jean Ayres' theory revisted. In A. C. Bundy, S. J. Lane, & E. A. Murray (Eds.), *Sensory integration: Theory and practice* (2nd ed., pp. 3-33). Philadelphia: F. A. Davis.

Case-Smith, J. (1995). The relationships among sensorimotor components, fine motor skills, and functional performance in preschool children. *American Journal of Occupational Therapy, 49,* 645-652.

Cataldo, M. F., & Harris, J. (1982). The biological basis for self-injury in the mentally retarded. *Analysis and Intervention in Developmental Disabilities, 2,* 21-39.

Cermak, S. A., & Daunhauer, L. A. (1997). Sensory processing in the postinstitutionalized child. *American Journal of Occupational Therapy, 51,* 500-507.

Charlop-Christy, M. H., & Haymes, L. K. (1998). Using objects of obsession as token reinforcers for children with autism. *Journal of Autism and Developmental Disorders, 28,* 189-198.

Colman, R. S., Frankel, R., Ritvo, E., & Freeman, B. J. (1976). The effects of fluorescent and incandescent illuminations upon repetitive behaviors in autistic children. *Journal of Autism and Childhood Schizophrenia, 6,* 157-162.

Coster, W. (1998). Occupation-centered assessment of children. *American Journal of Occupational Therapy, 52,* 337-344.

Dawson, G., & Lewy, A. (1989). Arousal, attention, and the socioemotional impairments of individuals with autism. In G. Dawson (Ed.), *Autism: Nature, diagnosis, and treatment* (pp. 49-74). New York: Guilford.

Dawson, G., Osterling, J., Meltzoff, A., & Kuhl, P. (2000). Case study of the development of an infant with autism from birth to 2 years of age. *Journal of Applied Developmental Psychology, 21,* 299-313.

Dempsey, I., & Foreman, P. (2001). A review of educational approaches for individuals with autism. *International Journal of Disability, Development and Education, 48,* 103-116.

Dunn, W. (1997). The impact of sensory processing abilities on the daily lives of young children and their families: A conceptual model. *Infants and Young Children, 9,* 23-35.

Dunn, W. (2001). The sensations of everyday life: Empirical, theoretical, and pragmatic considerations, 2001 Eleanor Clarke Slagle lecture. *American Journal of Occupational Therapy, 55,* 608-620.

Dunn, W., Myles, B. S., & Orr, S. (2002). Sensory processing issues associated with Asperger syndrome: A preliminary investigation. *The American Journal of Occupational Therapy, 56,* 97-102.

Dura, J. R., Mulick, J. A., & Rasnake, L. K. (1987). Prevalence of stereotypy among institutionalized nonambulatory profoundly mentally retarded people. *American Journal of Mental Deficiency, 91,* 548-549.

Edelson, S. M. (1984). Implications of sensory stimulation in self-destructive behavior. *American Journal of Mental Deficiency, 89,* 140-145.

Edelson, S. M., Edelson, M. G., Kerr, D. C. R., & Grandin, T. (1999). Behavioral and physiological effects of deep pressure on children with autism: A pilot study evaluating the efficacy of Grandin's Hug Machine. *American Journal of Occupational Therapy, 53,* 145-152.

Epstein, L. J., Taubman, M. T., & Lovaas, O. I. (1985). Changes in self-stimulatory behaviors with treatment. *Journal of Abnormal Child Psychology, 13,* 281-294.

Fentress, J. C. (1976). Dynamic boundaries of patterned behavior: Interaction and self-organization. In P. Bateson & R. Hinde (Eds.), *Growing points in ethology* (pp. 135-169). New York: Cambridge University Press.

Fisher, A., & Murray, E. (1991). Introduction to sensory integration theory. In A. Fisher, E. Murray, & A. Bondy (Eds.), *Sensory integration theory and practice* (pp. 3-27). Philadelphia: Davis.

Fox, C. R. (1999). Special senses 3: The visual system. In H. Cohen (Ed.), *Neuroscience for rehabilitation* (2nd ed., pp. 169-194). Philadelphia: Lippincott, Williams & Wilkins.

Freeman, W. J. (1991). The physiology of perception. *Scientific American, 264,* 78-85.

Grandin, T. (1996). Brief report: Response to National Institutes of Health Report. *Journal of Autism and Developmental Disabilities, 26,* 185-187.

Guess, D. (1966). The influence of visual and ambulation restriction on stereotyped behavior. *American Journal of Mental Deficiency, 70,* 542-547.

Guess, D., & Carr, E. (1991a). Emergence and maintenance of stereotypy and self-injury. *American Journal on Mental Retardation, 96,* 299-319.

Guess, D., & Carr, E. (1991b). Rejoinder to Lovaas and Smith, Mulick and Meinhold, and Baumeister. *American Journal on Mental Retardation, 96,* 335-344.

Guess, D., Helmstetter, E., Turnbull, H. R., & Knowlton, S. (1987). *Use of aversive procedures with persons who are disabled: An historical review and critical analysis.* Seattle, WA: Association for Persons with Severe Handicaps.

Hagopian, L. P., & Adelinis, J. D. (2001). Response blocking with and without redirection for the treatment of pica. *Journal of Applied Behavior Analysis, 34,* 527-530.

Hagopian, L. P., Farrell, D. A., & Amari, A. (1996). Treating total liquid refusal with backward chaining and fading. *Journal of Applied Behavior Analysis, 29,* 573-575.

Hayes, R. W., & Gordon, A. G. (1977). Auditory abnormalities in autistic children. *Lancet, 2,* 767.

Hirsch, N., & Myles, B. S. (1996). The use of a pica box in reducing pica behavior in a student with autism. *Focus on Autism and Other Developmental Disabilities, 11,* 222-225.

Hirstein, W., Iversen, P., & Ramachandran, V. S. (2001). Autonomic responses of autistic children to people and objects. *Proceedings of the Royal Society of London B, 268,* 1883-1888.

Hoch, T. A., Babbitt, R. L., Coe, D. A., Krell, D. M., & Hackbert, L. (1994). Contingency contacting: Combining positive reinforcement and escape extinction procedures to treat persistent food refusal. *Behavior Modification, 18,* 106-128.

Hoehn, T. P., & Baumeister, A. A. (1994). A critique of the application of sensory integration therapy to children with learning disabilities. *Journal of Learning Disabilities, 27,* 338-350.

Howlin, P. (1998). *Children with autism and Asperger syndrome: A guide for practitioners and careers.* Chichester, UK: Wiley.

Hubel, D. H., & Wiesel, T. N. (1963). Receptive fields of cells in striate cortex of very young, visually inexperienced kittens. *Journal of Neurophysiology, 26,* 994-1002.

Hung, D. W. (1978). Using self-stimulation as reinforcement for autistic children. *Journal of Autism and Childhood Schizophrenia, 8,* 355-366.

Hutt, C., & Hutt, S. J. (1965). Effects of environmental complexity upon stereotyped behaviors in children. *Animal Behavior, 13,* 1-4.

Hutt, C., & Hutt, S. J. (1970). Stereotypies and their relation to arousal: A study of autistic children. In S. J. Hutt & C. Hutt (Eds.), *Behavior studies in psychiatry* (pp. 175-204). New York: Pergamon Press.

Jason, L. A. (1977). Preventing accidents: A simple but effective approach toward maintaining driving wakefulness. *Behavior Therapy, 8,* 498-499.

Jensema, C. K. (1980). The use of positive practice to reduce self-stimulatory behaviors. *American Annals of the Deaf, 125,* 524-526.

Joseph, R. (1999). Environmental influences on neural plasticity, the limbic system, emotional development, and attachment: A review. *Child Psychiatry and Human Development, 29,* 189-208.

Joseph, R. & Casagrande, V. A. (1980). Visual deficits and recovery following monocular lid closure in a prosimian primate. *Behavior and Brain Research, 1,* 165-186.

Kalaska, J. F. (1988). The representation of arm movements in postcentral and parietal cortex. *Canadian Journal of Physiology and Pharmacology, 66,* 455-463.

Kandel, E., Schwartz, J., & Jessell, T. (2000). *Principles of neural science.* New York: McGraw-Hill.

Kanner, L. (1943). Autistic disturbances of affective contact. *The Nervous Child, 2,* 217-250.

Kaplan, B. J., Polatajko, H. J., Wilson, B. N., & Faris, P. D. (1993). Reexamination of sensory integration treatment: A comparison of two efficacy studies. *Journal of Learning Disabilities, 26,* 342-347.

Kientz, M. A., & Dunn, W. (1997). A comparison of the performance of children with and without autism on the sensory profile. *The American Journal of Occupational Therapy, 51,* 530-537.

Kimball, J. G. (1999). Sensory integration frame of reference: Theoretical base, function/dysfunction continua, and guide to evaluation. In P. Kramer & J. Hinojosa (Eds.), *Frames of reference for pediatric occupational therapy* (pp. 119-168). Philadelphia: Lippincott, Williams & Wilkins.

Kinnealey, M., & Fuiek, M. (1999). The relationship between sensory defensiveness, anxiety, depression, and perception of pain in adults. *Occupational Therapy International, 6,* 195-206.

Kinnealey, M., Oliver, B., & Wilbarger, P. (1995). A phenomenological study of sensory defensiveness in adults. *American Journal of Occupational Therapy, 49,* 444-451.

Kingsley, R. E. (2000). *Concise text of neuroscience.* Philadelphia: Lippincott Williams & Wilkins.

Klin, A. (1992a). Listening preference in regard to speech: A possible characterization of the symptom of social withdrawal. *Journal of Autism and Developmental Disorders, 21,* 29-42.

Klin, A. (1992b). Listening preferences in regard to speech in four children with developmental disabilities. *Journal of Child Psychology & Psychiatry & Allied Disciplines, 33,* 763-769.

Klin, A., Jones, W., Schultz, R., Volkmar, F., & Cohen, D. (2002a). Defining and quantifying the social phenotype in autism. *The American Journal of Psychiatry, 159,* 895-908.

Klin, A., Jones, W., Schultz, R., Volkmar, F., & Cohen, D. (2002b). Visual fixation patterns during viewing of naturalistic social situations as predictors of social competence in individuals with autism. *Archives of General Psychiatry, 59,* 809-816.

Koegel, R. L., & Covert, A. (1972). The relationship of self-stimulation to learning in autistic children. *Journal of Applied Behavior Analysis, 5,* 381-387.

Kootz, J. P., Marinelli, B., & Cohen, D. J. (1981). Sensory receptor hypersensitivity in autistic children. *Archives of General Psychiatry, 38,* 271-273.

Kootz, J. P., Marinelli, B., & Cohen, D. J. (1982). Modulation of response to environmental stimulation in autistic children. *Journal of Autism and Developmental Disabilities, 12,* 185-193.

Landry, R., & Bryson, S. E. (2004). Impaired disengagement of attention in young children with autism. *Journal of Child Psychology and Psychiatry, 45,* 1115-1122.

Lane, S. J. (2002). Structure and function of the sensory systems (pp. 35-70) & Sensory modulation (pp. 101-122). In A. C. Bundy, S. J. Lane, & E. A. Murray (Eds.), *Sensory integration: Theory and practice* (2nd ed.). Philadelphia: F. A. Davis.

Leuba, C. (1955). Toward some integration of learning theories: The concept of optimal stimulation. *Psychological Reports, 1,* 27-32.

Levin, L., & Carr, E. G. (2001). Food selectivity and problem behavior in children with developmental disabilities: Analysis and intervention. *Behavior Modification, 25,* 443-470.

Lewis, M. H., & Baumeister, A. A. (1982). Stereotyped mannerisms in mentally retarded persons: Animal models and theoretical analyses. In N. R. Ellis (Ed.), *International Review of Research in Mental Retardation* (Vol. 11, pp. 123-161). New York: Academic Press.

Lewis, M. H., Baumeister, A. A., & Mailman, R. B. (1987). A neurobiological alternative to the perceptual reinforcement hypothesis of stereotyped behavior: A commentary on "Self-stimulatory behavior and perceptual reinforcement." *Journal of Applied Behavior Analysis, 20,* 253-258.

Lord, C. (1995). Follow-up of two-year-olds referred for possible autism. *Journal of Child Psychology and Psychiatry, 36,* 1365-1382.

Losche, G. (1990). Sensorimotor and action development in autistic children from infancy to early childhood. *Journal of Child Psychology and Psychiatry, 31,* 749-761.

Lourie, R. S. (1949). The role of rhythmic patterns in childhood. *American Journal of Psychiatry, 105,* 653-660.

Lovaas, O. I. (1981). *Teaching developmentally disabled children: The ME book.* Austin, TX: Pro-Ed.

Lovaas, O. I. (2003). *Teaching individuals with developmental delays: Basic intervention techniques.* Austin, TX: ProEd.

Lovaas, O. I., Newsom, C., & Hickman, C. (1987). Self-stimulatory behavior and perceptual reinforcement. *Journal of Applied Behavior Analysis, 20,* 45-68.

Luiselli, J. K., Ricciardi, J. N., & Gilligan, K. (2005). Liquid fading to establish milk consumption by a child with autism. *Behavioral Interventions, 20,* 155-163.

MacLean, W. E., & Baumeister, A. A. (1981). Effects of vestibular stimulation on motor development and stereotyped behavior of developmentally delayed children. *Journal of Abnormal Child Psychology, 10,* 229-245.

Mathiowetz, V., & Haugen, J. B. (1995). Evaluation of motor behavior: Traditional and contemporary views. In C. A. Trombly (Ed.), *Occupational therapy for physical dysfunction* (pp. 157-185). Baltimore: Williams & Wilkins.

Matson, J. L., & Love, S. R. (1990). A comparison of parents-reported fear for autistic and nonhandicapped age-matched children and youth. *Australia & New Zealand Journal of Developmental Disabilities, 16,* 349-357.

McIntosh, D., Miller, L. J., Shyu, V., & Hagerman, R. J. (1999). Sensory modulation disruption, electrodermal responses and functional behaviors. *Developmental Medicine and Child Neurology, 41,* 608-615.

Meyer, L., & Evans, I. (1989). *Nonaversive intervention for behavior problems: A manual for home and community.* Baltimore: Brookes.

Missiuna, C., & Polatajko, H. (1995). Developmental dyspraxia by any other name: Are they all just clumsy children? *American Journal of Occupational Therapy, 49,* 619-654.

Montagu, A. (1978). *Touching: The human significance of the skin.* New York: Harper and Row.

Mudford, O. C., & Cullen, C. (2005). Auditory integration training: A critical review. In J. W. Jacobson, R. M. Foxx, & J. A. Mulick (Eds.), *Controversial therapies for developmental disabilities: Fad, fashion and science in professional practice.* (pp. 351-362). Mahwah, NJ: Erlbaum.

Mulligan, S. (2002). Advances in sensory integration research. In A. C. Bundy, S. J. Lane, & E. A. Murray (Eds.), *Sensory integration: Theory and practice* (2nd ed., pp. 397-411). Philadelphia: F. A. Davis.

Mundy, P., Sigman, M., & Kasari, C. (1994). Joint attention, developmental level, and symptom presentation in autism. *Development and Psychopathology, 6,* 389-401.

Muris, P., Steerneman, P., Merckelbach, H., Holdrinet, I., & Meesters, C. (1998). Comorbid anxiety symptoms in children with pervasive developmental disorders. *Journal of Anxiety Disorders, 12,* 387-393.

Palermo, M. T., & Curatolo, P. (2004). Pharmacologic treatment of autism. *Journal of Child Neurology, 19,* 155-164.

Parham, L. D., & Mailloux, Z. (2001). Sensory integration. In J. Case-Smith (Ed.), *Occupational therapy for children* (pp. 329-381). St. Louis, MO: Mosby.

Perrett, D. I., Smith, P. A., Potter, D. D., Mistlin, A. J., Head, A. S., Milner, A. D., et al. (1985). Visual cells in temporal cortex sensitive to face view and gaze direction. *Proceedings of the Royal Society of London Basic Biological Sciences, 223,* 293-317.

Piazza, C. C., Fisher, W. W., Hanley, G. P., LeBlanc, L. A., Worsdell, A. S., Lindauer, S. E., et al. (1998). Treatment of pica through multiple analyses of its reinforcing functions. *Journal of Applied Behavior Analysis, 31,* 165-189.

Polatajko, H. J., Kaplan, B. J., & Wilson, B. N. (1992). Sensory integration treatment for children with learning disabilities: Its status 20 years later. *Occupational Therapy Journal of Research, 12,* 323-341.

Rago, W., & Case, J. (1978). Stereotyped behavior in special education teachers. *Exceptional Children, 44,* 342-344.

Rapin, I. (Ed.). (1996). Preschool children with inadequate communication: Developmental language disorder, autism, low IQ. *Clinics in Developmental Medicine, No. 139.* London: Mac Keith Press.

Rattaz, C., Goubet, N., & Bullinger, A. (2005). The calming effect of a familiar odor on full-term newborns. *Developmental and Behavioral Pediatrics, 26,* 86-92.

Repp, A. C., Barton, L. E., & Gottlieb, J. (1983). Naturalistic studies of institutionalized profoundly or severely mentally retarded persons: The relationship of density and behavior. *American Journal of Mental Deficiency, 87,* 441-447.

Repp, A. C., Karsh, K. G., Deitz, D. E. D., & Singh, N. N. (1992). A study of the homeostatic level of stereotypy and other motor movements of persons with mental handicaps.

Journal of Intellectual Disability Research, 36, 61-75.

Rincover, A. (1978). Sensory extinction: A procedure for eliminating self-stimulatory behavior in developmentally disabled children. *Journal of Abnormal Child Psychology, 6,* 299-310.

Riordan, M. M., Iwata, B. A., Wohl, M. K., & Finney, J. W. (1980). Behavioral treatment of food refusal and selectivity in developmentally disabled children. *Applied Research in Mental Retardation, 1,* 95-112.

Robb, R. M., Mayer, D. L., & Moore, B. D. (1987). Results of early treatment of unilateral congenital cataracts. *Journal of Pediatric Opthalmology and Strabismus, 24,* 178-181.

Rogers, S. J., Hepburn, S., & Wehner, E. (2003). Parent reports of sensory symptoms in toddlers with autism and those with other developmental disorders. *Journal of Autism and Developmental Disorders, 33,* 631-642.

Rosenblatt, J., Bloom, P., & Koegel, R. L. (1995). Overselective responding: Description, implications, and intervention. In R. L. Koegel & L. K. Koegel (Eds.), *Teaching children with autism: Strategies for initiating positive interactions and improving learning opportunities* (pp. 33-42). Baltimore: Brookes.

Schanberg, S. M., & Field, T. M. (1988). Sensory deprivation stress and suplemental stimulation in the rat pup and preterm human neonate. *Child Development, 58,* 1431-1447.

Schmidt, R. A. (1999). *Motor control and learning: A behavioral approach.* Champaign, IL: Human Kinetics.

Schwartz, S. S., Gallagher, R. J., & Berkson, G. (1986). Normal repetitive and abnormal stereotyped behavior of non-retarded infants and young mentally retarded children. *American Journal of Mental Deficiency, 90,* 625-630.

Simpson, R. L., de Boer-Ott, S. R., Griswold, D. E., Myles, B. S., Byrd, S. E., Ganz, J. B., et al. (2005). *Autism spectrum disorders: Interventions and treatments for children and youth.* Thousand Oaks, CA: Corwin Press.

Smith, M. D. (1986). Use of similar sensory stimuli in the community-based treatment of self-stimulatory behavior in an adult disabled by autism. *Journal of Behavior Therapy and Experimental Psychiatry, 17,* 121-125.

Smith, E. A., & Van Houten, R. (1996). A comparison of the characteristics of self-stimulatory behaviors in "normal" children and children with developmental delays. *Research in Developmental Disabilities, 17,* 253-268.

Solomon, P., Kubzansky, P. E., Leiderman, P. H., Mendelson, J. H., Trumball, R., & Wexler, D. (Eds.). (1961). *Sensory deprivation.* Cambridge: Harvard University Press.

Soussignan, R., Schaal, B., Schmit, G., & Nadel, J. (1995). Facial responsiveness to odours in normal and pervasively developmentally disordered children. *Chemical Senses, 20,* 47-59.

Sugai, G., & White, W. J. (1986). Effects of using object self-stimulation as a reinforcer on the prevocational work rates of an autistic child. *Journal of Autism and Developmental Disorders, 16,* 459-471.

Tang, J. C., Kennedy, C. H., Koppekin, A., & Caruso, M. (2002). Functional analysis of stereotypical ear covering in a child with autism. *Journal of Applied Behavior Analysis, 35,* 95-98.

Thelen, E. (1979). Rhythmical stereotypies in normal human infants. *Animal Behavior, 27,* 699-715.

Thelen, E. (1981). Kicking, rocking, and waving: Contextual analysis of rhythmical stereotypies in normal human infants. *Animal Behavior, 29,* 3-11.

Tsai, L. Y. (1998). Medical interventions for students with autism. In R. L. Simpson & B. S. Myles (Eds.), *Educating children and youth with autism: Strategies for effective practice* (pp. 277-314). Austin, TX: Pro-Ed.

Vargas, D. L., & Camilli, G. (1999). A meta-analysis of research on sensory integration treatment. *American Journal of Occupational Therapy, 53,* 189-198.

Volkmar, F. R., Carter, A., Grossman, J., & Klin, A. (1997). Social development in autism. In D. Cohen & F. Volkmar (Eds.), *Handbook of autism and pervasive developmental disorders* (2nd ed., pp. 173-194). New York: Wiley.

Volkmar, F. R., Cohen, D. J., & Paul, R. (1986). An evaluation of *DSM-III* criteria for infantile autism. *Journal of the American Academy of Child Psychiatry, 25,* 190-197.

Warren, S. A., & Burns, N. R. (1970). Crib confinement as a factor in repetitive and stereotyped behavior in retardates. *Mental Retardation, 8,* 25-28.

Wiesel, T. N., & Hubel, D. H. (1963). Single-cell responses in striate cortex of kittens deprived of vision in one eye. *Journal of Neurophysiology, 26,* 1003–1017.

Wilson, B. N., Kaplan, B. J., Fellowes, S., Gruchy, C., & Faris, P. (1992). The efficacy of sensory integration treatment compared to tutoring. *Physical and Occupational Therapy in Pediatrics, 12,* 1–36.

Wing, L. (1969). The handicaps of autistic children: A comparative study. *Journal of Child Psychology and Psychiatry, 10,* 1–40.

Wong, V., & Wong, S. N. (1991). Brainstem auditory evoked potential study in chil-dren with autistic disorder, *Journal of Autism and Developmental Disorders, 21,* 329–340.

Zentall, S. S., & Zentall, T. R. (1983). Optimal stimulation: A model of disordered activity and performance in normal and deviant children. *Psychological Bulletin, 94,* 446–471.

Zigmond, M. J., Bloom, F. E., Landic, S. C., Roberts, J. L., & Squire, L. R. (1999). *Fundamental neuroscience.* Boston: Academic Press.

Zuckerman, M. (1994). *Behavioral expressions and biosocial bases of sensation seeking.* New York: Cambridge University Press.

CHAPTER 6

Using Applied Behavior Analytic Instructional Strategies

KEY TERMS

Baseline Data	Intertrial Interval
Blocking	Massed Trials
Collective Trials	Prompts
Discriminative Stimulus	Prompt Dependency
Distributed Trials	Response Maintenance
Fading	Satiation
Generalization	Stimulus Generalization

❖ LEARNING WITH MS. HARRIS: Ms. Nelson Finds a Cure

Ms. Harris had just finished reviewing the day with her students. As they lined up at the door to leave, Andy's mom, Ms. Nelson, rushed into the room waving a piece of paper. "Ms. Harris! Look what I just printed from the Internet! It's about the cure for my son!" Ms. Harris greeted Andy's mother and scanned the paper, stifling a sigh. Which one of the many empty promises could it be? But she knew that if she were the parent of a child with ASD, she would be drawn to any treatment that offered hope.

The website did indeed promise a cure for ASD! This particular site lauded the virtues of "ABA." Only the creators of the website weren't using the term to refer to the principles of the science of applied behavior analysis. As in so many websites, books, and daily discussions, the term was being used to refer specifically to Discrete Trial Training (DTT). The paper documented links to curricula and techniques as well as contact information for specially trained people who could provide the miraculous intervention.

"Can you do ABA?" asked Andy's mother. "Oh, boy," Ms. Harris thought to herself. "I am using applied behavior analytic instruction every day with Andy. How do I explain to Ms. Nelson the difference between ABA and DTT?"

Arguments about the use of applied behavior analysis (ABA) for students with Autism Spectrum Disorders have consumed vast amounts of time, effort, and professional resources. Most of those arguments are not actually about ABA, but about whether or not an applied behavior analytic strategy called *Discrete Trial Training (DTT)* can enable children with ASD to achieve normal educational and intellectual functioning as described by Lovaas (1987). The effectiveness of interventions based on the science of ABA is supported by copious research, and these are considered by many to be the only scientifically validated approaches for students with ASD. However, these interventions encompass much more than just DTT.

This chapter describes and defines ABA and then explains DTT within ABA's broader context. It also covers the general approach for conducting DTT and provides examples of applied behavior analytic strategies shown to be effective with students on the autism spectrum.

APPLIED BEHAVIOR ANALYSIS DEFINED

ABA takes an empirical approach to promoting learning and development. Principles and procedures known to affect learning and skill acquisition are used to promote enhanced functioning in a measurable way. Many of these principles and procedures have been recognized by social scientists for centuries, but it was not until 1968 that a group of researchers applied the principles as defined by Skinner (1953) to socially significant human behavior and articulated the key dimensions of ABA.

In 1968, Baer, Wolf, and Risley, in the first issue of the *Journal of Applied Behavior Analysis*, described ABA as "the process of applying sometimes tentative principles of behavior to the improvement of specific behaviors, and simultaneously evaluating whether or not any changes noted are indeed attributable to the process of application—and if so, to what parts of the process" (p. 91). In this article and in a subsequent reanalysis in 1987, the authors defined the five dimensions that must be present in an intervention for it to be considered ABA. These dimensions are:

- Applied and effective
- Technological
- Behavioral
- Analytic and conceptual
- Generality

Applied and Effective

For any procedure to be considered ABA, it must make a meaningful difference in the life of the person receiving the intervention. This means that the goals of the intervention must be important to the individual and that any changes must result in a better quality of life (Wolf, 1978). The dimension of applied and effective is ascertained though an analysis of goals, procedures, and outcomes.

Goals. The goals of the intervention must be viewed as worthwhile by the individual receiving the treatment and by those making decisions about the quality of life for the person receiving the treatment. The goals should take into consideration what would lead to more independence for the individual as well as what meets societal norms for behavior.

For example, it would not be meaningful to create a goal for a kindergarten-aged student who is decoding on the third-grade level to decode on a fourth-grade level if that student is not toilet trained, does not initiate social interactions, and comprehends only on the preprimer level. According to the applied and effective dimension of ABA, goals for this student need to address areas of self-help, social initiations, and comprehension of written material. Such goals would promote the student's independence and emphasize behaviors that allow the student to access a broader range of environments.

In regard to goals, we ask: **Will the specific behavioral goals benefit the student, and are the goals valued by the community?**

Procedures. The procedures used in an intervention must be only as intrusive or invasive as the context warrants (Green, 2001). Applied behavior analysts would challenge the idea that the end justifies the means. For example, the teacher could stop students who are talking out by slapping them each time they open their mouths. However, others might not be in favor of such an aversive procedure (Durand, 2005). The use of reinforcement to shape students' behavior so that they raise their hands and wait to be acknowledged before speaking is more likely to be perceived as acceptable.

It must be noted that some individuals are subject to invasive procedures such as restraint or contingent electric shock. However, these situations are exceptions rather than the rule. The use of aversive procedures is appropriate only after all other options are exhausted and human protection clearances are obtained.

In addition to being ethical, the cost and practicality of procedures must be reasonable for the desired outcomes. In regard to procedures, we ask: **Are the procedures as minimally invasive as possible, and would other people consider them acceptable in terms of the outcome?**

Outcomes. Successful outcomes are those viewed as valuable by all involved and any unexpected negative outcomes are tolerable. For example, the use of some procedures that result in a student being able to touch body parts on command might also provoke an aggressive reaction. Identifying body parts may be a meaningful outcome for the student, but it is not acceptable that the student hits the person asking him to identify the body parts. So, while the intervention provided some benefit, it would be worthwhile to consider if there is an alternative that does not produce undesirable outcomes.

The most common way to document the acceptability of outcomes is to consider social validity (Wolf, 1978). Social validity measures the degree to which the student and/or those who interact with the student are satisfied with *all* the outcomes and procedures used in the intervention.

Some students are unable to verbally describe their satisfaction with the outcomes. However, analysis of their behavior can provide an indication of their satisfaction. Likewise, surveys of family members, teachers, therapists, peers, and others can provide indications of satisfaction with procedures and outcomes.

Sometimes interventions actually affect the persons providing the intervention more than the recipients. For example, interventions that take place over many hours, days, or weeks can seriously disrupt the lives of family members, as in the case of a parent who quits a job to provide an intervention. Although the intervention may produce some desirable outcomes, the cost to the family may not be worth the effort, especially if there are other ways to accomplish similar goals.

In regard to outcomes, the question is: **Are *all* the outcomes and procedures acceptable in improving the quality of life for everyone involved?**

Although many published research studies meet the dimension of applied and effective for individuals with ASD, citing a few across several decades provides examples of the breadth of the meaningful differences that have been targeted. These include increased engagement and social interactions (Garfinkle & Schwartz, 2002; Kamps et al., 1992; Krantz & McClannahan, 1998; Massey & Wheeler, 2000; Pierce & Schreibman, 1997; Reinhartsen, Garfinkle & Wolery, 2002), learning new skills such as self-help, communication, and socialization (Brady, Shores, McEvoy, Ellis, & Fox, 1987; Matson, Taras, Sevin, Love, & Fridley, 1990; Ross & Greer, 2003; Yoder & Layton, 1988), maintaining appropriate levels of behavior through self-control and self-monitoring (Shearer, 1996; Strain, Kohler, Storey, & Danko, 1994), generalizing skills learned (Koegel, Camarata, Valdez-Menchaca, & Koegel, 1998; O'Neill & Sweetland-Baker, 2001; Ross & Greer, 2003), reducing the number of environments in which challenging behavior occurs (Carr, Dozier, Patel, Adams, & Martin, 2002), and decreasing interfering behaviors such as self-injurious behaviors, stereotypies, aggression, tantrums, pica, grabbing, spitting, inappropriate touching, and destroying property (Carr & Durand, 1985; Wacker et al., 1990).

Technological

To be considered ABA, interventions need to use technologies (strategies) that have been shown to be effective for learning and behavior change in all animals, including humans. The learning principles that underlie most of these technologies are centuries old and date back to times when the principles were used intuitively. Today, of course, they are defined and studied.

For example, it is reported that ancient Romans put eels in the bottom of wine cups to discourage excessive drinking, and monks in A.D. 610 gave out little dough scraps baked in the shape of praying hands (pretzels) to encourage children to learn their prayers (Alberto & Troutman, 2003). Most technologies used in applied behavior analytic approaches derive from operant learning theory, which has verified that behavior is occasioned by what occurs before the behavior (antecedent) and is influenced by what follows the behavior (consequence) (Skinner, 1953). It would take volumes to define and describe all of the validated technologies, so instead three procedures will be described as they relate to learning: reinforcement, prompting, and discrete trials.

Reinforcement. Operant learning theorists define *reinforcement* as anything that follows a behavior that maintains or increases the occurrence of the behavior. As such, there are no universal reinforcers. For some students, praise for completing a task increases or maintains task completion. For other students, praise does neither, but instead reduces the number of tasks completed. In that case, praise is not reinforcing; it is punishing.

One of the great behavioral challenges is the recognition that reinforcement is not a "thing" but an effect. For example, if cheese crackers are used to increase the number of times a student will sit down when directed to do so by the teacher, and the number of times the student sits down increases, then cheese crackers are reinforcing. If the number of times the student sits down decreases, then cheese crackers are not reinforcing. People who make statements such as, "In-seat behavior is not increasing even though I'm reinforcing the student with cheese crackers" do not really understand the technology of reinforcement.

For students with ASD, it is documented that sensory activities and access to objects of obsession may be as effective as food or praise (Charlop-Christy & Haymes, 1998; Ferrari & Harris, 1981) and may even produce higher numbers of correct responses than other types of reinforcement (Rincover & Newsom, 1985). Indeed, the opportunity to engage in self-stimulatory behaviors can serve to increase acceptable behaviors (making it a reinforcement; Hung, 1978), without increasing the number of self-stimulatory behaviors in other contexts (Charlop-Christy & Haymes, 1998; Wolery, Kirk, & Gast, 1985). Even when the reinforcer is delivered less frequently, individuals with autism continue to use the skills that were learned (Dunlap, Marshall, Plienis, & Williams, 1987).

Prompting. **Prompts** are additional supports that increase the likelihood that a behavioral response is learned. For example, when teaching young children to write their names, adults sometimes put their hands over the children's hands to guide them through the movements. This hand-over-hand guidance is a prompt.

ABA technology uses various types of prompts and includes several ways of implementing them. For students with ASD, some of these are tactile prompts (i.e., a pager-like device that vibrates) that help increase verbal initiations (Shabani et al., 2002; Taylor & Levin, 1998), picture prompts to increase ability to follow routines (Hall, McClannahan, & Krantz, 1995), written and audiotaped scripts that help promote more elaborate verbalizations (Krantz & McClannahan, 1998; Stevenson, Krantz, & McClannahan, 2000), video modeling that helps teach conversation skills (Charlop & Milstein, 1989) as well as purchasing (Haring, Kennedy, Adams, & Pitts-Conway, 1987), and self-operated auditory prompts that help increase academic and vocational on-task behaviors (Tabor, Seltzer, Heflin, & Alberto, 1999).

Prompts can increase the rate and accuracy of learning skills, but they may also cause dependency (i.e., the student waits for the prompt before engaging in the behavior). For this reason, the technology includes specific suggestions for fading prompts.

Discrete Trials. A trial is the basic unit of instruction. It presents a structured opportunity for a student to respond in the presence of a particular antecedent and consequence (Heflin & Alberto, 2001). Discrete Trial Training (DTT) is covered more thoroughly later in this chapter, but it is important to highlight that the discrete trial is just one of a number of technologies used in ABA.

Behavioral

This dimension takes a functional view of behavior, asserting that behavior always occurs for a reason, and the reason is directly related to the environments where the behavior occurs. Understanding the influence of context on behavior often leads to developing interventions that include changes in the environment (Dunlap, Kern, & Worcester, 2001) and an appreciation of the function(s) the behavior serves (Johnston & O'Neill, 2001).

Everyone behaves in ways that maximize gain and pleasure and minimize loss and pain. The desire to experience certain consequences and avoid other consequences is directly related to the environmental context. For example, students study and complete assignments in order to get good grades and avoid failing. Similarly, people brush their teeth to preserve them and avoid getting cavities.

Identifying what students want or do not want in a specific context is crucial to developing effective interventions. To do so involves conducting a functional behavior assessment (FBA), described in more detail in Chapter 7.

Analytic and Conceptual

This dimension of ABA regards accountability and being able to demonstrate that the interventions used are responsible for the learning of new skills and other changes in behavior. To link student outcomes to instruction and

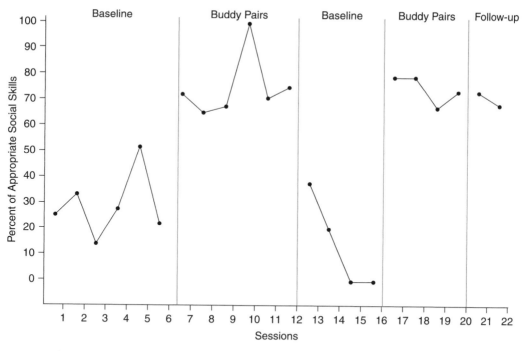

FIGURE 6.1
ABAB Design

Source: Kluwer Academic Publishers, *Journal of Autism and Developmental Disorders, 30,* 2000, p. 189, Enhancing social skills of kindergarten children with autism through the training of multiple peers as tutors, K. M. Laushey & L. J. Heflin, Figure 1, © 2000. With kind permission of Springer Science and Business Media.

interventions requires collecting data on behaviors that are observable and measurable, and the data must be collected frequently enough to be useful in evaluating the instruction and interventions.

In ABA, the methodology used to analyze data for instructional decision making is typically presented in single-subject designs that allow conclusions to be drawn from the data. There are two types of single-subject designs. "Teaching designs" allow conclusions to be drawn about whether the measured behavior is changing. "Research designs" demonstrate that the changes in behavior occur as a result of the intervention (Kennedy, 2005). Figure 6.1 displays a research design graph.

Both teaching and research designs present **baseline data** first, which are data collected prior to an intervention (usually referred to as the A phase). During intervention, data continue to be collected and are recorded as the B phase. With two phases, a teaching design called the *AB design* is being used.

An example of using an AB design is with a student who is initiating few interactions with his peers. The teacher targets a time when initiations could occur, such as at lunch, and collects baseline data to verify that the number of initiations is low. On Monday during lunch the student made 0 initiations; on Tuesday, 1 initiation; on Wednesday, 0 initiations; on Thursday, 0 initiations; and on Friday, 2 initiations. Given that other students in the same class initiate interactions an average of 12 times during lunch, the teacher decides to implement an intervention to increase the number of student initiations.

As the teacher continues to collect and graph data on the behavior during the intervention, the data show an increase in the number of initiations. Although it is impossible to conclude that the behavior is changing because of the intervention (which is why this is a teaching design), it is possible to document a behavioral change. If the number of initiations increases slightly but is still below the average number for the peers, the teacher may change something about the intervention to see if the number of initiations can be increased further. At this point, the AB design becomes an ABC design because there are two interventions: the first one (B) and the second one (C).

A visual inspection of graphs from teaching designs may confirm that there is behavioral change, but the design used cannot guarantee that the change occurred because of the intervention. A research design must be used to demonstrate that the behavior changed because of the intervention. There are several to choose from, including the ABAB (withdrawal) design that was shown in Figure 6.1.

In the ABAB design, if the intervention results in the desired behavior change after the first AB, the intervention is withdrawn to see if the behavior returns to baseline levels (second A). If so, the intervention is reinstated to determine if the behavioral performance improves (second B). If the baseline phases (the A phases) result in about the same levels of behavior, and the intervention phases (the B phases) produce the same levels of behavior, there is a demonstrated functional relationship between the intervention and the performance. Such is the case with the graph shown. John had a higher percentage of appropriate social skills when he participated in an intervention in which typically developing kindergarten children were taught to engage children with autism as compared to the baseline conditions (no intervention).

This graph provides visual evidence that not only was the intervention effective (the percentage of appropriate social skills used by John was much higher when the buddy-pair intervention was in place), but it was also responsible for the changes in the demonstration of social skills (when the intervention was removed, the percentage of appropriate social skills decreased). The graph also shows that when follow-up data were collected for John during the first six weeks of his next school year, the percentage of appropriate social skills was still much higher than during the baseline period. The concept of maintenance across time is important and will be discussed more fully in the section on the final dimension of ABA, generality.

The other research designs used to demonstrate a functional relationship between intervention and behavior as well as various data collection techniques will not be described here. Kennedy (2005) provides complete descriptions of both teaching and research single-subject designs and data collection techniques. Suffice it to say that data must be collected and analyzed for an intervention to be considered ABA. Although analysis usually occurs through a visual inspection of graphed data, other methodologies are available for linking changes in behavior to interventions.

Group designs compare the results of a group of students who receive a treatment to a similar group of students who do not receive the treatment (Kazdin, 2001). Group designs are not used as frequently with students with ASD because the population is so heterogeneous. Whether using the results of single-subject designs or group designs, analysis of data creates a self-correcting feedback loop for applied behavior analytic interventions (Anderson & Romanczyk, 1999). If data do not show desired changes in behavior, the intervention should be discarded or modified.

Generality

In a now classic statement, Baer, Wolf, and Risley (1968, p. 97) wrote, "Generalization should be programmed, rather than expected or lamented." This dimension of ABA suggests that even with a socially valid goal, appropriate techniques that consider the environmental context of behavior, and a research design that demonstrates the intervention is responsible for changing behavior, the intervention does not meet all the dimensions to be considered ABA if the student doesn't demonstrate the behavior outside of the teaching setting.

Generality (or **generalization**) means that the skills learned in teaching situations are then used in nonteaching situations. For example, if a student reliably responds to only one person who asks, "What's your name?" but does not respond if anyone else asks the same question, then the student has failed to generalize the skill. Unfortunately, individuals with ASD are characterized by their inability to generalize. They may not use a skill learned in the classroom in other situations, even other classrooms. Or they may not use the skill with people other than the person who taught them the skill. These are issues of **stimulus generalization** (Anderson & Romanczyk, 1999; Heflin & Alberto, 2001) in which new stimuli (places or people) do not occasion the behavior that is reliably demonstrated in the teaching situation. Fortunately, there are a number of strategies for promoting stimulus generalization. These include teaching the behavior using a variety of instructions (e.g., "What's your name?" "Who are you?" "Are you Steven?") as well as using a variety of materials to teach concepts, having different people provide the instructions, and conducting the instructional interactions in different settings.

Stimulus generalization is also enhanced by gradually withdrawing any prompts that have been introduced (known as **fading**), shaping the controlling stimuli so that more natural ones precede the desired behavior (e.g., gradually change from "Steven, go stand by the door" to "Steven, go line up" to "Everybody line up" to "It's time to go"), and practicing the behavior in natural environments with natural contingencies (e.g., standing in line in the cafeteria so you can get your food).

Another type of generalization is response maintenance. **Response maintenance** occurs when students continue to use a skill across time and across contexts, even when the teacher does not practice it with them on a frequent basis. It is not uncommon to lose a skill when it is not practiced. For some individuals on the autism spectrum, the amount of time it takes to forget a skill is short. For this reason, ways to promote response maintenance must be incorporated into instructional planning.

Specific strategies are effective for promoting response maintenance. Practicing the skill at various times across several days can promote response generalization (Anderson, Taras, & Cannon, 1996). Pairing primary reinforcers (e.g., food, drink) with secondary reinforcers (e.g., praise, smile) can help teach the value of the secondary reinforcer since those are the ones that tend to occur naturally (Alber, Heward, & Hippler, 1999). Likewise, gradually and systematically reducing the use of primary reinforcers and the frequency of reinforcement ("thinning of reinforcement") can also promote generalization across time (Skinner, 1969). This dimension of ABA requires that strategies for facilitating stimulus generalization and response maintenance be considered in the development of instructional interventions.

SUMMARY OF APPLIED BEHAVIOR ANALYSIS

ABA is a theoretical framework for promoting behavioral change, not a specific technique. The principles of ABA have been used effectively to teach everyone, not just those with ASD. There are many applied behavior analytic interventions. To be considered an applied behavior analytic intervention, the five dimensions articulated by Baer, Wolf, and Risley (1968; 1987) must be present:

- Socially significant behaviors are changed to a meaningful degree by using acceptable techniques with demonstrated effectiveness.
- The intervention must consider the influence of the environment on the behavior and must incorporate techniques designed to promote the continued use of the skill with other people and in other environments.
- Collected data must be analyzed to demonstrate that the instructional intervention is responsible for the change in the behavior.

Some applied behavior analytic interventions are stronger in regard to some dimensions than other dimensions, but all five dimensions need to be present for the intervention to be considered ABA. Confusion emerges when people use the term *ABA* to refer to a specific methodology, not the broad theoretical framework. This is what happened to Andy's mother in the vignette that opened this chapter, when she stumbled onto a misapplication of the term on the Internet. The website she found uses the term *ABA* to refer to a specific methodology, not the theoretical framework. Ms. Harris's response to Ms. Nelson, inquiring if she can "do ABA," should be that she incorporates the dimensions of ABA in her instruction every day. What was actually being discussed on the website Ms. Nelson found was Discrete Trial Training (DTT) rather than ABA.

DISCRETE TRIAL TRAINING

A discrete trial is a basic unit of instruction that falls under the technological dimension of ABA. DTT refers to the "intensive application of ABA principles within a structured teaching environment to teach specific skills" (Frea, 2000). For the population of individuals with ASD, DTT was first studied intensely to determine effectiveness for teaching expressive language (Lovaas, Berberich, Perloff, & Schaeffer, 1966; Lovaas, Freitag, Nelson, & Whalen, 1967). Using discrete trials, speech sounds were shaped into words to label objects. Today, however, a glance at any one of the published DTT curricula reveals that DTT is used to teach a variety of imitation, communication, socialization, and compliance skills (Leaf & McEachin, 1999; Lovaas, 2003; Maurice, Green, & Foxx, 2001; Maurice, Green, & Luce, 1996; Sundberg & Partington, 1998). The carefully modulated trials, which emphasize rote learning, can be effective for acquiring skills. Indeed, most people learn basic "facts" (e.g., multiplication tables, friends' names, telephone numbers) through what is essentially DTT.

The goal of DTT is to teach students to respond when directed, but not to respond if not directed ("stimulus dependency"). Chapter 4 defined a stimulus as something that occasions a particular response. Stimulus control means that the same behavioral response occurs whenever the stimulus is present. For example, if students are under stimulus control, they will comply with the directive, "Line up!" as quickly as it is given. Stimulus dependency means that students will not get in line unless the teacher directs them to do so. The behavioral response (getting in line) depends on the stimulus of the teacher's words.

There are a number of variations on DTT. For the purpose of introducing the methodology, DTT will be described as occurring in five steps. Although DTT has been divided into as few as three or as many as eight steps, all discrete trials contain the same basic components. The basic components for conducting DTT are:

- Attention
- Presentation of stimulus
- Student response
- Feedback
- Intertrial interval

Attention

To establish stimulus dependency, the student needs to attend to the stimulus. To begin a trial, the student's attention must be captured or he may miss the stimulus. Typically, the teacher is in close proximity to the student and may say the student's name, make eye contact, touch the student, or hold up something that attracts the student.

There are important things to consider in gaining the student's attention. Whatever is done should be effective the first time. For example, say the student's name only if it is known that she will orient to the speaker. Adults, unfortunately, teach children at an early age to ignore talking. Children playing outside rarely come inside for dinner the first time they are called. Most ignore the directive until the caregiver uses the first, middle, and last names in a shrill and no-nonsense tone, at which point they scurry inside the house. The same phenomenon occurs in many classrooms today. Teachers often have to make several requests with a concomitant change in tone and volume before everyone in the class complies with the direction given.

It may be best to avoid using the student's name every time to get attention. In the real world, directions are not always prefaced by names. Always using the student's name may inadvertently teach the student not to attend unless he hears his name. For initial discrete trials, holding up something the student likes, such a toy or a favorite food, may result in the student attending very intently.

In choosing a stimulus, it is important to remember that students with ASD are frequently reluctant to make eye contact. As discussed in a previous chapter, individuals with ASD can become overwhelmed by sensory input. For a student with ASD, looking at other people's faces, particularly their eyes, can result in a high level of sensory stimulation. They may instead rely more on peripheral vision (looking out from the sides of their eyes) to reduce the amount of visual input. Sometimes, a student on the autism spectrum may give full attention when she is beside the teacher using her peripheral vision, but not make direct eye contact. In fact, the absence of eye contact may increase the likelihood that she will pay more attention to what is being said. One high-functioning adult with autism has indicated that she can either make eye contact or listen, but not both, because the amount of sensory stimulation becomes too overwhelming (Grandin, 1996). Before presenting the stimulus, use whatever strategy gains the student's attention the first time.

Presentation of Stimulus

After gaining attention, give the instruction or direction. The technical term for the instruction is **discriminative stimulus.** This is what informs the student that a particular response is expected. For example, most people will say the discriminative stimulus for getting up in the morning is the sound of the alarm clock. However, how many people get up when the alarm clock goes off? Most will say that the actual discriminative stimulus for getting up is a certain number of hits on the snooze button or a specific time on the clock. In DTT, the discriminative stimulus for the student's response is determined in advance, remembering that the discriminative stimulus will be learned more quickly if it is the same every time (consistent); doesn't contain too much information (concise); and specifies exactly what needs to occur (clear).

An example of an inappropriate discriminative stimulus would be for a teacher to say, "Why don't you come over here and sit in this blue chair next to me?" An appropriate discriminative stimulus that provides the same information but is clear and concise is, "Come sit." To establish stimulus control, those exact words would be used every time. To prevent teaching students to ignore the discriminative stimulus, give it only once and say nothing else.

Student Response

After presenting the discriminative stimulus, wait for the student's response. There are only three responses possible: correct, incorrect, or no response at all. In DTT, the teacher should carefully consider how to maximize the likelihood that the student will respond correctly. One way is to engineer the environment so that there are few distractions and to be in close proximity so that the student can be quickly redirected if he tries to leave the area. Another is to make sure that the behavior selected for the trial is within the student's repertoire.

For example, if the student likes to throw things, the teacher might say "Open box" while holding out a box containing a lid. The student may reach for the box to throw it, but the teacher is holding the box tightly enough so that the student can grab only the lid, which he throws. Because the discriminative stimulus was to open the box, the student has responded correctly. Later, the student's behavior can be shaped so that he places the lid on the table after removal. The important concept is that the behavior is one that the student has the potential to perform, and the environment, including how materials are presented, is carefully engineered to enhance the probability that the correct stimulus will be attended to and the correct behavior will occur.

Even with careful selection of the behavior and good instructional control, the student may not respond with the correct behavior. He may instead engage in another behavior such as waving his hands in front of his face or talking about a favorite movie. He may try to leave the area. Or he may just sit without moving. The feedback provided next is contingent on the type of response the student gives.

One variation of DTT is to provide a prompt along with the discriminative stimulus to encourage errorless learning. Providing a prompt with the discriminative stimulus helps guarantee that the student responds correctly. For example, guiding the student's finger to his nose using a full physical prompt when giving the discriminative stimulus "Touch nose" results in a correct response without allowing for error.

Other types of prompts are useful for reducing or eliminating errors. The teacher may use **blocking** to prevent an incorrect response by restricting access to incorrect choices, such as covering all but the correct picture when asking the student to identify a particular picture. Within-stimulus prompts provide an exaggeration of relevant components of a stimulus, such as highlighting the word "Name" on students' papers to prompt them to write their names. A carpet freshening powder can be sprinkled on the floor to serve as a visual prompt for the areas left to be vacuumed. Although some advocate for the use of errorless learning (Heckaman, Alber, Hooper, & Heward, 1998), most DTT allows students to perform unassisted the first time, with prompts being given after the response in an error-correction procedure.

Feedback

The teacher provides a consequence after the student responds. If the student's response is correct, the feedback provides reinforcement. If the student is incorrect or gives no response, the feedback corrects the error by prompting the student to respond as directed.

To deliver feedback, identify and have available whatever the student finds reinforcing. The reinforcement must be delivered immediately upon demonstration of a correct response in order to develop the association between the discriminative stimulus and the response. Identifying reinforcers can be tricky for students with ASD. As discussed earlier in this chapter, reinforcement is not a "thing," but an effect. Something is reinforcing only if it maintains or increases the occurrence of a behavior. To identify potential reinforcers, analyze what the student likes and desires. Sometimes this is a particular food or drink, such as raisins or soda. Sometimes the student likes to listen to music or hold a particular object.

Potential reinforcers will be unique to the student. Teachers have reported that students on the autism spectrum have liked things that may seem unusual, such as picking up staples off the floor, holding pieces of laminating film, and smelling socks. Charlop-Christy and Haymes (1998) found that globes, map books, toothpaste caps, coffee swizzle sticks, toy helicopters, and balloons were preferred by the participants in their study. The array of potential reinforcers is endless. Knowing the student is the best way to start to identify potential reinforcers. For some students, identifying potential reinforcers can be particularly challenging because the things they like most do not lend themselves well to a DTT interaction. For example, some students like to go on walks, ride in the car, or swing. The challenge, then, is to try to identify potential reinforcers that do not last too long and that can be delivered in small quantities to avoid **satiation** (being satisfied and not wanting more).

Primary reinforcers that can be given in controlled quantities are ideal, such as a few ounces of soda or a single cheese puff. Wind-up or animated toys that are active for a short duration are also good. When the action stops, there is a logical transition to the next trial. The critical aspect is that the reinforcer is delivered immediately after the correct response occurs.

To identify reinforcers and to verify that the items identified are still relevant as reinforcers, conduct preference assessments (Cannella, O'Reilly, & Lancioni, 2005). This can be as simple as holding out two items and observing which one the student reaches or asks for. Preference assessments can also be more rigorous. For example, identify a number of items and then systematically offer them in pairs to determine the relative order of preference. Then consider what the student has preferred historically and make a judgment about the effect of motivating operations.

Motivating operations affect the relevance of the consequence based on recent experiences (Laraway, Snycerski, Michael, & Poling, 2003). For example, if the student has just finished a large lunch, then food items may be less desirable as reinforcers. However, those same food items may be of great interest to the student if she has not eaten in a while. In providing reinforcement, the teacher must be confident that the consequence delivered after a correct response is something the student desires.

If the student gives an incorrect response or no response at all, the feedback given provides error correction followed by reinforcement. Prompts delivered by another person exist on a hierarchy from least intrusive to more intrusive as follows:

* *Visual:* The teacher shows the student a picture, icon, word, or object representing the desired response.
* *Gestural:* The teacher gestures toward what is to be done.
* *Model:* The teacher performs the expected behavior for the student to watch.
* *Partial physical:* The teacher touches the student to get the requested motion started.
* *Full physical:* The teacher physically guides the student through the performance of the action.

One of the less intrusive prompts, the verbal prompt, has been purposely omitted from this listing. A verbal prompt is not the restatement of the discriminative stimulus. A verbal prompt contains comments that offer additional information. For the discriminative stimulus "Line up!" a verbal prompt might consist of "Stand up and walk to the door." Since most students with ASD have auditory processing difficulties, verbal prompts are contraindicated because they add verbal information that further strains the ability to comprehend.

Initially, the reinforcement for a prompted response is the same as the reinforcement for an independent response. The idea is to teach the student that when the response occurs after a particular instruction (discriminative stimulus), it is followed by something the student finds desirable (reinforcement).

Prompts must be used with caution to avoid prompt dependency. **Prompt dependency** occurs when the student waits for a prompt before responding and is said to be dependent upon the prompt. To avoid prompt dependency, after several trials with prompting, reduce or eliminate the

Discrete Trial Teaching

Student: **Nebil**   Trainer: **JT**

Objective: Color identification
Condition: Sitting across from Nebil and giving him a field of 3 options
Sd: "Touch _____" (fill in blue, red, yellow, green)
Criteria: 80% accuracy with Sd only (no prompting) for three consecutive sessions
Reinforcement Schedule: (1:1)   1:2 , 1:3   Intermittent   Other:

Date	9/7	Date	9/8	Date	9/9	Date	9/10	Date	9/13
	Prompt		Prompt		Prompt		Prompt		Prompt
~~10~~	F	10		~~10~~	G	(10)		10	
~~9~~	F	9		~~9~~	G	~~9~~	G	9	
~~8~~	F	~~8~~	P	~~8~~	G	~~8~~	P	8	
~~7~~	F	~~7~~	P	~~7~~	G	⑦		7	
~~6~~	F	~~6~~	P	~~6~~	P	⑥		6	
~~5~~	F	~~5~~	P	~~5~~	G	~~5~~	P	⑤	
~~4~~	F	~~4~~	F	~~4~~	P	[4]	G	[4]	
~~3~~	F	~~3~~	P	~~3~~	P	③		③	
~~2~~	F	~~2~~	F	~~2~~	P	~~2~~	G	~~2~~	G
~~1~~	F	~~1~~	F	~~1~~	P	~~1~~	G	①	
0%		0%		0%		40%		80%	
>f prompt: F 100 %		>f prompt: P 63 %		>f prompt: G/P 50 %		>f prompt: G 66 %		>f prompt: G 100 %	

Prompts: G = gestural
M = model
P = partial physical
F = full physical

Marking: ---- incorrect
    o correct
    □ total correct for session
*If a prompt is used, the trial is marked
    incorrect.

Comments:

FIGURE 6.2
DTT Data Collection for Nebil

186

reinforcement. Show but do not give the student the reinforcement after the error correction procedure. The next trial gives the student the opportunity to perform the response independently and receive the reinforcement.

Intertrial Interval

The **intertrial interval** is a brief period of time between trials during which the student enjoys the reinforcement received for a correct response and the teacher records the data for the trial. The intertrial interval is what gives the methodology its name. (The word *discrete* refers to something with a clear beginning and a clear end, and shouldn't be confused with *discreet*, which refers to something secretive or covert.)

After the intertrial interval, ensure that the student is still attending and provide another discriminative stimulus (the same as previously or different). Traditionally, a teacher removed any materials during the intertrial interval so that they could be presented distinctly at the beginning of the next trial. In applied settings, the materials may not always be removed. Intertrial intervals may last a few seconds but can be longer or shorter depending on the student. Indeed, for students with short attention spans or who are difficult to reengage after a break, the intertrial interval may be very brief (Lovaas, 2003). Short intertrial intervals have been shown to increase correct responding while reducing off-task behavior (Dunlap, Dyer, & Koegel, 1983).

If the length of the intertrial interval appropriate for the student allows, the accuracy of the student's response may be recorded during the intertrial interval. Data collection may be as simple as recording a plus if the student has responded correctly or a minus if the student has not responded correctly. More sophisticated forms of data collection record the level of prompting used in the error correction procedure. Figure 6.2 provides an example of a self-graphing data collection sheet that contains complete information about the task and responses. Although most data collection sheets are set up to collect data in sets of 10, that is only for the convenience of converting data to percentages and nothing more.

If a student provides correct responses for three trials in a row, switch to another discriminative stimulus. When asked to demonstrate a response that has already been done correctly several times, the student may become bored or resistant and the response will decay.

❖ LEARNING WITH MS. HARRIS: Teaching Gabe to Label Pictures

The IEP team decides Gabe needs to increase his receptive vocabulary and identify verbs. He is currently using one-word utterances (nouns) to identify things he would like to have. Since learning verbs is critical for language development, Ms. Harris has gathered pictures that portray people performing a variety of common acts (e.g., eating, sleeping, drinking, washing, running, swinging). Ms. Harris carefully arranged the environment so that she and Gabe could sit at a table in an area free of distractions. Gabe's chair backs up to the wall, so it will be difficult for him to leave the area.

Ms. Harris has several items that she knows Gabe likes. Sitting down at the table, Gabe starts to reach for the candy. Ms. Harris removes all the items from the table but keeps the candy in front of her. After making sure that she has Gabe's attention, Ms. Harris holds up the picture of a person walking and says, "Point to walking." If Gabe fails to respond, Ms. Harris repeats the discriminative stimulus and uses a full physical prompt to help Gabe point to the picture before she gives Gabe a small piece of candy while praising him.

After Gabe reliably points to the pictures when directed, Ms. Harris presents two pictures simultaneously and asks Gabe to point to the one that depicts a particular action. If Gabe correctly discriminates between the two pictures, Ms. Harris reinforces and praises him. If Gabe is incorrect, Ms. Harris repeats the discriminative stimulus and guides Gabe's hand to touch the correct picture. Then she gives him some candy, but watches Gabe closely to see if it looks as if he is waiting for her to prompt him. She certainly doesn't want to create prompt dependence!

Once in a while, Ms. Harris holds up two new items that are potential reinforcers to see which one Gabe might be interested in. If he doesn't reach for or label either one of them, Ms. Harris tries two different items. She knows it is important to vary the reinforcers to prevent Gabe from becoming satiated, which decreases his motivation for responding as requested. Across days and weeks, the series of trials continues until Gabe can correctly identify common verbs when they are presented in a field of three pictures with 90% accuracy over a two-week period and with at least two different teachers.

Variations

There is no controversy regarding the effectiveness of DTT as a basic methodology. However, variations on the basic methodology as well as recommendations regarding different types of DTT have resulted in considerable controversy.

One of the major variations relates to when prompts should be used. Some people recommend students not be prompted after the first incorrect/ no response. Instead, after an incorrect/no response, the teacher should say "no," look away, and remove the materials (Lovaas, 2003; Smith, 2001). Others hold the student's hands on the table for a brief period of time after an incorrect/no response (Pérez-González & Williams, 2002). Leaf and McEachin (1999) indicate that students should be allowed to give two incorrect responses before receiving a prompt for the correct response. These variations have led to disagreements regarding which method is most effective for teaching behavioral responses. Unfortunately, research has yet to be conducted to answer the question of which may be more effective and for whom.

There are also variations in the types of discrete trials. There are three types of discrete trials, with each having advantages and disadvantages: massed, distributed, and collective trials. In **massed trials,** the teacher uses the same discriminative stimulus many times consecutively in order to occasion the same response. An example of a massed discrete trial is asking the student to touch her nose 10 times in a row. The advantage of massed discrete trials is that they are useful for teaching a skill very quickly. The disadvantage is that the information tends to be quickly forgotten. Cramming for an exam is an example of a massed discrete trial. Students who have an exam on Thursday may start studying in earnest on Wednesday night and learn the information sufficiently to pass the exam. However, students cannot remember the information weeks, days, or even hours after taking the exam.

Another disadvantage of massed discrete trials is that people tend to get irritated when asked to perform the same response several times in a row (Koegel & Koegel, 1995). This irritability can manifest as noncompliance or even aggression. Some parents have claimed that the use of massed discrete trials has led to behavioral problems in their children and even symptoms of post-traumatic stress ("Open Letter," 1999).

To avoid resistance and promote greater retention of behavioral responses, trials can be distributed throughout and across days instead of massed. Instead of being asked to touch his nose 10 times in a row (massed trials), the student might be asked to touch his nose once in the morning while brushing his teeth, once when singing a song, once when waiting in line, and so forth (**distributed trials**). Or the trials might be distributed throughout a training session.

Although it will take longer for the student to learn the response with distributed trials, the advantage is that once the student learns the response, particularly if the trials have been distributed across settings and people, he will be more likely to retain it across time (Koegel, O'Dell, & Koegel, 1987; McGee, Krantz, & McClannahan, 1984). In the previous example of cramming for an exam and then forgetting the information, students would have retained much more of that information if they had studied and reviewed it each week of the semester leading up to the exam. Distributed trials have been found to be superior to massed trials when it is important for the information to be retained (Dellarosa & Bourne, 1985; Dempster, 1988; Lee & Genovese, 1988; Reynolds & Glaser, 1964).

A third type of discrete trial is **collective trials,** which distribute the trials across students. This is a common occurrence in classrooms. Students have been given the same assignment and the teacher solicits answers. The teacher asks a student for the answer to the first question (gain attention and present discriminative stimulus). The teacher acknowledges a correct answer and corrects an incorrect answer or calls on someone else to answer (response and consequence provided). Then another student is asked to answer the next question. An advantage of collective trials is sharing the spotlight. Also, collective trials allow students to learn from each other and benefit from modeling. Disadvantages are that students may not pay attention if they are not being questioned directly, and some students may not notice what others are doing, so they may not learn from the modeling. Distributing trials throughout the day and using different types of trials has been shown to be effective (Egel, Shafer, & Neef, 1984; McMorrow & Foxx, 1986).

PROS AND CONS OF DISCRETE TRIAL TRAINING

DTT is used in almost every learning situation. When a child is learning to speak, a caregiver points to a cat and says, "What's that?" to which the child replies, "Kitty" and is told, "Yes, it is!" (We'll assume that verbal praise from a caregiver increases the child's speaking and is therefore reinforcing.)

As children age, they are exposed to various types of DTT (probably massed for spelling words and multiplication facts) as well as other types of instruction. When analyzing the highly structured type of DTT that has been presented here, there are some pros and cons to take into consideration when deciding on how the methodology may be used in the classroom.

The pros include:

1. Students have many opportunities to learn and practice responses. Since trials are so short, the student could respond up to 12 times per minute (Smith, 2001).
2. The discriminative stimulus is clearly defined and all other distractions are eliminated. This helps the student attend to what is relevant.
3. Important skills are broken down into their discrete parts (task analyzed) so that each component can be specifically taught.
4. Correct behavior is determined in advance and reinforced immediately.
5. The methodology can be replicated across people so that everyone uses the same approach with the student.

In addition to the benefits inherent in highly structured DTT interactions, there are some cautions to consider.

The cons include:

1. Skills learned during massed discrete trials may not generalize to other settings or to people not involved in the training.
2. Exclusive emphasis on DTT may limit learning and result in unwanted side effects. Some students respond to intensive DTT by becoming resistant (Howard, Sparkman, Cohen, Green, & Stanislaw, 2005; Newman, Needelman, Reinecke, & Robek, 2002). Additionally, since the goal of DTT is to create stimulus dependency, the emergence of independent and adaptive behaviors may be inhibited (Birnbrauer & Leach, 1993; Rogers, 1999).
3. Stimulus dependency (responding to the discriminative stimulus when it is given, but only when it is given), may result in students learning

the wrong cues for behaviors, such as waiting for the teacher to tell them to play rather than playing in the presence of the toys themselves (Smith, 2001).

4. Some students may benefit more from DTT than others. Students with measured IQs of less than 50 are less likely to benefit from intensive DTT (Anderson et al., 1987; Fenske, Zalenski, Krantz, & McClannahan, 1985; Harris and Handleman, 2000; Lovaas, 1987) than students with IQs above 50.

SUMMARY OF DISCRETE TRIAL TRAINING

Strong empirical evidence supports the effectiveness of a variety of applied behavior analytic interventions. The data on the effectiveness of DTT are less conclusive (Gresham & Macmillan, 1997). Although everyone learns through the process of associating consequences with behaviors in the presence of certain stimuli, providing many hours of massed discrete trial may not produce generalized use of skills and improve adaptive functioning. Researchers have documented that DTT is more effective for younger children (younger than 4 years of age) with IQs above 50 (Lovaas, 1987). Gains equal to or better than those found in the seminal 1987 study by Lovaas have been noted in similar populations who did not receive DTT (Eaves & Ho, 2004; Gabriels, Hill, Pierce, Rogers, & Wehner, 2001), leading to the conclusion that characteristics of the children influenced outcomes more than the intervention (Lord, Cook, Leventhal, & Amaral, 2000). In particular, IQ appears to be the best predictor of responsiveness to intervention (Eikeseth, Smith, Jahr, & Eldevik, 2002).

As the NRC (2001) noted, family characteristics as well as child characteristics may confound research findings. Howard et al. (2005) found that intensive DTT was not effective for everyone; some students across all three of their comparison groups made progress. Students in their intensive DTT group made the most progress but were differentiated in terms of their families. The researchers used intact groups of children who were receiving intervention at three locations (private intensive DTT, public special education classroom, and public early intervention program), which indicates that the children were not living in similar home environments. As would be predicted, the parents who placed their children in the intensive DTT program had 1–2 more years of education than the parents in the other two groups. The children in the intensive DTT program had been diagnosed younger and had started intervention sooner. Four children originally in the intensive DTT group dropped out of the study; two because the intervention led to behavior problems and the parents chose to discontinue, one because the parent could not provide the home programming, and one whose family moved. Attrition in the two comparison groups occurred for different reasons. Of the four children who dropped out, one parent refused to allow testing at follow-up and three parents could not be contacted. The parents in the three groups also differed in terms of ethnicity and marital status, with almost half in the public early intervention program being unmarried. More analysis needs to be done to determine how family demographics influence response to intervention, including intensive DTT.

Some of the problems with early programs using DTT, such as cue dependency, lack of self-initiation, rote responding, and failure to generalize (Schreibman, 2000), have led to modifications in the methodology. For example, Smith, Eikeseth, Klevstrand, and Lovaas (1997) added a component of parent training to try to minimize some of the concerns. At the end of one year, no statistically significant differences were noted between a group of students receiving DTT and those receiving an "eclectic" special education program (Eikeseth et al., 2002). Intensive DTT has been found to accelerate learning but not to cure individuals of their autism (Rogers, 1998). This leads to the conclusion that:

> DTT is a necessary but not sufficient element of ABA treatment for children with autism. . . . other instructional approaches [will be needed to teach them how to] initiate the use of the skills they have acquired, transfer those skills to new settings, and reduce their reliance on cues from the teacher. (Smith, 2001, p. 91)

OTHER EFFECTIVE ABA INTERVENTIONS

Over the last thirty years, thousands of studies have been published that demonstrate the effectiveness of applied behavior analytic procedures for changing behavior in persons with and without disabilities in home, school, and community settings. Some of these procedures have been studied specifically with individuals with ASD. This book profiles many of the applied behavior analytic procedures used effectively with students on the autism spectrum. Chapter 4 describes applied behavior analytic interventions related to environmental arrangement and manipulation, the use of static and animated visual strategies, priming, choice making, and establishing stimulus control.

Chapter 7 describes the applied behavior analytic approach to support adaptive behavior by determining behavioral function and designing positive behavioral supports. That chapter discusses Pivotal Response Training (PRT) and Functional Communication Training (FCT), which meet the five dimensions of ABA. Chapter 8 discusses applied behavior analytic interventions for promoting the development of communication and verbal behavior through such procedures as incidental teaching, Natural Language Paradigm (NLP), Joint Action Routines (JARS), and Picture Exchange Communication System (PECS).

Chapter 9 describes applied behavior analytic strategies for supporting social development in the forms of peer-mediated and adult-mediated approaches. Chapters 10 and 11 discuss the application of applied behavior analytic interventions to support skill acquisition in academic content areas as well as those based on promoting engagement.

❖ LEARNING WITH MS. HARRIS: An Answer for Ms. Nelson

After great reflection, Ms. Harris sends Andy's mother the following e-mail:

Hi! Andy had a great day today, as you can tell from the work that was sent home! During centers, he traded seven objects with three different peers.

By the way, you asked if I could do ABA with Andy. You'll be happy to know that the majority of Andy's day is spent in applied behavior analytic (ABA) instruction. Even the PECS you're using at home is an applied behavior analytic strategy (as is that toilet training program we talked about).

You'll probably be pleased to know that some of Andy's instruction is provided in the form of Discrete Trial Training. Rather than using massed trials, I use distributed and collective trials. I'm using these to support Andy's use of the skills he is learning in other settings and with other people. We learned the lesson the hard way that when I practiced "What's your name?" with Andy over and over, he became good at answering me, but he didn't answer anyone else who asked him! Distributed trials are more likely to be maintained over time and are less likely to interfere with Andy's adaptive behavior development.

As hard as we're all working, we want to make sure to use approaches that provide the most benefit. Andy is making good progress through the use of a variety of applied behavior analytic strategies!

Hope you all have a great weekend! Ms. H

CONCLUSION

Interventions based on the principles of applied behavior analysis have strong empirical data to support their effectiveness with students with ASD. To be considered an ABA approach, the intervention must meet specified criteria related to social significance and contextual considerations affecting the generalized adaptability of behavior. Interventions based on ABA must be validated through collection of data that demonstrate their impact on the behavior. DTT is one of the many ABA interventions that have been used with students with ASD. DTT is effective for promoting skill acquisition but has limitations that necessitate that it be used in combination with other ABA interventions in order to teach important and relevant skills with generalized use to students with ASD.

DISCUSSION QUESTIONS AND ACTIVITIES

1. At an IEP meeting a parent turns to you and says, "I want you to do ABA with my child!" What do you say?

2. Identify a research article that describes an intervention that modified the behavior of a student with an ASD. Compare the intervention against the five dimensions of ABA and determine how adequately it meets all criteria.

3. Think of at least five skills you have learned using DTT. Describe how each of the five steps occurred in your experiences.

4. Most behavior is learned through the power of reinforcement. Describe a variety of strategies you could use to conduct reinforcer assessments with your students.

5. Discuss what needs to occur during and after instruction to enhance the student's ability to generalize the skills being learned.

REFERENCES

Alber, S. R., Heward, W. L., & Hippler, B. J. (1999). Teaching middle school students with learning disabilities to recruit positive teacher attention. *Exceptional Children, 65,* 253-270.

Alberto, P. A., & Troutman, A. C. (2003). *Applied behavior analysis for teachers* (6th ed.). Upper Saddle River, NJ: Merrill/Prentice Hall.

Anderson, G. M., Freedman, D. X., Cohen, D. J., Volkmar, F. R., Hoder, E. L., McPhedran, P., et al. (1987). Whole blood serotonin in autistic and normal subjects. *Journal of Child Psychology & Psychiatry & Allied Disciplines, 28,* 885-900.

Anderson, S. R., & Romanczyk, R. G. (1999). Early intervention for young children with autism: Continuum-based behavioral models. *Journal of the Association for Persons with Severe Handicaps, 24,* 162-173.

Anderson, S. R., Taras, M., & Cannon, B. O. (1996). Teaching new skills to young children with autism. In C. Maurice (Ed.), *Behavioral intervention for young children with autism: A manual for parents and professionals* (pp. 181-194). Austin, TX: Pro-Ed.

Baer, D. M., Wolf, M. M., & Risley, T. (1968). Current dimensions of applied behavior analysis. *Journal of Applied Behavior Analysis, 1,* 91-97.

Baer, D. M., Wolf, M. M., & Risley, T. (1987). Some still-current dimensions of applied behavior analysis. *Journal of Applied Behavior Analysis, 20,* 313-328.

Birnbrauer, J. S., & Leach, D. J. (1993). The Murdoch Early Intervention Program after 2 years. *Behaviour Change, 10,* 63-74.

Brady, M. P., Shores, R. E., McEvoy, M. A., Ellis, D., & Fox, J. J. (1987). Increasing social interactions of severely handicapped autistic children. *Journal of Autism and Developmental Disorders, 17,* 375-390.

Cannella, H. I., O'Reilly, M. F., & Lancioni, G. E. (2005). Choice and preference assessment research with people with severe to profound developmental disabilities: A review of the literature. *Research in Developmental Disabilities, 26,* 1-14.

Carr, J. E., Dozier, C. L., Patel, M., Adams, A. N., & Martin, N. (2002). Treatment of automatically reinforced object mouthing with noncontingent reinforcement and response blocking: Experimental analysis and social validation. *Research in Developmental Disabilities, 23,* 37-44.

Carr, E. G., & Durand, V. M. (1985). Reducing behavior problems through functional communication training. *Journal of Applied Behavior Analysis, 18,* 111-126.

Charlop, M. H., & Milstein, J. P. (1989). Teaching autistic children conversational speech using video modeling. *Journal of Applied Behavior Analysis, 22,* 275-285.

Charlop-Christy, M. H., & Haymes, L. K. (1998). Using objects of obsession as token reinforcers for children with autism. *Journal of Autism and Developmental Disorders, 28,* 189-198.

Dellarosa, D., & Bourne, L. E. (1985). Surface form and the spacing effect. *Memory and Cognition, 13,* 529-537.

Dempster, F. N. (1988). The spacing effect: A case study in the failure to apply the results of psychological research. *American Psychologist, 43,* 627-634.

Dunlap, G., Dyer, K., & Koegel, R. L. (1983). Autistic self-stimulation and intertrial interval duration. *American Journal of Mental Deficiency, 88,* 194-202.

Dunlap, G., Kern, L., & Worcester, J. (2001). ABA and academic instruction. *Focus on Autism and Other Developmental Disabilities, 16,* 129-136.

Dunlap, G., Marshall, U., Plienis, A. J., & Williams, L. (1987). Acquisition and generalization of unsupervised responding: A descriptive analysis. *Journal of the Association for Persons with Severe Handicaps, 12,* 274–279.

Durand, V. M. (2005). Past, present, and emerging directions in education. In D. Zager (Ed.), *Autism spectrum disorders* (3rd ed., pp. 89–109). Mahwah, NJ: Erlbaum.

Eaves, L. C., & Ho, H. H. (2004). The very early identification of autism: Outcome to age 4-5. *Journal of Autism and Developmental Disorders, 34,* 367–378.

Egel, A. L., Shafer, M. S., & Neef, N. A. (1984). Receptive acquisition and generalization of prepositional responding in autistic children: A comparison of two procedures. *Analysis and Intervention in Developmental Disabilities, 4,* 285–298.

Eikeseth, S., Smith, T., Jahr, E., & Eldevik, S. (2002). Intensive behavioral treatment at school for 4- to 7-year-old children with autism. *Behavior Modification, 26,* 49–68.

Fenske, E. C., Zalenski, S., Krantz, P. J., & McClannahan, L. E. (1985). Age at intervention and treatment outcome for autistic children in a comprehensive intervention program. *Analysis and Intervention for Developmental Disabilities, 5,* 49–58.

Ferrari, M., & Harris, S. L. (1981). The limits and motivating potential of sensory stimuli as reinforcers for autistic children. *Journal of Applied Behavior Analysis, 14,* 339–343.

Frea, W. D. (2000). Behavioral interventions for children with autism. In J. Austin & J. E. Carr (Eds.), *Handbook of applied behavior analysis* (pp. 247–273). Reno, NV: Context Press.

Gabriels, R. L., Hill, D. E., Pierce, R. A., Rogers, S. J., & Wehner, B. (2001) Predictors of treatment outcome in young children with autism. *Autism, 5,* 407–429.

Garfinkle, A. N., & Schwartz, I. S. (2002). Peer imitation: Increasing social interactions in children with autism and other developmental disabilities in inclusive preschool classrooms. *Topics in Early Childhood Special Education, 22,* 26–38.

Grandin, T. (1996). Brief report: Response to National Institutes of Health Report. *Journal of Autism and Developmental Disabilities, 26,* 185–187.

Green, G. (2001). Behavior analytic instruction for learners with autism: Advances in stimulus control technology. *Focus on Autism and Other Developmental Disabilities, 16,* 72–86.

Gresham, F. M., & Macmillan, D. L. (1997). Autistic recovery? An analysis and critique of the empirical evidence on the early intervention project. *Behavioral Disorders, 22,* 185–201.

Hall, L. J., McClannahan, L. E., & Krantz, P. J. (1995). Promoting independence in integrated classrooms by teaching aides to use activity schedules and decreased prompts. *Education & Training in Mental Retardation & Developmental Disabilities, 30,* 208–217.

Haring, T., Kennedy, C., Adams, M., & Pitts-Conway, V. (1987). Teaching generalization of purchasing skills across community settings to autistic youth using videotape modeling. *Journal of Applied Behavior Analysis, 20,* 89–96.

Harris, S. L., & Handleman, J. S. (2000). Age and IQ at intake as predictors of placement for young children with autism: A four- to six-year follow-up. *Journal of Autism and Developmental Disorders, 30,* 137–142.

Heckaman, K. A., Alber, S., Hooper, S., & Heward, W. L. (1998). A comparison of least-to-most prompts and progressive time delay on the disruptive behavior of students with autism. *Journal of Behavioral Education, 8,* 171–201.

Heflin, L. J., & Alberto, P. A. (2001). Establishing a behavioral context for learning with students with autism. *Focus on Autism & Other Developmental Disabilities, 16,* 93–101.

Howard, J. S., Sparkman, C. R., Cohen, H. G., Green, G., & Stanislaw, H. (2005). A comparison of intensive behavior analytic and eclectic treatments for young children with autism. *Research in Developmental Disabilities, 26,* 359–383.

Hung, D. W. (1978). Using self-stimulation as reinforcement for autistic children. *Journal of Autism and Childhood Schizophrenia, 8,* 355–366.

Johnston, S., & O'Neill, R. E. (2001). Searching for effectiveness and efficiency in conducting functional assessments: A review and proposed process for teachers and other practitioners. *Focus on Autism and Other Developmental Disabilities, 16,* 205–214.

Kamps, D. M., Leonard, B. R., Vernon, S., Dugan, E., Delquadri, J. C., Gershon, B., et al.

(1992). Teaching social skills to students with autism to increase peer interactions in an integrated first-grade classroom. *Journal of Applied Behavior Analysis, 25,* 281-288.

Kazdin, A. E. (2001). *Behavior modification in applied settings* (6th ed.). Belmont, CA: Wadsworth/Thomson.

Kennedy, C. H. (2005). *Single-case designs for educational research.* Boston: Allyn & Bacon.

Koegel, L. K., Camarata, S. M., Valdez-Menchaca, M., & Koegel, R. L. (1998). Setting generalization of question-asking by children with autism. *American Journal on Mental Retardation, 102,* 346-357.

Koegel, L. K., & Koegel, R. L. (1995). Motivating communication in children with autism. In E. Schopler & G. B. Mesibov (Eds.), *Learning and cognition in autism* (pp. 73-87). New York: Plenum.

Koegel, R. L., O'Dell, M. C., & Koegel, L. K. (1987). A natural language teaching paradigm for nonverbal autistic children. *Journal of Autism and Developmental Disorders, 17,* 187-200.

Krantz, P. J., & McClannahan, L. E. (1998). Social interaction skills for children with autism: A script-fading procedure for beginning readers. *Journal of Applied Behavior Analysis, 31,* 191-202.

Laraway, S., Snycerski, S., Michael, J., & Poling, A. (2003). Motivating operations and terms to describe them: Some further refinements. *Journal of Applied Behavior Analysis, 36,* 407-414.

Laushey, K. M., & Heflin, L. J. (2000). Enhancing social skills of kindergarten children with autism through the training of multiple peers as tutors. *Journal of Autism and Developmental Disorders, 30,* 183-193.

Leaf, R., & McEachin, J. (Eds.). (1999). *A work in progress: Behavior management strategies and a curriculum for intensive behavioral treatment of autism.* New York: DRL Books.

Lee, T. D., & Genovese, E. D. (1988). Distribution of practice in motor skill acquisition: Learning and performance effects reconsidered. *Research Quarterly for Exercise and Sport, 59,* 277-287.

Lord, C., Cook, E. H., Leventhal, B., & Amaral, D. G. (2000). Autism spectrum disorders. *Neuron, 28,* 355-363.

Lovaas, O. I. (1987). Behavioral treatment and normal education and intellectual functioning in young autistic children. *Journal of Consulting and Clinical Psychology, 55,* 3-9.

Lovaas, O. I. (2003). *Teaching individuals with developmental delays: Basic intervention techniques.* Austin, TX: ProEd.

Lovaas, O. I., Berberich, J. P., Perloff, B. F., & Schaeffer, B. (1966). Acquisition of imitative speech in schizophrenic children. *Science, 151,* 705-707.

Lovaas, O. I., Freitag, G., Nelson, K., & Whalen, C. (1967). The establishment of imitation and its use for the development of complex behavior in schizophrenic children. *Behaviour Research and Therapy, 5,* 171-181.

Massey, N. G., & Wheeler, J. J. (2000). Acquisition and generalization of activity schedules and their effects on task engagement in a young child with autism in an inclusive preschool classroom. *Education and Training in Mental Retardation and Developmental Disabilities, 35,* 326-335.

Matson, J. L., Taras, M. E., Sevin, J. A., Love, S. R., & Fridley, D. (1990). Teaching self-help skills to autistic and mentally retarded children. *Research in Developmental Disabilities, 11,* 361-378.

Maurice, C., Green, G., & Foxx, R. (2001). *Making a difference: Behavioral intervention for autism.* Austin, TX: Pro-Ed.

Maurice, C., Green, G., & Luce, S. C. (Eds.). (1996). *Behavioral intervention for young children with autism: A manual for parents and professionals.* Austin, TX: Pro-Ed.

McGee, G. G., Krantz, P. J., & McClannahan, L. E. (1984). Conversational skills for autistic adolescents: Teaching assertiveness in naturalistic game settings. *Journal of Autism & Developmental Disorders, 14,* 319-330.

McMorrow, M. J., & Foxx, R. M. (1986). Some direct and generalized effects of replacing an autistic man's echolalia with correct responses to questions. *Journal of Applied Behavior Analysis, 19,* 289-297.

National Research Council. (2001). *Educating children with autism.* Committee on Educational Interventions for Children with Autism. Division of Behavioral and Social Sciences and Education. Washington, DC: National Academy Press.

Newman, B., Needelman, M., Reinecke, D. R., & Robek, A. (2002). The effect of providing choices on skill acquisition and competing behavior of children with autism during discrete trial instruction. *Behavioral Interventions, 17,* 31–41.

O'Neill, R. E., & Sweetland-Baker, M. (2001). Brief report: An assessment of stimulus generalization and contingency effects in functional communication training with two students with autism. *Journal of Autism and Developmental Disorders, 31,* 235–240.

"Open letter." (1999). *The Communicator, 10*(1), 4.

Perez-Gonzalez, L. A., & Williams, C. (2002). Multicomponent procedure to teach conditional discriminations to children with autism. *American Journal of Mental Retardation, 107,* 293–330.

Pierce, K., & Schreibman, L. (1997). Using peer trainers to promote social behavior in autism? Are they effective at enhancing multiple social modalities? *Focus on Autism and Other Developmental Disabilities, 12,* 207–218.

Reinhartsen, D. B., Garfinkle, A. N., & Wolery, M. (2002). Engagement with toys in two-year-old children with autism: Teacher selection versus child choice. *Research & Practice for Persons with Severe Disabilities, 27,* 175–187.

Reynolds, R. E., & Glaser, R. (1964). Effects of repetition and spaced review upon retention of a complex learning task. *Journal of Educational Psychology, 55,* 297–308.

Rincover, A., & Newsom, C. D. (1985). The relative motivational properties of sensory and edible reinforcers in teaching autistic children. *Journal of Applied Behavior Analysis, 18,* 237–248.

Rogers, S. J. (1998). Empirically supported comprehensive treatments for young children with autism. *Journal of Clinical Child Psychology, 27,* 138–145.

Rogers, S. J. (1999). Intervention for young children with autism: From research to practice. *Infants and Young Children, 12,* 1–16.

Ross, D. E., & Greer, R. D. (2003). Generalized imitation and the mand: Inducing first instances of speech in young children with autism. *Research in Developmental Disabilities, 24,* 58–74.

Schreibman, L. (2000). Intensive behavioral/psychoeducational treatments for autism: Research needs and future directions. *Journal of Autism and Developmental Disorders, 30,* 373–378.

Shabani, D. B., Katz, R. C., Wilder, D. A., Beauchamp, K., Taylor, C. R., & Fischer, K. J. (2002). Increasing social initiations in children with autism: Effects of a tactile prompt. *Journal of Applied Behavior Analysis, 35,* 79–83.

Shearer, D. D. (1996). Promoting independent interactions between preschoolers with autism and their nondisabled peer: An analysis of self-monitoring. *Early Education and Development, 7,* 205–220.

Skinner, B. F. (1953). *Science and human behavior.* New York: Macmillan.

Skinner, B. F. (1969). *Contingencies of reinforcement.* East Norwalk, CT: Appleton-Century-Crofts.

Smith, T. (2001). Discrete trial training in the treatment of autism. *Focus on Autism and Other Developmental Disabilities, 16,* 86–92.

Smith, T., Eikeseth, S., Klevstrand, M., & Lovaas, O. I. (1997). Intensive behavioral treatment for preschoolers with severe mental retardation and pervasive developmental disorder. *American Journal on Mental Retardation, 102,* 238–249.

Stevenson, C. L., Krantz, P. J., & McClannahan, L. E. (2000). Social interaction skills for children with autism: A script-fading procedure for nonreaders. *Behavioral Interventions, 15,* 1–19.

Strain, P. S., Kohler, F. W., Storey, K., & Danko, C. D. (1994). Teaching preschoolers with autism to self-monitor their social interactions: An analysis of results in home and school settings. *Journal of Emotional and Behavioral Disorders, 2,* 78–88.

Sundberg, M. L., & Partington, J. W. (1998). *Teaching language to children with autism or other developmental delays.* Pleasant Hill, CA: Behavior Analysts.

Tabor, T. A., Seltzer, A., Heflin, L. J., & Alberto, P. A. (1999). Use of self-operated auditory prompts to decrease off-task behavior for a student with autism and moderate mental retardation. *Focus on Autism and Other Developmental Disabilities, 14,* 159–167.

Taylor, B. A., & Levin, L. (1998). Teaching a student with autism to make verbal initiations: Effects of a tactile prompt. *Journal of Applied Behavior Analysis, 31,* 651–654.

Wacker, D. P., Steege, M. W., Northrup, J., Sasso, G., Berg, W., Reimers, T., et al. (1990). A component analysis of functional communication training across three topographies of severe behavior problems. *Journal of Applied Behavior Analysis, 23,* 417–429.

Wolery, M., Kirk, K., & Gast, D. L. (1985). Stereotypic behavior as a reinforcer: Effects and side effects. *Journal of Autism and Developmental Disorders, 15,* 149–161.

Wolf, M. (1978). Social validity: The case for subjective measurement or how applied behavior analysis is finding its heart. *Journal of Applied Behavior Analysis, 11,* 203–214.

Yoder, P. J., & Layton, T. L. (1988). Speech following sign language training in autistic children with minimal verbal language. *Journal of Autism and Developmental Disorders, 18,* 217–230.

CHAPTER 7

Programming for Challenging Behavior

KEY TERMS

Attention/Access

Avoid/Escape

Differential Reinforcement (DR)

Direct Data Collection

Extinction (EXT)

Extinction Burst

Functional Analysis (FA)

Functional Behavior Assessment (FBA)

Functional Communication Training (FCT)

Indirect Data Collection

Noncontingent Reinforcement (NCR)

Operational Definition

Pain Attenuation

Pivotal Response

Positive Behavior Support (PBS)

Self-Management

Sensory-Based

❖ LEARNING WITH MS. HARRIS: A Bad Day

Ms. Harris collapsed into a heap on the floor. The end of the school day had come just in the nick of time. Now that all the students were gone, Ms. Harris had the chance to reflect on the day. As she ruefully surveyed the large bruise on her shin and lifted the ice pack off her arm to examine the teeth marks, Ms. Harris mentally reviewed the sequence of events that led to each injury. Gabe had arrived at school more agitated than usual. In the note written in the communication book, Gabe's mother informed Ms. Harris that "someone" had tried to take the VCR apart the night before and it was broken. Gabe was unable to watch his videos before bedtime and threw tantrums most of the night. He got very little sleep (and caused considerable damage to his room). Gabe was also unable to watch his usual videos before leaving for school in the morning. Gabe's mom wrote that she was going to get a replacement VCR before Gabe returned home and wished Ms. Harris good luck. That morning, Ms. Harris attempted to engage Gabe in the typical class routines but he kept running to the VCR in the room and screaming, "I want Thomas! Thomas in!" Ms. Harris decided that she would remove the VCR from the room. As she was wheeling it out, Gabe became violent and began to hit and kick Ms. Harris, leaving several tender spots and one large bruise on her shin.

Ms. Harris acquired the bite on her arm when she tried to help Donald finish his work. He had repeatedly thrown the work materials off the table, and when Ms. Harris tried to use hand-over-hand guidance to help Donald finish the work, he leaned forward and bit her. And then there was Steven, who took forever to finish his writing tasks because he held up his pencil between every letter and wiggled it in front of his eyes.

Ms. Harris was keenly aware of the neurological differences that made it difficult for students with ASD to understand the world, but she was going to have to do something to address these interfering behaviors if the students were going to make progress on their IEP goals.

One of the most daunting issues that all teachers face (general education and special education) is managing students' behavior in order to provide instruction. Some of the minor misbehavior exhibited by students can be dealt with by getting closer to the student, giving students the "teacher look," or giving directions with a warning tone. However, many students with Autism Spectrum Disorders (ASD) are not able to interpret the "look" or the voice tone because of their socialization and communication deficits. For students who use spoken language as well as those who do not, the communication deficits are likely to precipitate instances of misbehavior because students have no other reliable way to communicate their messages. This chapter will discuss challenging behavior in context and how teachers can decipher what the behavior is communicating. The process for doing this is called a Functional Behavior Assessment (FBA). The chapter then describes the process for using information gained from the FBA in order to develop Positive Behavioral Support (PBS) plans that have a higher likelihood of effectively managing student behavior so that instruction can be provided.

WHAT PRECIPITATES CHALLENGING BEHAVIOR?

All behavior tells a story, and the teacher's challenge is to decipher what a given behavior is communicating (Donnellan, Mirenda, Mesaros, & Fassbender, 1984). Behavior communicates information about an individual's internal state and about the individual's response to external events. In regard to the internal state, behaviors can provide clear indications of developmental maturity. For example, 2-year-old children commonly bite when they get frustrated. However, as children age, they learn other ways of communicating frustration. If an 11-year-old is still biting when he gets frustrated, it clearly communicates a delayed level of maturation.

Behaviors can also have a neurological basis. Individuals may bark or twitch or make abrupt arm movements as a symptom of a tic disorder, which indicates unusual electrical activity in the brain. They may fall asleep suddenly as a result of narcolepsy, which also occurs because of unusual brain functioning. They may engage in behaviors that provide sensory feedback, which the brain registers as needed or pleasurable, as in Steven's pencil wiggling.

In addition to behaviors that emanate from a neurological basis, individuals will be less interested in engaging in instructional activities if they are hungry or, as in Gabe's case, very tired and upset (O'Reilly, 1995; Kennedy & Meyer, 1996). Most people have had the experience of not performing at their best when suffering seasonal allergies or not feeling well. At times, people become sleepy as a result of medications taken for allergies and illness, exacerbating a lack of interest in engaging in expected behaviors. Teachers must examine behaviors to see what is being communicated about the internal state of the student (Romanczyk & Matthews, 1998).

Behaviors can also communicate information about the interaction between an individual and the environment (Durand & Merges, 2001). Behavior can indicate the person's preferences and reactions to events. For example, Donald communicated that he did not want to engage in the instructional activity by throwing the materials and then by biting when provided with assistance. Individuals may communicate through their behavior that others are too close to them or that they want to be around (or want to avoid) particular people. Many individuals smile or laugh to communicate when there is something occurring in the environment that they enjoy. Others, like those with ASD, may squeal, flap their hands, or jump when they get excited. For some individuals with ASD, laughter indicates that they are uncomfortable or stressed, rather than happy. Unless they make a conscious decision not to, people spontaneously make a face if presented with food that smells or looks particularly unappealing. In the presence of particular sounds or in noisy environments, some people cover their ears with their hands, communicating that they do not want to hear the sounds. Behaviors communicate preferences for activities and people as well as for sensory stimuli in the environment that are pleasant or aversive. Therefore, behavior is logically related to the environment in which it occurs (Kern & Dunlap, 1998).

In addition to analyzing behavior for what it communicates about internal states and reactions to external events, behaviors must be scrutinized to determine their relationship to consequences (Skinner, 1953). All behavior occurs for a reason; without a reason there would be no behavior. People brush their teeth to have fresh breath and avoid having to spend time in the dentist's office. People give money to charity because it gives them intrinsic pleasure and/or because it provides them with a tax deduction. People purchase and read textbooks so they can learn useful information and/or because it is required of them to earn a passing grade and then to acquire a degree or teaching credential. The key to addressing challenging behavior is to identify the reason behind the behavior (Carr et al., 1999). The reason is usually referred to as the "goal" or "function" of the behavior.

FUNCTIONS OF BEHAVIOR

There are four broad categories of functions of behavior (Iwata, Dorsey, Slifer, Bauman, & Richman, 1982/1994):

- Get (attention/access)
- Avoid (escape)
- Sensory-based
- Pain attenuation

In the category of **attention/access,** behaviors occur so the individual can obtain something that is desired. Sometimes it is attention and sometimes it is access to an object, food, or activity. Discerning between behaviors that are demonstrated to get attention and those that occur to gain access may be difficult because both may be accomplished at the same time. For example, if a student hits another student who is working on the computer in order to gain access to the computer, the action usually attracts some attention. The teacher reprimands the student for hitting. In the opening vignette, Gabe hit and kicked Ms. Harris because she denied him access to something he wanted: the opportunity to watch videos. Other students may call out in class because they want the teacher's or peers' attention. In this broad category, behaviors occur because they allow the individual to get something that is desired, whether it is social attention or access to an object or activity.

In the category of **avoid/escape,** behavior occurs to allow the individual to escape something that is undesirable. Individuals may want to avoid work that is perceived as too hard, too boring, or uninteresting. Donald bit Ms. Harris out of frustration and because of previous associations of biting and removal; Donald learned that if he bit Ms. Harris, he would be removed from the activity and therefore escape doing something he did not want to do. Students may become aggressive toward their peers so that they can be sent to the office and avoid an unwanted activity. Students may engage in behaviors so they can escape being the center of attention or having peers close to them. Or students may engage in behaviors so they will be removed from or avoid being in environments they find undesirable for a variety of reasons (e.g., smells, noises, expectations).

If the function is **sensory-based,** behavior occurs to solicit pleasurable feedback. Individuals chew gum because they like the sensory feedback. People rock or ride roller coasters because they like the feeling that it gives them.

As discussed in Chapter 5, sensory feedback may be intrinsically pleasurable or it may modulate the individual's internal regulation. Gum chewing may be enjoyable, and it may be used as an attempt to increase levels of arousal to try to stay awake. Rocking may provide pleasant feedback or it may engage the proprioceptive and vestibular systems to reduce levels of stress. Behaviors have a sensory basis if they serve the function of providing pleasurable or modulating feedback.

Pain attenuation must be considered as a possible function of behavior, but it requires medical, not educational, intervention. To attenuate something is to make it seem less. With pain attenuation, a behavior occurs so that a pain does not hurt as much. For example, many people scratch a mosquito bite to attenuate the itch. However, scratching a mosquito bite is not an effective treatment and may even cause more problems if the bite becomes inflamed or infected. Many people rub their temples if they get a headache in an attempt to attenuate the pain. Again, this effort does not provide a remedy for the pain, but temporarily it makes the pain seem less daunting. For some individuals, particularly those with communication impairments, hitting the jaw may attenuate the pain of a toothache just as head banging may attenuate the pain of a headache (Fisher & Dunn, 1983; O'Reilly, 1997). Pain-attenuating behaviors occur less frequently than the other three functions, but must be considered so that they can be ruled out prior to developing a behavioral support plan. If the function of the behavior is pain attenuation, the behavior will occur fairly consistently across multiple contexts and appear to have little logical relationship to the external environment. Individuals with behaviors that serve to attenuate pain need to be examined by a medical practitioner who can design an appropriate treatment.

Before describing the process of determining behavioral function, it is important to provide several cautionary notes. First, it is possible for behaviors to have multiple functions (Lalli & Casey, 1996). Donald may bite when he wants to escape a nonpreferred activity, and he also may bite when he wants the teacher's attention. Second, it is possible that several behaviors can serve the same function. For example, Donald may bite in order to escape a nonpreferred activity, or he may scream, kick, or throw a tantrum to escape a nonpreferred activity. Finally, as all behavior is dynamic, the function of a behavior can change over time (Lerman, Iwata, Smith, Zarcone, & Vollmer, 1994). People who play a musical instrument, like the piano, probably started playing in order to get their parents' approval (attention/access) and avoid their parents' disapproval (and possibly punishment; escape/avoid). Over time, they may have been motivated to continue playing in order to attract the attention of an audience and hear its applause or to avoid having to participate in sports. Years later, those same people may play the piano because of the sense of satisfaction that it provides them or the pleasure they gain when they perceive they are contributing to their community by playing piano for a choir. When considering functions of behavior, it is important to remember that one behavior can serve multiple functions (usually contingent upon the context); several behaviors can serve the same function; and the functions of behavior can change over time.

DETERMINING FUNCTIONS OF BEHAVIOR

Teachers must determine the function(s) of behavior to develop effective support plans (Foxx, 1996; Horner & Carr, 1997). Functional behavioral assessments and functional analyses are used to determine function. Although the terms *functional behavioral assessment* and *functional analysis* are often used interchangeably, they denote very different processes. A **Functional Behavioral Assessment (FBA)** is the process of gathering data and arriving at some conclusion regarding the probable function. A **Functional Analysis (FA)** is the process of verifying the probable function by manipulating what typically occurs before (*antecedents*) or after (*consequences*) the problem behavior (Horner, 2000). The processes for conducting FBAs will be conceptualized in three steps:

1. Operationally define the problem behavior.
2. Collect data on the behavior:
   a. Indirect data to get an idea of the possible function
   b. Direct observation data, including the student's responses to typical consequences
3. Analyze data to create a relationship statement (hypothesize function).

Operationally Define the Problem Behavior

It would be difficult to address all misbehavior simultaneously. Therefore, a priority behavior needs to be selected. Priority can be determined based on the severity of the behavior or based on the occurrence of the behavior early in an escalating chain. For example, some behaviors are so severe that they threaten the safety of the student (e.g., self-injurious behaviors) or the safety of others (e.g., aggressive behaviors). The severity of the behavior may elevate it to the status of priority. Sometimes, a behavior that occurs early in an escalating chain is selected as the priority behavior. For example, prior to becoming aggressive, a student may always begin to rock back and forth. Then rocking behavior may be targeted in the hopes that affecting this behavior interrupts the progression of the behavioral chain. Prioritize a single behavior or very few behaviors for the most accurate FBA results. Targeting more than three behaviors at a time invites confusion and makes the task more difficult.

After selection, the priority behavior must be operationally defined. An **operational definition** of a behavior is one that is written in terms that are observable, measurable, and can be clearly understood by anyone reading the definition (Kazdin, 2001). The behavior "refuses to do work" is not operationally defined, because that description can mean different things to different people. An operational definition of "refuses to do work" might read: "Roy crosses his arms across his chest, looks away from the teacher, and says, 'no,' 'I'm not going to do that,' or another negating comment." For another student, "refusing to do work" may be operationally defined as: "Meredith crawls under her desk and puts her head on her knees." The operational definition of the problem behavior is specific to the individual student and describes exactly what the behavior looks like in terms that are observable and measurable.

Collect Data on the Behavior

Once the problem behavior has been operationally defined, descriptive data are collected to determine the contexts that usually surround the occurrence of the behavior. Data collection also identifies the contexts in which the behavior *never* occurs, allowing comparison and contrast of occurrences and nonoccurrences (Horner, 2000; Kern & Dunlap, 1998). Sufficient data must be collected to formulate answers to the following six questions critical to determining function (O'Neill, et al., 1997):

1. How often does the behavior occur or how long does it usually last?
2. Where does the behavior usually occur and where does it never occur?
3. Who is usually present when the behavior occurs and who never sees the behavior?
4. What is going on when the behavior occurs and what are the activities during which the behavior never occurs?
5. When is the behavior most likely to occur and when is the behavior least likely to occur?
6. What is the student's reaction to the consequences that typically follow the occurrence of the problem behavior?

To formulate answers to these questions, practitioners collect descriptive data. Descriptive data are of two types: indirect and direct. **Indirect data collection** involves asking questions of people who know the student well to solicit their perceptions of the behavior. The results of indirect data collection can open a dialogue about the behavior and provide cursory impressions of the function of the behavior. Indirect assessments may fail to accurately identify the function (Crawford, Brockel, Schauss, & Miltenberger, 1992; Zarcone, Rodgers, Iwata, Rourke, & Dorsey, 1991) because of reliance on subjective memories that may be biased (Lennox & Miltenberger, 1989). Because of these influences, indirect assessments are a good starting place for determining function, but not sufficient for the creation of a positive behavior support plan.

Several instruments are commonly used to collect indirect data. These include the Functional Analysis Screening Tool (FAST; Florida Center on Self-Injury, 1996); the Motivation Assessment Scale (MAS; Durand & Crimmins, 1992); and the Problem Behavior Questionnaire (PBQ; Lewis, Scott, & Sugai, 1994). Figure 7.1 contains an older version of the MAS that has been completed on Natasha, a student who frequently puts work materials in her mouth.

MOTIVATION ASSESSMENT SCALE

Name: Natasha   **Rater:** _____ **Date:** _____

Description of Behavior (be specific): puts materials in mouth, throws materials, clears surfaces

Setting Description: classroom at her own table

Instructors: The MAS is a questionaire designed to identify those situations where an individual is likely to behave in specific ways. From this information, more informed decisions can be made about the selections of appropriate replacement behaviors. To complete the MAS, select one behavior of specific interest. Be specific about the behavior. For example "is aggressive" is not as good a description as "hits other people". Once you have specified the behavior to be rated, read each question carefully and circle the one number that best describes your observations of this behavior.

QUESTIONS	ANSWERS						
	Never	Almost Never	Seldom	Half the Time	Usually	Almost Always	Always
1. Would the behavior occur continuously if this person was left alone for long periods of time?	Never 0	Almost Never 1	(Seldom) (2)	Half the Time 3	Usually 4	Almost Always 5	Always 6
2. Does the behavior occur following a request to perform a difficult task?	Never 0	Almost Never 1	Seldom 2	(Half the Time 3)	Usually 4	Almost Always 5	Always 6
3. Does the behavior seem to occur in response to your talking to other persons in the room/area?	Never 0	Almost Never 1	Seldom 2	Half the Time 3	(Usually 4)	Almost Always 5	Always 6
4. Does the behavior ever occur to get a toy, food, or an activity that this person has been told he/she can't have?	Never 0	Almost Never 1	(Seldom 2)	Half the Time 3	Usually 4	Almost Always 5	Always 6
5. Would the behavior occur repeatedly, in the same way, for long periods of time if the person was alone? (e.g. rocking back & forth for over an hour)	(Never 0)	Almost Never 1	Seldom 2	Half the Time 3	Usually 4	Almost Always 5	Always 6
6. Does the behavior occur when any request is made of this person?	Never 0	Almost Never 1	Seldom 2	(Half the Time 3)	Usually 4	Almost Always 5	Always 6
7. Does the behavior occur whenever you stop attending to this person?	Never 0	Almost Never 1	Seldom 2	Half the Time 3	Usually 4	(Almost Always 5)	Always 6
8. Does the behavior occur when you take away a favorite food, toy or activity?	Never 0	Almost Never 1	(Seldom 2)	Half the Time 3	Usually 4	Almost Always 5	Always 6
9. Does it appear to you that the person enjoys doing the behavior? (It feels, tastes, looks, smells, sounds pleasing).	Never 0	Almost Never 1	(Seldom 2)	Half the Time 3	Usually 4	Almost Always 5	Always 6
10. Does this person seem to do the behavior to upset or annoy you when you are trying to get him/her to do what you ask?	Never 0	Almost Never 1	(Seldom 2)	Half the Time 3	Usually 4	Almost Always 5	Always 6
11. Does this person seem to do the behavior to upset or annoy you when you are not paying attention to him/her? (e.g. you are in another room, interacting with another person.)?	Never 0	Almost Never 1	Seldom 2	Half the Time 3	Usually 4	(Almost Always 5)	Always 6
12. Does the behavior stop occurring shortly after you give the person food, toy or requested activity?	Never 0	Almost Never 1	(Seldom 2)	Half the Time 3	Usually 4	Almost Always 5	Always 6
13. When the behavior is occurring does this person seem calm and unaware of anything else going on around her/him?	(Never 0)	Almost Never 1	Seldom 2	Half the Time 3	Usually 4	Almost Always 5	Always 6
14. Does the behavior stop occurring shortly after (one to five minutes) you stop working with or making demands of this person?	Never 0	(Almost Never 1)	Seldom 2	Half the Time 3	Usually 4	Almost Always 5	~~Always 6~~
15. Does this person seem to do the behavior to get you to spend some time with her/him?	Never 0	Almost Never 1	Seldom 2	Half the Time 3	Usually 4	Almost Always 5	(Always 6)
16. Does the behavior seem to occur when this person has been told that he/she can't do something he/she had wanted to do?	Never 0	Almost Never 1	(Seldom 2)	Half the Time 3	Usually 4	Almost Always 5	Always 6

FIGURE 7.1

MAS for Natasha

Source: Motivation Assessment Scale and Guide, Copyright 1992, Monaco & Associates Incorporated, 1-800-798-1309, *www.monacoassociates.com.*

The MAS completed by the teacher suggests that the function of Natasha's behavior is attention. Natasha's speech-language pathologist (SLP), paraprofessional, and mother also independently rated Natasha using the MAS. The results indicate that the SLP and the mother perceive the function of Natasha's behavior to be escape-based, while the paraprofessional's responses predicted attention as the function. Independently completed indirect assessments rarely produce exactly the same results, even when the behavior is clearly operationally defined.

Teachers use indirect assessments to initiate a dialogue about a problem behavior and serve as a catalyst for initial collection of perceptions about a student's behavior, but direct observation data need to be collected to generate a viable relationship statement regarding the function of the behavior (Horner & Carr, 1997). The standard analogue data collection format developed by Bijou, Peterson, and Ault (1968) structures space to record the antecedent, problem behavior, and consequences. For the purpose of determining function, this standard format has been modified to include a place to record the student's reaction to the consequences that typically follow the behavior. Figure 7.2 contains a **direct data collection** format that has been used effectively by hundreds of teachers (adapted from Smith & Heflin, 2001). A time-saving addition is a key that condenses full descriptions to a single letter, reducing the amount of writing required during direct observations.

The options for context, antecedents, consequences, and student's reaction are fairly predictable in educational environments. Figure 7.3 provides a nonexhaustive list of commonly reported options collected from teachers in one state across more than 10 years.

How much direct data need to be collected? Sufficient data so that there is a high degree of confidence in the ability to hypothesize the function of the behavior. For some students, it will take relatively little data (e.g., 10–15 separate incidents), whereas for other students, it will take much more. Sufficient data need to be collected to answer the six questions posed earlier and to identify patterns in the data.

Analyze Data to Create a Relationship Statement

Data that have been collected need to be analyzed to identify patterns and determine if there is any predictability in the behavior. The ability to predict the occurrence of a problem behavior provides a good basis for determining function. Consider for example, the sample of direct observation data collected on Natasha in Figure 7.4.

Recall that the results of Natasha's indirect assessments indicated that the teacher and paraprofessional rated attention as the most probable function, while the SLP and mother rated escape as the most probable function. The direct data collected reflect highly predictive patterns of behavior. Natasha was more likely to put her work materials in her mouth when her teacher was not giving her attention and was likely to stop the behavior if her

BEHAVIORAL OBSERVATION FORM

STUDENT: _____

DATE: _____ PAGE: _____

Circle One: Mon Tues Wed Thurs Fri   Full day Absent   Partial day: In _____ Out _____

TIME/ Duration	CONTEXT/ACTIVITY	ANTECEDENT/ SETTING EVENTS	IDENTIFIED TARGET BEHAVIORS	CONSEQUENCE/ OUTCOME	STUDENT REACTION	STAFF INITIALS

KEY:	KEY:	KEY:	KEY:	KEY:	
A.	A.	1.	A.	A.	
B.	B.	2.	B.	B.	
C.	C.	3.	C.	C.	
D.	D.		D.	D.	
E.	E.		E.	E.	
F.	F.		F.	F.	
G.	G.		G.	G.	
H.	H.		H.	H.	
I.	I.		I.	I.	
J.	J.		J.	J.	
K.	K.		K.	K.	
L.	L.		L.	L.	

CONTEXT/ACTIVITY: The student's environmental surroundings (*people, places, events*)

ANTECEDENT/SETTING EVENTS: Describe **exactly** what occurred in the environment just **before** targeted behavior was exhibited.

BEHAVIOR: Types of behavior displayed during incident

CONSEQUENCE/OUTCOME: What happened in the environment immediately **after** behavior was exhibited?

STUDENT REACTION: How did the student react **immediately** following the **initial** consequence being delivered?

FIGURE 7.2

Direct Observation Data Collection Form

Source: Adapted from Smith & Heflin (2001).

BEHAVIORAL ASSESSMENT FORM: COMMON ENTRIES

Context	Antecedent	Behaviors	Consequences/Outcome	Student Reaction
Classroom	Transition	(List target behaviors)	Ignored	Stopped
Bus Area	Teacher attention to others		Redirect	Continued
Bathroom	Redirection		Verbal reprimand/warning	Intensified
Hallway	Praise		Time-out	Remorse
Pre/voc activity	Request by teacher		Applied restraints	Apologized
Home Living	Seizure activity		Sent to office	Cried
Academics	Told "No"		Sent home	Different behavior
CBI	Close physical proximity		Chair time-out	Moved away
Lunchroom	Easy task given		Physical restraint	Laughed
Outside/playground	Difficult task given		Physical assist	Slept
Gym/P.E.	Physically assist		Removal of materials	
Music	Food presentation		Removal of reinforcement	
Speech	Down time/waiting		Peer attention	
Art	Denied access		Head on desk	
Leisure activity	Individual work time		Change/delayed activity	
Centers	Rest time		Gave personal space	
Story time	Break time		Natural consequence	
Choices	Attempt to communicate		Reflection	
Group	Tangible removal		Problem solving	
Individual	Corrective feedback		Stated rules	
Computer lab	Peer interaction		Gave choice	

FIGURE 7.3

Common Entries for Direct Observation Data Collection Form

Source: From "Supporting positive behavior in public schools: An intervention program in Georgia" by M. L. Smith, and L. J. Heflin (2001), *Journal of Positive Behavioral Interventions, 3,* pp. 39–47. Copyright (2001) by PRO-ED, Inc. Reprinted with permission.

BEHAVIORAL OBSERVATION FORM

STUDENT: Natasha

Circle One: Mon (Tues) Wed Thurs Fri DATE: 9 - 23 (Full day) Absent Partial day: In____ Out____ PAGE: 1

TIME/Duration	CONTEXT/ACTIVITY	ANTECEDENT/SETTING EVENTS	IDENTIFIED TARGET BEHAVIORS	CONSEQUENCE/OUTCOME	STUDENT REACTION	STAFF INITIALS
9:15	B	B, I	1	A	A, B	
9:16	B	B	1	A	A, B	
9:18	B	C	1	A, B	A, B, C	
9:20	B	A	1	D	A	
9:23	B	D	1	C	G	
9:24	B	D	1	B	A, C	
9:26	B	C	1	A	A, B	
9:27	B	B	1	D	D	

KEY:	KEY:	KEY:	KEY:	KEY:
A. Group Instruction	A. Teacher leave	1. Materials in mouth	A. Tchr. reprimand	A. Stopped
B. Individual---easy	B. Teacher look away	2.	B. Tchr. ask for materials	B. Laugh
C. Individual---hard	C. Tchr. attend to others	3.	C. Withhold materials	C. Withhold materials
D. Hallway	D. Request by teacher		D. Ignore	D. Continue
E. bathroom	E. Physical contact		E. Physical assist	E. Intensify
F. bus area	F. waiting		F. Change activity	F. Cry
G. gym	G. denied access		G. Time-out	G. Change behavior
H. cafeteria	H. Told "no"		H.	H. Move away
I. snack area	I. Tchr. pick up materials		I.	I.
J. transition	J.		J.	J.
K.	K.		K.	K.
L.	L.		L.	L.

CONTEXT/ACTIVITY: The student's environmental surroundings (*people, places, events*)

ANTECEDENT/SETTING EVENTS: Describe **exactly** what occurred in the environment just **before** targeted behavior was exhibited.

BEHAVIOR: Types of behavior displayed during incident

CONSEQUENCE/OUTCOME: What happened in the environment immediately **after** behavior was exhibited?

STUDENT REACTION: How did the student react immediately following the **initial** consequence being delivered?

Adapted from Smith & Heflin (2001)

FIGURE 7.4
Direct Observation Data for Natasha

TABLE 7.1
Summary of Direct Observation Data for Natasha

Antecedents	Letter	Frequency	Ratio	% Involved
Teacher leaves	A	9	9/43	21%
Teacher looks away	B	14	14/43	33%
Teacher attention to others	C	8	8/43	19%
Request by teacher	D	11	2/43	4%
Physical contact	E	0	0	0
Waiting	F	10	10/43	23%
Denied access	G	0	0	0
Told "no"	H	0	0	0

Consequence	Letter	Tally	Student Reaction		% Effective
			Stop	Continue	
Reprimand	A	24	22	2	92%
Ask for material	B	5	3	2	60%
Redirect	C	3	3		100%
Ignore	D	6		6	0%
Physical assist	E	3	3		100%
Change activity	F				
Time out	G	2		2	0%

teacher reprimanded or redirected her. If the teacher ignored the behavior, Natasha was likely to continue the behavior and even add additional behaviors that would be considered undesirable in the instructional setting. Table 7.1 offers a summary of the complete direct observation data collected on Natasha.

Given that the most common antecedent for Natasha's problem behavior was lack of attention, and the consequence that was likely to result in stopping the behavior was attention in the form of a reprimand, it is likely that the function of Natasha's behavior of putting her work materials in her mouth is to get attention. To further support this hypothesis, the data suggest that when attention was withheld (i.e., ignoring), the problem behavior was likely to escalate until she received attention. Table 7.2 provides a very general summary of antecedents and reactions to consequences that are predictive of specific functions.

From the analysis of data, a relationship statement (hypothesis) is developed. The relationship statement specifies:

When _____, the student will
　　　　(antecedent)

_____ in order to _____.
(problem behavior)　　　　　　　(consequence/function)

TABLE 7.2
Summary of Common Antecedents and Reactions by Function

Function	Antecedents	Reactions to Consequences
Attention/Access	• No specific attention being paid to student or attention being given to someone else	• Behavior escalates if student is ignored • Behavior stops if teacher/peer attention is gained (even if the attention is "negative" as in reprimand or taunting)
	• Prevented from having access to preferred item/activity	• Behavior escalates
	• Access to item/activity obtained	• Behavior stops
Escape/Avoid	• Asked to complete or given a nonpreferred task (too hard, too easy, done previously), particularly if the student is hungry, tired, or agitated	• Behavior escalates if additional demands are placed on the student to complete the task
	• Told to stop a preferred activity to transition to another activity	• Behavior stops if task is removed or student removed from activity (sent to desk, "time out," principal's office)
Sensory Stimulation	• Required to be in an activity that has no meaning or required to wait quietly with nothing to do • Experience stressful situation (e.g., noisy, unclear expectations)	• Engage in behavior that provides pleasure/stimulation (e.g., drawing, muscle tense & release, echo video script)

In Natasha's case, the relationship statement would read: "When the teacher is not attending to her, Natasha will put materials in her mouth in order to get the teacher's attention as a redirection, reprimand, or physical assist."

The three components just described as the FBA process help teachers isolate antecedents that are likely to occasion behavior and identify consequences that are maintaining behavior. An intervention plan developed by the teacher based on this information has a greater chance of being successful. The possibility exists, however, that the correct function of the behavior has not been identified during the FBA process. A Functional Analysis (FA) can be used to verify that the correct behavioral function has been identified.

FUNCTIONAL ANALYSIS

An experimental Functional Analysis requires systematic modification of antecedents and consequences within stringently controlled conditions (Iwata et al., 1982/1994) to develop or verify a hypothesis regarding the function of behavior. However, controlled conditions may fail to capture naturally occurring variables that affect behavior (Iwata, Vollmer, & Zarcone, 1990). Variations of experimental FAs are less time consuming and more readily conducted in classroom settings (Sasso et al., 1992; Zanolli, Daggett, Ortiz, & Mullins, 1999). But even these modified formats may induce the problem behavior, which will then have to be handled in the classroom. The simplest way to conduct an FA in a classroom is to modify the antecedents to see if the behavior can be prevented from occurring. With Natasha, an FA might consist of the teacher giving exclusive and constant attention for a prescribed period of time (e.g., 15 minutes) to see if this will stop Natasha from putting materials in her mouth. For a student who throws a tantrum every time he is asked to do his math (escape/avoid), no math assignments will be given for a day to see if any tantrums occur. In applied settings, educators modify the antecedents to see if the problem behavior can be prevented. If the behavior does not occur, the FA has verified the relationship statement.

POSITIVE BEHAVIOR SUPPORT

Once the function of the behavior has been determined, a positive behavior support plan can be developed to address the challenging behavior. The **positive behavior support (PBS)** plan considers how the environment can be changed to better support the student (O'Neill et al., 1997) before determining what the student needs to be able to do to be successful in the instructional environment. Changes to the environment can reduce the likelihood that challenging behavior will occur and teaching the student the skills necessary to be successful can further reduce the occurrence of the problem behavior. The function of behavior identified through the FBA and FA processes is recognized as indicating relevant motivation useful for creating behavior change. Behavior change occurs through the use of three key strategies, all based in reinforcement:

- Noncontingent reinforcement (NCR)
  (reduces behavior)

- Differential reinforcement (DR)
  (replaces behavior)

- Extinction (EXT)
  (eliminates behavior)

Noncontingent reinforcement (NCR) allows access to reinforcement without making it contingent on the student doing anything in particular. This can reduce problem behavior. **Differential reinforcement (DR)** is used to increase desired behaviors by reinforcing them instead of inadvertently reinforcing the undesired behaviors. This can replace an undesired behavior with one that is more acceptable. **Extinction (EXT)** means that reinforcement is withheld when the behavior occurs in order to reduce future occurrences. If whatever is reinforcing is withheld, the behavior is likely to stop. Extinction usually occurs in combination with differential reinforcement. Desired behaviors are differentially reinforced while undesired behaviors experience extinction so that they receive no reinforcement whatsoever, which is a very powerful combination for eliminating one behavior and increasing a replacement behavior. Consider Ms. Harris' exposure to the three key strategies.

❖ LEARNING WITH MS. HARRIS: A Lesson in Changing Behavior

Ms. Harris, still limping slightly and sporting scabs on the back of her hand, has the opportunity to attend an inservice presented by the behavioral consultant, Ms. Briggs. During the inservice, Ms. Briggs asks for a volunteer to demonstrate the power of reinforcement on reducing, replacing, and eliminating behavior. Ms. Harris quickly volunteers and the demonstration proceeds.

Ms. Briggs: *Ms. Harris is a teacher at Phillips Elementary. We all know that she went into teaching because she was motivated to make a difference in the lives of students. However, there is another motivation that drives Ms. Harris. What can it be? Right—it's her paycheck. If money were her only motivation, Ms. Harris would have gone into a profession other than teaching. However, without the motivation of her paycheck, it would be hard for her to continue in her current position. For the sake of the demonstration, let's consider that the function of Ms. Harris's work behavior is to earn a paycheck, so the reinforcer is money. Let's see if I can reduce Ms. Harris's work behavior. Ms. Harris, I have in my hand the winning lotto ticket— $24,000,000. It's yours! Now Ms. Harris has lots of what she finds reinforcing—money—and it is not contingent upon her behavior.*

Ms. Harris: *Where will you be next Monday?*

Ms. Harris: *Probably Tahiti.*

Ms. Briggs: *Right! I can reduce your working behavior by giving you lots of what you find reinforcing, without making you demonstrate any work behavior to get it. That's called noncontingent reinforcement. It may not totally stop your teaching behavior; after all, you went into teaching for reasons in addition to the paycheck. You may even use some of your millions of dollars to open your own school and work with kids. Or you may squander your money and need more, so you will return to seek a teaching position. Noncontingent reinforcement only reduces levels of behavior; it won't totally stop the behavior.*

Let's see if I can replace your behavior. Currently, you work at Phillips Elementary. You can choose to continue to work there.

> *Your classroom is all set up, the children like you, the other teachers like you, the principal likes you; however, you won't get a paycheck unless you show up at Simpson Elementary on Monday. Remember, everything can stay the same at Phillips, but you just won't get a paycheck. If you go to Simpson, you will get a paycheck. Where will you be on Monday?*

Ms. Harris: *I guess I'll be at Simpson!*

Ms. Briggs: *By differentially reinforcing Ms. Harris, I can replace her work behavior so that she is teaching at Simpson rather than at Phillips. I haven't stopped her behavior—I have only led to its occurrence at a different location by changing the conditions under which she is reinforced. That's differential reinforcement.*

> *Now let's see if I can totally stop her behavior. Ms. Harris, I am sorry to be the bearer of bad tidings, but the school district has experienced major budget cuts. All money is gone for first-year teachers. However, your class is all set up, your students are making good progress, and the principal would love for you to keep working at Phillips. You just won't get paid. And, no, there is no money for benefits either. So no money whatsoever, but it would be great if you would keep teaching. Will you?*

Ms. Harris: *Uhh . . . well, no salary? Uhh . . . I think I'd better go apply at the grocery store.*

Ms. Briggs: *Of course you wouldn't continue to engage in a behavior for which you receive no reinforcement. By withholding reinforcement (which is the definition of extinction), I can totally eliminate your work behavior. There you have it, the three key strategies for changing behavior: noncontingent reinforcement to reduce behavior, differential reinforcement to replace behavior, and extinction to eliminate behavior.*

To effectively use the three key strategies of noncontingent reinforcement, differential reinforcement, and extinction, educators must identify what is reinforcing to the student. Some of the most powerful reinforcers are those evident in the function of behavior. To reduce and replace the problem behavior, the student should have noncontingent access to, or differentially receive the function of, the behavior. To eliminate a problem behavior, the function of the behavior has to be withheld. Consider the use of reinforcement and withholding of reinforcement in the functions of behavior as depicted in Table 7.3.

A note of caution: Extinction usually creates a temporary increase in behavior. The **extinction burst** (Kazdin, 2001, p. 250) is an elevated level of behavior designed to accomplish the function of behavior. If the soda machine doesn't produce a drink after money is put in, some people will push buttons frantically or even hit the machine. The reinforcer (soda) was

TABLE 7.3
Reinforcement and Extinction by Function

Function	Reinforcement	Extinction (Withholding Reinforcement)
Attention/Access	Get attention Get access	Attention withheld (ignoring) Deny access
Escape/Avoid	Getting out of an activity Avoiding something undesired	Not allowing the student to get out of or avoid something that is undesired
Sensory Stimulation	Receiving the sensory feedback that is sought	Sensory feedback is blocked (e.g., rocking stopped, eyes covered, sound muffled)

withheld, so behavior escalates in an attempt to get the soda. Teachers must prepare to handle a temporary increase in the problem behavior when extinction is used.

Knowledge of the function of the behavior can provide insight into one of the most salient reinforcers available. For example, if the function of the behavior is to avoid work, then work avoidance can be used as a reinforcer for demonstrating more appropriate behavior.

DEVELOPING POSITIVE BEHAVIOR SUPPORT PLANS

After the function of the behavior has been identified so that the maintaining consequences (and powerful reinforcers) have been determined, it is time to develop a support plan to address the challenging behavior. A behavior support plan will not only address the challenging behavior but also change the environment and enhance the student's skills and competence (Guess & Carr, 1991b). Two caveats apply:

1. Misbehavior provides feedback about the environment. Misbehavior can be evaluated to gain an understanding of the student's perspective on such variables as physical environment, scheduling and movement, interactions, curricula, and instructional modalities.
2. The environment needs management, not the student. Although powerful contingencies can be arranged, it is almost impossible to make someone do something without negative repercussions. The impetus, therefore, is not on how educators can "change" the student, but on how to manage the environment to reduce the need for misbehavior and increase the likelihood that desirable behaviors will be demonstrated (Horner, 2000).

With those caveats in mind, consider the steps for developing a positive behavior support plan:

1. Consider antecedent modifications.
2. Teach acceptable behaviors that serve the same function as the misbehavior.

3. Identify the consequences for misbehavior and develop backup plans should the misbehavior escalate.
4. Plan for generalization.

Consider Antecedent Modifications

Given that behavior is usually linked to the environment, the first step is to carefully consider environmental adjustments that can be made to reduce the need for the misbehavior. For students with ASD, this means examining sensory stimuli, considering the use of visually based methods of presenting behavioral expectations and the sequence of activities, and establishing predictable routines. Many environmental modifications that can be effective for students with ASD were described in Chapters 4 and 5.

As another proactive measure, learning new skills can enhance the student's ability to cope with the environment. One of the most important skills is reliable communication. Without the ability to communicate needs, wants, and desires, students will use what will be viewed as misbehavior to accomplish the attainment of those critical objectives (Donnellan et al., 1984; Horner, 2000). Using a combination of effective interventions for developing communication (described in Chapter 8), students need to be taught to communicate their wants and preferences. Compensatory strategies can also be taught, such as inserting earplugs when the noise level becomes annoying or politely asking a peer to give a little more space.

Pivotal Response Training (PRT) has been used to proactively teach skills that produce enhanced functioning and responsiveness to stimuli in typical environments (Koegel, Koegel, & McNerney, 2001). A **pivotal response** is a behavior that leads to generalized improvements in other behaviors and is maintained by naturally occurring consequences (Koegel & Koegel, 1995). Using applied behavior analytic principles, the selected pivotal response is systematically taught in natural contexts using discrete trials that incorporate materials preferred by the child to allow for more natural reinforcement of attempts (Koegel, Koegel, & Carter, 1999). PRT also incorporates "child choice, frequent task variation, interspersing previously learned tasks with new acquisition tasks, using less intrusive prompting, reinforcing the child's attempts, and incorporating turn-taking within the interactions" (Koegel, Koegel, Harrower, & Carter, 1999, p. 178).

Pivotal responses that have been successfully taught include motivation (Koegel, O'Dell, & Kogel, 1987); responsivity to multiple cues (Schreibman, Charlop, & Koegel, 1982); self-initiations (Koegel, Koegel, Shoshan, & McNerney, 1999); language skills (Pierce & Schreibman, 1997); symbolic play skills (Stahmer, 1995); and self-management (Koegel & Koegel, 1990). PRT has also been shown to be more effective for developing generalized use of behavior than traditional discrete trial training formats (Koegel, Camarata, Koegel, Ben-Tall, & Smith, 1998). Figure 7.5 summarizes strategies for incorporating PRT in instruction.

Pivotal Response	Intervention	Examples
Motivation	Provide child choice.	Child chooses order of assignments. Child chooses writing instruments. Child chooses book to be read to class.
	Vary tasks and intersperse maintenance tasks.	Vary tasks often by following a short duration of reading with a short duration of art time. Vary task size by providing frequent breaks. Modify pacing of task by decreasing the interval of time between student's responses and presentation of the next instruction. Intersperse a learned task such as counting with a new task such as learning money.
	Reinforce attempts.	Provide verbal praise for all responses to questions asked. Provide written praise on homework papers and other assignments.
	Use natural reinforcers.	When learning to tell time, let the child learn the times of favorite activities. When teaching money, have the children purchase small favorite items.
Multiple cues	Encourage multiple cue learning and responses.	Furnish a number of different colors of construction paper, crayous, pencils, etc. during art time and have children ask for which they'd like. Ask questions during story time which require the children to respond using multiple cues. For mathematics assignments or practicing writing alphabet letters, provide a number of different writing utensils (e.g., a blue pen, a black pen, & yellow pencil, etc.), and have the children request the utensil they'd prefer.
Self-initiated responses	Teach question asking.	Teach informations-seeking initiations such as questions about the name and location of items. Teach assistance-seeking initiations, such as asking for help.
Self-management	Teach children to discriminate their own behaviors and to record the occurrence or absence of the behaviors.	Have child put a check mark on a piece of paper for every page turned during story time when sitting quietly. Have child use a repeat chronograph alarm wristwatch to self-evaluate periods of on-task behavior during in class mathematics or other assignments.

FIGURE 7.5
Strategies for Teaching Pivotal Responses

Source: Koegel, R. L., Koegel, L. K., & Carter, C. M. (1999). Pivotal teaching interactions for children with autism. *School Psychology Review, 28*, pp. 588–589. Copyright 1999 by the National Association for School Psychologists, Bethesda, MD. Reprinted with permission of the publisher.

Using the steps described by Koegel, Camarata, Valdez-Menchaca, & Koegel (1998), consider how PRT could be used to teach a student the pivotal skill of asking questions.

❖ LEARNING WITH MS. HARRIS: Using PRT with Craig

Although Craig communicated using spoken language and had an expressive vocabulary that was typical for someone his age, he rarely asked questions. Ms. Harris decided to use PRT to teach Craig to spontaneously ask questions. First, she put one of Craig's favorite items, a plastic dinosaur, in a paper sack. Next, she prompted him to ask "What's that?" in order to be shown what was in the sack, and then gave him a few minutes to hold the dinosaur. Ms. Harris presented the bag several times during the day (varying the favorite objects that were in the sack) and gradually faded the prompt so that Craig was spontaneously asking "What's that?" when he saw the sack. Over time, Ms. Harris substituted Craig's favorite items with common items that he wasn't really interested in (like a pencil) and with items that he probably didn't know the label for (such as a manual can opener). She also started eliminating the paper sack by cutting it so that it became smaller and smaller. Through the strategy, Craig began to spontaneously ask, "What's that?" when he came across items he didn't know the label for and even began to use the question with his parents. In addition to learning how to appropriately inquire about something unfamiliar to him, Craig also increased his vocabulary by learning more object labels.

An important consideration in the development of a positive behavior support plan is to be proactive in determining how to modify antecedents and how to enhance the student's skills by reducing the need for inappropriate behavior. These proactive strategies can include antecedent modifications such as varying the task demands and method of instruction. They can also be as simple as identifying distractions in the environment. A critical aspect of proactive modifications is teaching students methods of reliable communication and using techniques such as PRT to facilitate the students' competence in the environment. Figure 7.6 contains a nonexhaustive list of antecedent modifications that can be proactively implemented.

Teach Acceptable Behaviors That Serve the Same Function as the Misbehavior

Once proactive modifications and strategies have been implemented, design the educative component of the positive behavior support plan. In the educative component, the student learns a replacement behavior that serves the same function as the problem behavior (Durand & Crimmins, 1987). The replacement behavior must be more efficient and equally effective as the problem behavior and must produce the same results (Horner & Day, 1991). Asking for a break is much easier than engaging in a tantrum but

- Assess the environment to modify stimuli that could be aversive or distracting to the student.
- Evaluate the schedule for predictability and length and sequencing of activities. Insert preferred activities into the schedule, based on the needs of the student.
- Reduce the amount of down time/waiting.
- Consider the task demands to determine if they are too easy, too hard, boring, and so forth.
- Incorporate opportunities for the student to make choices.
- Provide instruction in ways that engage the student by modifying presentation and incorporating special interests.
- Incorporate noncontingent reinforcement based on the function of the behavior.
- Establish visual methods of communicating expectations as well as for presenting information.
- Provide additional assistance to support transitions and self-control.
- Teach compensatory strategies.
- Use precorrection to highlight behaviors expected in the next activity.
- Establish clear expectations and be consistent in use of contingencies for meeting or violating expectations.
- Establish powerful contingencies to motivate the demonstration of appropriate behavior.
- Use "First/Then" visual reminders.
- Teach reliable communication skills, including how to request help.
- Teach pivotal responses.

FIGURE 7.6
Proactive Modifications

can serve the same function of escape. An analysis of competing behavior pathways (O'Neill et al., 1997) can be helpful for identifying the intermediate and long-term objectives.

	↗	Desired behavior		
Antecedent	→	Replacement behavior	↘	**Same Function**
	↘	Problem behavior	↗	

Many teachers want the replacement behavior and the desired behavior to be the same. For example, Ms. Harris would greatly prefer that Donald complete his work instead of bite. However, Donald's biting gets him out of doing his work. Ultimately, the desired behavior of working independently will be shaped and subsequently maintained by naturally occurring consequences. But initially, a replacement behavior that is more acceptable, yet serves the same function as biting (in this example, escape) must be taught. This is referred to as **Functional Communication Training (FCT)**. The student is taught a replacement behavior that accomplishes the same function (outcome) but is more socially acceptable (Carr & Durand, 1985).

Depending on the student, verbal or nonverbal methods of communicating can be taught. Verbal methods involve teaching a particular phrase (e.g., "I want a break," "Talk to me"); nonverbal methods have included teaching sign language, exchanging icons, and using speech-generating devices (SGD) (Durand, 1993; Wacker et al., 1990).

The student must always meet with success when learning the replacement behavior or she will revert back to the behavior she knows will accomplish the desired result. For example, if a student has historically hit other students in order to gain access to the computer, the student will politely ask the peer for a turn (or inform the teacher she would like to use the computer) only if the behavior is effective and efficient. If not, the student will hit because that works. Therefore, replacement behavior must be designed to be effective and during the learning stage must always accomplish the function. As the student reliably demonstrates the replacement behavior, delay strategies can be used to systematically increase the amount of time between a student's request for attention, access, escape, or sensory activity and when the desired outcome is actually provided (Dunlap, Koegel, Johnson, & O'Neill, 1987; Fisher, Thompson, Hagopian, Bowman, & Krug, 2000).

As described earlier in this chapter, the problem behavior is replaced with a more acceptable alternative through a combination of differential reinforcement and extinction. Reinforcement (the accomplishment of the function: attention, access, escape, sensory) follows demonstrations of the replacement behavior, while extinction (the withholding of reinforcement) follows instances of the inappropriate behavior. Figure 7.7 presents considerations for using FCT (as adapted from Durand & Merges, 2001).

❖ LEARNING WITH MS. HARRIS: FCT for Donald

Ms. Harris determined that Donald bit to avoid doing certain tasks, specifically those that involved sustained fine motor effort. Figure 7.8 contains the competing behavior model Ms. Harris drew for Donald.

Ms. Harris decided that it would be better for the instructional environment to allow Donald to take a brief break when he requested it rather than to put herself (and others) in danger of being bitten. She also knew that teaching Donald a more socially acceptable way of refusing an activity would be beneficial for him in the long run. After considering antecedent modifications that included looking for alternatives to fine motor tasks and incorporating Donald's interests in the tasks, Ms. Harris was ready to teach Donald the replacement behavior.

She laminated an index card containing the word "Break" and put it close to Donald. Then she brought one of Donald's least favorite fine motor tasks to his desk. Before she put it on his desk, she prompted him to give her the "Break" card. She said, "You want a break? OK!" returned the card to his desk, and left immediately with the fine motor task. After allowing Donald to sit contentedly at his desk for a minute, Ms. Harris approached him with the task, again prompting him to give her the break

Considerations	Descriptors
Response Match (For initial reductions in behavior)	Does the replacement communicative behavior match the function of the challenging behavior?
Response Mastery (For initial reductions, generalizations, and maintenance)	Does the replacement behavior achieve the desired outcome? Consider the following: 1. response efficiency—the new behavior needs to achieve the desired outcome faster (efficiency) and easier (effective) than the challenging behavior 2. response acceptability—the new behavior needs to be accepted by others in the environment 3. response recognizability—the new behavior needs to be easily recognized by familiar and unfamiliar people
Response Milieu	Can the replacement behavior serve the same function as the challenging behavior across environments? Are there opportunities for the student to make choices in these environments?
Consequences for Challenging Behavior	Are response-independent consequences being used (i.e., continue working with the student as if the challenging behavior did not occur)? Is the challenging behavior becoming nonfunctional in the environment?

FIGURE 7.7
Considerations for Using FCT
Source: Adapted from Durand & Merges (2001).

card and responding the same way. After a couple more times, Donald began grabbing the break card and handing it to Ms. Harris as she approached him. No more biting! Ms. Harris would just have to be sure that the break card was always available.

She would also have to begin to shape the behavior so that Donald would complete nonpreferred tasks. She would do this by implementing

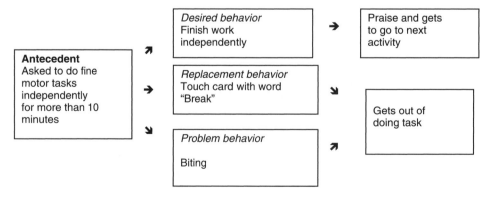

FIGURE 7.8
Competing Behavior Model for Donald's Escape-Based Behavior

progressively longer delays between when Donald asked for a break and when he actually received it. She would start by saying, "You want a break? OK—just pick up the blue one first," and, upon completion, would leave with the task and allow Donald his escape. Gradually, she would expect more work from Donald. If he reverted to biting, Ms. Harris would have to withhold reinforcement (escape) and continue to present the task while prompting Donald to hand her the break card. She would differentially reinforce the appropriate behavior and withhold escape until Donald demonstrated the replacement behavior.

Identify Consequences for Misbehavior and Develop Backup Plans

Even with effective proactive antecedent modifications and systematic teaching of an acceptable replacement behavior, misbehavior will occur. Whenever misbehavior occurs, the student should be encouraged to perform the replacement behavior. If the inappropriate behavior escalates, contingencies designed to reduce future occurrences of the problem behavior need to be developed. Just like the antecedent modifications and the replacement behavior, the contingencies need to be built on the function of the inappropriate behavior. Behavior reduction strategies, described in detail in resources like Kazdin (2001), Maag (2004), and Miltenberger (2001), include consequences such as:

- Extinction (withholding reinforcement)
- Response cost (loss of privileges or tokens)
- Overcorrection (practicing the correct behavior or restoring the environment)
- Time out

Time out is frequently used as a consequence for typically developing students and those with other disabilities, but may inadvertently reinforce some students' inappropriate behaviors, especially those students with ASD. The concept of "time out from reinforcement" indicates that the activities in which the student is currently engaged are reinforcing and that removal from those activities would be distressing. However, many students with ASD would rather be sent away from the group than engage in activities they do not like. When the function of the behavior is escape, time out is reinforcing and the behaviors will likely continue or increase. Additionally, if the function of the inappropriate behavior is sensory stimulation, sending a student to "time out" may allow her the opportunity to engage in self-stimulatory behaviors without interruption. Therefore, time out is a consequence that should be used only when the function of the behavior is attention or access, and used judiciously (Nelson & Rutherford, 1983; Yell, 1990).

Plans for minimizing damage rather than providing instruction need to be developed for the times when a challenging behavior escalates. The time to plan for crisis management is before the behavior occurs. Take care not to inadvertently reinforce a student for escalating behaviors or the student will learn to demonstrate the escalated behaviors in order to obtain attention, escape, access, or sensory stimulation (Guess & Carr, 1991a; Sigafoos, 1998). For example, a student who wants the teacher's attention may learn that talking out is not as efficient as throwing a book. The teacher may ignore the talking out but reprimand the student for throwing a book. The student, reinforced, learns that it is more efficient to start with throwing a book than talking out to get the teacher's attention.

The collaboration of all members of the IEP team and even possible input from behavioral specialists (if not already part of the IEP team) is important before deciding to use behavior reduction strategies. Some of the behavior reduction strategies are invasive, and everyone needs to be in agreement that all other options have been tried. The team needs to set parameters for the use of invasive strategies and monitor the implementation and effects closely. If the team decides that a student should be removed from the instructional setting in the event of specific behavior, the school district's policies regarding removal of students from instructional settings need to be followed. The team should establish a specific set of steps to be followed in the event that a student's behavior becomes dangerous. Physical management (restraint) is an option of last resort to be used with extreme caution (Ryan & Peterson, 2004) when the student is doing harm to self or to others. Personnel should use only those physical management techniques their district has trained them to use. Frequent refresher courses are needed for personnel who implement physical management. Because of the possibility of causing harm or being harmed, physical management should not be used if the student is damaging property. Property can be replaced. Additionally, some students with ASD find the sensory feedback from physical management very reinforcing and may act in ways they know will result in adults holding them (Favell, McGimsey, & Jones, 1978).

Plan for Generalization

During the process of designing positive behavior support, make plans for promoting generalization so that the student can function independently in multiple environments. Generalization involves fading external supports and transferring responsibility for behavioral control to the student. Fading external supports involves providing less frequent feedback and thinning the reinforcement schedule. Rather than reducing the reinforcement that is available, teachers should expect more of the desired behavior before providing the reinforcement. For example, instead of a student having to answer three questions prior to earning a token and earning five tokens before being able to spend time on the computer, the requirement can be modified so that the student must now answer five questions before earning a token. Or perhaps the schedule can be modified so that it takes seven tokens to earn computer time. Reinforcers can never be eliminated totally, but the goal is to fade the intensity of the feedback so that it begins to approximate naturally occurring contingencies.

The process of monitoring and evaluating behavior can also be transferred to the student. Transferring control involves teaching the student to self-manage his behavior (Maag, 2004). **Self-management** involves teaching students to:

- Discriminate between acceptable and unacceptable behavior
- Record demonstrations of expected behavior
- Recruit reinforcement for meeting expected criteria (Koegel, Koegel, & McNerney, 2001)

Students can be taught to discriminate between acceptable and unacceptable behavior through the use of modeling and examples. Correct responses should be reinforced. Visual depictions of the correct and incorrect behaviors may be helpful. Modeling and example are also used to teach students to record their behavior. Again, reinforcement is used to strengthen the occurrence of accurate recording. When the recorded behaviors meet an established criterion (e.g., above a certain number for behaviors that need to increase, or below a certain number for behaviors that need to decrease), students can ask for or access predetermined reinforcement. As described in Chapter 6, students with ASD may have strong preferences for unusual reinforcers.

Self-management has been shown to positively affect behavior, including increased time engaged with activities, decreased disruptive behavior, and enhanced socialization (Callahan & Rademacher, 1999; Koegel, Harrower, & Koegel, 1999; Koegel, Koegel, Hurley, & Frea, 1992; Koegel, Koegel, & Surratt, 1992; Mancina, Tankersley, Kamps, Kravits, & Parrett, 2000; Newman et al., 1995; Shearer, 1996; Stahmer & Schreibman, 1992; Strain, Kohler, Storey, & Danko, 1994). Self-management has been used with individuals of various ages and in worksites (Hughes & Scott, 1997) and community settings (Koegel & Koegel, 1990) as well as schools, and is an effective strategy for promoting generalization of behavioral improvement.

❖ LEARNING WITH MS. HARRIS: Collaborative Problem Solving

After the inservice, which theoretically reduced, replaced, and eliminated Ms. Harris's work behavior, Ms. Harris went to dinner with one of her friends who taught community-based instruction (CBI) to high school students. The teacher was complaining because one of her students required high levels of supervision to accomplish vocational tasks that he was capable of performing independently. Ms. Harris helped her devise a strategy to teach the young man to self-manage his behavior. Using an available napkin, they sketched out the following plan:

1. Create a master list of the seven tasks that Thomas must complete on the worksite. Draw a square in front of each task. At the bottom of the page, write the word "Soda." Put the paper on a bright purple clipboard (Thomas's favorite color).

2. *At the worksite, show the list to Thomas. Help him partially complete the first task. Show him the clipboard and ask if he is finished with #1. He will say no. Wait until he finishes the task and ask him again if he is finished. When he says yes, show him how to put a check mark in the box. Show him the next task on the list and help him get started.*

3. *When he is almost finished with the second activity, stop him and ask him if he is finished. He will say no and you will say, "Oh, then you may not check the box!" Encourage him to finish, and ask him if he can put a check in the box. Go to the third task and repeat as above. Make sure he understands when it is time to put a check in the box.*

4. *Once Thomas has checked all the boxes, show him where the soda is stored and give him some time to drink and enjoy.*

5. *Practice the process for several days with Thomas, ensuring that he knows where to store the clipboard and that he marks the boxes only after he has completed the task. Gradually reduce the amount of prompting until Thomas is completing all the tasks and accessing the reinforcement (soda) independently.*

Ms. Harris and her colleague are excited about teaching Thomas how to self-manage his vocational behavior because they know that such skills will be greatly appreciated by potential employers.

Efforts to promote generalization are enhanced through collaboration. If particular supports have been used across environments, then all involved in those environments need to systematically alter the level of support that is provided. For example, if the student was receiving a token for every 5 minutes of work completed and the intent is to fade the frequency of feedback to 10 minutes, then everyone using the system needs to provide tokens for 10 minutes of completed work. If adults across environments were prompting the student to check his schedule, and it is decided the prompt should be modified from a verbal to a gestural prompt, then everyone should use the gestural prompt. Slowing fading the frequency of feedback and removing the external control can lead to more generalized use of skills and behaviors. When creating the external systems of support and motivation, all adults involved with the student need to plan how the support and motivation will be eventually faded so that the student functions as independently as possible. However, as mentioned earlier, it is unrealistic to think that *all* external reinforcement can be faded (as Ms. Harris learned during the inservice, few teachers would go to work if their paycheck were faded). However, reinforcement can be provided on a less frequent basis and may be shaped to approximate more natural consequences.

CONCLUSION

All behavior occurs for a reason. Identifying the reason for behavior is instrumental in reducing problem behavior. Four general functions serve to motivate behavior: attention/access (get), escape/avoid, sensory, and pain attenuation. Efforts to shape challenging behavior so that it is more adaptive will be more effective if the function of the behavior is considered. Functional Behavioral Assessment (FBA) is the process of collecting data on behavior in order to determine function. Indirect methods of data collection, such as questionnaires and interviews, can provide a general impression of possible function that needs to be verified through the collection and analysis of direct observation data. Examination of data is used to generate a statement describing the relationship between the behavior and the environment. A Functional Analysis may be used to verify or generate the function of behavior. Once that relationship is understood, teachers have insight into environmental contexts that need to be altered and powerful sources of motivation that can be used to support learning of efficient behavior.

Positive behavior support is not intended to be used to eliminate problem behavior (Iovannone, Dunlap, Huber, & Kincaid, 2003). Reductions in problem behavior are a side effect of the use of strategies that create supportive environments that encourage participation and use of teaching skills, which enables students to achieve their goals in acceptable ways. Generalization of skill acquisition can be promoted through the use of behavior analytic strategies such as Pivotal Response Training (PRT) and self-management. Positive behavior support increases the range of activities and relationships available to the individual as well as the independence that can be exerted in making personal choices (Horner, 2000).

DISCUSSION QUESTIONS AND ACTIVITIES

1. Nikki spits. Why does she do this? List as many communicative intents (not necessarily functions) as you can think of to explain this behavior.

2. For the following students, identify a replacement behavior that meets the same function as the problem behavior. Describe how you will teach the student to demonstrate the replacement behavior. Also identify the desired behavior that the student will ultimately be taught to use that will be maintained by naturally occurring consequences.

   • Cecil hits other students so he can take their toys (function = access).

   • Roberta "tantrums" every time a demand is placed on her, such as when she is asked to complete a task, sit down, move away, stop, and so forth (function = escape).

   • During instruction, Hans suddenly stands up and walks around the room, trying to engage the teacher in a discussion about his favorite subject. The longer he can negotiate with her about sitting down, the happier he seems (function = attention).

3. Observe a classroom that includes students with ASD. Select one student who could benefit from learning one of the pivotal responses presented in Figure 7.5. Develop a plan for teaching the pivotal response to the student.

4. Think of an example from your own life when your behavior was modified through noncontingent reinforcement. Identify another example when your behavior was shaped through differential reinforcement. Finally, describe a time when a behavior was eliminated through extinction.

5. For each of the following simple examples, take a guess at the possible function of the behavior. (Note: Each example contains a single line of data. More data would be necessary in order to have confidence in speculating about function.)

Antecedent	Behavior	Consequence	Student Reaction	Function
Student told to get to work	Tantrum	Sent to time out	Tantrum stops	
Student alone	Hand stim	Increased stimulation	Stim continues	
Teacher talking to another student	Screams	Teacher gets onto student	Screaming stops	
Another student at computer	Hitting	Other student runs to teacher	Student gets on computer	
Time to go to PE	Yelling and surface clearing	Not allowed to go to PE	Student calms down	
Clock indicates 9:59	Crawls under table and covers head	Does not hear bell that rings at 10:00	Comes out from under table at 10:01	

REFERENCES

Bijou, S. W., Peterson, R. F., & Ault, M. H. (1968). A method to integrate descriptive and experimental field studies at the level of data and empirical concepts. *Journal of Applied Behavior Analysis, 1,* 175–191.

Callahan, K., & Rademacher, J. A. (1999). Using self-management strategies to increase the on-task behavior of a student with autism. *Journal of Positive Behavior Interventions, 1,* 117–122.

Carr, E. G., & Durand, V. M. (1985). Reducing behavior problems through functional communication training. *Journal of Applied Behavior Analysis, 18,* 111–126.

Carr, E. G., Horner, R. H., Turnbull, A., Marquis, J., Magito-McLaughlin, D., McAtree, M. L., et al. (1999). *Positive behavior support as an approach for dealing with problem behavior in people with developmental disabilities: A research synthesis.* Washington, DC:

American Association on Mental Retardation Monograph Series.

Crawford, J., Brockel, B., Schauss, S., & Miltenberger, R. G. (1992). A comparison of methods for the functional assessment of stereotypic behavior. *Journal of the Association for Persons with Severe Handicaps, 17,* 77–86.

Donnellan, A. M., Mirenda, P. L., Mesaros, R. A., & Fassbender, L. L. (1984). Analyzing the communicative functions of aberrant behavior. *Journal of the Association for Persons with Severe Handicaps, 9,* 201–212.

Dunlap, G., Koegel, R. L., Johnson, J., & O'Neill, R. E. (1987). Maintaining performance of autistic clients in community settings with delayed contingencies. *Journal of Applied Behavior Analysis, 20,* 185–191.

Durand, V. M. (1993). Functional communication training using assistive devices: Effects on challenging behavior and affect. *Augmentative and Alternative Communication, 9,* 168-176.

Durand, V. M., & Crimmins, D. B. (1987). Assessment and treatment of psychotic speech in an autistic child. *Journal of Autism and Developmental Disorders, 17,* 17-28.

Durand, M. V., & Crimmins, D. (1992). *Motivation Assessment Scale (MAS).* Topeka, KS: Monaco & Associates.

Durand, V. M., & Merges, E. (2001). Functional communication training: A contemporary behavior analytic intervention for problem behaviors. *Focus on Autism & Other Developmental Disorders, 16,* 110-119.

Favell, J. E., McGimsey, J. F., & Jones, M. L. (1978). The use of physical restraint in the treatment of self-injury and as positive reinforcement. *Journal of Applied Behavior Analysis, 11,* 225-241.

Fisher, A. F., & Dunn, W. (1983). Tactile defensiveness: Historical perspectives, new research: A theory grows. *Sensory Integration Special Interest Section Newsletter, 6,* 1-2.

Fisher, W. W., Thompson, R. H., Hagopian, L. P., Bowman, L. G., & Krug, A. (2000). Facilitating tolerance of delayed reinforcement during functional communication training. *Behavior Modification, 24,* 3-29.

Florida Center on Self-Injury. (1996). *Functional analysis screening tool (FAST).* Author.

Foxx, R. M. (1996). Twenty years of applied behavior analysis in treating the most severe problem behavior: Lessons learned. *Behavior Analyst, 19,* 225-235.

Guess, D., & Carr, E. (1991a). Emergence and maintenance of stereotypy and self-injury. *American Journal on Mental Retardation, 96,* 299-319.

Guess, D., & Carr, E. (1991b). Rejoinder to Lovaas and Smith, Mulick and Meinhold, and Baumeister. *American Journal on Mental Retardation, 96,* 335-344.

Horner, R. H. (2000). Positive behavior supports. *Focus on Autism and Other Developmental Disabilities, 15,* 97-105.

Horner, R. H., & Carr, E. G. (1997). Behavioral support for students with severe disabilities: Functional assessment and comprehensive intervention. *Journal of Special Education, 31,* 84-104.

Horner, R. H., & Day, H. M. (1991). The effects of response efficiency on functionally equivalent competing behaviors. *Journal of Applied Behavior Analysis, 24,* 719-732.

Hughes, C., & Scott, S. V. (1997). Teaching self-management in employment settings. *Journal of Vocational Rehabilitation, 8* 43-53.

Iovannone, R., Dunlap, G., Huber, H., & Kincaid, D. (2003). Effective educational practices for students with autism spectrum disorders. *Focus on Autism and Other Developmental Disabilities, 18* 150-165.

Iwata, B. A., Dorsey, M. F., Slifer, K. J., Bauman, K. E., & Richman, G. S. (1982/1994). Toward a functional analysis of self-injury. *Journal of Applied Behavior Analysis, 27* 197-209.

Iwata, B. A., Vollmer, T. R., & Zarcone, J. R. (1990). The experimental (functional) analysis of behavior disorders: Methodology, applications, and limitations. In A. Repp & N. Singh (Eds.), *Perspectives on the use of nonaversive and aversive interventions for persons with developmental disabilities* (pp. 301-330). Sycamore, IL: Sycamore.

Kazdin, A. E. (2001). *Behavior modification in applied settings* (6th ed.). Belmont, CA: Wadsworth/Thomson.

Kennedy, C. H., & Meyer, K. A. (1996). Sleep deprivation, allergy symptoms, and negatively reinforced problem behavior. *Journal of Applied Behavior Analysis, 29* 133-135.

Kern, L. & Dunlap, G. (1998). Curricular modifications to promote desirable classroom behavior. In J. K. Luiselli & M. J. Cameron (Eds.), *Antecedent control: Innovative approaches to behavioral support* (pp. 289-307). Baltimore: Paul H. Brooks.

Koegel, R. L., Camarata, S., Koegel, L. K., Ben-Tall, A., & Smith, A. (1998). Increasing speech intelligibility in children with autism. *Journal of Autism and Developmental Disorders, 28,* 241-251.

Koegel, L. K., Camarata, S. M., Valdez-Menchaca, M., & Koegel, R. L. (1998). Setting generalization of question-asking by children with autism. *American Journal on Mental Retardation, 102,* 346-357.

Koegel, L. K., Harrower, J., & Koegel, R. L. (1999). Support for children with developmental disabilities participating in full-inclusion classrooms through self-management. *Journal of Positive Behavioral Interventions, 1,* 26-34.

Koegel, R. L., & Koegel, L. K. (1990). Extended reductions in stereotypic behavior of students with autism through a self-management treatment package. *Journal of Applied Behavior Analysis, 23,* 119-127.

Koegel, L. K., & Koegel, R. L. (1995). Motivating communication in children with autism. In E. Schopler and G. B. Mesibov (Eds.), *Learning and cognition in autism* (pp. 73-87). New York: Plenum.

Koegel, R. L., Koegel, L. K., & Carter, C. M. (1999). Pivotal teaching interactions for children with autism. *School Psychology Review, 28,* 576-594.

Koegel, L. K., Koegel, R. L., Harrower, J. K., & Carter, C. M. (1999). Pivotal response intervention I: Overview of approach. *Journal of the Association for Persons with Severe Handicaps, 24,* 174-185.

Koegel, L. K., Koegel, R. L., Hurley, C., & Frea, W. D. (1992). Improving social skills and disruptive behavior in children with autism through self-management. *Journal of Applied Behavior Analysis, 25,* 341-353.

Koegel, R. L., Koegel, L. K., & McNerney, E. K. (2001). Pivotal areas in intervention for autism. *Journal of Clinical Child Psychology, 30,* 19-32.

Koegel, L. K., Koegel, R. L., Shoshan, Y., & McNerney, E. (1999). Pivotal response intervention II: Preliminary long-term outcome data. *Journal of the Association for Persons with Severe Handicaps, 24,* 186-198.

Koegel, R. L., Koegel, L. K., & Surratt, A. (1992). Language intervention and disruptive behavior in children with autism. *Journal of Autism and Developmental Disorders, 22,* 141-152.

Koegel, R. L., O'Dell, M. C., & Koegel, L. K. (1987). A natural language teaching paradigm for nonverbal autistic children. *Journal of Autism and Developmental Disorders, 17,* 187-200.

Lalli, J. S., & Casey, S. D. (1996). Treatment of multiple controlled problem behavior. *Journal of Applied Behavior Analysis, 29,* 391-395.

Lennox, D. B., & Miltenberger, R. G. (1989). Conducting a functional assessment of problem behavior in applied settings. *Journal of the Association for Persons with Severe Handicaps, 14,* 304-311.

Lerman, D. C., Iwata, B. A., Smith, R. G., Zarcone, J. R., & Vollmer, T. R. (1994). Transfer of behavioral function as a contributing factor in treatment relapse. *Journal of Applied Behavior Analysis, 27,* 357-370.

Lewis, T. J., Scott, T., & Sugai, G. (1994). The Problem Behavior Questionnaire: A teacher based instrument to develop functional hypotheses of problem behavior in general education classrooms. *Diagnostique, 19,* 103-115.

Maag, J. W. (2004). *Behavior management: From theoretical implications to practical applications* (2nd ed.). Belmont, CA: Wadsworth/Thomson.

Mancina, C., Tankersley, M., Kamps, D., Kravits, T., & Parrett, J. (2000). Brief report: Reduction of inappropriate vocalizations for a child with autism using a self-management treatment program. *Journal of Autism and Developmental Disorders, 30,* 599-606.

Miltenberger, R. G. (2001). *Behavior modification: Principles and procedures* (2nd ed.). Belmont, CA: Wadsworth.

Nelson, C. M., & Rutherford, R. B., Jr. (1983). Timeout revisited: Guidelines for its use in special education. *Exceptional Education Quarterly, 3*(4), 56-67.

Newman, B., Buffington, D. M., O'Grady, M. A., McDonald, M. E., Poulson, C. L., Hemmes, N. S. (1995). Self-management of schedule following in three teenagers with autism. *Behavioral Disorders, 20,* 190-196.

O'Neill, R. E., Horner, R. H., Albin, R. W., Sprague, J. R., Storey, K., & Newton, J. S. (1997). *Functional assessment and program development for problem behavior: A practical handbook*. Pacific Grove, CA: Brooks/Cole.

O'Reilly, M. F. (1995). Functional analysis and treatment of escape maintained aggression correlated with sleep deprivation. *Journal of Applied Behavior Analysis, 28,* 225-226.

O'Reilly, M. F. (1997). Functional analysis of episodic self-injury associated with otitis media. *Journal of Applied Behavior Analysis, 30,* 165-167.

Pierce, K., & Schreibman, L. (1997). Using peer trainers to promote social behavior in autism: Are they effective at enhancing multiple social modalities? *Focus on Autism and Other Developmental Disabilities, 12,* 207-218.

Romanczyk, R. G., & Matthews, A. L. (1998). Physiological state as antecedent: Utilization in functional analysis. In J. K. Luiselli & M. J. Cameron (Eds.), *Antecedent control: Innovative approaches to behavioral support* (pp. 115-138). Baltimore: Paul H. Brooks.

Ryan, J. B., & Peterson, R. L. (2004). Physical restraint in school. *Behavioral Disorders, 29,* 154-168.

Sasso, G. M., Reimers, T. M., Cooper, L. J., Wacker, D., Berg, W., Steege, M. W., et al. (1992). Use of descriptive and experimental analyses to identify the functional properties of aberrant behavior in school settings. *Journal of Applied Behavior Analysis, 25,* 809-821.

Schreibman, L., Charlop, M. H., & Koegel, R. L. (1982). Teaching autistic children to use extra stimulus prompts. *Journal of Experimental Child Psychology, 33,* 475-491.

Shearer, D. D. (1996). Promoting independent interactions between preschoolers with autism and their nondisabled peers: An analysis of self-monitoring. *Early Education and Development, 7,* 205-220.

Sigafoos, J. (1998). Choice making and personal selection strategies. In J. K. Luiselli & M. J. Cameron (Eds.), *Antecedent control: Innovative approaches to behavioral support* (pp. 187-221). Baltimore: Paul H. Brooks.

Skinner, B. F. (1953). *Science and human behavior.* New York: Macmillan.

Smith, M. L., & Heflin, L. J. (2001). Supporting positive behavior in public schools: An intervention program in Georgia. *Journal of Positive Behavioral Interventions, 3,* 39-47.

Stahmer, A. C. (1995). Teaching symbolic play to children with autism using pivotal response training. *Journal of Autism and Developmental Disorders, 25,* 123-141.

Stahmer, A. C., & Schreibman, L. (1992). Teaching children with autism appropriate play in unsupervised environments using a self-management treatment package. *Journal of Applied Behavior Analysis, 25,* 447-459.

Strain, P. S., Kohler, F. W., Storey, K., & Danko, C. D. (1994). Teaching preschoolers with autism to self-monitor their social interactions: An analysis of results in home and school settings. *Journal of Emotional and Behavioral Disorders, 2,* 78-88.

Wacker, D. P., Steege, M. W., Northrup, J., Sasso, G., Berg, W., Reimers, T., et al. (1990). A component analysis of functional communication training across three topographies of severe behavior problems. *Journal of Applied Behavior Analysis, 23,* 417-429.

Yell, M. L. (1990). The use of corporal punishment, suspension, expulsion, and timeout with behaviorally disordered students in public schools: Legal considerations. *Behavioral Disorders, 15,* 100-109.

Zanolli, K., Daggett, J., Ortiz, K., & Mullins, J. (1999). Using rapidly alternating multiple schedules to assess and treat aberrant behavior in natural settings. *Behavior Modification, 23,* 358-378.

Zarcone, J. R., Rodgers, T. A., Iwata, B. A., Rourke, D., & Dorsey, M. F. (1991). Reliability analysis of the Motivational Assessment Scale: A failure to replicate. *Research in Developmental Disabilities, 12,* 349-360.

CHAPTER 8

Encouraging Communication and Verbal Behavior

KEY TERMS

Augmentative and Alternative Communication

Communication

Communicative Competence

Intentional Communication

Joint Attention

Language

Leading

Mand

Nonverbal Communication

Pedantic

Pragmatics

Preintentional

Prelinguistic

Tact

❖ LEARNING WITH MS. HARRIS: Differences Between Talking and Communicating

Ms. Harris knows that her students with ASD have deficits in communication. She has read their IEPs and has met with the speech-language pathologist, Ms. Patel, to make sure she understands the difference between phonology and prosody. It amazes her to see how the clinical terms in the students' files come to life in the classroom. Take Milo, for example. Milo is exhibiting readiness skills and responding well to instruction based on applied behavior analytic methods. However, he never initiates an interaction with peers or an adult, even if they have something he really likes and would obviously like to have. At times he becomes aggressive for no obvious reason and, seemingly out of the blue, he lunges and grabs items from others. Ms. Harris knows that Milo can say words—she and Ms. Patel keep a running list of the words he says and in what context. Indeed, they've heard him sing an entire song from a Disney movie and repeat verbatim a 15-minute segment from a popular cartoon. Ms. Harris wonders what she can do to encourage him to ask her or a classmate for the computer, a snack, or a turn on the swing. He behaves well in his exploratory classes and sits quietly with his general education homeroom during story time, but he doesn't talk to anyone. It's time Milo began to communicate with others!

When educators search for an approach to promote communication skills in students with autism spectrum disorders, they are often overwhelmed with the available options (Diehl, 2003; Gerber, 2003; Heflin & Simpson, 1998a). Should they focus on one specific type of intervention or should they consider integrating a variety of strategies? As a developmental disability that typically appears during the first three years of life (APA, 2000), ASD affects verbal and nonverbal communication, as well as social interaction and play (Wing, 2001; Wolfberg, 2003). During this crucial time of development, language emerges and children recognize that the words they use communicate intentions and information to others (Bernstein & Levey, 2002; Prizant, Wetherby, Rubin, & Laurent, 2003). In fact, the acquisition of spoken language has been identified as a predictor of long-term positive outcomes for students with ASD (Gillberg, 1991; Lord & Paul, 1997). This chapter discusses the development of communication, language acquisition, and how they differ in individuals with ASD. The chapter also describes various interventions to help children develop communication and verbal behavior.

EARLY COMMUNICATION DEVELOPMENT

The ability to communicate is considered essential for participation within families and communities. **Communication** has been defined as the ability to receive, send, process, and comprehend concepts of verbal, nonverbal, and graphic symbol systems. Failure to communicate can be the result of a disorder that may be evident in the processes of hearing, language, and/or speech and may range in severity from mild to profound. Finally, individuals may demonstrate one or any combination of communication disorders (ASHA, 1997). Early communication development is directly linked to the ways infants use their eyes, make vocal noises, and use gestures.

Eye Gaze

An infant communicates through physical and/or facial gestures such as eye gaze. By $3\frac{1}{2}$ months of age, infants' visual-motor systems are fully mature, and they use eye gaze to learn about the relationships between objects, people, and events as well as to indicate interests and emotions (Tiegerman & Primavera, 1984).

Eye gaze behavior in young children with ASD is usually different from that of typical peers. They may stare fixedly at specific objects and not integrate the surrounding visual stimuli (Dawson, Meltzoff, Osterling, Rinaldi, & Brown, 1998; Rincover & Ducharme, 1987). They may become preoccupied with parts of objects, rather than the whole (Boucher & Lewis, 1992). The child may direct less eye gaze at people (Snow, Hertzig, & Shapiro, 1987), preferring to look at geometric patterns rather than human faces. Or children with ASD may gaze in a person's direction, but appear to look right through him or her. Deviations in eye gaze may signal problems understanding the world and may negatively affect communication development. Baron-Cohen, Baldwin, and Crowson, (1997) found that toddlers with autism do not pay attention to the direction of a speaker's eye gaze and thus do not know to what the speaker is referring. Obviously, problems with eye gaze interfere with development of communication in children with ASD.

Babbling

Communication evolves as infants begin babbling (vocalizing speechlike sounds) at around 6 to 7 months. As early as 7 months, infants appear to be capable of analyzing and indicating their awareness of the language present in their environments. Infants begin to match the intonation and some basic speech sounds of their communicative partners. Typically developing infants who are babbling want to share what they find interesting with others. Vocalizations increase in frequency during the second year of life (Baron-Cohen, Wheelwright, & Jolliffe, 1997; Lederberg, 2003).

In contrast, children with ASD fail to indicate an awareness of language spoken in their environments. Parents report taking their children for hearing screenings because they "act as if they are deaf" and do not orient to someone talking to them or even to their names being called (Werner, Dawson, Osterling, & Dinno, 2000). Children with ASD have been noted to have a preference for nonspeech sounds as opposed to speech (Kuhl, Coffey-Corina, Padden, & Dawson, 2005). Although some young children with ASD match a speaker's intonation and language during episodes of echolalia, babbling may be different or nonexistent and rarely used to share interests. Lack of babbling by the age of 12 months is one of the "red flags" for further evaluation of potential developmental delays including ASD (Filipek et al., 2000).

Gestures

At 9 months, typically developing infants use gestures such as reaching to indicate their intent, and adults typically respond to the communication attempts (Bates, Benigni, Bretherton, Camaioni, & Volterra, 1979). Infants progress to pointing at around 12 to 13 months and then to pantomime gestures at around 17 months. With the development of meaningful gestures, toddlers are able to participate in conversational turn taking and object-focused interactions with their caregivers (even before they speak real words). Bates et al. (1979, p. 328) report that young children use "coordinated attention" between the adult and the object even while vocalizing or gesturing. The gestures and vocalizations that are used to gain adults' attention and directing that attention to a desired object or event are referred to as **intentional communication.**

Rather than gesturing, young children with ASD may use a technique called **leading** to obtain a desired object (Wetherby & Prizant, 2005). For example, when the child desires assistance in obtaining something, she may push an adult's hand or arm toward the item. Although leading does indicate a desire, it is not a type of interactive communication: The child does not interact with the adult; she only uses the adult as a tool. Children with ASD may also use pointing to indicate that they want something, but they tend not to use pointing to try to get someone else to look at something (Baron-Cohen et al., 1996).

In addition to failing to use pointing to direct another's attention, children with ASD may not use gestures such as showing, waving, or pantomiming (Luyster et al., 2005; Rogers, Bennetto, McEvoy, & Pennington, 1996; Stone, Ousley, Yoder, Hogan, & Hepburn, 1997). Lack of referential gestures may be predictive of ASD (Vostanis et al., 1998). Young children with ASD and mental retardation tend to engage more frequently in nonmeaningful gestures (repetitive motor movements) than communicative gestures (Osterling, Dawson, & Munson, 2002). Since the children's gestures fail to communicate a message, they may escalate into problem behavior as the children become frustrated in conveying intent (Keen, 2005).

BASICS FOR LANGUAGE DEVELOPMENT

Communication refers to the message being sent and received; language is one of the mediums used to communicate. "**Language** is a set of arbitrary symbols defined by an individual's culture in which ideas are conveyed for the purpose of communication" (Stone & Yoder, 2001, p. 341). These arbitrary symbols are evident in spoken language, sign language, and written expression. To communicate effectively with a broad audience, an individual should possess some level of "language." There are three variables identified as predictors of spoken language development in children with and without disabilities: motor imitation, joint attention, and object play (Mundy, Sigman, & Kasari, 1990; Stone, Ousley, & Littleford, 1997).

Motor Imitation

According to Stone and Yoder (2001), motor imitation requires a child to attend to another person and form a mental representation of that person's behavior so that it can be imitated. Imitation skills precipitate a child's ability to process language spoken by others and thus acquire and develop the language of the people around him (Stone & Yoder, 2001). Children with ASD are noted for having difficulty imitating (Williams, Whiten, & Singh, 2004) that varies by developmental level (Receveur et al., 2005). When imitation does occur, some individuals with ASD make an unusual error by imitating actions exactly as they see them, such as turning the palm of the hand toward their faces when imitating someone waving at them (Ohta, 1987). Failures to imitate a model and pay attention to relevant stimuli have significant negative implications for the development of communication and language (Smith & Bryson, 1994).

Joint Attention

Joint attention occurs when children are able to identify what another person is attending to and can also be seen in their ability to draw another person's attention toward something of interest to them (Prizant et al., 2003). The number of joint attention acts has been found to predict later expressive language development (Mundy et al., 1990; Prizant & Wetherby, 1993; Sigman & Ruskin, 1999). Researchers suggest three reasons why joint attention correlates with language acquisition. First, joint attention signals a child's desire for interaction, and if responded to, links to his language development (Koegel, Camarata, Valdez-Menchaca, & Koegel, 1998). This occurs, for example, when a child holds out an object and the mother calls it "Barney." The child begins to learn the name for the object.

Second, joint attention helps children elicit language from others for the purpose of developing language (McCathren, Yoder & Warren, 1999). For example, when a child touches the refrigerator and looks at his mother and she responds by saying, "Oh, do you want some milk?" the child receives a model of a word for what he was seeking. Finally, children solicit joint attention to share their experiences with adults in their environment (Mundy, 1995), further supporting the development of language.

Joint attention is problematic among children with ASD and possibly one of its hallmark characteristics (Wetherby, Prizant & Schuler, 2000). Students with ASD are unlikely to respond to another's attempt to solicit joint attention and do not try to get another person to look at an object or event for social purposes (McArthur & Adamson, 1996). The absence of joint attention has implications for social, cognitive, and language development. Joint attention involves not only making a connection between another person and an object or event, but also sharing of emotional states. Students functioning on the higher end of the autism spectrum may connect the gaze between people and objects and share some positive emotions, but tend not to obtain another's attention for the purpose of sharing (Wetherby et al., 2000).

Object Play

How a child plays with objects can provide valuable information regarding development. According to Piaget (1962), the foundation for the development of symbolic play and language relies on a child's ability to use one object to represent another. Typically developing children spontaneously learn how to vary and combine actions from repetitively exploring and manipulating objects or people within their environments. Symbolic or pretend play becomes more complex as children create imaginative play scripts using objects, others, and themselves (Boucher, 1999). Functional play becomes more complex and frequent as children imitate acts they observe outside of their immediate environments.

Children with ASD have difficulties with symbolic as well as functional play (Dawson & Adams, 1984). Children with ASD may not pretend an object is another object and engage in imaginative play nor even use toys in the way they are intended. For example, a child with an ASD may put all the toy animals in a row rather than arrange them as if they were in a zoo or pretend they are interacting with each other. The absence of symbolic or functional play has negative implications for receptive and expressive language (Sigman & Ruskin, 1999).

LANGUAGE ACQUISITION

A child's first word typically appears around the age of 10 to 13 months. Children expand their vocabularies with new words as they spend more time engaged in joint attention and playing with people and objects (Wolfberg, 2003). At 4 years, typically developing preschoolers make statements and ask questions, whereas children with slower development and/or with disabilities are more likely to state directives toward others. As typically developing preschoolers use more words to express themselves, they use fewer gestures.

Engaging in familiar activities and routines contributes to a child's cognitive and language development (Tomasello, 2002). Children learn new words based on routine conversations with familiar adults (Masur, 1997) and rely on the intentions and social cues specific to their culture (Tomasello, 1992). Learning new words depends on a person's ability to infer the intentions of others (Bloom & Markson, 1998). In addition to the importance of social interactions and familiar routines, the repetition of familiar sounds supports language and vocabulary development (Gray, 2003; Storkel & Morrisette, 2002).

In children with ASD the absence of joint attention, play, and social interactions impedes the development of language, particularly language used for interacting with others. Likewise, these children tend to have difficulty inferring the intentions or thoughts of others, which can further hinder the development of communication and language. A child is at risk for a language-based developmental delay, including ASD, if the child does not (1) babble or coo by 12 months, (2) gesture by 12 months, (3) say single words by 16 months, (4) say two-word phrases on his or her own by 24 months, and/or (5) regress in any language or social skill at any age. Further assessment is required if any of these characteristics are observed (Filipek et al., 1999; Filipek et al., 2000). Research indicates that children achieve better outcomes the earlier they are diagnosed and receive appropriate intervention (NRC, 2001; Woods & Wetherby, 2003).

Components of Language

Language is characterized according to content (semantics), form (grammar), and use (pragmatics) (Lahey, 1988). Language may be spoken, signed, and drawn graphically. At the most basic level, the semantics of language refer to vocabulary and comprise both receptive and expressive forms. The rules of grammar for a particular language dictate how the words are sequenced and modified so that the form is correct. When children begin to manipulate the order of words to become more grammatically correct, they are able to direct the present and future actions of others and express events that have happened in the past by using appropriate past verb tenses. **Pragmatics** involves how the vocabulary is used, decisions speakers make about the timing and delivery of their message, and nonverbal features that accompany the message, which are all used in an attempt to convey the desired message (Prutting & Kirchner, 1987). Pragmatics are learned through social interactions and may vary by culture (Mundy & Markus, 1997). An example of language use occurs when a 15-month-old child says "Mommy up" (semantics) in a pleading tone with an earnest look accompanied by raising his arms (pragmatics), which probably indicates a request for a desired action. Although not grammatically correct as a complete sentence, the young child's grammar is appropriate for his age. Concern about grammar would be generated if a 15-year-old adolescent used the phrase "Mommy up" to describe her mother as standing.

For children with ASD, content (vocabulary), form (grammar), and use (pragmatics) can be areas of great difficulty. Any delays in the development of these areas will have an impact on a child's comprehension and spoken language development (Gerber, 2003). Approximately 35–40% of individuals with ASD do not develop any functional or communicative language (Mesibov, Adams, & Klinger, 1997). Those who develop spoken language may use language that is advanced in terms of vocabulary but may continue to have difficulty with pragmatic components, such as eye gaze, body language, and facial expressions (Loveland & Tunali-Kotoski, 1997; Safran, Safran, & Ellis, 2003; Young, Diehl, Morris, Hyman, & Bennetto, 2005).

Parents report noticing deficits in language skills among their children with ASD as early as 18 months when their children fail to do such things as point, share attention, imitate others, or play appropriately with people or objects (Stone & Lemanek, 1990; Wolfberg, 2003). As the children grow, they exhibit problems with vocal quality, intensity, and/or intonation (Lord & Paul, 1997). Individuals with ASD may exhibit differences in pitch and volume (e.g., speaking with a high, squeaky voice or speaking very loudly or softly), differences in vocal quality (e.g., using a "breathy" voice), differences in intonation (e.g., speaking in monotone, sounding like a robot), and differences in prosody (e.g., putting the stress on the wrong syllable, using rising inflection at the end of statements so that everything sounds like a question, failing to differentiate between talking to a baby vs. an authority figure) (Shriberg et al., 2001). Children with ASD also exhibit **nonverbal communication** anomalies that include inconsistent eye gaze (Tiegerman-Farber, 2002), minimal acts of joint attention (Baron-Cohen, Baldwin, & Crowson, 1997), and staying too far away from or getting too close to their listeners.

Levels of Communication

Children with limited or no spoken language are described as functioning at preintentional and prelinguistic levels of communication (Schuler, Prizant, & Wetherby, 1997). **Preintentional** describes students who do not realize the *importance* of communicating with others, while **prelinguistic** describes students who have *not yet developed* spoken language as a means of communication. Therefore, students who do not appear to care about asking for a drink are preintentional and unmotivated to acquire and use spoken language. This may negatively influence their overall communication competence; they may demonstrate inappropriate behaviors such as screaming, displaying self-injurious behaviors (SIB), or appearing noncompliant or argumentative with others (Carr & Durand, 1985; Tiegerman-Farber, 2002; Wetherby & Prizant, 2000), and they may exhibit inappropriate social interaction skills—all of which can interfere with instruction.

Echolalia

Students who are prelinguistic do communicate, but they tend to operate within a more restricted range of communicative functions by repeating words or phrases (echolalia) and/or using gestures rather than words. In the past, echolalia was considered meaningless jargon (Tiegerman-Farber, 2002). However, immediate echolalia provides evidence of comprehension and serves functional purposes (Prizant & Duchan, 1981). Delayed echolalia can aid social interactions in various ways (Prizant & Rydell, 1984). If others understand the student's intent expressed in the echolalia and respond adequately to the message, then the student has demonstrated communicate competence (Rydell & Prizant, 1995) regardless of the means. Table 8.1 provides a description of the forms of echolalia and probable functions.

Students with ASD are also often described as using words in unconventional ways. For example, Baron-Cohen, Baldwin and Crowson (1997, p. 49) reported an example from Leo Kanner's 1973 description of autism and a 2-year-old boy's "unconventional," "nonsensical," and "irrelevant" expressions. The mother of this 2-year-old boy diagnosed with autism related that once while she was reciting the nursery rhyme "Peter, Peter Pumpkin Eater," she dropped a saucepan. From that point on, whenever her son saw a saucepan he referred to it as "Peter eater." This is a classic example of how some students with ASD tend to use words or phrases that seem irrelevant

TABLE 8.1
Functions of Immediate and Delayed Echolalia

Functional Categories of Immediate Echolalia (Prizant & Duchan, 1981)

Category	Description
Interactive	
Turn-taking	Utterances used as turn fillers in an alternating verbal exchange
Declarative	Utterances labeling objects, actions, or location (accompanied by demonstrative gestures)
Yes-answer	Utterances used to indicate affirmation of prior utterance
Request	Utterances used to request objects or others' actions. Usually involves mitigated echolalia
Noninteractive	
Nonfocused	Utterances produced with no apparent intent, and often in states of high arousal (such as fear, pain)
Rehearsal	Utterances used as a processing aid, followed by utterance or action indicating comprehension of echoed utterance
Self-regulatory	Utterances that serve to regulate one's own actions. Produced in synchrony with motor activity

Functional Categories of Delayed Echolalia (Prizant & Rydell, 1984)

Category	Description
Interactive	
Turn-taking	Utterances used as turn fillers in alternating verbal exchange
Verbal completion	Utterances that complete familiar verbal routine initiated by others
Providing information	Utterances offering new information not apparent from situational context (may be initiated or respondent)
Labeling (interactive)	Utterances labeling objects or actions in environment
Protest	Utterances protesting actions of others. May be used to prohibit others' actions
Request	Utterances used to request objects of actions
Calling	Utterances used to call attention to oneself or to establish/maintain interaction
Affirmation	Utterances used to indicate affirmation of previous utterance
Directive	Utterances (often imperatives) used to direct others' actions
Noninteractive	
Nonfocused	Utterances with no apparent communicative intent or relevance to the situational context
Situation association	Utterances with no apparent communicative intent, which appear to be triggered by an object, person, situation, or activity
Self-directive	Utterances used to regulate one's own actions. Produced in synchrony with motor activity
Rehearsal	Utterances produced with low volume followed by louder interactive production. May be practice for subsequent production
Label (noninteractive)	Utterances labeling objects or actions in environment with no apparent communicative intent. May be a form of practice for learning language

Source: © Barry Prizant, Ph.D., CCC-SLP, Childhood Communication Services, Cranston, RI.

to a listener. Although the association may be meaningful for the child, such occurrences can slow vocabulary development.

Additional Considerations with Asperger Syndrome

Asperger Syndrome (AS) falls under the same clinical classification as autism (Pervasive Developmental Disorders [PDD]) but presents differently. In AS, characteristics are less severe and, according to the *DSM-IV-TR*, there are no language delays. Difficulties using communication socially among individuals with AS include problems with reciprocal conversations, limiting conversations to a small range of topics and interests, inability to initiate and/or maintain conversations, and appearing to "talk at" others rather than talking "with" listeners (Landa, 2000). Wing (1981) described the **pedantic** speech of individuals with AS as having a "bookish" quality in which the speaker uses formal and obscure words rather than relying on colloquial or less formal speech. In a preliminary study, Ghaziuddin and Gerstein (1996) found that the majority of individuals with AS display pedantic speech regardless of levels of intelligence.

Unlike many students with autism, students with AS appear to want acceptance by their peers but do not possess the skills to effectively accomplish this goal (Attwood, 1998). They may appear to lack empathy since they do not understand conventional social rules, are unaware of people's hidden agendas, and misunderstand nonliteral or figurative expressions (i.e., humor, sarcasm, idioms) (Myles & Simpson, 2001; Myles & Southwick, 1999; Safran et al., 2003). Although they may perseverate and seem to be knowledgeable in a variety of adultlike topics, students with AS use their excellent rote memory skills to store pieces of information that have no relevance to their conversations with others (e.g., details of toilet manufacturers). Finally, students with AS tend to talk more like adults than peers (Attwood), lack inflection and prosody (Safran et al.), and may use extreme vocal pitches when agitated.

COMMUNICATION BREAKDOWNS AND REPAIR STRATEGIES

Intentional communication (prelinguistic and linguistic) is characterized by an awareness that communicative acts are supposed to produce an effect and result in persistent efforts to produce those effects (Bates, 1979; Wetherby & Prizant, 1989). Not every attempt to communicate with another person is successful. A communication attempt may fail because the message is not received or not understood. Even when others hear and understand a message, they may not respond or they may respond by changing the topic (Halle, Brady, & Drasgow, 2004). Communication breakdowns can occur as a result of: (1) extraneous background noise, (2) overly complex communicative signals or language, (3) highly complex social context, (4) lack of a communicative partner's ability to request clarification of the message, and (5) lack of motivation to communicate in a reciprocal manner (Prizant, 2002).

Individuals with disabilities who have communication deficits may not speak intelligibly or may use unconventional or unusual methods of communicating, leading to communication breakdowns (Yont, Hewitt, & Miccio, 2000). In a descriptive study, Geller (1998) noted that lack of intelligibility and lack of audibility hindered the communicative attempts of five verbal children with autism. However, problems with semantics (lack of specificity when referencing items) and absence of joint attention were the major causes of communication breakdowns for these participants. Young students with disabilities may experience very low rates of success with initial attempts to communicate (Wetherby, Alexander, & Prizant, 1998).

During a communication breakdown, the speaker is likely to use verbal and/or nonverbal strategies to reestablish the conversational exchange. These repair strategies are based on an awareness of common social conventions (Rubin & Lennon, 2004). Infants older than 8 months and children as young as 2 years of age have been found to attempt to repair communication breakdowns (Alexander, 1995; Ferrier, Dunham, & Dunham, 2000). Sophistication of repairing communication breakdowns differs, with the youngest children relying on gestures. By 27 months and 33 months of age, typically developing toddlers are capable of repairing breakdowns by repeating their message or modifying their original message.

The five verbal children with autism in the Geller (1998) study did try to repair 73% of their communication breakdowns, demonstrating persistence in attempts to communicate. The repairs used were not consistent with their developmental levels, and the children had difficulty adding linguistic information. In the six children with autism studied by Keen (2005), repair strategies included repetition and substitutions to convey the message. Gestures and vocalizations that were used tended to be accompanied by increased emphasis and inflection and could be perceived by some as evolving into undesirable behavior.

The repair of communication breakdowns requires communication skills and social recognition that a message has not been received (Alexander, 1995). Due to social deficits, individuals with ASD may have difficulty recognizing that a breakdown has occurred. Communication deficits can also hinder the ability to request clarification when experiencing a breakdown and modify a message when trying to repair a communication breakdown. Figure 8.1 provides suggestions that educators can use when communicating with students to try to prevent communication breakdowns from occurring as well as suggestions for encouraging students to persist in their communicative attempts.

Strategies for identifying and repairing communication breakdowns should be taught as soon as the student demonstrates weaknesses in this area. Educators need to encourage students to repair communication breakdowns, rather than providing the repair themselves (Geller, 1998). Within the context of motivational activities, educators can pause and wait for students to provide a repair. Since typically developing children tend to use gestures in initial attempts to repair communication breakdowns,

To reduce breakdowns and repair those that occur when YOU are talking TO the student:

- Always secure student's attention prior to signaling or speaking.
- Monitor signs of comprehension:
  - Student performs appropriate action or begins to scan choices provided.
  - Student attempts to respond appropriately with verbal behavior or augmentative system.
- If you are not sure the student comprehends, repeat the message, allow time to respond, and then paraphrase the message.
- If the student appears to be attending and comprehending but still does not respond, ask the student to repeat your message.
- Teach the student to indicate lack of comprehension and to request clarification when appropriate (e.g., teach him to say, "I don't understand" or "Say that again, please").

To support the continuation of the communication when the student unsuccessfully initiates communication:

- Be a good listener—get on the student's level and wait expectantly.
- Teach the student to secure others' attention prior to communicating.
- If the message is incomplete, repeat what the student said and wait.
- If the message is unintelligible, say "I don't understand, tell me again" with nonverbal signals indicating lack of comprehension. When unintelligibility is due to specific factors such as rate, add appropriate information such as "Please speak slowly."
- If student doesn't respond, ask to be shown ("show me") and then provide appropriate language model.
- Encourage the use of backup augmentative device or written word if speech is not successful.
- When all else fails, make your best guess on how to respond and monitor the student's reaction.

FIGURE 8.1
Repairing Communication Breakdowns
Source: Adapted from Prizant (2002).

intervention may need to focus on teaching students to use gestural repairs (Alexander, 1995). Providing explicit instruction to teach conventional gestural and spoken communication can help reduce the number of breakdowns students experience (Halle et al., 2004). Students can even be taught typical forms of repair (e.g., pointing at what they want; learning to say "What?" when they don't understand).

During late childhood and adolescence, students with ASD may be particularly vulnerable to communication breakdowns. During these times, typical peers are noted to use more sarcasm, nonliteral or figurative language, and teasing remarks as responses (Rubin & Laurent, 2004). As a result, students with ASD may misread these responses and react emotionally. Direct instruction targeting recognition of communication breakdowns and the use of repair strategies may be more beneficial if conducted within groups of supportive peers. Peers can be trained to use more literal language and to clarify their intentions when communicating (Rubin & Laurent, 2004). Chapter 9 contains more information on peer-mediated strategies.

ASSESSMENT OF COMMUNICATION SKILLS

As a component of determining eligibility for special education services, most students with ASD will have participated in a comprehensive communication assessment. Speech-language pathologists (SLPs) are skilled at determining students' communicative competence and are critical members on IEP teams (Wetherby, Prizant, & Hutchinson, 1998). Assessments conducted by SLPs should identify opportunities for communicating, interactive styles of communicating partners, degree of structure in a specific activity, and whether or not there are available resources to assist in scaffolding conversations (Schuler et al., 1997). Rate of communicating, evidence of communication repair strategies, and use of social signals also need to be assessed.

Formal language assessments have limited utility in evaluating communication deficits in students with ASD (Wetherby et al., 2000), although tests of speech production and oral-motor functioning can help determine if the student has motor-planning deficits that affect the development of spoken language. Questionnaires and checklists provide information about the student's language development and current communication level (Bailey, McWilliam, Winton, & Simeonsson, 1992). SLPs will have access to a variety of resources for evaluating communicative competence and language in students with ASD.

Evaluation of the traditional components of language and levels of play are equally important. For students who use little language interactively, it is suggested that educators compile a list of the words the students use and identify under what circumstances the words are used (Sundberg & Michael, 2001). SLPs will assist educators in assessing students' receptive language, evaluating their level of comprehension, nonlinguistic responses, and processing, as well as language-related cognitive skills such as play, attention, imitation, and understanding of routines (Bailey et al., 1992; Crais, 1993; Schuler et al., 1997). The assessments will provide more reliable and useful information if conducted in a variety of settings and with a diverse group of communicative partners. Assessment is valuable only to the extent that the results can be used to develop goals and outcome measures for strategies to enhance communication (Wetherby & Prizant, 2005).

ENCOURAGING VERBAL BEHAVIOR
❖ LEARNING WITH MS. HARRIS: Insight into Echolalia

Ms. Harris is getting a better understanding of what the results from the communication assessments conducted by Ms. Patel actually mean. She recognizes that Milo does not seem aware that he can use communication to interact with others in the environment. She knows that he possesses a fairly extensive vocabulary, but only in the context of echolalic repetition. Ms. Harris has studied the functions of echolalia and is beginning to be able to tell when Milo repeats words in an attempt to calm or entertain himself rather than when he is using the words he associates with an event to try to get something to happen. For example, just yesterday, Ms. Harris took away the toy that Milo was playing with and he became very angry. In his anger, he looked at Ms. Harris and said, "Get a rope!" echoing a phrase from a popular hot sauce television commercial in which some cowboys are shown getting angry at their cook and using that phrase in a threatening manner.

Ms. Harris is quite sure that Milo doesn't comprehend many of the words he hears in his environment, and this is significantly interfering with his ability to build a meaningful vocabulary. Ms. Harris has read about strategies for supporting the development of communication and has talked with Ms. Patel to get her ideas. Together they devise a plan for teaching and encouraging Milo to communicate with others.

Typical language development depends on the presence of varied and integrated components for the acquisition of communicative competence. The language of individuals with ASD does not develop typically—unusual eye gaze and play as well as lack of joint attention, motor imitation, and gestures hinder development. Communication by students with ASD is quantitatively and qualitatively different from typically developing students. Language development and use is different when compared with other clinical populations, suggesting a genetic basis (Kjelgaard & Tager-Flusberg, 2001). Differences in language among individuals with ASD cannot be explained solely by IQ (Chan, Cheung, Leung, Cheung, & Cheung, 2005). The analysis of verbal behavior (i.e., language) provided by Skinner (1957) provides guidance for teaching students with ASD to communicate.

Skinner (1957) identified the importance of considering outcomes of verbal behavior in terms of their relationship with the environment. A **mand** is verbal behavior followed by a specific reinforcement (e.g., student says. "cookie" and is given one). A **tact** is verbal behavior followed by nonspecific reinforcement (e.g., student says "cookie" when shown a picture and is told "Good job" or given a raisin). Very generally, a mand can be thought of as a request and a tact can be thought of as a label. Skinner's analysis goes beyond the division of language into nouns, verbs, and so forth. "Cookie" is a noun according to language analysis, but in terms of verbal behavior, "cookie" is a tact if the student is naming it and a mand if the student is requesting it.

Typical language acquisition is based on the idea that if students learn the names of objects or activities (tacts), they will be able to ask for them in the absence of those objects or activities. Individuals with ASD have extreme difficulty doing this. Applying the constructs of verbal behavior can be beneficial in promoting the development of language.

The National Research Council (2001) reported that no one specific intervention is effective for all individuals with ASD and that integrating multiple approaches is better. What follows are descriptions of several approaches that have been used for developing communication and verbal behavior in students with ASD. Each approach targets either tacts or mands initially and moves toward the communicative use of both. Some were developed specifically for students without spoken language, and others capitalize on emerging or existent language. Two approaches that focus on the development of language and communication are described in other chapters. They are Discrete Trial Training (DTT) and Functional Communication Training (FCT). A brief summary will be useful here, but readers are referred to the individual chapters for more complete information.

Discrete Trial Training (DTT)

Described in Chapter 6, DTT targets the development of tacts. DTT has been used to teach the entire range of communication from gestural communication (Buffington, Krantz, McClannahan, & Poulson, 1998) to increasingly complex spoken language skills such as sentences (Krantz, Zalewski, Hall, Fenski, & McClannahan, 1981). Disappointing results with the transfer of skills learned in training settings have led to a reconceptualization of how DTT may best be used to facilitate language development. Researchers are facilitating generalization of language skills by interspersing trials and embedding training trials across the day (Egel, Shafer, & Neef, 1984; Secan, Egel, & Tilley, 1989). Chapter 6 provides a more complete discussion of DTT.

Functional Communication Training (FCT)

Functional Communication Training (FCT), described in Chapter 7, targets the development of mands to reduce behavioral problems. FCT is based on the perspective that challenging behavior may reflect the only means some individuals have to control what happens to them in their environments and should be analyzed based on what it communicates (Carr & Durand, 1985). FCT has been empirically validated for reducing problem behavior while increasing communication skills (Buckley & Newchok, 2005; Durand & Merges, 2001). Teaching the use of functional equivalents to problem behavior in a variety of natural contexts has been shown to facilitate generalization and produce more long-term effects (Durand & Carr, 1992). Chapter 7 provides a more complete discussion of FCT.

The applied behavior analytic approaches described in this chapter are:

- Augmentative and Alternative Communication
- Sign Language
- Picture Exchange Communication System
- Natural Language Paradigm
- Joint Action Routines
- Incidental Teaching

Augmentative and Alternative Communication (AAC)

Augmentative and Alternative Communication uses services and devices such as graphics, text-based flash cards, or voice recordings to enhance an individual's communication. The ultimate goal for AAC users is to establish a communication system that is functional and effective. It is equally important for AAC users to have a system that demonstrates their expressive and receptive language skills, as well as a way to expand vocabulary to include educational or vocational terms. As the term implies, AAC systems can supplement (augment) and/or replace (be an alternative for) an existing communication mode. The systems can be "low-tech," referring to devices that can be readily obtained, simple to make, or inexpensive (e.g., pictures, cards containing the printed word "yes," Touch Talk 4®), or "high-tech," which are usually more complex and more expensive (e.g., Dynawrite®, Dynavox®, Liberator®). The low- and high-tech systems can involve the use of graphics (pictures and text), manual signals (signs and gestures), acoustics (recordings), or tactile articles (e.g., object boards).

If a student uses a speech-generating device (SGD) that speaks a message when she pushes a button, her language is considered aided. In contrast, if she primarily uses gestures and signs, her communication is considered unaided. In addition, when an SGD or communication board has symbols on it that require the assistance of another person to change them so that another group of symbols are available, those symbols are considered static. However, if a student uses an SGD that switches screens automatically when the screen is accessed, those symbols are considered dynamic. Most individuals use multiple forms of communication. Individuals with typical speech and language skills use spoken language and nonverbal gestures, body language, voice tone, and varying inflections to convey their meaning. Therefore, it is critical that AAC users have the same opportunities. For example, if using an SGD with recordable messages, have someone of the same gender and age group as the AAC user record the messages using appropriate inflections.

Some students with ASD benefit from using AAC. AAC can target tacts, mands, and even interverbal behaviors (e.g., responding to questions, making comments). Augmentative communication that employs visual stimuli that are available for prolonged examination may capitalize on the visual processing strengths present in many individuals with ASD (Mirenda & Schuler, 1988). Pictures, icons, objects, and written words are examples of visual stimuli that may be useful for promoting communication development. For example, three children with ASD were taught to use a card containing the question, "Can I play?" to successfully communicate a desire to join play activities (Johnston, Nelson, Evans, & Palazolo, 2003).

Although limited research has been conducted on the use of SGDs with students with ASD, they have been well researched for individuals with other disabilities (Schlosser & Blischak, 2001). The effective use of an SGD was generalized from the training setting to the home for a 12-year-old with autism (Sigafoos, O'Reilly et al. 2004). An SGD was also used to teach two students with developmental disabilities to repair communication breakdowns that occur when others do not notice gestural initiations (Sigafoos et al. 2004). A comprehensive assessment of communication systems is necessary to identify the AAC that best meets the student's needs. Additionally, it is imperative that the system be used in all contexts (settings, speakers, and tasks), so that the student always has a means of communication. Everyone interacting with the student must use the system simultaneously. For the system to be consistently and effectively used the student's team will need to plan for maintenance, durability, and generalization.

Schepis, Reid, and Behrman (1996) describe some of the potential benefits of using a speech-generating device such as AAC. The SGD provides a typical and understandable message to listeners, in contrast to sign language, which may not be understood, or pictures that may provide a label but not a desired action. By providing an auditory signal, the SGD serves to capture others' attention so that the communicative initiation is recognized. This circumvents the problems encountered with students who gesture for what they want but no one sees the action. Finally, the SGDs can be programmed to provide very precise messages so that the listener does not have to guess the speaker's intention. Icons and printed words may also be effective for communicating a message as long as the students are taught to give them directly to a listener in order to capture attention.

There are a few limitations to be aware of when considering AAC for students with ASD. First, due to a tendency to perseverate, some students fixate on pressing the buttons on an SGD or pulling the pictures on and off a board with Velcro in order to hear the sounds. Second, whether using an AAC system or spoken language, students must learn to establish joint attention and indicate intent. Since this is an area of inherent deficit for most students with ASD, it is vital to teach the proper use of the ACC device. For some students, having an SGD act as an intermediary relieves the social aspect of the act of communicating. For students with ASD who are non-speaking or extremely limited in their speech, the use of an AAC system could be beneficial even if used only at certain times of the day. For example, using an AAC system during a joint action routine is ideal for encouraging a student with an ASD to interact with his peers. Even if all he does is perseverate on pushing the buttons, the buttons can be programmed to reflect a variety of age-appropriate topics or objects that his peers find interesting. In a natural setting, when he pushes those buttons, the peers may respond and create the context for interaction.

Sign Language

For individuals who have the capacity to use spoken language, sign language is considered a low-tech, unaided type of augmentative communication if used with spoken language or an alternative communication if used in the absence of spoken language. Teaching individuals with ASD to use manual signing as an AAC has generated some controversy, which deserves attention. Decades of research have produced consistent findings that individuals with ASD can successfully use manual signs to communicate with others (Goldstein, 2002; Seal & Bonvillian, 1997). Early hesitation to teach students to sign revolved around the concern that using manual signs might somehow suppress the emergence of spoken language. Indeed, the opposite has proven true. Using manual signs within a total communication approach (spoken language + sign; Barrera & Sulzer-Azaroff, 1983) has demonstrated that learning sign language may facilitate the emergence of spoken language (Layton & Watson, 1995; Tincani, 2004). However, some individuals will not develop spoken language, but will rely on the use of manual sign to communicate with others (Layton, 1988).

Another issue that has generated discussion relates to whether individuals with ASD have the imitation and motor abilities to learn manual signs. Seal and Bonvillian (1997) found that the size of the sign vocabulary and the accuracy of sign formation was negatively affected by poor motor skills in their 14 participants with ASD, although the variability in acquiring sign language is similar to the variability seen in acquisition of spoken language in individuals with ASD. Mirenda and Erickson (2000) suggest that the use of symbol systems in which students point to what they want is motorically less demanding and, thus, may be more beneficial. Additionally, pictures and icons may be more universally recognized than sign language (Rotholz, Berkowitz, & Burberry, 1989). Concerns related to motor abilities and the potential need for an interpreter have led some to conclude that sign language is not a viable communication option for students with ASD.

In contrast, others have emphasized that the benefits of teaching manual signs may outweigh those concerns. Sign language requires the use of the hands, which are always available; may be easier to teach than spoken language (because signs are easier to prompt); is closely associated with spoken language; and is received by the visual system through a means that is less transient than spoken language (Goldstein, 2002; Shafer, 1993; Sundberg, 1993). The empirical research supports the effectiveness of teaching sign language to individuals with ASD as one the options for AAC. Educators will need to collaborate with SLPs and families to determine if sign language is a worthwhile option to explore. Manual signs may be more effective for students with more limited communication abilities and should be used as a part of a total communication approach (i.e., the use of manual sign without accompanying speech is contraindicated) (Goldstein, 2002). Working together, teams may want to consider teaching signs that more closely represent the actual item or action, such as "eat" and "drink" (Mirenda & Erickson, 2000), or synonymous terms that are motorically easier to produce, such as "treat" instead of "cookie" (Seal & Bonvillian, 1997). A student's fine motor control and imitation may need to be considered in making a decision about the use of sign language (Tincani, 2004).

Individuals with developmental disabilities have been successfully taught to use sign language to initiate requests (Duker, Kraaykamp, & Visser, 1994; Tincani, 2004) and can produce and comprehend signs as well as typically developing controls matched by mental age (Soorya, 2004). Using a discrete trial training approach (see Chapter 6), a 2-year old with autism quickly learned manual signs and began to use the signs spontaneously (Bartman & Freeman, 2003).

The challenge in developing communicative competence through the use of AAC is determining which method will be more effective for augmenting or providing an alternative to students' current communicative functioning. SLPs have training and experience in evaluating students to determine which system or systems have the highest likelihood of successful use (Diehl, 2003). Students with poor verbal imitation abilities may benefit from using AAC to support their expressive language (NRC, 2001); however, consideration of the potential utility of AAC needs to be given to all students with communication deficits (Beukelman & Mirenda, 1998), and the use of augmented communication could enhance the development of spoken language, even in students older than 5 years (Romski & Sevcik, 1996). The ultimate goal for students with ASD is to help them develop and maintain the use of their communication system. This can be achieved by arranging situations in which they receive consistent access to desired reinforcers by using communication, whether it occurs via spoken language or through augmented or alternative means.

Picture Exchange Communication System (PECS)

In contrast to an AAC, which can be used over a life span, the Picture Exchange Communication System (PECS) is a strategy designed to teach intentional communication and can eventually be faded for some students. PECS was developed at the Delaware Autistic Program by Bondy and Frost (1994) to teach individuals without spoken language to initiate spontaneously with others in their environment, thereby expressing their communicative intent. Influenced by Skinner's framework, PECS establishes mands, as students exchange a picture or object for a desired item or activity (Bondy, Tincani, & Frost, 2004). In contrast to other communication approaches, the student is expected to initiate by seeking out a communicative partner and exchanging the picture or object.

One advantage of using PECS with students who are nonspeaking or minimally verbal is flexibility. Since PECS uses pictures, a fairly universal language, a student can communicate with anyone in any setting. PECS does not require the student to imitate spoken language or motor movements as do speech training and sign language. Nor does PECS require the student to maintain eye contact. Eye gaze emerges naturally through the process of the exchange.

There are six phases involved in PECS training (Bondy & Frost, 1994). Phase I involves the request for an item or activity with the exchange of a picture or object. In Phase II the distance between the student and the communication notebook, board, or picture is increased, and the student is taught to retrieve the picture or object and express intent by exchanging it with someone in the environment. In Phase III, students are taught to discriminate between pictures so that they can have more choices. Phase IV involves requesting; Phase V, answering "What do you want?"; and Phase VI, commenting in response to questions. There are also opportunities to

FIGURE 8.2
PECS Notebook in Phase III
Source: Heflin and Alaimo

acquire new vocabulary, make spontaneous comments, and respond to yes/no questions (Bondy & Frost, 1994). Figure 8.2 illustrates an example of a PECS book set up for Phase III. Notice the sentence strip at the bottom. The book contains pages of additional picture cards that are meaningful for the student, categorized for ease of use.

A possible disadvantage of PECS is that two instructors are necessary during the initial training phase. Since the goal is spontaneous initiations, the communication partner cannot be the same person as the person who prompts the student to exchange the picture. For example, in Phase I, the communication partner holds something the student really likes. A picture of the item is placed between the communication partner and the student. The prompter, who is usually behind the student and not participating in the communicative exchange, wordlessly helps the student pick up the picture and place it in the communication partner's hand. Immediately the communication partner labels the object and gives it to the student (i.e., "Cheese ball. I want cheese ball"), responding enthusiastically to the student's exchange of the picture. If the communication partner had started the exchange by saying, "What do you want?" it would only teach the student to wait for someone to ask her if she wants something.

Although only the early phases require the use of two people, it is sometimes difficult to find two people who are available at the same time. However, since the goal of PECS is spontaneous communication with a variety of people in a variety of settings, the two people do not always have to be the same. Bus drivers have been willing to return to school after their routes and help train for 20 to 30 minutes two or three times weekly. Since the training does not rely on a specific number of responses or a specific amount of time, clinic workers or custodians are also usually happy to assist. As in any classroom, parent or classroom volunteers can also help. Educators can offer names of students who might be willing to serve as communication partners for PECS training when they complete their work earlier than others, arrive at school earlier, or stay later in the afternoon. The local high school can provide a list of students who are required to perform hours of service for a class or extracurricular organization. High school students enrolled in vocational-technical work programs or the students who participate in Community-Based Instruction can also be very effective PECS trainers.

As mentioned earlier, the greatest benefit of PECS is the focus on spontaneous initiation without verbal prompting. Although initially an open-hand cue is used to train the child, the prompt is systematically faded (Bondy & Frost, 1994) to reduce the possibility of the student becoming prompt-dependent. The beginning phases of training never include verbal prompting.

PECS has been used effectively with students who are minimally verbal, echolalic, or who use jargon, as well as with those who do not exhibit spoken language. The language used during the exchange includes labeling the item followed by a statement involving "I" so that the student will hear the appropriate pronoun in reference to self. PECS has been found to enhance vocabulary, improve general communicative functioning, and increase spontaneity across a variety of settings and people (Schwartz & Garfinkle, 1998).

As educators look for ways to help improve the quality of life for students with ASD, consideration must be given to strategies addressing functional communication. Through an expanding body of empirical research, it appears that PECS may meet this need based on its effectiveness for training spontaneous initiation of speech, encouraging the acquisition of spoken language, decreasing problem behaviors, and increasing communicative behaviors in play and academic settings (Charlop-Christy, Carpenter, Le, LeBlanc, & Kellet, 2002). PECS may be mastered quickly by some students (Magiati & Howlin, 2003) and has been shown to facilitate imitation of simple sounds (Cummings & Williams, 2000). Use of PECS may facilitate social interaction (Kravits, Kamps, Kemmerer, & Potucek, 2002) and promote the emergence of spoken language (Ganz & Simpson, 2004; Tincani, 2004). In a study of 66 children (5 years old and younger) with ASD, 73% developed functional spoken language after one to five years of using PECS (Bondy & Frost, 1995).

❖ LEARNING WITH MS. HARRIS: Milo Requests Cheese Balls

As a team, Milo's mom, Ms. Harris, and the SLP have decided that they want to teach Milo that he can intentionally communicate to get things he wants. Ms. Harris and the SLP use their Boardmaker computer program to create black and white pictures representing some of the things Milo likes most. They decide to start with cheese balls since Milo just can't seem to get enough of them. Milo's mom takes turns being the prompter and the communicative partner. They create an index card to highlight the following key information:

1. *Provide powerful reinforcement systems.*
2. *Remember, don't ask "What do you want?" (That can be done in Phase IV.)*
3. *Respond immediately (unless you're working on waiting).*
4. *Plan for generalization and maintenance with specific objectives in mind.*
5. *Begin by prompting (communicative partner has open hand extended, prompter uses full physical guidance to help Milo pick up and release card into the hand of the communicative partner).*
6. *Fade prompts as quickly as possible.*

Milo becomes highly proficient at finding the picture of the cheese balls and handing it to any adult within range of the cheese ball container. He's spontaneously initiating a clear request in a very appropriate manner. Milo's mom is thrilled, and she and Ms. Harris make a duplicate set of the pictures for Milo to use at home.

The next three communication strategies, Natural Language Paradigm (NLP), Joint Action Routines (JARs), and Incidental Teaching, combine an applied behavior analytic approach in natural contexts that highlight interactions between the adult and the student while using motivating reinforcers. Considered within the concept of milieu teaching (Goldstein, 2002), the strategies integrated within NLP, JARs, and Incidental Teaching primarily target mands. They share the common features of encouraging turn-taking between partners, natural consequences, and using familiar objects and activities (Koegel, O'Dell, & Koegel, 1987). NLP, JARs, and Incidental Teaching are typically incorporated into daily activities, reducing the need to program for generalization (Koegel et al., 1998).

Natural Language Paradigm (NLP)

NLP is a child-initiated strategy (Green, 2001) in which the adult waits until a student is paying attention and showing interest in an object or activity before commenting, requesting, or prompting for a desired response. Adults have a clear role in NLP as they systematically prompt for verbalizations, model expected responses, and reinforce all approximate responses during play and school activities (Laski, Charlop, & Schreibman, 1988). The teachable moment, however, occurs only after the student uses a mand (through spoken or nonverbal means) to request an object or activity (Detrich, 1999). If the student does not use a mand, the teacher may model the verbal behavior for the student to repeat (echoic behavior). Educators set up the environment to provide opportunities for the student to want to communicate, thereby increasing his motivation to keep the interaction going.

Four parameters are useful for enhancing communication through the use of NLP (Koegel et al., 1987).

- *Stimulus item:* things selected by the student through verbal or nonverbal means to indicate her attention and intent. An array of stimulus items needs to be available so that they can be interchanged depending on the interest of the child.
- *Prompts:* a verbal model provided by the adult, who simultaneously plays with the object. If the student does not respond, the adult models once again.
- *Response:* acceptance of all approximations. If the student looks at, reaches for, or touches the item, makes a verbal approximation of the name of the item, or says the name of the item, he receives the reinforcer.
- *Consequences:* reinforcement for the student through the opportunity to play with the object and by receiving social praise.

NLP's effectiveness depends on the direct reinforcement of verbal attempts through shared control and taking turns with the toys. The teacher also varies the tasks and provides numerous examples to facilitate vocabulary development (Laski et al., 1988).

Studies show that NLP is effective in promoting spoken language. Students with ASD who demonstrated no verbal behavior showed an increase in their imitative verbalizations and subsequently used spontaneous verbalizations in settings other than where they were trained (Koegel et al., 1987). Children of parents who had been trained to implement NLP responded more, showed no increases in echolalia, and generalized their language skills at home with their siblings (Laski et al., 1988).

Although it may be difficult to implement NLP into a general education classroom because it is more difficult to follow and respond to the student's lead (Detrich, 1999), using applied behavior analytic techniques within naturally occurring situations ultimately enhances the social and communicative competence of the student (Quill, 2000). Ogletree (1998) states that NLP techniques are often used within a Joint Action Routine.

Joint Action Routines (JARs)

Snyder-McLean, Solomonson, McLean, and Sack (1984) developed Joint Action Routines (JARs) to support the language development of students with severe impairments. JARs rely on the consistency and reliability of familiar routines that provide cues for the students to acquire new responses or use accepted responses at the appropriate times (Earles, Carlson, & Bock, 1998). When routines are repeated often, the event becomes more meaningful, the student gains a sense of control, and the student engages in the cognitive tasks of the activity (Stremel, Bixler, Morgan, & Layton, 2002). Situations are set up to encourage the student's use of mands, tacts, echoic, and ultimately, intraverbal behavior. The repetitiveness of routines offers frequent opportunities to practice communication strategies that promote acquisition, maintenance, and generalization. Since the routines occur in natural environments, other people in that setting know about the routines and can easily initiate and respond accordingly. Some examples of daily routines in the home are making the bed, brushing teeth, and cleaning. School routines include snack time, calendar time, and guided constructive play.

Following is a summary of considerations for implementing JARs adapted from Earles et al. (1998) and Snyder-McLean et al. (1984).

1. When choosing a theme for the routine, make sure it is meaningful and familiar to all participants.
2. Present the routine frequently throughout the day with many opportunities to interact and communicate with others.
3. Specify an outcome.
4. Make certain the routine follows a sequence, with a clear beginning and end.
5. Identify a definite signal to represent the beginning and end of the routine.
6. Do not expect mastery immediately, and be prepared to model the language and routine to help students with their roles.
7. Plan on repeating the routine on a daily basis and add variations gradually.
8. Include props in the routines to help students distinguish between roles and reduce the need for verbal prompting by an adult.

Once there is a theme, create a script that lists what each participant is expected to say as well as how to respond in the situation (Earles et al., 1998). The style and content of the script should take into consideration the student's current language and abilities so that there is encouragement for the student to extend her use of language. The final element requires that the routines have natural, explicit roles that remain the same each time and can be switched easily between participants (Snyder-McLean et al., 1984). Perhaps the roles might be a dentist and a patient. When the student plays the role of the dentist she reinforces the steps to brush her teeth, and when she plays the patient, she practices brushing her teeth and may ask questions, such as "Is this how you do it?" Matching the language with a mental representation of brushing teeth maps both the language and events (Snyder-McLean et al., 1984).

Drew et al. (2002) taught parents to engage their preschoolers with disabilities based on a JARs type of approach. Although the outcomes should be interpreted with caution, they noted that language skills improved in terms of words understood, words spoken, and total gestures used. Although there is little empirical evidence to substantiate the effectiveness of JARs with students with ASD, the constructs of encouraging students to communicate by providing motivational and predictable experiences gives the approach face validity (Simpson et al., 2005).

❖ LEARNING WITH MS. HARRIS: JARs/NLP for Milo

Ms. Harris calls her class to the calendar area to start the daily routine. They have used the calendar activity for several months and the routine is always the same. She has decided to use a variation of JARs and NLP to further encourage Milo's language development. She says, "This morning, Milo is going to be the teacher!"

Milo stands in front of the group and looks at Ms. Harris. Ms. Harris turns him toward the calendar and says to Milo, "You say, 'Let's see what today is'" (a phrase she always uses to start the routine). Milo repeats the phrase and moves toward the calendar, mimicking the movements Ms. Harris has made so many times. He stops suddenly and begins to look around. Ms. Harris, knowing that he is looking for the stick she uses to point to the calendar, asks him if he needs something. He holds out his hand but says nothing. Ms. Harris, reaching behind her where the pointer is hidden, says, "Do you need the pointer? Say 'pointer.'" Milo says, "Pointer" and is given the stick. He turns to the calendar and begins to count the days, touching each numeral as he does so. (Ms. Harris is struck by how much he actually sounds like her!) He stops, repeatedly touching the empty spot that should contain that day's date. He starts rummaging in the stack of numerals by the calendar, and Ms. Harris asks, "Do you need the number?" while holding up the correct card. He reaches for it and she pulls it back, looking at him expectantly. Milo says, "Number" and she hands it to him. He sticks the card on the calendar and proceeds through the year, season, and weather.

Ms. Harris has sabotaged something within each routine so that Milo has to ask for or request the missing pieces. All in all, Milo does a very good job being "the teacher" during the calendar routine. He even asks his other peers the same questions Ms. Harris would have. Best of all, Milo seems to be enjoying himself, and he is using a lot of language!

Incidental Teaching

Typically developing children transfer skills acquired in one setting to other situations with relative ease. Because Mr. Michaels tells them to sit in their seats and be quiet, they infer that they should do the same in Ms. Lesley's class. Students with ASD experience difficulty continuing to use their skills (Carr, 1985) and generalizing skills learned in one environment to another environment. Similar to NLP and JARs, Incidental Teaching provides structure in natural environments to alleviate this discrepancy. Originally defined for aiding language development in children living in poverty (Hart & Risley, 1968), Incidental Teaching occurs when a student's natural environment is intentionally organized to lure students to preferred objects or activities. An adult responds to students' interests with praise, and then prompts them to expand ideas.

Incidental Teaching has been used successfully to meet the needs of a variety of students who use spoken and/or have limited language to communicate. Incidental Teaching has helped some students improve their receptive language skills while simultaneously improving their vocational skills (McGee, Krantz, Mason, & McClannahan, 1983); increase their peer interactions (McGee, Almeida, Sulzer-Azaroff, & Feldman, 1992); improve their abilities to make appropriate requests and responses (Farmer-Dougan, 1994); and increase their joint attention, play, and social communication skills (McGee, Morrier, & Daly, 1999; Mundy & Crowson, 1997; Oswald & Lignugaris, 1990).

McGee et al. (1983) modified Hart and Risley's original format to contain an easier prompt sequence and used the strategy in isolated contexts (e.g., play). Advanced planning helps optimize instructional time with the student and allows a variety of goals to be addressed simultaneously (McGee et al., 1999; Krantz, 2000). Examples include organizing a classroom center to include play activities targeting different forms of vehicles, and placing the student's favorite car in sight but out of reach. A lotto game at an instructional table nearby is set up to target correct articulation of /k/ in "car." Table 8.2 provides suggestions for implementing Incidental Teaching in a classroom (adapted from McGee et al., 1999).

A form of modified Incidental Teaching has been described by Ostrosky, Drasgow, and Halle, (1999) that may be useful for teaching students to repair

TABLE 8.2
Implementing Incidental Teaching

Curricular Targets	Expressive verbal language
	Engagement with toys
	Social responsiveness to adults
	Social tolerance/limitation of peers
	Independence in daily living
Environmental Modifications	Goals embedded in natural activities
	Supplemental one-to-one instruction in natural contexts
	Child-selected teaching materials
	Systematic display and rotation of toys
Incidental Teaching Procedures	Vigorous speech shaping
	Active social instruction
	Wait-ask-say-show-do
	Promotion of engagement
	Checklist-based performance appraisals

Source: Adapted from McGee, G. G., Morrier, M. J., & Daly, T. (1999). An incidental teaching approach to early intervention for toddlers with autism. *Journal of the Association for Persons with Severe Handicaps, 24,* 133–146.

TABLE 8.3
Comparison of Instructional Strategies for Communication and Language

Instructional Strategy	Lesson Control	Type of Presentation	Target(s)
Direct teaching (e.g., DTT)	Teacher led	Multiple opportunities to practice; structured	tacts
Activity based (e.g., NLP, JARs)	Teacher led	Embedded in thematic structure	mands tacts echoic intraverbal
Incidental Teaching	Child directed	Uses any opportunity to model and prompt communication	mands tacts echoic intraverbal
Functional Communication Training	Teacher prompted	Redirect student to functional behavioral equivalent and respond accordingly	mands

communication breakdowns. After identifying situations in typically occurring routines that are characterized by frequent communication breakdowns (or engineering such opportunities), educators prompt students to produce repairs that are appropriate for their functioning and useful in most environments. Inserting the instruction at motivating moments enhances the likelihood that the child will form associations between the repair strategy and the communicative context.

As mentioned earlier, it would be unusual to use only one strategy exclusively with a child to increase his communicative competence. Most often, a combination and even a blending of approaches is necessary to produce the desired outcome. The strategies described in this chapter vary in the amount of empirical support available to substantiate their use, but all have at least face validity. The approaches also vary in purpose and process. Table 8.3 provides a brief comparison of the communication strategies commonly used with students with ASD.

Using a combination of communication and language interventions provides opportunities for initiation, flexibility, and spontaneity, which are important in the communication process and prove beneficial for students with ASD (Frea, 1996; Gerber, 2003; Olley & Reeve, 1997). The ultimate goal for all individuals with language delays and impairments is to develop communicative competence. **Communicative competence** involves an individual's use of both verbal and nonverbal communication for effective expression (Rollins, 1999). Overall communicative competence provides a good prognosis for positive outcomes (Garfin & Lord, 1986; McEachin, Smith, & Lovaas, 1993).

As a result of identifying what will make a student a competent communicator, effective communication strategies can be taught to reduce challenging behaviors (Buschbacher & Fox, 2003; Durand & Carr, 1991; Fisher, Thompson, Hagopian, Bowman, & Krug, 2000; Reichle & Johnston, 1993); encourage appropriate social skills (Frea, 1996; Koegel, 1996; Sasso, Garrison-Harrell, McMahon, & Peck, 1998; Quill, 2000, 1995); teach functional communication skills (Carr & Durand, 1985; Fisher et al., 2000; Kahng, Hendrickson, & Vu, 2000; Keen, Sigafoos, & Woodyatt, 2001); establish educational goals that strengthen the student's social communication with peers and adults across settings (Wetherby & Prizant, 2000); and improve their comprehension of academic content (Chen & Bernard-Optiz, 1993; National Research Council, 2001).

CONCLUSION

An awareness of typical communication and language development allows educators to identify the foundational skills, such as gestures, joint attention, imitation, and object play, that may be lacking in their students with ASD. Directly teaching and encouraging the use of these foundational skills may promote positive communication outcomes (Jones & Carr, 2004). A number of strategies have been shown to be effective for increasing verbal behavior in students with ASD. For those students who do not develop spoken language, communication can be facilitated by teaching them to vocalize, gesture, sign, and/or point to or exchange objects or pictures. The use of these visually based means of communication, including manual sign, has not been shown to inhibit the emergence of spoken language. Echolalia, a common characteristic among students with ASD with verbal behavior, occurs for a variety of reasons contingent upon context. Educators are encouraged to identify the functions of echolalia and use that knowledge to shape more conventional verbal behavior.

Strategies common to many of the interventions for enhancing communication development include the following (Buffington et al., 1998; McCathren, 2000; Wetherby & Prizant, 2005; Woods & Wetherby, 2003):

- Arrange the environment so that students need to communicate to access preferred items and activities
- Pause frequently or sabotage routines during highly preferred activities so that the student is motivated to communicate
- Use teaching strategies demonstrated to be effective such as modeling, waiting to see if the student will respond ("time delay"), and prompting
- Imitate the student's gestures and vocalizations
- Provide natural reinforcement by allowing access to objects or activities in which the student has expressed an interest and remove undesired objects or discontinue activities if the student protests

As summarized by Goldstein (2002, p. 393), "Effective communication interventions will depend on good decision making on a variety of fronts. For example, careful programming is needed: to select useful objectives, to provide environments that set the occasion for meaningful communication, to provide functional reinforcers that eventually are available with regularity in the natural environment, and to provide scaffolds (models, prompts, corrections, and encouragement) that are faded to promote independent and spontaneous communication." Educators need to work closely with families and rely heavily on the expertise of speech-language pathologists in determining students' communication needs and implementing systematic interventions that promote the development of communicative competence. Communication is a dynamic process and students' needs will change over time, so educators, families, and SLPs need to collaborate to ensure the most positive communication outcomes.

DISCUSSION QUESTIONS AND ACTIVITIES

1. Go to a park or playground where there are typically developing young children. Observe the children and notice how they use eye gaze, gestures, babbling, and motor imitation. Also look for evidence of joint attention and coordinated attention and observe how they play with objects.

2. Describe the differences and similarities between PECS and visually cued instruction (Chapter 4).

3. Describe how you would implement Phase I of PECS training.

4. Looking at Table 8.1, select one category from immediate echolalia and one category from delayed echolalia and relate each to a student who demonstrates similar patterns of echolalia. Describe how you could shape the echolalia into functional verbal behavior that would fall into the same category.

5. Identify a daily routine and discuss how you would implement JARs, following the guidelines provided in the chapter.

REFERENCES

Alexander, D. (1995). *The emergence of repair strategies in chronologically and developmentally young children.* Unpublished doctoral dissertation, Florida State University, Tallahassee.

American Psychiatric Association. (2000). *Diagnostic and statistical manual of mental disorders* (4th ed., text revision). Washington, DC: Author.

American Speech-Language-Hearing Association Ad Hoc Committee on Service Delivery in the Schools (1997). Definitions of communication disorders and variations. *ASHA, 35* (Suppl. 10), 108-108a).

Attwood, T. (1998). *Asperger's syndrome: A guide for parents and professionals.* London: Jessica Kingsley.

Bailey, D., McWilliam, P., Winton, P., & Simeonsson, R. (1992). *Implementing family-centered services in early intervention: A team-based model for change.* Cambridge, MA: Brookline.

Baron-Cohen, S., Baldwin, D. A., & Crowson, M. (1997). Do children with autism use the speaker's direction of gaze strategy to crack the code of language? *Child Development, 68,* 48-57.

Baron-Cohen, S., Cox, A., Baird, G., Swettenham, J., Drew, A., Nightingale, N., et al. (1996). Psychological markers of autism at 18 months of age in a large population. *British Journal of Psychiatry, 168,* 158-163.

Baron-Cohen, S., Wheelwright, S., & Jolliffe, T. (1997). Is there a "language of the eyes"?

Evidence from normal adults, and adults with autism or Asperger syndrome. *Visual Cognition, 4,* 311-331.

Barrera, R. D., & Sulzer-Azaroff, B. (1983). An alternating treatment comparison of oral and total communication training programs with echolalic autistic children. *Journal of Applied Behavior Analysis, 16,* 379-394.

Bartman, S., & Freeman, N. (2003). Teaching language to a two-year-old with autism. *Journal on Developmental Disabilities, 10,* 47-53.

Bates, E. (1979). Intentions, conventions, and symbols. In E. Bates, L. Benigni, I. Bretheron, L. Camaioni, & V. Volterra (Eds.), *The emergence of symbols* (pp. 33-42). New York: Academic Press.

Bates, E., Benigni, L., Bretherton, I., Camaioni, L., & Volterra, V. (1979). *The emergence of symbols: Cognition and communication in infancy.* New York: Academic Press.

Bernstein, D. K., & Levey, S. (2002). Language development: A review. In D. K. Bernstein & E. Tiegerman-Faber (Eds.), *Language and communication disorders in children* (5th ed., pp. 27-94). Boston: Allyn & Bacon.

Beukelman, D. R., & Mirenda, P. (1998). *Augmentative and alternative communication.* Baltimore: Paul H. Brookes.

Bloom, P., & Markson, L. (1998). Capacities underlying word learning. *Trends in Cognitive Sciences, 2,* 67-73.

Bondy, A. S., & Frost, L. A. (1994). The picture exchange communication system. *Focus on Autistic Behavior, 9*(3), 1-20.

Bondy, A., & Frost, L. (1995). Educational approaches in preschool: Behavior techniques in a public school setting. In E. Schopler & G. Mesibov (Eds.), *Learning and cognition in autism* (pp. 311-333). New York: Plenun.

Bondy, A., Tincani, M., & Frost, L. (2004). Multiply controlled verbal operants: An analysis and extension to the picture exchange communication system. *Behavior Analyst, 27,* 247-261.

Boucher, J. (1999). Editorial: interventions with children with autism—methods based on play. *Child Language Teaching and Therapy, 15*(1), 1-6.

Boucher, J., & Lewis, V. (1992). Unfamiliar face recognition in relatively able autistic children. *Journal of Child Psychology and Psychiatry, 33,* 843-859.

Buckley, S. D., & Newchok, D. K. (2005). Differential impact of response effort within a response chain on use of mands in a student with autism. *Research in Developmental Disabilities, 26,* 77-86.

Buffington, D. M., Krantz, P. J., McClannahan, L. E., & Poulson, C. L. (1998). Procedures for teaching appropriate gestural communication skills to children with autism. *Journal of Autism and Developmental Disorders, 28,* 535-545.

Buschbacher, P. W., & Fox, L. (2003). Understanding and intervening with the challenging behavior of young children with autism spectrum disorder. *Language, Speech, & Hearing Services in Schools, 34,* 217-228.

Carr, E. G. (1985). Behavioral approaches to language and communication. In E. Schopler & G. B. Mesibov (Eds.), *Communication problems in autism.* New York: Plenum, 37-57.

Carr, E. G., & Durand, V. M. (1985). Reducing behavior problems through functional communication training. *Journal of Applied Behavior Analysis, 18,* 111-126.

Chan, A. S., Cheung, J., Leung, W. W. M., Cheung, R., & Cheung, M. (2005). Verbal expression and comprehension deficits in young children with autism. *Focus on Autism and Other Developmental Disabilities, 20*(2), 117-124.

Charlop-Christy, M. H., Carpenter, M., Le, L., LeBlanc, L. A., & Kellet, K. (2002). Using the Picture Exchange Communication System (PECS) with children with autism: Assessment of PECS acquisition, speech, social-communicative behavior, and problem behavior. *Journal of Applied Behavior Analysis, 35,* 213-231.

Chen, S. H., & Bernard-Optiz, A. V. (1993). Comparison of personal and computer-assisted instruction for children with autism. *Mental Retardation, 31,* 368-376.

Crais, E. (1993). Families and professionals as collaborators in assessment. *Topics in Language Disorders, 14,* 29-40.

Cummings, A. R., & Williams, W. J. (2000). Visual identity matching and vocal imitation training with children with autism: A surprising finding. *Journal on Developmental Disabilities, 7,* 109-122.

Dawson, G., & Adams, A. (1984). Imitation and social responsiveness in autistic children. *Journal of Abnormal Child Psychology, 12,* 209-226.

Dawson, G., Meltzoff, A. N., Osterling, J., Rinaldi, J., & Brown, E. (1998). Children with autism fail to orient to naturally occurring social stimuli. *Journal of Autism and Developmental Disorders, 28,* 479–485.

Detrich, R. (1999). Increasing treatment fidelity by matching interventions to contextual variables within the educational setting. *School Psychology Review, 28,* 608–620.

Diehl, S. F. (2003). The SLPs role in collaborative assessment and intervention for children with ASD. *Topics in Language Disorders: Children and Young Adults with Autism Spectrum Disorder, 23,* 95–115.

Drew, A., Baird, G., Baron-Cohen, S., Cox, A., Slonims, V., Wheelwright, S., et al. (2002). A pilot randomized control trial of a parent training intervention for preschool children with autism. *European Child & Adolescent Psychology, 11,* 266–272.

Duker, P. C., Kraaykamp, M., & Visser, E. (1994). A stimulus control procedure to increase requesting with individuals who are severely/profoundly intellectually disabled. *Journal of Intellectual Disability Research, 38,* 177–186.

Durand, V. M., & Carr, E. G. (1991). Functional communication training to reduce challenging behavior: Maintenance and application in new settings. *Journal of Applied Behavior Analysis, 24,* 251–264.

Durand, V. M., & Carr, E. G. (1992). An analysis of maintenance following functional communication training. *Journal of Applied Behavior Analysis, 25,* 777–794.

Durand, V. M., & Merges, E. (2001). Functional communication training: A contemporary behavior analytic intervention for problem behaviors. *Focus on Autism & Other Developmental Disorders, 16,* 110–119.

Earles, T. L., Carlson, J. K., & Bock, S. J. (1998). Instructional strategies to facilitate successful learning outcomes for students with autism. In R. L. Simpson & B. S. Myles (Eds.), *Educating children and youth with autism: Strategies for effective practice* (pp. 55–105). Austin, TX: Pro-Ed.

Egel, A. L., Shafer, M. S., & Neef, N. A. (1984). Receptive acquisition and generalization of prepositional responding in autistic children: A comparison of two procedures. *Analysis and Intervention in Developmental Disabilities, 4,* 285–298.

Farmer-Dougan, V. (1994). Increasing requests by adults with developmental disabilities using incidental teaching by peers. *Journal of Applied Behavior Analysis, 27,* 533–544.

Ferrier, S., Dunham, P., & Dunham, F. (2000). The confused robot: Two-year-olds' responses to breakdowns in conversation. *Social Development, 9,* 337–348.

Filipek, P. A., Accardo, P. J., Ashwal, S., Baranek, G. T., Cook, Jr., E. H., Dawson, G., et al. (2000). Practice parameter: Screening and diagnosis of autism: Report of the Quality Standards Subcommittee of the American Academy of Neurology and the Child Neurology Society. *Neurology, 55,* 468–479.

Filipek, P. A., Pasquale, J. A., Baranek, G. T., Cook, Jr., E. H., Dawson, G., Gordon, B., et al. (1999). The screening and diagnosis of autistic spectrum disorders. *Journal of Autism and Developmental Disorders, 29,* 439–484.

Fisher, W. W., Thompson, R. H., Hagopian, L. P., Bowman, L. G., & Krug, A. (2000). Facilitating tolerance of delayed reinforcement during functional communication training. *Behavior Modification, 24,* 3–29.

Frea, W. D. (1996). Social-communicative skills in higher-functioning children with autism. In R. L. Koegel & L. K. Koegel (Eds.), *Teaching children with autism: Strategies for initiating positive interactions and improving learning opportunities* (pp. 53–66). Baltimore: Paul H. Brookes.

Ganz, J. B., & Simpson, R. L. (2004). Effects on communicative requesting and speech development of the picture exchange communication system in children with characteristics of autism. *Journal of Autism and Developmental Disorders, 34,* 395–409.

Garfin, & Lord, C. (1986). Communication as a social problem in autism. In E. Schopler & G. Mesibov (Eds.), *Social behavior in autism* (pp. 237–261). New York: Plenum.

Geller, E. (1998). An investigation of communication breakdowns and repairs in verbal autistic children. *The British Journal of Developmental Disabilities, 44,* 71–85.

Gerber, S. (2003). A developmental perspective on language assessment and intervention for children on the autistic spectrum. *Topics in Language Disorders, 23,* 74–94.

Ghaziuddin, M., & Gerstein, L. (1996). Pedantic speaking style differentiates Asperger syndrome from high-functioning autism. *Journal of Autism and Developmental Disorders, 26,* 585–595.

Gillberg, C. (1991). Outcome in autism and autistic-like conditions. *Journal of the American Academy of Child and Adolescent Psychiatry, 30,* 375–382.

Goldstein, S. (2002). Review of the *Asperger Syndrome Diagnostic* scale. *Journal of Autism and Developmental Disorders, 32,* 611–614.

Gray, S. (2003). Word-learning by preschoolers with specific language impairment: What predicts success? *Journal of Speech, Language, and Hearing Research, 46,* 56–67.

Green, G. (2001). Behavior analytic instruction for learners with autism: Advances in stimulus control technology. *Focus on Autism and Other Developmental Disabilities, 16,* 72–86.

Halle, J., Brady, N. C., & Drasgow, E. (2004). Enhancing socially adaptive communicative repairs of beginning communicators with disabilities. *American Journal of Speech-Language Pathology, 13,* 43–54.

Hart, B. M., & Risley, T. R. (1968). Establishing use of descriptive adjectives in the spontaneous speech of disadvantaged preschool children. *Journal of Applied Behavior Analysis, 1,* 109–120.

Heflin, L. J., & Simpson, R. L. (1998a). Interventions for children and youth with autism: Prudent choices in a world of exaggerated claims and empty promises. Part I: Intervention and treatment option review. *Focus on Autism and Other Developmental Disabilities, 13,* 194–211.

Johnston, S., Nelson, C., Evans, J., & Palazolo, K. (2003). The use of visual supports in teaching young children with autism spectrum disorder to initiate interactions. *AAC: Augmentative & Alternative Communication, 19,* 86–103.

Jones, E. A., & Carr, E. G. (2004). Joint attention in children with autism: Theory and intervention. *Focus on Autism & Other Developmental Disabilities, 19,* 13–26.

Kahng, S. W., Hendrickson, D. J., & Vu, C. P. (2000). Comparison of single and multiple functional communication training responses for the treatment of problem behavior. *Journal of Applied Behavior Analysis, 33,* 321–324.

Keen, D. (2005). The use of nonverbal repair strategies by children with autism. *Research in Developmental Disabilities, 26,* 243–254.

Keen, D., Sigafoos, J., & Woodyatt, G. (2001). Replacing prelinguistic behaviors with functional communication. *Journal of Autism and Developmental Disorders, 31,* 385–398.

Kjelgaard, M. M., & Tager-Flusberg, H. (2001). An investigation of language impairment in autism: Implications for genetic subgroups. *Language and Cognitive Processes, 16,* 287–308.

Koegel, L. K. (1996). Communication and language intervention. In R. L. Koegel & L. K. Koegel (Eds.), *Teaching children with autism: Strategies for initiating positive interactions and improving learning opportunities* (pp. 17–32). Baltimore: Paul H. Brookes.

Koegel, L. K., Camarata, S. M., Valdez-Menchaca, M., & Koegel, R. L. (1998). Setting generalization of question-asking by children with autism. *American Journal on Mental Retardation, 102,* 346–357.

Koegel, R. L., O'Dell, M. C., & Koegel, L. K. (1987). A natural language teaching paradigm for nonverbal autistic children. *Journal of Autism and Developmental Disorders, 17,* 187–200.

Krantz, P. J. (2000). Commentary: Interventions to facilitate socialization. *Journal of Autism and Developmental Disorders, 30,* 411–413.

Krantz, P. J., Zalewski, S., Hall, L., Fenski, E., & McClannahan, L. (1981). Teaching complex language to autistic children. *Analysis & Intervention in Developmental Disabilities, 1,* 259–297.

Kravits, T. R., Kamps, D. M., Kemmerer, K., & Potucek, J. (2002). Brief report: Increasing communication skills for an elementary-aged student with autism using the picture exchange communication system. *Journal of Autism and Developmental Disorders, 32,* 225–230.

Kuhl, P. K., Coffey-Corina, S., Padden, D., & Dawson, G. (2005). Links between social and linguistic processing of speech in preschool children with autism: Behavioral and electrophysiological measures. *Developmental Science, 8,* F1–F12.

Lahey, M. (1988). *Language disorders and language development.* New York: Macmillan.

Landa, R. (2000). Social language use in Asperger syndrome and high-functioning autism. In A. Klin, F. Volkmar, & S. Sparrow

(Eds.), *Asperger syndrome* (pp. 125-158). New York: Guilford Press.

Laski, K. E., Charlop, M. H., & Schreibman, L. (1988). Training parents to use the natural language paradigm to increase their autistic children's speech. *Journal of Applied Behavior Analysis, 21,* 391-400.

Layton, T. (1988). Language training with autistic children using four different modes of presentation. *Journal of Communication Disorders, 21,* 333-350.

Layton, T., & Watson, L. (1995). Enhancing communication in nonverbal children with autism. In K. A. Quill (Ed.), *Teaching children with autism: Strategies to enhance communication and socialization* (pp. 73-101). New York: Delmar.

Lederberg, A. R. (2003). Expressing meaning: From communicative intent to building a lexicon. In M. Marshark & P. Spencer (Eds.), *Oxford handbook of deaf studies, language, and education* (pp. 247-260). New York: Oxford University Press.

Lord, C., & Paul, R. (1997). Language and communication in autism. In D. Cohen & F. Volkmar (Eds.), *Handbook of autism and pervasive developmental disorders* (2nd ed., pp. 195-225). New York: Wiley.

Loveland, K. A., & Tunali-Kotoski, B. (1997). The school-age child with autism. In D. J. Cohen & F. R. Volkmar (Eds.), *Handbook of autism and pervasive developmental disorders* (2nd ed., pp. 283-308). New York: Wiley.

Luyster, R., Richler, J., Risi, S., Hsu, W. L., Dawson, G., Bernier, R., et al. (2005). Early regression in social communication in autism spectrum disorders. *Developmental Neuropsychology, 27,* 311-326.

Magiati, I., & Howlin, P. (2003). A pilot evaluation study of the Picture Exchange Communication System (PECS) for children with autistic spectrum disorders. *Autism: The International Journal of Research & Practice, 7,* 297-321.

Masur, E. F. (1997). Maternal labeling of novel and familiar objects: Implications for children's development of lexical constraints. *Journal of Child Language, 24,* 427-439.

McArthur, D., & Adamson, L. B. (1996). Joint attention in preverbal children: Autism and developmental language disorder. *Journal of Autism and Developmental Disorders, 26,* 481-496.

McCathren, R. B. (2000). Teacher-implemented prelinguistic communication intervention. *Focus on Autism & Other Developmental Disabilities, 15,* 21-29.

McCathren, R. B., Yoder, P. J., & Warren, S. F. (1999). Prelinguistic pragmatic functions as predictors of later expressive vocabulary. *Journal of Early Intervention, 22,* 205-216.

McEachin, J. J., Smith, T., & Lovaas, O. I. (1993). Long-term outcome for children with autism who received early intensive behavioral treatment. *American Journal on Mental Retardation, 97,* 359-372.

McGee, G. G., Almeida, M. C., Sulzer-Azaroff, B., & Feldman, R. S. (1992). Promoting reciprocal interactions via peer incidental teaching. *Journal of Applied Behavior Analysis, 25,* 117-126.

McGee, G., Krantz, P. J., Mason, D., & McClannahan, L. E. (1983). A modified incidental teaching procedure for autistic youth: Acquisition and generalization of receptive object labels. *Journal of Applied Behavior Analysis, 16,* 329-338.

McGee, G. G., Morrier, M. J., & Daly, T. (1999). An incidental teaching approach to early intervention for toddlers with autism. *Journal of the Association for Persons with Severe Handicaps, 24,* 133-146.

Mesibov, G. B., Adams, L. W., & Klinger, L. G. (1997). *Autism: Understanding the disorder.* New York: Plenum.

Mirenda, P., & Erickson, K. (2000). Augmentative communication and literacy. In A. M. Wetherby & B. M. Prizant (Eds.), *Autism spectrum disorders: A transactional developmental perspective* (pp. 333-367). Baltimore: Paul H. Brooks.

Mirenda, P., & Schuler, A. L. (1988). Augmenting communication for persons with autism: Issues and strategies. *Topics in Language Disorders, 9,* 24-43.

Mundy, P. (1995). Joint attention and social-emotional approach behavior in children with autism. *Development and Psychopathology, 7,* 63-82.

Mundy, P., & Crowson, M. (1997). Joint attention and early social communication: Implications for research on intervention with autism. *Journal of Autism and Developmental Disorders, 27,* 654-676.

Mundy, P., & Markus, J. (1997). On the nature of communication and language impairment in autism. *Mental Retardation and*

Developmental Disorders Research Reviews, 3, 343-349.

Mundy, P., Sigman, M., & Kasari, C. (1990). A longitudinal study of joint attention and language development in autistic children. *Journal of Autism and Developmental Disorders, 20,* 115-129.

Myles, B. S., & Simpson, R. L. (2001). Understanding the hidden curriculum: An essential social skill for children and youth with Asperger syndrome. *Intervention in School & Clinic, 36,* 279-287.

Myles, B. S., & Southwick, J. (1999). *Asperger syndrome and difficult moments: Practical solutions for tantrums, rage, and meltdowns.* Shawnee Mission, KS: Autism Asperger.

National Research Council. (2001). *Educating children with autism.* Committee on Educational Interventions for Children with Autism. Division of Behavioral and Social Sciences and Education. Washington, DC: National Academy Press.

Ogletree, B. T. (1998). The communicative context of autism. In R. L. Simpson & B. S. Myles (Eds.), *Educating children and youth with autism* (pp. 141-172). Austin, TX: Pro-Ed.

Ohta, M. (1987). Cognitive disorders of infantile autism: A study employing the WISC, spatial relationship conceptualization, and gesture imitation. *Journal of Autism and Developmental Disorders, 17,* 45-62.

Olley, J. G., & Reeve, C. E. (1997). Issues of curriculum and classroom structure. In D. J. Cohen & F. R. Volkmar (Eds.), *Handbook of autism and pervasive developmental disorders* (2nd ed., pp. 484-508). New York: Wiley.

Osterling, J. A., Dawson, G., & Munson, J. A. (2002). Early recognition of 1-year-old infants with autism spectrum disorder versus mental retardation. *Development and Psychopathology, 14,* 239-251.

Ostrosky, M. M., Drasgow, E., & Halle, J. W. (1999). "How can I help you get what you want?" A communication strategy for students with severe disabilities. *Teaching Exceptional Children, 31,* 56-61.

Oswald, L. K., & Lignugaris, B. (1990). The effects of incidental teaching on the generalized use of social amenities at school by a mildly handicapped adolescent. *Education and Treatment of Children, 13,* 142-153.

Piaget, J. (1962). *Play, dreams, and imitation in childhood.* New York: Norton.

Prizant, B. M., Wetherby, A. M., Rubin, E., & Laurent, A. C. (2003). A transactional, family-centered approach to enhancing communication and socioemotional abilities of children with autism spectrum disorder. *Infants and Young Children, 16,* 296-316.

Prizant, B. M. (2002, February). The SCERTS model: Enhancing communicative and socioemotional competence in young children with autistic spectrum disorders. Presentation given in Charlotte, NC.

Prizant, B. M., & Duchan, J. F. (1981). The functions of immediate echolalia in autistic children. *Journal of Speech and Hearing Disorders, 46,* 241-249.

Prizant, B. M., & Rydell, P. J. (1984). An analysis of the functions of delayed echolalia in autistic children. *Journal of Speech and Hearing Research, 27,* 183-192.

Prizant, B. M., & Wetherby, A. M. (1993). Communication in preschool autistic children. In E. Schopler, M. van Bourgondien, & M. Bristol (Eds.), *Preschool issues in autism* (pp. 95-108). New York: Plenum.

Prutting, C., & Kirchner, D. M. (1987). A clinical appraisal of the pragmatic aspects of language. *Journal of Speech and Hearing Disorders, 52,* 105-119.

Quill, K. A. (1995). *Teaching children with autism: Strategies to enhance communication and socialization.* New York: Delmar.

Quill, K. A. (2000). *DO-WATCH-LISTEN-SAY: Social and communication intervention for children with autism.* Baltimore: Paul H. Brookes.

Receveur, C., Lenoir, P., Descombre, H., Roux, S., Barthelemy, C., & Malvy, J. (2005). Interaction and imitation deficits from infancy to 4 years of age in children with autism. *Autism: The International Journal of Research & Practice, 9,* 69-83.

Reichle, J., & Johnston, S. (1993). Replacing challenging behavior: The role of communication intervention. *Topics in Language Disorders, 13,* 61-76.

Rincover, A., & Ducharme, J. M. (1987). Variables influencing stimulus overselectivity and "tunnel vision" in developmentally delayed children. *American Journal of Mental Deficiency, 91,* 422-430.

Rogers, S. J., Bennetto, L., McEvoy, R., & Pennington, B. F. (1996). Imitation and pantomime in high-functioning adolescents with autism spectrum disorders. *Child Development, 67,* 2060–2073.

Rollins, P. R. (1999). Early pragmatic accomplishments and vocabulary development in preschool children with autism. *American Journal of Speech-Language Pathology, 8,* 181–190.

Romski, M. S., & Sevcik, R. A. (1996). *Breaking the speech barrier: Language development through augmented means.* Baltimore: Paul H. Brookes.

Rotholz, D., Berkowitz, S., & Burberry, J. (1989). Functionality of two modes of communication in the community by students with developmental disabilities: A comparison of signing and communication books. *Journal of the Association for Persons with Severe Handicaps, 14,* 227–233.

Rubin, E., & Laurent, A. C. (2004). Implementing a curriculum-based assessment to prioritize learning objectives in Asperger syndrome and high-functioning autism. *Topics in Language Disorders, 24,* 298–315.

Rubin, E., & Lennon, L. (2004). Challenges in social communication in Asperger syndrome and high-functioning autism. *Topics in Language Disorders, 24,* 271–285.

Rydell, P. J., & Prizant, B. M. (1995). Assessment and intervention strategies for children who use echolalia. In K. A. Quill (Ed.), *Teaching children with autism* (pp. 106–132). Albany, NY: Delmar.

Safran, S. P., Safran, J. S., & Ellis, K. (2003). Intervention ABCs for children with Asperger syndrome. *Topics in Language Disorders, 23,* 154–165.

Sasso, G. M., Garrison-Harrell, L., McMahon, C. M., & Peck, P. (1998). Social competence of individuals with autism: An applied behavior analysis perspective. In R. L. Simpson & B. S. Myles (Eds.), *Educating children and youth with autism* (pp. 173–190). Austin, TX: Pro-Ed.

Schepis, M. M., Reid, D. H., & Behrman, M. M. (1996). Acquisition and functional use of voice output communication by persons with profound multiple disabilities. *Behavior Modification, 20,* 451–468.

Schlosser, R. W., & Blischak, D. M. (2001). Is there a role for speech output in interventions for persons with autism? A review. *Focus on Autism and Other Developmental Disabilities, 16,* 170–178.

Schuler, A. L., Prizant, B. M., & Wetherby, A. M. (1997). Enhancing language and communication development: Prelinguistic approaches. In D. J. Cohen & F. R. Volkmar (Eds.), *Handbook of autism and pervasive developmental disorders* (2nd ed., pp. 539–571). New York: Wiley.

Schwartz, I. S., & Garfinkle, A. N. (1998). The Picture Exchange Communication System: Communicative outcomes for young children with disabilities. *Topics in Early Childhood Special Education, 18,* 144–160.

Seal, B., & Bonvillian, J. (1997). Sign language and motor functioning in students with autistic disorder. *Journal of Autism and Developmental Disorders, 27,* 437–466.

Secan, K. E., Egel, A. L., & Tilley, C. S. (1989). Acquisition, generalization, and maintenance of question-answering skills in autistic children. *Journal of Applied Behavior Analysis, 22,* 181–196.

Shafer, E. (1993). Teaching topography-based and selection-based verbal behavior to developmentally disabled individuals: Some considerations. *The Analysis of Verbal Behavior, 11,* 117–133.

Shriberg, L. D., Paul, R., McSweeney, J. L., Klin, A., Cohen, D. J., & Volkmar, F. R. (2001). Speech and prosody characteristics of adolescents and adults with high-functioning autism and Asperger syndrome. *Journal of Speech, Language, and Hearing Research, 44,* 1097–1115.

Sigafoos, J., Drasgow, E., Halle, J. W., O'Reilly, M., Seely-York, S., Edrisinha, C., et al. (2004). Teaching VOCA use a communicative repair strategy. *Journal of Autism and Developmental Disorders, 34,* 411–422.

Sigafoos, J., O'Reilly, M. F., Seely-York, S., Weru, J., Son, S. H., Green, V. A., et al. (2004). Transferring AAC intervention to the home. *Disability and Rehabilitation, 26,* 1330–1334.

Sigman, M., & Ruskin, E. (1999). Continuity and change in the social competence of children with autism, Down syndrome, and developmental delays. *Monographs of the Society in Research in Child Development, 64,* 1–114.

Simpson, R. L., de Boer-Ott, S. R., Griswold, D. E., Myles, B. S., Byrd, S. E., Ganz, J. B., et al. (2005). *Autism spectrum disorders: Interventions and treatments for children and youth.* Thousand Oaks, CA: Corwin Press.

Skinner, B. F. (1957). *Verbal behavior.* Upper Saddle River, NJ: Prentice Hall.

Smith, I. M., & Bryson, S. E. (1994). Imitation and action in autism: A critical review. *Psychological Bulletin, 116,* 259-273.

Snow, M. E., Hertzig, M. E., & Shapiro, T. (1987). Expressions of emotion in young autistic children. *Journal of the American Academy of Child and Adolescent Psychiatry, 27,* 647-655.

Snyder-McLean, L. K., Solomonson, B., McLean, J. E., & Sack, S. (1984). Structuring joint action routines: a strategy for facilitating communication and language development in the classroom. *Seminars in Speech and Language, 5,* 213-225.

Soorya, L. V. (2004). *Evaluation of motor proficiency and apraxia in autism: Effects on sign language acquisition.* Unpublished doctoral dissertation, State University of New York at Binghamton.

Stone, W. L., & Lemanek, K. L. (1990). Parental report of social behaviors in autistic preschoolers. *Journal of Autism and Developmental Disorders, 20,* 513-522.

Stone, W. L., Ousley, O. Y., & Littleford, C. (1997). Motor imitation in young children with autism: What's the object? *Journal of Abnormal Child Psychology, 25,* 475-485.

Stone, W. L., & Yoder, P. J. (2001). Predicting spoken language level in children with autism spectrum disorders. *Autism, 5,* 341-361.

Stone, W. L., Ousley, O. Y., Yoder, P. J., Hogan, K. L., & Hepburn, S. L. (1997). Nonverbal communication in two- and three-year-old children with autism. *Journal of Autism and Developmental Disorders, 27,* 677-696.

Storkel, H. L., & Morrisette, M. L. (2002). The lexicon and phonology: Interactions in language acquisition. *Language, Speech, and Hearing Services in Schools, 33,* 24-37.

Stremel, K., Bixler, B., Morgan, S., & Layton, K. (2002). *Communication fact sheet for parents.* Eric Document Reproduction Service No. ED 475 791.

Sundberg, M. (1993). Selecting a response form for nonberbal persons: Facilitated communication, pointing systems, or sign language? *The Analysis of Verbal Behavior, 11,* 99-116.

Sundberg, M. L., & Michael, J. (2001). The benefits of Skinner's analysis of verbal behavior for children with autism. *Behavior Modification, 25,* 698-724.

Tiegerman-Farber, E. (2002). Autism spectrum disorders: Learning to communicate. In D. K. Bernstein & E. Tiegerman-Faber (Eds.), *Language and communication disorders in children* (5th ed., pp. 510-564). Boston: Allyn & Bacon.

Tiegerman, E., & Primavera, L., (1984). Imitating the autistic child: Facilitating communicative gaze behavior. *Journal of Autism and Developmental Disorders, 14,* 27-38.

Tincani, M., (2004). Comparing Picture Exchange Communication System (PECS) and sign language training for children with autism. *Focus on Autism and Other Developmental Disabilities, 19,* 152-164.

Tomasello, M. (1992). The social bases of language acquisition. *Social Development, 1,* 67-87.

Tomasello, M. (2002). Things are what they do: Katherine Nelson's functional approach to language and cognition. *Journal of Cognition and Development, 3,* 4-19.

Vostanis, P., Smithe, B., Corbett, J., Sungum-Paliwal, R., Edwards, A., Gingell, K., et al. (1998). Parental concerns of early development in children with autism and related disorders. *Autism, 2,* 229-242.

Werner, E., Dawson, G., Osterling, J., & Dinno, N. (2000). Brief report: Recognition of autism spectrum disorder before 1 year of age: A retrospective study based on home videotapes. *Journal of Autism and Other Developmental Disorders, 30,* 157-167.

Wetherby, A. M., Alexander, D. G., & Prizant, B. M. (1998). The ontogeny and role of repair strategies. In A. M. Wetherby, S. F. Warren, & J. Reichle (Vol. Eds.), *Communication and language intervention series: Vol. 7. Transition in prelinguistic communication* (pp. 135-161). Baltimore: Paul H. Brookes.

Wetherby, A. M., & Prizant, B. M. (1989). The expression of communicative intent: Assessment guidelines. *Seminars in Speech and Language, 10,* 77-91.

Wetherby, A. M., & Prizant, B. M. (2000). *Autism spectrum disorders: A developmental, transactional perspective.* Baltimore: Paul H. Brookes.

Wetherby, A. M., & Prizant, B. M. (2005). Enhancing language and communication development in autism spectrum disorders: Assessment and intervention guidelines. In D. Zager (Ed.), *Autism spectrum disorders* (3rd ed., pp. 327-365). Mahwah, NJ: Erlbaum.

Wetherby, A. M., Prizant, B. M., & Hutchinson, T. A. (1998). Communicative, social/

affective and symbolic profiles of young children with autism and pervasive developmental disorders. *American Journal of Speech-Language Pathology, 7,* 77–91.

Wetherby, A. M., Prizant, B. M., & Schuler, A. L. (2000). Understanding the nature of communication and language impairments. In A. M. Wetherby & B. M. Prizant (Eds.), *Autism spectrum disorders: A transactional developmental perspective* (pp. 109–142). Baltimore: Paul H. Brookes.

Williams, J. H. G., Whiten, A., & Singh, T. (2004). A systematic review of action imitation in autistic spectrum disorder. *Journal of Autism and Developmental Disorders, 34,* 285–299.

Wing, L. (1981). Asperger's syndrome: A clinical account. *Psychological Medicine, 11,* 115–129.

Wing, L. (2001). *The autistic spectrum: A parents' guide to understanding and helping your child.* Berkeley, CA: Ulysses Press.

Wolfberg, P. J. (2003). *Peer play and the autism spectrum.* Shawnee Mission, KS: Autism Asperger.

Woods, J. J., & Wetherby, A. M. (2003). Early identification of and intervention for infants and toddlers who are at risk for autism spectrum disorder. *Language, Speech, & Hearing Services in Schools, 34,* 180–194.

Yont, K. M., Hewitt, L. E., & Miccio, A. W. (2000). A coding system for describing conversational breakdowns in preschool children. *American Journal of Speech-Language Pathology, 9,* 300–309.

Young, E. C., Diehl, J. J., Morris, D., Hyman, S. L., & Bennetto, L. (2005). The use of two language tests to identify pragmatic language problems in children with autism spectrum disorders. *Language, Speech, and Hearing Services in Schools, 36,* 62–72.

CHAPTER 9

Enhancing Socialization and Social Competence

KEY TERMS

Acquisition Deficits

Adult-Mediated Instruction and Interventions (AMII)

Behavior Sampling

Comic Strip Conversations™

Concept Mastery

Elicited Responses

Hidden Social Curriculum

Masquerading

Peer-Mediated Instruction and Interventions (PMII)

Performance Deficits

Social Autopsies

Social Competence

Social Skills Instruction

Social Stories™

Social Reciprocity

❖ LEARNING WITH MS. HARRIS: Craig Joins In—Badly

Throughout the year, Ms. Harris has documented how much her students have achieved: adjusting to changes in their schedules and settings, following rules and routines, paying attention during academic tasks, and attending activities and content classes in general education. There has been an increase in the frequency of spontaneous initiations, negations, and requests. The use of the broad range of applied behavior analytic interventions has resulted in the development of skills that are enhancing the functioning of students in her class.

Ms. Harris was feeling good about life until she rounded the hall and saw groups of students waiting for the bus. Five of the "cool" boys were standing off to one side, balancing their notebooks on their heads and challenging each other to move without dropping them. Craig noticed the boys and Ms. Harris could tell that he wanted to join the activity. In his excitement to join in, Craig stumbled into two of the boys, making them drop their notebooks. They yelled at Craig, who by now had his notebook on his head. The yelling attracted the attention of the bus monitor, who approached the group, causing all the boys to scatter except for Craig, who was turning around with his notebook on his head, calling for the other boys to come back. It was obvious that the bus monitor was shocked, and getting angry that Craig had not also responded to her approach by stopping his silliness and going back to his place in line. Walking faster, Ms. Harris hoped she could get there before the woman had time to start assigning detention.

Students with Autism Spectrum Disorders may have pronounced deficits recognizing and interpreting social cues that modulate behavior, not only resulting in social isolation but also provoking negative consequences, as in Craig's case. The social understanding that comes so naturally to individuals who are neurotypical may be elusive to individuals with ASD. Some students with ASD appear to be disinterested in social interactions, while others may be desperately interested but unable to engage successfully. This chapter reviews social differences and social competence in students with ASD and discusses methods to assess and enhance socialization.

SOCIAL DIFFERENCES IN ASD

Both Kanner (1943) and Asperger (1944) described the children and youth they studied as having marked differences in their abilities to interact socially. For many individuals with ASD, their unusually strong preferences for and attachment to objects are in sharp contrast to the absence of relatedness to other people (Dawson, Meltzoff, Osterling, Rinaldi, & Brown, 1998; Volkmar et al., 1994). By 3 to 5 years of age, children may show preferences for their caregivers over strangers (Sigman, Dijamco, Gratier, & Rozga, 2004) but the way they demonstrate these preferences may be unusual (Rogers, Ozonoff, & Maslin-Cole, 1993). From an early age, most individuals with ASD appear to relate differently to other people. Since children with ASD initiate less (verbally and nonverbally), make fewer spontaneous requests, perseverate on a topic or toy, and usually remain on the periphery or totally isolated, there are fewer occasions for **social reciprocity** (the give and take that occurs within interactions) (Kohler, Strain, & Shearer, 1992; Wolfberg, 2003).

Social acceptance of some students with ASD may be further impeded by their failure to express and understand emotions and perceptions (Attwood, 1998; Myles & Adreon, 2001; Myles & Simpson, 1998), which may result in undesirable behavior (Myles, Barnhill, Hagiwara, Griswold, & Simpson,

2001; Prizant, Wetherby, Rubin, Laurent, & Rydell, 2002) as well as stereotypic behaviors (Schopler & Mesibov, 1985). Therefore, as breakdowns occur in the ability to communicate and regulate their emotions, students with ASD have fewer opportunities to develop and maintain friendships (Boucher, 1999), and the chances of their being included in a peer group are weighted against them (Kohler et al., 1992). As children with ASD engage less with peers, fewer attempts are made by peers to initiate with them, which then provides fewer opportunities for students with ASD to interact socially, resulting in more time isolated from their peers.

Chapter 1 described the triad of core deficits for individuals with ASD as comprising differences in communication, socialization, and range of interests and activities. The *Diagnostic and Statistical Manual of Mental Disorders* (4th ed., text revision [*DSM-IV-TR*]; APA, 2000, pp. 70–71) describes a "lack of varied spontaneous make-believe play or social imitative play appropriate to developmental level" and the "failure to develop peer relationships appropriate to developmental level" as explicit diagnostic criteria for autistic disorder. Problems with socialization for students with ASD result from their difficulty with interpersonal communication, their inability to be flexible, their need to be literal, their tendency to be disorganized, and their lack of ability to generalize (Lewis & Boucher, 1995; Libby, Powell, Messer, & Jordan, 1997; Terpstra, Higgins, & Pierce, 2002).

Some students with ASD do not understand social conventions and expectations. Typically developing students learn very quickly how to behave around certain people and what behaviors to avoid in order to stay out of trouble or seem different. Since these skills are not taught directly, but must be inferred and learned by trial and error, they are referred to as the **hidden social curriculum** (Myles & Simpson, 2001). Because of their neurological differences, most students with ASD do not have the ability to access the hidden social curriculum. These students may engage in behaviors that are considered socially unacceptable by others, such as picking their nose when others are around. These students do not have any concept of how people are expected to behave in different contexts and therefore have no behavioral inhibitions.

Students functioning on the higher end of the spectrum may be successful in storing the specific words or rules that apply to social situations, but are unable to recall, use, and then apply them appropriately in other situations (Kunce & Mesibov, 1998; Wolery & Garfinkle, 2002). Unfortunately, since many students with ASD can repeat social rules verbatim, teachers assume the students should be able to retrieve and apply the information at any time. For example, a student may be able to recall and repeat that it is not appropriate to barge into the middle of a group of people and begin talking about Egyptian mummies, but he may fail to recognize when a break in the conversation occurs or know how to initiate a discussion (Attwood, 1998; Myles & Adreon, 2001). At these times, teachers who do not have an understanding of ASD may make statements that indicate they believe the student knew exactly what he was to do and was just being rude or manipulative (Tsatsanis, Foley, & Donehower, 2004).

Some students functioning on the higher end of the spectrum who try to tell others how to follow the rules are perceived by peers and teachers as being egocentric, rude, and bossy. Few teachers appreciate being corrected in front of a class, even if they have made a mistake. These perceptions of willful behavior may result in some students with ASD being disciplined unnecessarily and subject to peer and teacher rejection. Students with ASD tend to be unaware of people's hidden agendas (Myles & Simpson, 2001; Myles & Southwick, 1999) and misunderstand nonliteral or figurative expressions (i.e., humor, sarcasm, idioms) (Safran, Safran, & Ellis, 2003). Demonstrating poor social inhibition, engaging in behaviors others consider "gross," and misinterpreting others' social behaviors can result in students with ASD being ignored, or worse, teased and bullied (Heerey, Capps, Keltner, & Kring, 2005; Little, 2001). Being disciplined for failure to identify and engage in correct social behaviors as well as being rejected by peers can lead to students with ASD becoming anxious and depressed (Bellini, 2004; Myles & Simpson, 1998; Tantam, 2000), further diminishing their motivation to learn and use social skills.

Among students with ASD, there is a tendency to exhibit behaviors associated with attention deficit hyperactivity disorder, combined type (Gillberg & Ehlers, 1998; Loveland & Tunali-Kotoski, 1997), which also influences social development. In addition to the inattentiveness, impulsivity, and hyperactivity associated with attention deficit hyperactivity disorder (ADHD), individuals often demonstrate difficulties in social relationships (Frick & Lahey, 1991; Matthys, Cuperus, & van Engeland, 1999; McFadyen-Ketchum & Dodge, 1998). Approximately 50% of the students with ADHD as compared with 15%–30% of the same-aged sample of typical students have difficulty with interpersonal interactions (Guevremont & Dumas, 1994). Students who demonstrate concomitant social impairment may experience future problems, such as fewer friends and attendance at fewer social activities (Barkley, Anastopolous, Guevremont, & Fletcher, 1991); poor school performance (Eccles & Roeser, 1999; Ladd, 1990; Robin, 1998; Zeigler-Dendy, 2000); and poor self-esteem into adulthood (Wheeler & Carlson, 1994).

SOCIAL COMPETENCE

An individual's social competence is typically defined by the perceptions of others (Dodge, Pettit, McClaskey, & Brown, 1986). In other words, people are socially competent if others view their behavior as appropriate. **Social competence** implies that the individual has the knowledge and skills to successfully navigate the constantly changing social landscape. Crick and Dodge (1994) identified three predictors for social competence in students: (1) the extent to which students are accepted by their peers, (2) the degree to which students are aggressive toward peers (fighting, hitting, pushing, or threatening), and (3) the degree to which students withdraw from peer interactions (playing alone rather than with peers). These researchers also determined that poor parent-child relationships, students' inability to understand others' emotions and solve problems, academic failure, social rejection, and the inability to get along in a group and to form friendships are major risk factors that interfere with the acquisition and performance of social skills.

SOCIAL SKILLS TRAINING
Assessment

Teachers usually have an inner sense when something appears amiss in a student's development. However, objective data need to be collected to document social strengths and skill deficits. Social deficits negatively affect a student's competence across contexts (i.e., people, places, and tasks). Teachers should use ecologically valid assessment approaches and tools to evaluate social skill deficits, approaches that consider the following factors (Prizant, 2002; Quill, 2000; Tsatsanis, 2004):

- Social skills of typically developing peers for comparison
- Evidence of the student's successful performance with similar skills that are on the assessment
- Various settings in which the student will be evaluated
- People who are usually in those settings
- Types of assessment tools

Social skills assessments may include observations in natural environments, behavior sampling, elicited responses, parent/teacher reports, student self-reports, and standardized testing (Prizant, 2002; Quill, 1995; Tsatsanis, 2004). The least intrusive approach to social skills assessment is the parent/teacher report, because there is no direct interaction with the student. However, parents and teachers may not be aware of social behaviors that occur when they are not around. Standardized testing is the most intrusive and may not solicit an authentic assessment. Observations in natural environments, behavior sampling, and elicited responses each offer different yet valuable information.

- *Observations in natural environments* do not alter activities or routines nor do they place the student in situations where she has to interact with unfamiliar adults or peers.
- **Behavior sampling** allows the evaluators to set up situations that make the student want to interact. Results show whether the student has a repertoire of strategies. They also provide information that can be related to normal development scales.
- **Elicited responses** assess the student's ability to respond to a variety of tasks including "wh" questions (e.g., who, why, when), inferential and factual questions, and/or motor tasks.

Quill (1995) recommends reviewing records and case histories that may provide background information regarding the student's developmental course (rate and sequence) across domains.

Examples of valid and reliable assessment tools include the following:

- The *Autism Diagnostic Observation Schedule* (ADOS), developed by Lord, Rutter, DiLavore, and Risi (1999), is accepted as the standard in research and is gaining prominence in clinical evaluations. Although it is an observational approach for recording social and communicative behavior, the protocol uses a standard administration, but the tasks are diverse, unstructured, and occur in the student's natural social contexts. Therefore, evaluators need to be trained. The ADOS usually takes about 40 to 60 minutes to complete and provides qualitative information on behaviors such as nonverbal communication, joint attention, reciprocity, aggression, disinhibition, or self-stimulation.
- The *Social Skills Rating Scale* (SSR), developed by Gresham and Elliot (1990), provides nationally standardized norms of prosocial skills (Farmer-Dougan & Kaszuba, 1999). It assesses five developmental domains in terms of the frequency with which the behaviors occur and the importance of the behaviors to successful classroom behavior. These domains are cooperation, assertiveness, internalizing behavior, externalizing behavior, and school-related behavior (Farmer-Dougan & Kaszuba, 1999). Similar to the ADOS, the SSR can be used across contexts and age levels (e.g., preschoolers during play; high school students during leisure time).
- *School Social Behavior Scales, 2nd edition* (SSBS-2; Merrell, 2002a) is a behavior rating scale for students in grades K–12, which the student's teacher(s) and other school personnel can complete within 10 minutes. Results are compared to nationally standardized norms of social competence and antisocial behavior in domains such as peer relations, self management/compliance, academic behavior, defiance/disruptiveness, hostility/irritability, and aggression.
- The *Home & Community Social Behavior Scales* (HCSBS; Merrell, 2002b) is a counterpart of the SSBS-2; however, parents, guardians, group home supervisors, or other individuals who are familiar with the student in either the home or community can complete the rating scale. The results are compared to nationally standardized norms of both social competence and antisocial behavior for children and adolescents, ages 5 to 18 years.

These measures can be used to gauge a student's social competence and identify which social skills are the most critical to achieve. Teachers and related professionals may feel more comfortable designing an intervention plan and developing goals and objectives that directly relate back to the corresponding assessment tool. Quill (2000), McGinnis and Goldstein (1997, 2003), and Goldstein and McGinnis (1997) have specific programming suggestions and activities that correlate with their respective assessments. The following sources provide objectives and detailed procedures that can be modified to target the individual student's specific social skills.

- *DO-WATCH-LISTEN-SAY Assessment of Social and Communication Skills with Autism*, found in the corresponding intervention program, *Do Watch Listen Say* (Quill, 2000), addresses social, communicative, and ritualistic behaviors such as exploratory, nonverbal social interaction; imitation; organizational, solitary play; social play; group skills; and community social skills in children with autism.
- The *Skillstreaming* series includes *Skillstreaming in Early Childhood* (McGinnis & Goldstein, 2003), *Skillstreaming the Elementary School Child* (McGinnis & Goldstein, 1997), and *Skillstreaming the Adolescent* (Goldstein & McGinnis, 1997). Teachers who use lessons from the *Skillstreaming* series employ modeling, role-playing, performance feedback, and transfer training (homework). This series comes with a manual that includes lessons and an informal developmental rating scale that assesses a broad range of social skills. In addition, the authors offer parallel intervention activities by providing program forms, student manuals, skill cards for role-playing and homework, and videos of a *Skillstreaming* session. *Skillstreaming in Early Childhood* assesses and addresses 40 prosocial skills divided into beginning social skills, school-related skills, friendship-making skills, dealing with feelings, alternatives to aggression, and dealing with stress. Additionally, the authors include strategies for managing problem behaviors of the younger child as well as suggestions for building positive relationships with parents. *Skillstreaming the Elementary School Child* assesses skills and contains 60 lessons that cover classroom survival skills, friendship-making skills, dealing with feelings, alternatives to aggression, and dealing with stress. Finally, *Skillstreaming the Adolescent* assesses skills and contains 50 lessons that address beginning social skills, advanced social skills, dealing with feelings, alternatives to aggression, dealing with stress, and planning skills.

Evaluations should not be merely an annual or triennial event. Instead, data should be collected on a student's social and communication skills, ability to regulate behavior, and use of transactional supports on an ongoing basis (Quill, 1995) across home, school, and community settings (Prizant, 2002).

Acquisition, Performance, and Generalization

Over the last 20 years, researchers have found that some students require direct instruction to acquire appropriate social skills while others need only support to perform these skills. According to Gresham (1997), poor social skills fall into three categories: acquisition deficits, performance deficits, and competing behavior. Wolery and Garfinkle (2002) provide a summary of these three categories. Acquisition refers to the initial and beginning stages of learning in which students are taught the skill. Students with **acquisition deficits** have not learned the skill. **Performance deficits** occur when students do not demonstrate the skills they have acquired. Performance of a skill can be examined on two levels, fluency and maintenance. *Fluency* is the act of performing a skill unhesitatingly and effortlessly. *Maintenance* represents a student's ability to perform a skill after instruction has ended. *Generalization* describes a student's ability to apply the skill across contexts, behaviors, and tasks. To be effective, social skills training must target the student's needs, whether in acquisition, performance, or the need to reduce competing behavior. Students will probably require social skills training involving a combination of all three areas.

STRATEGIES TO ENHANCE SOCIALIZATION AND SOCIAL COMPETENCE

Prior to introducing specific social skill training strategies the importance of prerequisite and communication skills should be considered. Some students with ASD may lack the prerequisite skills of imitation, play, and attending/engagement, which can facilitate the development of appropriate social skills (National Research Council, 2001; Wolery & Garfinkle, 2002). These students need direct instruction to remediate these skill deficits.

Some of the communication approaches discussed in Chapter 8 may be used to enhance socialization. For example, PECS can encourage socialization because it is effective in training students to initiate communication spontaneously, decrease concomitant behaviors, and increase interactive behaviors in play and academic settings (Charlop-Christy, Carpenter, Le, LeBlanc, & Kellet, 2002). For students with ASD who do not use spoken language or are extremely limited in their verbalizations, using an AAC system during Joint Action Routines (JARs) may encourage the student to interact with peers. Even if the student does not appear to understand the purpose of the AAC system and is inconsistent in its use, the system should be set up to reflect a variety of age-appropriate, high-interest topics. In a natural setting, such as a classroom or playground, peers can respond and create contexts for interaction if the student pushes a button on a speech-generating device (SGD).

Functional Communication Training (FCT), described in Chapter 7, integrates communication and social skills by addressing a variety of communicative functions, such as initiating, asking questions, refusing, commenting, and asking for help. Same-aged peers usually avoid students who display challenging behaviors along with severe communication problems. This certainly interrupts the development of social friendships (Fox, Dunlap, & Philbrick, 1997). FCT can be used for work-related tasks as well as social interaction. In addition to the benefit of reducing targeted behavior, increasing appropriate functional communication, and providing support for social communication, FCT affords the student the opportunity to communicate in a variety of settings.

As described in Chapter 8, the strategies used in NLP, JARs, and Incidental Teaching can encourage turn taking between partners by using familiar objects and activities (Koegel, O'Dell, & Koegel, 1987). Incidental Teaching also promotes peer interactions (McGee, Almeida, Sulzer-Azaroff, & Feldman,

1992); affords opportunities for appropriately requesting and responding (Farmer-Dougan, 1994); and improves joint attention, play, and social communication skills (McGee, Morrier, & Daly, 1999; Mundy & Crowson, 1997; Oswald & Lignugaris, 1990).

Discrete trials have been found to be an efficient strategy for controlling the presentation of stimuli and subsequent responses, and use highly motivating reinforcers to aid adults' attempts to encourage socialization. The drawbacks of using discrete trials to teach social skills, however, is the frequent failure to generalize the skills learned in training to other people and settings, including peer relationships. The use of applied behavior analytic techniques within naturally occurring contexts ultimately enhances the child's social and communicative competence (Delprato, 2001; Quill, 2000).

PEER-MEDIATED INSTRUCTION AND INTERVENTIONS

Many students with ASD are in general education classrooms in order to promote their socialization (Eckerman & Stein, 1990; Escalona, Field, Nadel, & Lundy, 2002). Teachers should not expect that placement in the general education setting automatically equates with successful socialization (Sontag, 1997). Peers should be educated, trained as social agents, and have opportunities to practice the strategies with schoolmates with ASD. One method of improving the social performance of students with ASD is the use of peer confederates (typically developing, same-age peers) during peer-mediated social skills instruction (Newcomb & Bagwell, 1995). In the 1970s, Strain and associates found that using peer confederates during dramatic activities increased the rate of social interactions among students with ASD when measured by social reciprocity (Newcomb & Bagwell, 1995).

Peer-Mediated Instruction and Interventions (PMII) derive from applied behavior analysis, mastery learning, Bandura's social learning theory, and process-product studies of effective instruction (Utley & Mortweet, 1997). PMII initially described a process in which classroom knowledge is reinforced through social interactions between student pairs. Originally these interventions were used to address the diverse needs of students in any classroom (Utley & Mortweet, 1997).

In PMII, competent peers, who are selected and trained, encourage the acquisition and performance of teacher-directed objectives within a student's natural environment (Kamps et al., 2002). To promote social and communicative competence, typical peers are taught to initiate and maintain engagement with students with disabilities through modeling, prompting, and providing reinforcement in order to help them achieve appropriate academic and social responses and play skills (Hundert & Houghton, 1992; Odom et al., 2003; Peck & Sasso, 1997). Most often they work on eye contact, play activities, initiating conversation, offering or requesting help, maintaining topics of social interaction, expanding the content of their interaction, and demonstrating affection (Utley & Mortweet, 1997). Peers are also taught to understand standard and nonstandard modes of communication. Adults provide explicit and direct support to the trained peers (Quill, 2000). Through the use of peer-mediated strategies (Newcomb & Bagwell, 1995; Quill, 1995), the social behavior of students with ASD may improve, as will teacher and peer acceptance (Gresham, 1997). Social acceptance may promote academic achievement and the development of friendships.

The term *peer-mediated* can be used to qualify an assortment of specific approaches. For example, peer-mediated instructional interventions can include peer tutoring (Kavale & Forness, 1999); peer modeling (Werts, Caldwell, & Wolery, 1996); classwide peer tutoring (CWPT) (Kamps, Barbetta, Leonard, & Delquadri, 1994; Mitchem, Young, West, & Benyo, 2001); cooperative groups (Dugan et al., 1995; Hill, 1999); Incidental Teaching (McGee et al., 1992); peer-assisted learning strategies (PALS) (Baker, Gersten, Dimino, & Griffiths, 2004; Fuchs, Fuchs, & Burish, 2000; Gersten & Dimino, 2001); and peer initiation training (Haring & Lovinger, 1989). Regardless of the PMII selected, the teacher alternates among delivering instruction, monitoring the student pairs, and supporting and improving peer-teaching activities.

The positive influence of peers as facilitators has been well documented. PMII were found effective in promoting student outcomes across content, skills, ages, and disabilities (Utley & Mortweet, 1997). For students with mild disabilities, this approach has been found to encourage generalization; however, for students with more severe disabilities, it has been less effective. A major disadvantage of this approach is that a considerable amount of teacher training is required for the program to be successful.

ADULT-MEDIATED INSTRUCTION AND INTERVENTIONS

In **Adult-Mediated Instruction and Interventions (AMII),** adults provide social skills instruction directly to the students. The instruction typically occurs in small-group settings. Some of the most commonly used adult-mediated approaches for students with ASD include facilitating play behavior, direct teaching of social skills, Social Stories™, Comic Strip Conversations™, Concept Mastery, and social autopsies. AMII can help students with ASD acquire new skills, after which peer-mediated approaches can be used to encourage the skill generalization.

Facilitating Play Behavior

Play has a direct impact on the acquisition of language, which affects social development. Therefore, it may be beneficial to teach play behavior to students with ASD. Evidence of the importance of play for socialization is well documented, as well as its strong correlation with normal language development (Rettig, 1994; Siller & Sigman, 2002; Stahmer, 1999; Terpstra, et al., 2002; Thorp, Stahmer, & Schreibman, 1995).

Terpstra et al. (2002) describe a hierarchy of three types of play: symbolic, functional, and sociodramatic. In typical play development, children spontaneously learn how to vary and combine actions from repetitive exploration and manipulation of objects or people within their environments. Children with ASD tend to continue with repetitive manipulation of objects and are often observed playing with toys or objects inappropriately, perseverating on the toy or object (for example, lining dinosaurs up in a specific manner), or engaging in repetitive, stereotyped behaviors (for example, playing with the string of a pull toy) (Boucher, 1999; Lewis & Boucher, 1995; Wolfberg, 2003). Although the exploratory behavior looks similar to that of typically developing children at very young ages (Baranek et al., 2005), as the children get older they do not progress to the next stage of play and their play behaviors may become noticeably different. Interventions that use behavioral strategies may be effective for teaching appropriate object play (Stahmer, Ingersoll, & Carter, 2003). These strategies include the use of discrete trial training, Pivotal Response Training, differentially reinforcing appropriate object play, and video modeling.

During symbolic or pretend play, children create imaginative play scripts using objects, others, and themselves (Boucher, 1999). Some students with ASD have the most difficulty with symbolic or pretend play (Lewy & Dawson, 1992; Libby et al., 1997; Rettig, 1994). After an analysis of empirical research on symbolic play in children with ASD, Jarrold, Boucher and Smith (1993) concluded that children with ASD have a capacity for symbolic play that is not exhibited spontaneously. Other researchers have noted the ability of children with ASD to demonstrate symbolic play in structured testing settings that is not generalized to natural settings (McDonough, Stahmer, Schreibman, & Thompson, 1997). Strategies that have been effective for facilitating the development of pretend play include the use of visual supports in the form of activity schedules, picture cures, and video models (Dauphin, Kinney, & Stromer, 2004).

Functional play occurs as children imitate acts they observe outside of their immediate environment. Students with ASD demonstrate play schemes that are simpler and more often observed within the present environment (Baranek et al., 2005; Terpstra et al., 2002; Wolfberg, 2003). For example, in a study that compared the functional play of 15 children with ASD, 15 children with Down syndrome, and 15 typically developing children (Williams, Reddy, & Costall, 2001), children with ASD produced slightly fewer acts of functional play but were noticeably different in the restricted nature of the functional acts. Functional acts performed by the children with ASD consisted almost entirely of simple acts with a single object (e.g., pushing a car or bringing a cup to the mouth). Little research has been conducted on facilitating the development of functional play; however, students with ASD were found to respond to prompting procedures to produce functional play acts (Charman & Baron-Cohen, 1997).

Direct Teaching of Social Skills

The assessment and remediation of social skills deficits have occurred for decades in programs serving students with disabilities, particularly those with behavioral disorders (Gresham, Cook, Crews, & Kern, 2004). Although such assessment and remediation are beneficial for modifying social behavior, concerns have been raised relative to generalization and long-term maintenance of the new skills (Gresham, 1997), resulting in the need for more research on factors that influence the impact of social skills instruction (Kavale, Mathur, Forness, Quinn, & Rutherford, 2000). Some research has been conducted on teaching social skills directly to students with ASD in the hopes of increasing the frequency or quality of social interactions. Typically, **social skills instruction** (consisting of explaining the social skill, modeling the social skill, and having the student practice the social skill) is provided in structured environments and then prompted and reinforced in other settings with the goal of bringing the social skill under control of reinforcing contingencies (McConnell, 2002). In this fashion, students with ASD are taught specific social skills and then prompted to demonstrate them in social situations and reinforced for doing so.

Effective teaching of social skills to students with ASD has used modeling and practice followed by reinforcement or corrective feedback (Barnhill, Cook, Tebbenkamp, & Myles, 2002; Jahr & Eldevik, 2002). Priming (as discussed in Chapter 5) has also been used to facilitate the demonstration of social skills. Sawyer, Luiselli, Ricciardi, and Gower (2005) used priming to teach the social skills of sharing. Prior to going to play settings with his peers, a 4-year-old boy with ASD practiced sharing with one peer and an adult. During play, the child was prompted to share and praised if he demonstrated the skill. As a result of the intervention, the child shared as frequently as his peers. Prompts have been described by Sontag (1997) as an important component of improving social skills in students with disabilities.

Direct teaching of social skills to students with ASD appears to be facilitated by the use of visual supports. Three preschool students with ASD were taught to ask "Can I play?" which was associated with graphic symbols. The students were taught the skill through modeling, prompting, practice, and reinforcement for demonstrating the skills. All three students successfully learned to request admission to play activities. Thiemann and Goldstein (2004) used written text to increase three different social skills for five elementary-aged students with ASD. The written cues were more effective for increasing demonstration of the social skills than training peers to elicit the skills. Krantz and McClannahan (1998) increased interactions with adults by adding prompts to "look" or "listen" in picture activity schedules.

In addition to pictures and text, visual cueing in the form of videotapes has been used to provide specific instruction in social skills. Self-evaluation using video feedback was added to written text and increased the interactive skills of five students with ASD (Thiemann & Goldstein, 2001). Nikopoulos and Keenan (2004) used videotapes showing a typically developing peer and adult interacting to play with a toy. Viewing the video increased social initiation and reciprocal play skills for three children with ASD, and the effects were still evident after three months. Clips taken from videotapes have also been used to teach students with ASD to discriminate between appropriate and inappropriate social behaviors (Simpson, Langone, & Ayres, 2004).

Four students with ASD used a computer-based program with embedded video clips that showed typically developing peers displaying examples and nonexamples of targeted social skills. All four students demonstrated improvements in social skills in the natural environment after the computer-based training.

Direct teaching of social skills can be effective for promoting acquisition of important skills for interacting with others. Modeling, practice, prompting, priming, and reinforcement have some demonstrated effectiveness for teaching social skills to students with ASD. Social skill acquisition may be supported through the use of visual strategies for prompting the occurrence of the behavior. Teaching students to self-record behaviors (described in Chapter 11) may promote maintenance and generalization of social skills (Koegel, Koegel, Hurley, & Frea, 1992).

Social Stories™

Social Stories™ and Comic Strip Conversations™ are two commonly used strategies for enhancing socialization in individuals with ASD, but there is little empirical support for their effectiveness. Lack of empirical validation is partly attributed to the use of a variety of written narratives that are referred to as Social Stories in published literature but which do not appear to be Social Stories according to the criteria established by the originator, Carol Gray. For example, the story written by Agosta, Graetz, Mastropieri, and Scruggs (2004) violates the guidelines for a descriptive Social Story as articulated by Gray (2004), yet it was effective for reducing yelling by a 6-year-old boy with ASD during morning circle time.

Copious anecdotal support guarantees continued use of interventions using Social Stories. In addition, published research that supports the effectiveness of using written text to change behavior of students with ASD would suggest that even if a story is not written as per the Social Story guidelines, there exists the possibility it will enhance student functioning (Crozier & Tincani, in press). However, more research using actual Social Stories needs to be conducted before drawing conclusions about the effectiveness of the methodology (Sansosti, Powell-Smith, & Kincaid, 2004).

According to Gray (2004), **Social Stories** are written not to change the student's behavior, but to facilitate understanding of social situations and the perspectives of others. Social Stories share information to explain events and expectations and may include illustrations. For every Social Story written to promote social understanding, Gray recommends that another story be written to recognize achievement. Social Stories answer "wh" questions (who, what, where, when, and how) to provide a concrete explanation. Social Stories are typically written from the first person (student's) perspective but may be written from a third person perspective, depending on the student. Six types of sentences are used in writing a Social Story. They are:

- Descriptive sentences that describe a situation, event, or expectation (who, what, when, where, and why)
- Directive sentences that describe the behaviors expected of the student

- Perspective sentences that describe what people might be feeling or believing or what they know
- Affirmative sentences that help identify important concepts
- Cooperative sentences that provide the student with a description of the roles others play in the situation
- Control sentences that are written by the student to assist in recall

Most Social Stories are developed to describe situations, not tell the student what to do. To maintain this focus, Gray (2004) developed a ratio for evaluating the adequacy of the story. To be a descriptive Social Story, the quotient of the number of descriptive, perspective, cooperative, and affirmative sentences in the story divided by the number of directive and control sentences must be greater than or equal to 2. More information about Social Stories is available at *www.thegraycenter.org/*.

Whether the interventions employ Social Stories or narrative text, some variation of the methodology has been used to help students with ASD prepare for novel events (Ivey, Heflin, & Alberto, 2004), reduce frustration related to doing homework (Adams, Gouvousis, VanLue, & Waldron, 2004), and facilitate choice-making (Barry & Burlew, 2004). Social Stories have been presented via computer (Hagiwara & Myles, 1999) and have been implemented in a student's home (Lorimer, Simpson, Myles, & Ganz, 2002).

Figure 9.1 contains a Social Story that was written for an elementary student with an ASD who did not understand the game that was being played

What Happens When We Play Igloo During PE?

I usuall o to on on a s an urs a s Coac u an Coac ain are m teac ers escri tive Sentences

ost c il ren li e la in it t e arac ute I li e t e arac ute too ers ective Sentences

ne ame e la in is I loo en e la I loo e are un er t e arac ute escri tive Sentences

Coac is outsi e t e arac ute Coac touc es our eet ut e on t no en e ill touc t em escri tive Sentences

Coac reten s to e a ear t at is tr in to et us escri tive Coo erative Sentences

e are all sa e Coac is not reall a ear ers ective an A irmative Sentences

I I on t ant m eet touc e I s oul tell Coac lease on t touc m toes irective Sentence

I ave un la in it t e arac ute ers ective Sentence

FIGURE 9.1
Social Story for Understanding a Game in PE

during physical education class, as evidenced by his behavioral problems and aggressive outbursts.

Comic Strip Conversations™

In addition to the traditional story approach, **Comic Strip Conversations™** (Gray, 1994) have been described anecdotally as being effective for helping students understand the literal and nonliteral information exchanged within a conversation. In a Comic Strip Conversation, the adult encourages and prompts the student to consider situational features of a specific conversation as the student draws the comiclike illustrations (Gray, 1994). Comic Strip Conversations may be useful for identifying alternatives to situations. They also provide a visual representation of social behavior, which taps into one of the processing strengths for many students with ASD. Using "frames," as in a typical comic strip, information is presented in smaller parts to make it easier for the student to process.

There is a set of eight standard "thought" and "word" balloons seen in typical Comic Strip Conversations (Gray, 1994). As shown in Figure 9.2, these symbols portray typical conversational skills such as thoughts or questions. Through this visual representation, individuals with ASD are able to focus on what other people may actually be thinking or feeling, as well as what may be motivating them.

A Comic Strip Conversation uses common language and requires only simple materials (Gray, 1994). Neither the student nor adult has to be a master artist. Stick figures are quick, easy, and readily recognized (Moyes, 2001). The use of color is recommended to provide a visual basis for understanding feelings, much like an "emotional palette" (Gray, 1994) or a "Feelings Thermometer" (Attwood, 1998). Students and teachers can use the colors associated with specific feelings as identified in the Comic Strip Conversations guide or decide for themselves which colors should represent which feelings.

The concept of using colors to provide visual representations for emotions was very helpful for Tommy, a first-grade student diagnosed with Asperger syndrome. Tommy spent 30 minutes daily in a small setting for resource support. During one session, Tommy's teacher placed a large assortment of colored markers in the middle of the table and asked Tommy to choose the color that reminded him of particular things and people that she knew provoked specific feelings (e.g., mad, happy, sad). They drew a rainbow with those colors and added the emotional labels. The following day, Tommy approached his teacher and told her he was "feeling brown" (mad) because she had not given him the opportunity to choose a color for feeling "okay." The teacher allowed him to choose a color for "okay" (which he identified as green) and Tommy added it to his rainbow. The teacher posted a color copy of the rainbow in each of his classrooms. In the following weeks, the rainbow was used to launch instruction on expressing "I" statements with Tommy describing how he was feeling. Figure 9.3 contains a copy of Tommy's rainbow.

Conversation Symbols Dictionary

FIGURE 9.2
Comic Strip Conversation Symbols
Source: Gray, C. (1994). *Comic Strip Conversations.* Arlington, TX: Future Horizons.
Reprinted with permission of Future Horizons, Inc.

A variation on the Comic Strip Conversations strategy is the "Bubble Dialogue" program reported by Rajendran and Mitchell (2000). The Bubble Dialogue program is presented on a computer. The program involves two characters interacting. Thoughts are entered into thought bubbles and spoken words into a graphic representing speech. Thoughts are presented visually

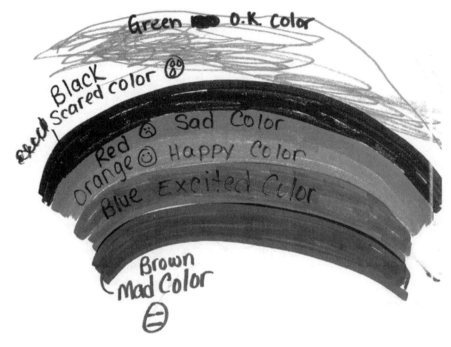

FIGURE 9.3
Tommy's Rainbow of Feelings
Source: Heflin and Alaimo

prior to speech. Individuals with ASD can interact with a neurotypical partner to experience how thoughts influence speech and how modifying what is said can affect thoughts. This method of presentation slows down social interactions and allows analysis of what occurred. Using the program, individuals with ASD have the opportunity to go back and change what they said to see if it affected the outcome. The methodology may have promise as a technique for supporting social skills development in students with ASD.

Concept Mastery

Although more commonly associated with teaching academic subjects, Concept Mastery routines have shown preliminary evidence of effectiveness for enhancing socialization in students with ASD. **Concept Mastery** routines consist of a systematic set of instructions that provide teachers with the structure to help students organize, understand, recall, and apply critical information (Bulgren & Lenz, 1996; Bulgren, Schumaker, & Deshler, 1988). As one of the routines, a graphic organizer called a *concept diagram* is created by the teacher and students to cover the three main components of Concept Mastery routines: definitions, characteristics, and examples of the concept (Deshler & Bulgren, 1998; Shaw, Thomas, Hoffman, & Bulgren, 1995).

To construct the concept diagram, the teacher helps the students identify characteristics that are always present in the concept and those that are never present. Teachers also solicit examples of characteristics that could sometimes be present. Together, the teacher and students generate a list of examples and nonexamples of the concept. The seven steps for creating a concept diagram spell the word "CONCEPT" (Bulgren, Schumaker, & Deshler, 1993):

Step 1: C—Convey the concept
Step 2: O—Offer the overall concept name
Step 3: N—Note key words
Step 4: C—Classify the characteristics
Step 5: E—Explore examples
Step 6: P—Practice with a new example(s)
Step 7: T—Tie down a definition

Concept Mastery routines have been effective for students receiving general education services in mathematics (Shaw et al., 1995), science, social studies, and language arts (Bulgren et al., 1988). Researchers have also documented benefit from using concept mastery for students who have learning disabilities (Bulgren et al., 1988) as well as gifted students with learning disabilities (Deshler & Bulgren, 1998). One study extends the use of Concept Mastery to teach social skills to students with ASD (Laushey, 2002).

Concept Mastery holds promise for students with ASD because the concept diagram provides a visual representation of explicit behavioral expectations. These visual representations provide opportunities for students with ASD to process the information at their own pace (Myles & Southwick, 1999) and to review the material whenever the need arises. Implementing Concept Mastery routines combines adult-mediated direct instruction of social skills with peer-mediated approaches that reinforce social skills. This may help students with ASD acquire and generalize social skills (Laushey, 2002). Figure 9.4 contains a completed concept diagram that resulted in improvements in social skills in four elementary-aged boys with ASD.

The concept diagram shown in Figure 9.4 is an instructional tool developed and researched at the University of Kansas Center for Research on Learning (Bulgren, Schumaker, & Deshler, 1988). It is one of a number of teaching devices designed for teachers to use as they teach content information to classes containing diverse student populations. A data-based teaching instrument, it has been found effective when used with a planning routine as well as a teaching routine that combines cues about the instruction, specialized delivery of the content, involvement of the students in the cognitive processes, and a review of the learning process and content material (Bulgren, Deshler, & Schumaker, 1993). It has not been shown to be an effective tool if it is simply distributed to students.

Social Autopsies

Another adult-mediated strategy that may help students with mild disabilities understand social errors in behavior is called the **social autopsy**

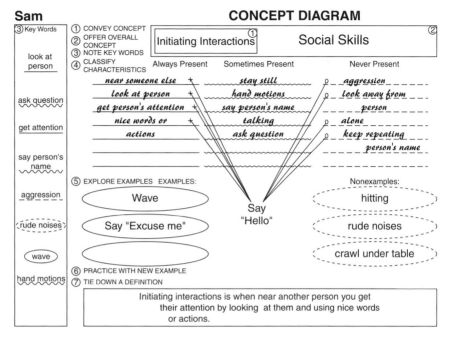

FIGURE 9.4

Concept Diagram for Teaching Initiation

Source: Laushey, K. M. (2002) and Bulgren, J. A., Schumaker, J. B., & Deshler, D. D. (1993). *The concept mastery routine*. Lawrence, KS: Edge Enterprises. Reprinted with permission. For more information on the training workshops that accompany the use of this book, contact the University of Kansas Center for Research on Learning, J. R. Pearson Hall, Lawrence, KS 66049 or call 785-864-4780.

(Myles & Adreon, 2001). Unlike Social Stories, which are designed to reduce future social dilemmas, the student completes social autopsies after a social error occurs. Similar to Life Space Crisis Intervention (LSCI; Long & Fecser, 1996) in its retrospective format, the student and teacher work together to describe the circumstances surrounding the error, identify the social error, identify who may have been hurt by the social error, consider solutions to the problem, and develop a plan to avoid future occurrences of the social error (Myles & Adreon, 2001).

One benefit of using social autopsies is that they may help establish cause and effect relationships between social behavior and the social consequences of that behavior. An additional benefit is that they provide immediate feedback and, therefore, reinforcement. Figure 9.5 illustrates the framework for a social autopsy.

For students who have difficulty with writing tasks, the social autopsy worksheet can be created as an electronic file so the student can type responses directly onto the form. Another alternative is to have the student dictate the response either into a recorder or to a scribe.

```
┌─────────────────────────────────────────────────────────────────┐
│  Social Autopsies Worksheet                                       │
│                                                                   │
│  What happened? _____ │
│  _____  │
│  _____  │
│  _____  │
│                                                                   │
│     What was the social error?      Who was hurt by the social error? │
│     _____           _____          │
│     _____           _____          │
│     _____           _____          │
│     _____           _____          │
│                                                                   │
│  What should be done to correct the error? _____ │
│  _____  │
│  _____  │
│  _____  │
│                                                                   │
│  What could be done next time? _____ │
│  _____  │
│  _____  │
│  _____  │
│                                                                   │
└─────────────────────────────────────────────────────────────────┘
```

FIGURE 9.5
Social Autopsy Worksheet
Source: Myles, B. S., & Adreon, D. (2001). *Asperger syndrome and adolescence: Practical solutions for school success*. Shawnee Mission, KS: Autism Asperger Publishing. Reprinted with permission of Autism Asperger Publishing Company.

STRATEGIES FOR ENHANCING FRIENDSHIPS

Some of the characteristics of students with ASD negatively affect their ability to make friends. Students with ASD have problems with reciprocal conversations, tend to focus conversations on their favorite topics, have difficulty starting and maintaining conversations, and appear to "talk at" others rather than "talking with" them. None of these behaviors is particularly endearing. Although some students with ASD appear to want acceptance by their peers, unfortunately, they do not possess the skills to effectively accomplish this goal (Attwood, 2002).

In addition to teaching students the skills that can promote social competence, strategies designed to encourage friendships can be implemented. If done with great care, the use of PMII can naturally support friendship development as students spend time together, as in "Stay, Play, & Talk".

Stay, Play, & Talk

Stay, Play, & Talk (English, Goldstein, Shafer, & Kaczmarek, 1997) is a strategy for promoting friendships between students with ASD and students without disabilities. It demonstrates the effectiveness of combining adult-mediated and peer-mediated approaches. Systematic instruction of social skills by adults is combined with trained, typically developing peers who act as social agents for eliciting appropriate social behaviors. Examples of social skills that have been successfully taught to kindergarteners with disabilities include: (1) requesting an object and responding to the communicative partner's answer, (2) gaining someone's attention by calling her name or tapping him on the shoulder, (3) waiting for one's turn, and (4) looking at or in the direction of another person who is speaking to you (Laushey & Heflin, 2000).

Rather than limiting the selection of peer confederates to only a few, the entire class is trained to use targeted social skills within the students' natural settings (e.g., free play, lunch, etc.). During instruction, all students are taught:

- Staying with a buddy means playing in the same area, taking turns playing with what each one wants to play with, and staying with that buddy no matter what.
- Playing with a buddy means that you play with each other by not only staying in the same area, but also by sharing the same types of toys or games. Playing with a buddy also means that you can join in your buddy's play, you can bring a toy to your buddy, or you can ask your buddy whether he would like to come and play with your toy or game.
- Talking with a buddy means that you stay together, play together, and talk to each other. You can talk about what you are playing with or you can play pretend games and talk to each other while playing pretend. And, even if the buddy does not talk back to you, try to talk to him.

Reinforcement is provided when students with and without disabilities are observed staying with, playing with, and talking with a peer buddy (English et al., 1997). As typical peers stay, play, and talk with students with ASD, there are greater opportunities to interact and to practice social skills (Laushey & Heflin, 2000), which may result in the development of friendships.

Additional Considerations for Developing Friendships

Some students with ASD do not appear to be affected by the presence or absence of friendships. Others appear to be concerned about their difficulties making friends. Individuals functioning on the higher end of the spectrum have been found to experience more loneliness than typically developing peers (Bauminger & Kasari, 2000), which may contribute to the high rates of anxiety and depression in the population (Bellini, 2004; Ghaziuddin, Ghaziuddin, & Greden, 2002; Ghaziuddin, Weidner-Mikhail, & Ghaziuddin, 1998). In a study involving 235 adolescents and adults with Aspergers, Orsmond, Krauss, and Seltzer (2004) discovered that 50% did not have any friends outside of prearranged activities (e.g., school, work). These researchers and others have found friendships that do develop tend to revolve around a specific interest such as computer games (Barnhill et al., 2002; Carrington, Templeton, & Papinczak, 2003).

The age and severity of ASD is associated with development of friendships; younger students who have less obvious social impairments are the most likely to have friends (Orsmond et al., 2004). Some adolescents with Aspergers may report having more friends than they do (called **masquerading;** Carrington & Graham, 2001), revealing an attempt to fit in and mask their deficits (Carrington et al., 2003). Although friendships cannot be forced, teaching students social skills to increase social competence and providing opportunities to practice the skills across environments can create bridges for the development of friendships. Connecting students to others who share their special interests can create an opportunity for the development of friendships (Barnhill et al., 2002). For students functioning on the higher end of the spectrum, helping them understand the nuances of social interactions as well as how to advocate for themselves in situations where they are being bullied can be crucial. No interventions can be implemented to guarantee the development of friendships. However, teachers can teach social skills, explain social expectations, and provide feedback during practice that may facilitate the potential for friendships for those students who desire them.

CONCLUSION

Individuals with ASD demonstrate differences in the way they interact with others from very early in life, leading some to view social deficits as the most pronounced feature of ASD. Social deficits are intimately related to the communication deficits discussed in the previous chapter. Communication deficits negatively affect opportunities for social interaction, which in turn reduces the opportunity to develop communication skills. Some students with ASD do not seem aware of the social conventions that dictate behavior. These students may engage in behaviors that others view as disgusting or strange, resulting in fewer attempts to engage the students. Other students with ASD appear to want to interact with others and develop friendships. However, they have difficulty accomplishing these goals because they are unaware of the hidden social curriculum and cannot identify and interpret the subtle social cues that occur during most interactions. These students may be ostracized or even teased and bullied, which can exacerbate coexisting conditions of anxiety and depression. Social reciprocity does not develop and they form few friendships.

Assessment verifies the presence of social impairments and identifies contexts that appear to be most problematic. Supporting the development of priority social skills for students with ASD provides the basis for their social competence. Although there is no cookbook approach to enhancing social competence and socialization, a variety of strategies have been validated as effective for promoting skill development. These strategies include Peer-Mediated Instruction and Interventions (PMII), in which socially competent peers encourage the demonstration of social skills. Adult-Mediated Instruction and Interventions (AMII) include the use of explicit instruction and reinforcement to facilitate the acquisition of skills. Some of the AMII strategies currently being used, which have varying amounts of empirical support, include facilitating play behavior, direct teaching of social skills, Social

Stories™, Comic Strip Conversations™, Content Mastery, and social autopsies. Students with ASD often demonstrate difficulty with generalizing skills they have been taught, so social skills need to be practiced across the various settings, people, and activities they meet throughout their day. Flexibility in using a combination of approaches holds the most promise for success.

Social skills can be reliably taught. However, acquisition does not automatically lead to the development of friendships. Combining AMII and PMII, as occurs in "Stay, Play, & Talk," may promote the development of friendships for younger students. For older students, using AMII to teach social skills and social understanding while helping students recognize how they come across to others may facilitate social interactions. Providing PMII along with the AMII provides structured opportunities for students to interact with others and may serve as a basis for friendship development. Identifying groups of people who share the same interests as students with ASD (in school and outside of school) may also provide the opportunity for friendships to develop.

Through the use of empirically based instructional approaches for students with autism, students with ASD may be viewed by others as more socially competent and therefore be more accepted by adults and peers. Social acceptance provides additional opportunities to learn and refine social skills and also creates the potential for the development of the social relationships desired by some individuals with ASD.

DISCUSSION QUESTIONS AND ACTIVITIES

1. Visit a school during an unstructured nonacademic time (e.g., lunch, PE) or attend an extracurricular activity (e.g., sports event, dance). Observe how the typically developing students interact with each other socially. Compare those interactions to the profile of socialization for individuals with ASD as described in this chapter and Chapter 1.

2. Pick an age group you would like to teach. Generate a list of behaviors in the hidden social curriculum for students of that age. What does it take to fit in? What are the unwritten rules for behavior? What are the behaviors that would automatically result in being ostracized by the group? How would you teach this hidden social curriculum to students with ASD?

3. Think of a student with ASD whom you know. Identify an important social skill that he or she does not currently demonstrate. Describe the process for directly teaching the social skill to the student, remembering to plan for strategies to promote generalization of the skill.

4. Bradley is a 14-year-old male who is eligible for special education under the eligibility of autism. Unless stressed, Bradley demonstrates fairly good receptive and expressive language (although he does not initiate). When upset, when emotionally aroused, or when the discussion includes novel information, Bradley is lost. Bradley's doctor has recently prescribed a medication that must be taken twice a day. Bradley refuses to take the medication. His mother has tried hiding it in food. Bradley swallows the

food and spits out the pill. If the pill is crushed and put in liquid or food, Bradley can detect it and refuses to consume the food. Bradley is going to have to take the pill, twice a day, for an extended period of time. Write a Social Story for Bradley addressing this issue.

5. Find a friend who has committed a social blunder. Work through the components of the social autopsy worksheet (Figure 9.5) to gain insight into how that tool can be used.

REFERENCES

Adams, L., Gouvousis, A., VanLue, M., & Waldron, C. (2004). Social story intervention: Improving communication skills in a child with an autism spectrum disorder. *Focus on Autism and Other Developmental Disabilities, 19,* 87-94.

Agosta, E., Graetz, J. E., Mastropieri, M. A., & Scruggs, T. E. (2004). Teacher-researcher partnerships to improve social behavior through social stories. *Intervention in School & Clinic, 39,* 276-287.

American Psychiatric Association. (2000). *Diagnostic and statistical manual of mental disorders* (4th ed., text revision). Washington, DC: Author.

Asperger, H. (1944/1991). Autistic psychopathy in childhood (Trans). In U. Frith (Ed.), *Autism and Asperger syndrome* (pp. 37-92). Cambridge, UK: Cambridge University Press.

Attwood, T. (1998). *Asperger syndrome: A guide for parents and professionals.* London: Jessica Kingsley.

Attwood, T. (2002, December). *How to teach social understanding: A one-day workshop.* Paper presented at the Southeastern Super Conference on Autism/Asperger's sponsored by Future Horizons, Atlanta, GA.

Baker, S., Gersten, R., Dimino, J. A., & Griffiths, R. (2004). The sustained use of research-based instructional practice. *Remedial and Special Education, 25,* 5-24.

Baranek, G. T., Barnett, C. R., Adams, E. M., Wolcott, N. A., Watson, L. R., & Crais, E. R. (2005). Object play in infants with autism: Methodological issues in retrospective video analysis. *The American Journal of Occupational Therapy, 59,* 20-30.

Barkley, R. A., Anastopolous, A. D., Guevremont, D. C., & Fletcher, K. E. (1991). Adolescents with ADHD: Patterns of behavioral adjustment, academic functioning and treatment utilization. *Journal of the American Academy of Child and Adolescent Psychiatry, 30,* 752-761.

Barnhill, G. P., Cook, K. T., Tebbenkamp, K., & Myles, B. S. (2002). The effectiveness of social skills intervention targeting nonverbal communication for adolescents with Asperger syndrome and related pervasive developmental delays. *Focus on Autism and Other Developmental Disabilities, 17,* 112-118.

Barry, L. M., & Burlew, S. B. (2004). Using social stories to teach choice and play skills to children with autism. *Focus on Autism and Other Developmental Disabilities, 19,* 45-51.

Bauminger, N., & Kasari, C. (2000). Loneliness and friendship in high-functioning children with autism. *Child Development, 71,* 447-456.

Bellini, S. (2004). Social skill deficits and anxiety in high-functioning adolescents with autism spectrum disorders. *Focus on Autism and Other Developmental Disabilities, 19,* 78-86.

Boucher, J. (1999). Editorial: Interventions with children with autism—Methods based on play. *Child Language Teaching and Therapy, 15*(1), 1-6.

Bulgren, J. A., & Lenz, B. K. (1996). Strategies instruction in the content areas. In D. D. Deshler, E. S. Ellis, & B. K. Lenz (Eds.), *Teaching adolescents with learning disabilities: Strategies and methods* (pp. 409-474). Denver, CO: Love.

Bulgren, J. A., Schumaker, J. B., & Deshler, D. D. (1988). Effectiveness of a concept teaching routine in enhancing the performance of LD students in secondary-level mainstream classes. *Learning Disability Quarterly, 11,* 3-17.

Bulgren, J. A., Schumaker, J. B., & Deshler, D. D. (1993). *The concept mastery routine.* Lawrence, KS: Edge Enterprises.

Carrington, S., & Graham, L. (2001). Perceptions of school by two teenage boys with Asperger syndrome and their mothers: A qualitative study. *Autism, 5,* 37–48.

Carrington, S., Templeton, E., & Papinczak, T. (2003). Adolescents with Asperger syndrome and perceptions of friendship. *Focus on Autism and Other Developmental Disabilities, 18,* 211–218.

Charlop-Christy, M. H., Carpenter, M., Le, L., LeBlanc, L. A., & Kellet, K. (2002). Using the Picture Exchange Communication System (PECS) with children with autism: Assessment of PECS acquisition, speech, social-communicative behavior, and problem behavior. *Journal of Applied Behavior Analysis, 35,* 213–231.

Charman, T., & Baron-Cohen, S. (1997). Brief report: Prompted pretend play in autism. *Journal of Autism and Developmental Disorders, 27,* 325–332.

Crick, N. R., & Dodge, K. A. (1994). A review and reformulation of social information-processing mechanisms in children's social adjustment. *Psychological Bulletin, 115,* 74–101.

Crozier, S., & Tincani, M. J. (in press). Using a modified social story to decrease disruptive behavior of a child with autism. *Focus on Autism and Other Developmental Disorders, 20*(3).

Dauphin, M., Kinney, E. M., & Stromer, R. (2004). Using video-enhanced activity schedules and matrix training to teach sociodramatic play to a child with autism. *Journal of Positive Behavior Interventions, 6,* 238–250.

Dawson, G., Meltzoff, A. N., Osterling, J., Rinaldi, J., & Brown, E. (1998). Children with autism fail to orient to naturally occurring social stimuli. *Journal of Autism and Developmental Disorders, 28,* 479–485.

Delprato, D. J. (2001). Comparisons of discrete-trial and normalized behavioral language intervention for young children with autism. *Journal of Autism and Developmental Disorders, 31,* 315–325.

Deshler, D. D., & Bulgren, J. A. (1998). Redefining instructional directions for the gifted students with learning disabilities. *Learning Disabilities, 8,* 121–132.

Dodge, K. A., Pettit, G. S., McClaskey, C. L., & Brown, M. M. (1986). Social competence in children. *Monographs of the Society for Research in Child Development, 51* (2, Serial No. 213).

Dugan, E., Kamps, D., Leonard, B., Watkins, N., Rheinberger, A., & Stackhaus, J. (1995). Effects of cooperative learning groups during social studies for students with autism and fourth-grade peers. *Journal of Applied Behavior Analysis, 28,* 175–188.

Eccles, J. S., & Roeser, R. W. (1999). School and community influences on human development. In M. H. Bornstein & M. E. Lamb (Eds.), *Developmental psychology: An advanced textbook* (4th ed., pp. 503–554). Hillsdale, NJ: Lawrence Erlbaum.

Eckerman, C. O., & Stein, M. R. (1990). How imitation begets imitation and toddlers' generation of games. *Developmental Psychology, 26,* 370–378.

English, K., Goldstein, H., Shafer, K., & Kaczmarek, L. (1997). Promoting interactions among preschoolers with and without disabilities: Effects of a buddy skills-training program. *Exceptional Children, 63,* 229–243.

Escalona, A., Field, T., Nadel, J., & Lundy, B. (2002). Imitation effects on children with autism. *Journal of Autism and Developmental Disorders, 32,* 141–144.

Farmer-Dougan, V. (1994). Increasing requests by adults with developmental disabilities using incidental teaching by peers. *Journal of Applied Behavior Analysis, 27,* 533–544.

Farmer-Dougan, V., & Kaszuba, T. (1999). Reliability and validity of play-based observations: Relationship between the PLAY behaviour observation system and standardized measures of cognitive and social skills. *Educational Psychology, 19,* 429–440.

Fox, L., Dunlap, G., & Philbrick, L. A. (1997). Providing individual supports to young children with autism and their families. *Journal of Early Intervention, 21*(1), 1–14.

Frick, P. J., & Lahey, B. B. (1991). The nature and characteristics of attention-deficit hyperactivity disorder. *School Psychology Review, 20,* 163–174.

Fuchs, D., Fuchs, L. S., & Burish, P. (2000). Peer-assisted learning strategies: An evidence-based practice to promote reading achievement. *Learning Disabilities Research & Practice, 15,* 85–91.

Gersten, R., & Dimino, J. (2001). The realities of translating research into classroom practice. *Learning Disabilities Research & Practice, 16,* 120-130.

Ghaziuddin, M., Ghaziuddin, N., & Greden, J. (2002). Depression in persons with autism: Implications for research and clinical care. *Journal of Autism and Developmental Disorders, 32,* 299-306.

Ghaziuddin, M., Weidner-Mikhail, E., & Ghaziuddin, N. (1998). Comorbidity of Asperger syndrome: A preliminary report. *Journal of Intellectual Disability Research, 42,* 279-283.

Gillberg, C., & Ehlers, S. (1998). High-functioning people with autism and Asperger syndrome. In E. Schopler, G. B. Mesibov, & L. J. Kunce (Eds.), *Asperger syndrome or high-functioning autism?* (pp. 79-106). New York: Plenum.

Goldstein, A. P., & McGinnis, E. (1997). *Skillstreaming the adolescent: New strategies and perspectives for teaching prosocial skills* (Rev. ed.). Champaign, IL: Research Press.

Gray, C. (1994). *Comic strip conversations.* Arlington: TX, Future Horizons.

Gray, C. (2004). Social Stories™ 10.0: The new defining criteria & guidelines. *Jennison Autism Journal, 15*(4), 2-21.

Gresham, F. M. (1997). Social competence and students with behavior disorders: Where we've been, where we are, and where we should go. *Education and Treatment of Children, 20,* 223-249.

Gresham, F. M., Cook, C. R., Crews, S. D., & Kern, L. (2004). Social skills training for children and youth with emotional and behavioral disorders: Validity considerations and future directions. *Behavioral Disorders, 30,* 32-46.

Gresham, F. M., & Elliot, S. N. (1990). *Social Skills Rating System.* Circle Pines, MN: American Guidance Service.

Guevremont, D. C., & Dumas, M. C. (1994). Peer relationship problems and disruptive behavior disorders. *Journal of Emotional & Behavioral Disorders, 2,* 164-173.

Hagiwara, T., & Myles, B. S. (1999). A multimedia social story intervention: Teaching skills to children with autism. *Focus on Autism and Other Developmental Disabilities, 14,* 82-95.

Haring, T. G., & Lovinger, L. (1989). Promoting social interaction through teaching generalized play initiation responses to preschool children with autism. *Journal for the Association for Persons with Severe Handicaps, 14,* 58-67.

Heerey, E. A., Capps, L. M., Keltner, D., & Kring, A. M. (2005). Understanding teasing: Lessons from children with autism. *Journal of Abnormal Child Psychology, 33,* 55-68.

Hill, S. (1999). Perspectives on cooperative learning. In L. E. Berk (Ed.), *Landscapes of development: An anthology of readings* (pp. 267-277). Stamford, CT: Thomson-Wadsworth.

Hundert, J., & Houghton, A. (1992). Promoting social interaction of children with disabilities in integrated preschools: A failure to generalize. *Exceptional Children, 58,* 311-320.

Ivey, M., Heflin, L. J., & Alberto, P. (2004). The use of social stories to promote independent behaviors in novel events for children with PDD-NOS. *Focus on Autism and Other Developmental Disabilities, 19,* 164-176.

Jahr, E., & Eldevik, S. (2002). Teaching cooperative play to typical children utilizing a behavior modeling approach: A systematic replication. *Behavioral Interventions, 17,* 145-157.

Jarrold, C., Boucher, J., & Smith, P. (1993). Symbolic play in autism: A review. *Journal of Autism and Developmental Disorders, 23,* 281-307.

Kamps, D. M., Barbetta, P. M., Leonard, B. R., & Delquadri, J. (1994). Classwide peer tutoring: An integration strategy to improve reading skills and promote peer interactions among students with autism and general education peers. *Journal of Applied Behavior Analysis, 27,* 49-61.

Kamps, D., Royer, J., Dugan, E., Kravits, T., Gonzalez-Lopez, A., Garcia, J., et al. (2002). Peer training to facilitate social interaction for elementary students with autism and their peers. *Exceptional Children, 69,* 173-187.

Kanner, L. (1943). Autistic disturbances of affective contact. *The Nervous Child, 2,* 217-250.

Kavale, K. A., & Forness, S. R. (1999). Effective intervention practices and special education. In G. N. Siperstein (Ed.), *Efficacy of special education and related services* (pp. 1-9). Washington, DC: American Association on Mental Retardation.

Kavale, K. A., Mathur, S. R., Forness, S. R., Quinn, M. M., & Rutherford, R. B. (2000). Right reason in the integration of group and single-subject research in behavioral disorders. *Behavioral Disorders, 25,* 142-157.

Koegel, L. K., Koegel, R. L., Hurley, C., & Frea, W. D. (1992). Improving social skills and disruptive behavior in children with autism through self-management. *Journal of Applied Behavior Analysis, 25,* 341-353.

Koegel, R. L., O'Dell, M. C., & Koegel, L. K. (1987). A natural language teaching paradigm for nonverbal autistic children. *Journal of Autism and Developmental Disorders, 17,* 187-200.

Kohler, F. W., Strain, P. S., & Shearer, D. D. (1992). The overtures of preschool social skill intervention agents. *Behavior Modification, 16,* 525-542.

Krantz, P. J., & McClannahan, L. E. (1998). Social interaction skills for children with autism: A script-fading procedure for beginning readers. *Journal of Applied Behavior Analysis, 31,* 191-202.

Kunce, L., & Mesibov, G. B. (1998). Educational approaches to high-functioning autism and Asperger syndrome. In E. Schopler, G. B. Mesibov, & L. J. Kunce (Eds.), *Asperger syndrome or high-functioning autism?* (pp. 227-291). New York: Plenum.

Ladd, G. W. (1990). Having friends, keeping friends, making friends, and being liked by peers in the classroom: Predictors of children's early school adjustment? *Child Development, 61,* 1081-1100.

Laushey, K. M. (2002). *Using a Concept Mastery routine to teach social skills to elementary children with high-functioning autism in order to facilitate acceptance.* Unpublished doctoral dissertation, Georgia State University, Atlanta.

Laushey, K. M., & Heflin, L. J. (2000). Enhancing social skills of kindergarten children with autism through the training of multiple peers as tutors. *Journal of Autism and Developmental Disorders, 30,* 183-193.

Lewis, V., & Boucher, J. (1995). Generativity in the play of young people with autism. *Journal of Autism and Developmental Disorders, 25,* 105-121.

Lewy, A. L., & Dawson, G. (1992). Social stimulation and joint attention in young autistic children. *Journal of Abnormal Child Psychology, 20,* 555-566.

Libby, S., Powell, S., Messer, D., & Jordan, R. (1997). Imitation of pretend play acts by children with autism and Down syndrome. *Journal of Autism and Developmental Disorders, 27,* 365-383.

Little, L. (2001). Peer victimization of children with Asperger spectrum disorders. *Journal of the American Academy of Child and Adolescent Psychiatry, 40,* 995-996.

Long, N. J., & Fecser, F. A. (1996). *Life space crisis intervention.* Minneapolis, MN: N. A. K. Production.

Lord, C., Rutter, M., DiLavore, P., & Risi, S. (1999). *Autism Diagnostic Observation Schedule (ADOS).* Los Angeles, CA: Western Psychological Services.

Lorimer, P. A., Simpson, R. L., Myles, B. S., & Ganz, J. B. (2002). The use of social stories as a preventative behavioral intervention in a home setting with a child with autism. *Journal of Positive Behavior Interventions, 4,* 53-60.

Loveland, K. A., & Tunali-Kotoski, B. (1997). The school-age child with autism. In D. J. Cohen & F. R. Volkmar (Eds.), *Handbook of autism and pervasive developmental disorders* (2nd ed., pp. 283-308). New York: Wiley.

Matthys, W., Cuperus, J., & van Engeland, H. (1999). Deficient social problem-solving in boys with ODD/CD, with ADHD, and with both disorders. *Journal of the American Academy of Child and Adolescent Psychiatry, 38,* 311-322.

McConnell, S. R. (2002). Interventions to facilitate social interaction for young children with autism: Review of available research and recommendations for educational intervention and future research. *Journal of Autism and Developmental Disorders, 32,* 351-372.

McDonough, L., Stahmer, A., Schreibman, L., & Thompson, S. J. (1997). Deficits, delays, and distractions: An evaluation of symbolic play and memory in children with autism. *Development and Psychopathology, 9,* 17-41.

McFadyen-Ketchum, S. A., & Dodge, K. A. (1998). Problems in social relationships. In E. J. Mash & R. A. Lamb (Eds.), *Treatment of childhood disorders* (2nd ed., pp. 338-365). New York: Guilford Press.

McGee, G. G., Almeida, M. C., Sulzer-Azaroff, B., & Feldman, R. S. (1992). Promoting reciprocal interactions via peer incidental teaching. *Journal of Applied Behavior Analysis, 25,* 117-126.

McGee, G. G., Morrier, M. J., & Daly, T. (1999). An incidental teaching approach to early intervention for toddlers with autism.

Journal of the Association for Persons with Severe Handicaps, 24, 133–146.

McGinnis, E., & Goldstein, A. P. (1997). *Skillstreaming the elementary school child: New strategies and perspectives for teaching prosocial skills.* Champaign, IL: Research Press.

McGinnis, E., & Goldstein, A. P. (2003). *Skillstreaming in early childhood: New strategies and perspectives for teaching prosocial skills* (rev. ed). Champaign, IL: Research Press.

Merrell, K. W. (2002a). *School Social Behavior Scales,* 2nd ed. Eugene, OR: Assessment-Intervention Resources.

Merrell, K. W. (2002b). *Home & Community Social Behavior Scales.* Eugene, OR: Assessment-Intervention Resources.

Mitchem, K. J., Young, K. R., West, R. P., & Benyo, J. (2001). CWPASM: A classwide peer-assisted self-management program for general education classrooms. *Education and Treatment of Children, 24,* 111–140.

Moyes, R. A. (2001). *Incorporating social goals in the classroom.* London: Jessica Kingsley.

Mundy, P., & Crowson, M. (1997). Joint attention and early social communication: Implications for research on intervention with autism. *Journal of Autism and Developmental Disorders, 27,* 654–676.

Myles, B. S., & Adreon, D. (2001). *Asperger syndrome and adolescence: Practical solutions for school success.* Shawnee Mission, KS: Autism Asperger.

Myles, B. S., Barnhill, G. P., Hagiwara, T., Griswold, D. E., & Simpson, R. L. (2001). A synthesis of studies on the intellectual, academic, social/emotional and sensory characteristics of children and youth with Asperger syndrome. *Education and Training in Mental Retardation and Development Disabilities, 36,* 304–311.

Myles, B. S., & Simpson, R. L. (1998). *Asperger syndrome: A guide for educators and parents.* Austin, TX: Pro-Ed.

Myles, B. S., & Simpson, R. L. (2001). Understanding the hidden curriculum: An essential social skill for children and youth with Asperger syndrome. *Intervention in School & Clinic, 36,* 279–287.

Myles, B. S., & Southwick, J. (1999). *Asperger syndrome and difficult moments: Practical solutions for tantrums, rage, and meltdowns.* Shawnee Mission, KS: Autism Asperger.

National Research Council. (2001). *Educating children with autism.* Committee on Educational Interventions for Children with Autism. Division of Behavioral and Social Sciences and Education. Washington, DC: National Academy Press.

Newcomb, A. F., & Bagwell, C. L. (1995). Children's friendship relations: A meta-analytic review. *Psychological Bulletin, 117,* 306–347.

Nikopoulos, C. K., & Keenan, M. (2004). Effects of video modeling on social initiations by children with autism. *Journal of Applied Behavior Analysis, 37,* 93–96.

Odom, S. L., Brown, W. H., Frey, T., Karasu, N., Smith-Canter, L. L., & Strain, P. S. (2003). Evidence-based practices for young children with autism: Contributions for single-subject design research. *Focus on Autism and Other Developmental Disabilities, 18,* 166–175.

Orsmond, G. I., Krauss, M. W., & Seltzer, M. M. (2004). Peer relationships and social and recreational activities among adolescents and adults with autism. *Journal of Autism and Developmental Disorders, 34,* 245–256.

Oswald, L. K., & Lignugaris, B. (1990). The effects of incidental teaching on the generalized use of social amenities at school by a mildly handicapped adolescent. *Education and Treatment of Children, 13,* 142–153.

Peck, J., & Sasso, G. M. (1997). Use of the structural analysis hypothesis testing model to improve social interactions via peer-mediated intervention. *Focus on Autism and Other Developmental Disabilities, 12,* 219–231.

Prizant, B. M. (2002, February). The SCERTS MODEL: Enhancing communicative and socioemotional competence in young children with autistic spectrum disorders. Charlotte, NC.

Prizant, B. M., Wetherby, A. M., Rubin, E., Laurent, A. C., & Rydell, P. (2002). The SCERTS model: Enhancing communication and socioemotional abilities of children with autism spectrum disorder. *Jenison Autism Journal, 14,* 2–19.

Quill, K. A. (1995). *Teaching children with autism: Strategies to enhance communication and socialization.* New York: Delmar.

Quill, K. A. (2000). *DO-WATCH-LISTEN-SAY: Social and communication intervention for children with autism.* Baltimore: Paul H. Brookes.

Rajendran, G., & Mitchell, P. (2000). Computer mediated interaction in Asperger syndrome: The bubble dialogue program. *Computers & Education, 35,* 189–207.

Rettig, M. A. (1994). Play behaviors of young children with autism: Characteristics and interventions. *Focus on Autistic Behavior, 9*(1), 1–7.

Robin, A. L. (1998). *ADHD in adolescents: Diagnosis and treatment.* New York: Guilford Press.

Rogers, S. J., Ozonoff, S., & Maslin-Cole, C. (1993). Developmental aspects of attachment behavior in young children with pervasive developmental disorders. *Journal of the American Academy of Child and Adolescent Psychiatry, 32,* 1274–1282.

Safran, S. P., Safran, J. S., & Ellis, K. (2003). Intervention ABCs for children with Asperger syndrome. *Topics in Language Disorders, 23,* 154–165.

Sansosti, F. J., Powell-Smith, K. A., & Kincaid, D. (2004). A research synthesis of social story interventions for children with autism spectrum disorders. *Focus on Autism and Other Developmental Disabilities, 19,* 194–204.

Sawyer, L. M., Luiselli, J. K., Ricciardi, J. N., & Gower, J. L. (2005). Teaching a child with autism to share among peers in an integrated preschool classroom: Acquisition, maintenance, and social validation. *Education & Treatment of Children, 28,* 1–10.

Schopler, E., & Mesibov, G. B. (1985). Introduction to communication problems in autism. In E. Schopler & G. B. Mesibov (Eds.), *Communication problems in autism* (pp. 1–13). New York: Plenum.

Shaw, J. M., Thomas, C., Hoffman, A., & Bulgren, J. (1995). Using concept diagrams to promote understanding in geometry. *Teaching Children Mathematics, 2,* 184–189.

Sigman, M., Dijamco, A., Gratier, M., & Rozga, A. (2004). Early detection of core deficits in autism. *Mental Retardation and Developmental Disabilities Research Reviews, 10,* 221–233.

Siller, M., & Sigman, M. (2002). The behaviors of parents of children with autism predict the subsequent development of their children's communication. *Journal of Autism and Developmental Disorders, 32,* 77–89.

Simpson, A., Langone, J., & Ayres, K. (2004). Embedded video and computer based instruction to improve social skills for students with autism. *Education and Training in Developmental Disabilities, 39,* 240–252.

Sontag, J. C. (1997). Contextual factors affecting the sociability of preschool children with disabilities in integrated and segregated classrooms. *Exceptional Children, 63,* 389–404.

Stahmer, A. C. (1999). Using pivotal response training to facilitate appropriate play in children with autistic spectrum disorders. *Child Language Teaching & Therapy, 15,* 29–40.

Stahmer, A. C., Ingersoll, B., & Carter, C. (2003). Behavioral approaches to promoting play. *Autism: The International Journal of Research & Practice, 7,* 401–413.

Tantam, D. (2000). Psychological disorder in adolescents and adults with Asperger syndrome. *Autism, 4,* 47–62.

Terpstra, J. E., Higgins, K., & Pierce, T. (2002). Can I play? Classroom-based interventions for teaching play skills to children with autism. *Focus on Autism and Other Developmental Disabilities, 17,* 119–126.

Thiemann, K. S., & Goldstein, H. (2001). Social stories, written text cues, and video feedback: Effects on social communication of children with autism. *Journal of Applied Behavior Analysis, 34,* 425–446.

Thiemann, K. S., & Goldstein, H. (2004). Effects of peer training and written text cueing on social communication of school-age children with pervasive developmental disorder. *Journal of Speech, Language & Hearing Research, 47,* 126–144.

Thorp, D. M., Stahmer, A. C., & Schreibman, L. (1995). Effects of sociodramatic play training on children with autism. *Journal of Autism and Developmental Disorders, 25,* 265–282.

Tsatsanis, K. D. (2004). Heterogeneity in learning style in Asperger syndrome and high-functioning autism. *Topics in Language Disorders, 24*(4), 260–270.

Tsatsanis, K. D., Foley, C., & Donehower, C. (2004). Contemporary outcome research and programming guidelines for Asperger syndrome and high-functioning autism. *Topics in Language Disorders, 24,* 249–259.

Utley, C. A., & Mortweet, S. L. (1997). Peer-mediated instruction and interventions. *Focus on Exceptional Children, 29*(5), 1–24.

Volkmar, F. R., Klin, A., Siegel, B., Szatmari, P., Lord, C., Campbell, M., et al. (1994). Field trial for autistic disorder in *DSM-IV. The American Journal of Psychiatry, 151,* 1361-1367.

Werts, M. G., Caldwell, N. K., & Wolery, M. (1996). Peer modeling of response chains: Observational learning by students with disabilities. *Journal of Applied Behavior Analysis, 29,* 53-66.

Wheeler, J., & Carlson, C. (1994). The social functioning of children with ADD with hyperactivity and ADD without hyperactivity: A comparison of their peer relations and social deficits. *Journal of Emotional & Behavioral Disorders, 2,* 2-13.

Williams, E., Reddy, V., & Costall, A. (2001). Taking a closer look at functional play in children with autism. *Journal of Autism and Developmental Disorders, 31,* 67-77.

Wolery, M., & Garfinkle, A. N. (2002). Measures in intervention research with young children who have autism. *Journal of Autism and Developmental Disorders, 32,* 463-478.

Wolfberg, P. J. (2003). *Peer play and the autism spectrum.* Shawnee Mission, KS: Autism Asperger.

Zeigler-Dendy, (2000). *Teaching teens with ADD and ADHD.* Bethesda: MD, Woodbine House.

CHAPTER 10

Promoting Academic Skill Acquisition

KEY TERMS

Assistive Technology (AT)

Auditory Processing Lag

Authoring Software

Computer-Assisted Instruction (CAI)

Continuous Speech Systems

Discrete Speech Systems

Decoding

Differentiated Instruction

Early Literacy Activities

Graphic Organizer

Hyperlexia

One-to-One Correspondence

Prewriting Strategies

Speech Recognition (SR) Software

Time Delay

❖ LEARNING WITH MS. HARRIS: Success in General Education Settings

Using strategies based in applied behavior analysis, Ms. Harris has made progress in improving the communication and social skills of her students. Their general education homeroom teachers have reported to Ms. Harris that they are impressed with the improvements in the students' behavior. Peers from the general education classes are looking for Ms. Harris in the hallways and cafeteria to ask when they can play with some of her students. Ms. Harris makes a mental note to encourage the peers to direct their requests directly to the students, but she is always excited with this informal feedback that suggests her students with ASD are becoming more socially competent.

Ms. Harris meets weekly with the individual teachers to discuss student progress, share data that are being collected to document progress on skills specified in each student's IEP, and share concerns. One week, just to prove that when it rains, it pours, it seemed as if all the teachers had concerns. Apparently, Craig was refusing to complete written assignments. He would tell the teacher the answers and even compose sentences, but he would not write them down. Laura didn't want to read the books that are part of her accelerated reader program. Chan's teacher is quite sure he could complete the assignments but Chan doesn't seem to pay any attention. The math teacher says that she is worried Anthony won't ever be able to add without using the counting bears. Ms. Harris starts thinking about strategies that are easy to put into practice that she can suggest to the general education teachers to promote her students' success and the teachers' own sense of accomplishment.

Students with ASD may challenge the adequacy of traditional instructional techniques. Age and levels of functioning can have an impact on availability for instruction. Issues related to the triad of core deficits in students with ASD can test the limits of teachers' patience and understanding. Chapter 4 described how teachers can establish instructional contexts conducive to learning. This chapter discusses the importance of IEP teams establishing meaningful learning objectives and how some of the features of ASD may require differentiated instruction. Additional considerations for content areas will be explored.

DETERMINING ACADEMIC OBJECTIVES

The success of educational programming is influenced as much by knowing *what* to teach as knowing *how* to teach. Effective teaching strategies have been well researched but if they are used to teach meaningless or useless skills, the effort is worthless. One of the critical aspects of applied behavior analysis is that any change in behavior must be of value to the individual. Learning constitutes changes in behavior. Therefore, teachers should carefully consider which skills to teach (Olley & Reeve, 1997). For students who may be eligible for special education services, the skill set is typically determined during Individualized Educational Program (IEP) planning meetings.

Students with Autism Spectrum Disorders (ASD) need to acquire many of the same skills as students without ASD. However, they have some unique instructional needs because of their disability. For students with ASD to benefit from interacting with their teachers and peers and achieve success in general education classes, the general education students and the students with ASD need to be working on similar skill objectives. The objectives need to be developmentally appropriate and curriculum based (Rubin & Laurent, 2004). For example, it would be age-appropriate for a preschool child with an ASD to work on identifying colors and categorizing common household objects (which is what most typically developing preschoolers are doing). Not only are those objectives important for language development, but they are also relevant to activities occurring in inclusive environments. If a preschool child with an ASD were working on multiplication problems, there would be an obvious discrepancy compared to her same-age peers.

In middle and high school, it continues to be critical to have reasonable, achievable, and age-appropriate learning objectives. It would not be beneficial to have a student with an ASD sit with a paraprofessional in an eighth-grade, general education history class working on a preschool-level map of the United States while the rest of the students are studying the Revolutionary War. IEPs are written to guide instruction toward attainment of realistic outcomes. Placement decisions are made based on providing the most appropriate means of achieving those outcomes.

In addition to considering the instructional expectations in the general education classroom and their applicability for the student with an ASD, instruction may need to emphasize skills that the student with an ASD needs to acquire but her typically developing peers do not. In these cases, the IEP team will probably decide that intensive intervention in a smaller setting will be more beneficial than putting the student in the back of a general education classroom learning to decode while the rest of the class discusses *Romeo and Juliet.* Therefore the learning goals for many students with ASD will target social interaction skills, functional spontaneous communication, verbal and nonverbal language use, cognitive development, and recreational skills (NRC, 2001; Olley, 1999).

DIFFERENTIATED INSTRUCTION

The wide diversity of learning profiles in students with ASD influence decisions about the type and manner of instruction. Learning profiles can influence which teaching styles may be most effective (Tsatsanis, 2004). **Differentiated instruction** involves tailoring the strategies and expectations to the learning profiles of individual students. Although IQ scores provide a gross indication of general functioning, instructional decisions should not be based solely on the students' cognitive profile (Myles, Barnhill, Hagiwara, Griswold, & Simpson, 2001). Furthermore, teachers need to be mindful that students who have better nonverbal than verbal skills are not necessarily lower functioning (Loveland & Tunali-Kotoski, 1997). Similarly, students who sound very bright because of their advanced vocabularies may have great difficulty comprehending what others are saying (Mayes, Calhoun, & Crites, 2001). Cognitive profiles can influence academic achievement but so can other characteristics associated with ASD such as difficulty initiating interactions with others, problems staying on the topic or making appropriate comments, lack of imaginary play, sensory integration difficulties, the need for rituals and routines, and difficulty with transitions.

As students with ASD age, they may be identified with other conditions that interfere with their ability to succeed. A substantial percentage of students with ASD may be diagnosed with attention deficit/hyperactivity disorder (ADHD), particularly at elementary school ages (Ghaziuddin,

Weidmer-Mikhail, & Ghaziuddin, 1998). Church, Alisanski, and Amanullah (2000) reported that 20% of students with ASD aged 6 to 11 years are diagnosed with attention deficit/hyperactivity disorder. As students with ASD get older, they may be more likely to experience depression (Ghaziuddin, Gaziuddin, & Greden, 2002) and be identified as having behavior disorders by the time they reach middle school (usually oppositional defiant or conduct disorder; Church et al., 2000). Students with Aspergers, because of their cognitive strengths and verbal abilities, may appear to be defiant and insubordinate as their social deficit negatively influences their ability to modulate responses (Tsatsanis, Foley, & Donehower, 2004). Confrontational interactions may further exacerbate depression and anxiety (Bellini, 2004). A majority of students functioning on the higher end of the spectrum are on medication to address these coexisting conditions, including obsessive compulsive disorders (Church et al., 2000). Coexisting conditions and the side effects of medications may need to be considered during instructional planning.

Students' ages may also have implications for instructional content and materials. Age influences instructional planning in two major ways: First, students with more significant impairments tend to be identified at younger ages than students with milder impairments (Howlin, 2003). Students on the higher functioning end of the spectrum may not be diagnosed until they are older because their impairments are less obvious (Baird et al., 2001). Indeed, students on the higher functioning end of the spectrum may not be identified until late elementary or middle school, or even as an adult (Williams, 1992). Therefore, the age at diagnosis can provide some insight into severity, and it is possible that even high school teachers may be working with students who have yet to be diagnosed with ASD.

Second, the age of the student needs to be considered when identifying materials and activities to be used for instruction. This may be particularly critical for students functioning on the lower end of the spectrum as they grow older. When older students are seen with toys associated with younger children, they suffer more social stigmatization. However, some students seem to prefer materials that are associated with younger children. For example, it may be prudent to teach an adolescent with an ASD that he can look at his "Little Golden Books" only when he is in a private setting.

Students' insistence on sameness of rules, routines, and rituals can be addressed by using external supports (e.g., visual schedules, written daily agendas). Known upcoming changes in the schedule can be reviewed well in advance. Students who are bothered when peers break classroom rules need to be taught that there are times when rules can be broken and how to self-monitor and regulate their emotional behavior in those situations. For students functioning on the higher end of the spectrum, teachers may have to provide explicit explanations about how and why mastering the content will be relevant to the students' lives (Myles & Simpson, 2001).

During high school, options for types of instruction and placement need to be carefully considered. By high school, the IEP teams, including the student as a member if possible, already should have had many discussions about realistic postschool outcomes for the student. In order to achieve those outcomes, the student might need a variety of instructional programs. Options can range from a traditional school program (general education inclusion, resource, or self-contained classrooms) to programs that involve attending a traditional school for core academic classes for half of a day and attending a vocational training program during the other half of the day. Additional variations include receiving academic instruction through combinations of traditional courses and independent course work done on campus, attending an alternative setting (e.g., night school), or enrolling in advanced courses at a local community college (Church et al., 2000). The option of accessing instruction online can mitigate the social barriers to learning for some students with ASD, and enrolling in advanced courses may better match the student's abilities.

The IEP team is responsible for establishing and monitoring relevant goals that promote independent functioning and successful performance. Characteristics of the population will influence the delivery of instruction. For students with ASD, differentiated instruction may include strategies that facilitate listening, enhance motivation to learn, and increase engagement through the use of assistive technology (including computer-assisted instruction).

Facilitating Listening

Students with ASD who do not *appear* to be paying attention to ongoing instruction (e.g., while the teacher is lecturing on science, the student puts his head down on the desk and closes his eyes) may actually be listening and learning. Conversely, intense attention may not indicate that the student focused on the lesson or that he heard what the teacher was saying. Many individuals with ASD have an **auditory processing lag** (Wong & Wong, 1991) in which they do not process auditory information as quickly as others so they need additional time to interpret verbal instructions. Students with ASD may also have difficulty processing auditory and visual information when presented simultaneously (Myles & Simpson, 1998). Students may need to be given time to process auditory information, and teachers should verify that the student is comprehending verbal explanations and instructions. It may be helpful to explain lesson outcomes and write them on the board as a reminder of the expectations. After explanations, directions, and instruction, teachers can judge the student's comprehension of the material. There are a variety of assessment measures (e.g., standard tests or quizzes, projects, reflection logs, presentations, or compilation of a portfolio) for verifying student comprehension.

Listening may be aided by providing students with tangible items related to the content. Students functioning on the lower end of the spectrum may need to hold objects related to the discussion. Teachers can vary their voice tone and use inflection and prosody that the student finds interesting. Students with ASDs may not respond well to information delivered in a monotone voice (Lamers & Hall, 2003). Students functioning on the higher end of the spectrum may benefit from having outlines of the material to study ahead of time. Koegel, Koegel, Frea, and Green-Hopkins (2003) found that priming by reviewing worksheets prior to class increased academic performance for two students with ASD. Similarly, teachers can prepare outlines of the information with key words and phrases missing (similar to cloze procedures) and prompt the student to fill in the blanks at the appropriate times.

For students functioning on the higher end of the spectrum, there are two commonly used options for taking notes during class sessions: recording the lecture and later transcribing or having someone transcribe the notes (Myles & Adreon, 2001), and having someone, such as a peer, take notes. If the student's IEP team recommends a notetaker, the person taking notes can use carbonless NCR paper (National Cash Register paper available from RIT Campus Connections, 585-475-2504; Hastings et al., 1997). This paper allows the peer to write notes, separate the two pages, and give the student an immediate copy of the lecture. Alternately, in classes with multiple sections, a good notetaker can take notes during the first section and photocopy the notes for the students with ASD who will be in subsequent sections. Using White-out® to conceal key words can encourage the student with an ASD to listen so that she can fill in those key words. The tactile properties of the White-out® serves as an additional cue that words are missing.

The use of visual cues and supplemental materials to accompany auditory presentation of content can facilitate engagement during instructional periods. As much as possible, teachers should use concise and concrete language to reduce confusion and maintain attention (Myles et al., 2001). Explanations of abstract concepts need to be accompanied by hands-on and realistic applications to help the students understand those concepts.

Enhancing Motivation to Learn

Teachers typically plan how they can motivate students to remain engaged and complete assigned tasks. This can be particularly challenging for students with ASD who may not be as invested in the social aspects of learning and uninterested in grades or praise. Incorporating special interests and topics can greatly enhance motivation. For students functioning at the higher end of the spectrum, instruction related to their topics of special interest or special skill not only benefits them, but the entire class as well (Safran & Safran, 2001). Students who are interested in aquariums may be more inclined to complete word problems that involve fish. Students who are fascinated by water may be willing to pick up blocks of specified colors from a water-filled container. All students and teachers might learn from a presentation on mummification given by a student with an ASD during a history unit on ancient Egypt or a science unit on decomposition.

There are times when even the most creative teacher finds it impossible to consistently incorporate the special interests of students with ASD. Still, the interests can be used to motivate the students if they are permitted access to the special interests contingent upon completing their work (Charlop-Christy & Haymes, 1996). A student fascinated by bricks can be allowed to go into the hall and look at the brick wall after he completes a task. Students fascinated with machinery can watch a few minutes of a NASCAR race or home improvement show if they make it through the day without correcting a teacher. Embedding special interests into instructional activities can enhance motivation and promote academic achievement.

Incorporating Assistive Technology

Interventions that employ technology are well suited for the learning styles of students with ASD (Heimann, Nelson, Tjus, & Gillberg (1995) and may increase their motivation to complete activities (Chen & Bernard-Opitz, 1993). IEP teams should meet and discuss assistive technology devices and/ or services for all students with ASD. **Assistive Technology (AT)** is defined in the Individuals Education Act of 1990 (IDEA) as:

> Any item, piece of equipment, or product system, whether acquired commercially, off the shelf, modified, or customized, that is used to increase, maintain, or improve the functional capabilities of children with disabilities. (34 CFR 300.16)

AT includes high-tech devices such as personal digital assistants (PDAs) and read/scan software (e.g., Kurzweil, 2004) as well as the use of low-tech devices such as slant boards and pencil grips. Students with deficits in reading and written expression can benefit from instruction that incorporates AT.

Students should be evaluated on a range of AT systems while performing meaningful, daily work tasks in order to determine the most useful devices and services. Since the learning profiles of students with ASD are so heterogeneous (Tsatsanis, 2004; Wing, 1997), AT methods need to be multi- and interdisciplinary (Hutinger, 1996). Speech-language pathologists and occupational therapists can collaborate during an AT evaluation for a student with significant deficits in written expression. While comparing manual handwriting, keyboarding, and speech recognition work samples across content areas, the SLP may focus on structure, spelling, and vocabulary; the OT may focus on organization as well as motor planning and execution (Diehl, 2003).

AT is used to enhance social skills, communication, and academic performance. AT in the form of a videotape was used to encourage dramatic play among preschoolers with autism (D'Ateno, Mangiapanello, & Taylor, 2003). The preschoolers watched play sequences and skills on videotape and were able to successfully participate in imaginative play situations. Using videotapes as an AT takes advantage of the strengths associated with autism (i.e., visual) and incorporates a highly motivating video medium.

For students with more moderate to severe autism, picture cues can be combined with adapted Augmentative and Alternative Communication (AAC) devices to provide both visual and auditory prompts. Mechling and Gast (1997) found that combining two self-prompting strategies, visual and auditory, was successful in helping students complete a variety of tasks in different school settings. More importantly, the students preferred using the auditory-visual prompting device, which facilitated motivation.

A student who is not using spoken language and has increased his spontaneous initiations through the use of PECS, but who is limited by the symbols in his communication notebook, may be able to use a speech- generating device (SGD) to expand his available language. A student functioning on the higher end of the spectrum who continues to have difficulty completing writing assignments because of difficulty with spelling may benefit from a talking word processor that helps with spelling (Blischak & Schlosser, 2003).

AT should not be used as an alternative for teacher instruction but as a means to provide additional experiences and opportunities for independence. The type of AT used by a student one day may not be successful tomorrow, next month, or in two years. As teachers expand their knowledge base regarding various low-tech and high-tech forms of AT, they can assure students of greater opportunities for success. As teachers establish higher expectations for students to produce more and more work, demand faster completion of written work, and insist on a quicker turnaround of written assignments, access to AT devices can enable students with ASD to participate successfully in instruction (Attwood, 1998).

Using Computer-Assisted Instruction

Another method of incorporating technology involves the use of computer-assisted instruction (NRC, 2001). Because computers require users to focus on a monitor, they may be particularly well suited for individuals with ASD who have difficulty screening out peripheral sensory information (Schlosser & Blischak, 2001). Computers are predictable, which provides a good match for the needs of students with ASD. Most students with ASD appear to be interested in computers, possibly because of the visual and unique auditory stimulation they offer. Computers can be used to increase levels of learning, motivation, attention, response rate, and problem solving.

One of the advantages of using computers is that they provide immediate feedback and reinforcement. They also reduce the amount of teacher or paraprofessional supervision needed (Frank, Wacker, Berg, & McMahon, 1985). Moreover, they can be customized to the student's level of performance and adjusted to the student's instructional pace. **Computer-assisted instruction (CAI)** has been found to be effective for promoting achievement in spelling and math (Baumgart & VanWalleghem, 1987; Podell, Tournaki-Rein, & Lin, 1992; Scruggs & Mastropieri, 1997; Stromer, Mackay, Howell, McVay, & Flusser, 1996), as well as enhancing problem-solving skills (Lancioni, VandenHof, Furniss, O'Reilly, & Cunha, 1999).

SUMMARY OF DIFFERENTIATED INSTRUCTION

Students with ASD bring unique learning styles and preferences to the classroom. Teachers can employ a variety of strategies that range from simple (e.g., augment lecture with visuals) to more complex (e.g., have student

> - Use individual sets of materials for each student.
> - Use a combination of verbal interaction (discussion format) and media.
> - Use five-minute rotations for media/concept presentation.
> - Use a minimum of three sets of materials to teach each concept.
> - Use frequent group (choral) responding.
> - Use fast-paced random responding.
> - Use serial responding—three to five quick responses per student.
> - Use frequent student-to-student interactions.
> - Change delivery style every 20 to 30 minutes (depending on the grade level).
> - Include visual supports to compensate for auditory processing deficits.
> - Incorporate cooperative learning groups.
> - Make use of available assistive technologies.

FIGURE 10.1
Additional Ideas for Differentiating Instruction for Students with ASD
Source: Adapted from Kamps, Dugan, Leonard, & Daoust (1994); Kamps, Leonard, Dugan, Boland, & Greenwood (1991).

evaluated for appropriate AT). Figure 10.1 provides a summary of recommended strategies that have demonstrated effectiveness for increasing engagement and improving critical academic and functional skills of students with ASD.

Unfortunately, little research has been done examining the effectiveness of various strategies for improving content area achievement in students with ASD. A limited number of studies have been conducted regarding basic literacy and numeral identification with students functioning on the lower end of the spectrum. Relatively more research has been conducted to evaluate the learning effects of instructional techniques for students functioning on the higher end of the spectrum, particularly those with Aspergers. What follows is a distillation of teaching implications from research conducted with students with ASD as well as with those with other disabilities. Four core content areas, writing and written expression, reading, spelling, and math will be addressed because of the challenges they present for students with ASD.

CORE CONTENT AREAS
Written Expression

When directed to complete an assignment involving writing, students with ASD often demonstrate frustration and anxiety, which may manifest as noncompliance and defiance (Church et al., 2000). Students with learning disabilities (LD) demonstrate similar difficulties with writing tasks (Gaskins, 1998; Graham, Harris, & Larsen, 2001; Isaacson & Gleason, 1997). One high school student with an ASD described writing as being "physically challenging" (Church et al., 2000, pg. 19). The act of writing requires not only the ability to pull from memory the knowledge of how to form letters, it also requires the ability to execute the motor movement to create letter shapes on paper. Students with ASD have difficulty with visual-motor coordination and controlling fine motor movements that may result in poor pencil control (Myles et al., 2001). Many students with ASD receive services from occupational therapists beginning at a young age and continuing throughout their school years to address fine motor deficits. As many as 58% of elementary students with ASD receive occupational therapy for fine motor deficits related to grasp, handwriting, manipulation of scissors, or the use of utensils (Church et al., 2000).

Another factor that interferes with students' ability to produce legible work is the writing device. Writing with crayons may be more difficult because of their roughness on paper. Instead, using a marker on a whiteboard may be easier for students to manage. Some students express an aversion to using old-fashioned yellow pencils (Myles, Cook, Miller, Rinner, & Robbins, 2000) because of the feel of the varnished outer shell. To compensate for these idiosyncrasies, teachers can supply fat pencils, mechanical pencils, pencil grips, or natural cedar pencils. When using mechanical pencils, note that students with ASD sometimes have difficulty modulating the amount of pressure they exert. Therefore, mechanical pencils, which have thin lead and fine tips, snap frequently and may cause more frustration for the student. Felt-tip pens are described as being easier to use. Their ink flows easily, and in addition felt-tip pens provide contrast to make the words stand out from the background.

Some students have difficulty writing legibly because of the position of the paper. Securing their paper on a slant board can make the difference in whether they complete the task (Myles et al., 2000). Positioning papers on a raised, tilted platform may promote accuracy during writing tasks as well as increase the visual field and reduce glare that may interfere with reading the text from the paper. For younger students, an occupational therapist may provide a table-top slant board that can collapse for transport into different settings. As students get older, they can purchase commercially manufactured slant boards that resemble a clipboard. Figure 10.2 shows a picture of a slant board that appears more age-appropriate for students in high school classes or in community-based instruction.

Cursive writing may be easier to produce than print for some students with ASD because they do not have to lift their pencils between each letter. Cursive writing also helps prevent problems learning how to adequately space between words because each letter is connected into a distinct unit.

If handwriting skills do not improve, even after changing the writing device, materials, support, and style, students with ASD may benefit from acquiring and/or improving their keyboarding skills (Brown, 2004) and producing written products using technology (MacArthur, 2000). Personal word processors (e.g., Alphasmarts, computer laptops, PDAs), speech recognition software, and authoring software may become increasingly important for students functioning on the higher end of the spectrum. Diehl (2003) found that using a

FIGURE 10.2
Slant Board
Source: Heflin and Alaimo

keyboard resulted in writing samples that were more cohesive and longer than those completed using manual handwriting.

Other ways for teachers to help students compensate for problems producing written products include reducing the amount of written work required (Mayes & Calhoun, 2003), perhaps by having a scribe write down responses (Attwood, 1998; Church et al., 2000). Students may be allowed to take notes using outlining (Myles & Simpson, 1998) or authoring software.

Authoring software can bypass the need to write assignments or master keyboarding yet still produces a printed version. **Speech recognition (SR) software,** such as Dragon Dictate™, Dragon Naturally Speaking™, and Voice Express™, have been found to effectively improve writing skills in students with mild disabilities and students with fine motor deficits and/or visual-motor coordination difficulties. SR software circumvents the traditional method of putting information into the computer. Instead of typing on a keyboard, writers speak into a microphone and the computer converts the speech into digitized form. **Discrete speech systems** require the writer to pause between words, while **continuous speech systems** permit connected, conversational speech (Cavalier & Ferretti, 1996). Discrete speech systems are better adapted for nonstandard speaking patterns and can compensate for students who have mild oral-motor deficits or articulation difficulties since the rate of speech is slower due to the required pause after each word (Higgins & Raskind, 2000). Students with ASD who might benefit from access to SR software are those who have word identification skills consistent with at least third-grade level and who can spell well enough to identify the first letter or two of most words.

SR systems allow students to read the text as it is composed. This may be beneficial for noticing errors and being more amenable to correcting them. De La Paz (1999, p. 181) reported that one high school student stated that "composing his assignments through an SR system did not help him get better grades, yet it did motivate him to finish more assignments because his work was completed more easily." The use of speech recognition software may circumvent the fine motor deficits and increase compliance for writing tasks.

In addition to the difficulties related to transcribing ideas on paper, students with ASD may have problems formulating what to write. Students with ASD functioning on the higher end of the spectrum often describe English as a difficult subject. Students report being challenged by the writing assignments (Church et al., 2000) and struggling to organize and develop their ideas. Students with Aspergers have been found to produce the same quantity of writing (although much less legible) as their typically developing peers, but the quality of the written product is noticeably different (Myles et al., 2003). Diehl (2003) speculated that students may have difficulty switching from the narrative writing style taught in elementary grades to the expository style valued in the upper grades.

Teaching students to use **prewriting strategies** (e.g., individualized visual organizers, color-coded assignment folders, planning charts) may help structure and support their ideas during writing tasks (Fullerton, Stratton, Coyne, & Gray, 1996). For example, students can organize and submit their outline or initial draft in a **graphic organizer** such as a visual web (Safran, Safran, & Ellis, 2003). Bedrosian, Lasker, Speidel, and Politsch (2003) found that the use of a "Story Grammar Map" (Figure 10.3) can facilitate written narrative abilities. The technique is based on a visual outline that is simple to follow. Afterwards, students can use the graphic organizer to more fully develop their writing into a narrative or expository text. Providing a word bank that includes essential terms/concepts may support written expression (Moyes, 2002). In order to evaluate the student's ability to synthesize and integrate related material, additional (unrelated) words may be added to the word bank. Skill in written expression evolves over a lifetime and requires a variety of skills including text-production skills and higher-order thought processes (Hunt-Berg, Rankin, & Beukelman, 1994).

Reading

Early literacy experiences can affect a child's development in reading, writing, and language (Hetzroni & Schanin, 2002). **Early literacy activities** begin when infants are exposed to print in a variety of reading materials. The length of time spent listening to stories at an early age influences

Setting

(?) 1. Who is the story about? _____

✗ 2. Where does the story take place? _____

(?) 3. When does the story take place? _____

Problem or Initiating Event

? ♪♪♪ 1. What happens first? _____

?(☹)? 2. What is the problem for the main character? _____

Internal Response

What does the main character feel/think about the problem? _____

Plan

What does the main character plan to do? _____

Attempt

? What does the main character try to do? _____

Consequence

Does the plan work, or not? _____

Reaction

How does the story end ? _____

Title of Story: _____

FIGURE 10.3
Story Grammar Map

Source: Bedrosian, J., Lasker, J., Speidel, K., & Politsch, A. (2003). Enhancing the written narrative skill of an AAC student with autism: Evidence-based research issues. *Topics in Language Disorders, 23,* 305-324. Used with permission of Lippincott, Williams & Wilkins and author.

development of reading skills. Important components of emergent literacy include access to print, opportunities for listening to stories and being exposed to printed text, and the quality of reciprocal interactions that occur during reading. Examples of emergent reading activities include looking at picture books, having students retell a story by memory, and "reading" the popular logos on signs in the community. Emergent literacy activities are beneficial for students with ASD (Koppenhaver & Erickson, 2003; Skoto, Koppenhaver, & Erickson, 2004).

Another way to involve students in literacy activities is through the use of interactive computer software programs (e.g., Interactive Living Books™). This type of computer-assisted instruction can encourage student interactions through the use of stories and drawing/writing tools for emergent reading and writing tasks (Hetzroni & Schanin, 2002). When students showed a preference for using an SGD or a talking word processing program, they demonstrated greater gains in literacy as well (Blischak & Schlosser, 2003).

Computers have also been used to teach word recognition through a stimulus fading procedure to children functioning on the lower end of the autism spectrum (Hetzroni & Shalem, in press). Preferred food items were identified for six students with ASD who did not use spoken language. The logo from the food package was transformed into typical graphic symbols (print) in seven incremental stages. The multilevel procedure was presented by the computer. Each student learned the words for eight favorite foods and most of them were able to recognize the words in natural environments.

Changes in the environment and in activities may help maximize the effect of emerging literacy activities on later academic performance. Suggestions include:

- Increase the quantity and variety of literacy tools and materials in the classroom.
- Make books readily available and keep word processing programs open on the computer.
- Make literacy tools and materials readily available throughout the day.
- Provide time for independent exploration.
- Model appropriate literacy behavior.
- Interact with the students as they engage in emergent reading and writing literacy activities.

Students progress from being exposed to printed text and listening to storybooks to being able to respond to simple comprehension questions based on pictures. Students are expected to exhibit phonological awareness by demonstrating their ability to match letters with sounds in the process of decoding.

Decoding. Lord and Paul (1997, p. 215) succinctly define **decoding** as "pronouncing written words without any requirement for meaning." Many students with ASD amaze their teachers with their astounding decoding and spelling skills. These students demonstrate **hyperlexia** (Grigorenko et al., 2002; Mayes & Calhoun, 1999; Needleman, 1982), which is the ability to speak written text with uncanny accuracy. Often, students with hyperlexia are also good spellers. The astounding decoding and spelling abilities seen in students with hyperlexia are in stark contrast to their poor comprehension skills. Decoding is not an issue for these students, and strategies to improve comprehension take priority.

Some students functioning on the lower end of the spectrum may learn to decode through their visual strengths (Brown, 2004). Teaching sight-word recognition using whole words reduces the demand on students' auditory processing capacities, which are necessary for segmenting and decoding words. Incorporating personal and meaningful vocabulary helps students relate the text to life experiences. Simple matching tasks using shapes, pictures, and so forth can set the stage for understanding correspondence and promote the development of early cognitive skills. Sight-word recognition and matching tasks should be conducted across contexts to promote generalization.

Establishing a functional sight-word vocabulary is important for students functioning at the lower end of the spectrum. As they learn to associate printed words with their meanings (Mirenda, 2003), the students become more independent in community-based instruction (CBI), creating a positive trajectory for postschool success.

Direct instruction (DI) may be useful for teaching decoding to students with ASD and may also be used to strengthen comprehension skills. DI, recognized as an effective instructional practice (Kavale & Forness, 1999), has been used successfully to help students with and without disabilities learn to read (Wilson, Martens, Arya, & Altwerger, 2004). DI incorporates a scripted set of instructional materials and behavioral procedures for teachers to use. These procedures provide a blueprint for the teacher's preparation, instruction, curriculum, and classroom management, and they can be effective for promoting mastery of functional reading skills (Brown, 2004). Although not demonstrated empirically as effective for students with ASD, DI contains a number of components that could be beneficial. For example, DI is structured and predictable. A variety of brief activities are presented and students must respond frequently. A complete description of DI procedures and opportunities for training is available at *www.nifdi.org/*.

Reading Comprehension. Reading comprehension problems are common among students with ASD. Students functioning on the higher end of the spectrum demonstrate strength in comprehending factual information (Myles et al., 2001), although they may become overenthralled with themes, characters, and settings involving fantasy. Students with ASD can improve both their reading comprehension and their phonological awareness of sound-symbol representations using CAI (Heimann et al., 1995). CAI has shown to be effective for students with ASD (Chen & Bernard-Opitz, 1993) and can increase their motivation to remain engaged in the reading tasks. Stein, Klin, and Miller (2004) found that recording reading material on tape or offering the opportunity to interact with books on tape can also help students with ASD complete reading tasks independently.

For students with ASD, stories one or two grade levels below the student's actual decoding and word recognition levels may provide a more accurate assessment of comprehension (Brown, 2004). The use of yes/no, true/false, and multiple choice questions may provide a more reliable measure of comprehension because they minimize the impact of additional language processing difficulties. If a student has difficulties responding verbally to questions, she can point to or circle her answers (Brown, 2004), use pictures that match the choices, and/or answer questions by drawing pictures (Kluth, 2004).

When reading aloud, the instructional, listening, and frustration levels are found to be on par with the grade levels of students functioning on the high end of the spectrum. Yet silent and independent reading skills are below grade level (Myles et al., 2002). Since students in upper elementary grades onward are expected to read independently (Mastropieri et al., 2001), general education teachers need to be encouraged to adapt materials for students with ASD.

❖ LEARNING WITH MS. HARRIS: Laura and the Media Specialist

Laura has been participating in the Accelerated Reader (AR) *program at her school and enjoys going to the media center weekly with a peer buddy from her general education classroom. The media specialist has been watching Laura carefully for the last month and is wondering why this little girl, who barely speaks to anyone else and is in Ms. Harris's classroom part of the day, always selects animal books that are beyond her grade level. She checks the program data and notes that Laura is very successful on her tests. The media specialist decides to ask Ms. Harris about Laura during the faculty meeting. There the media specialist and Ms. Harris decide that Laura could benefit by trying another type of book. The media specialist decides that she will guide Laura toward selecting one of the* Amelia Bedelia *stories.*

The next time Laura goes to the media center, the media specialist asks her to choose one of the Amelia Bedelia *stories. Immediately, Laura's respiration visibly increases, her vocal tone rises in pitch, and she begins to repeat, "No. Kodiak bear," as she inches away from the media specialist. The media specialist worries that she has caused Laura to become anxious and talking to her is not calming her down. The media specialist sends for Ms. Harris.*

As Ms. Harris enters the media center, she notices Laura's heightened anxiety and picks up one of the animal books to attract Laura's attention. She hands Laura the book and Laura hugs it tightly. Ms. Harris knows that talking to a student with an ASD is like pouring gasoline on a fire, so she waits until Laura is calm before initiating a discussion about a compromise. Laura and Ms. Harris agree that if Laura takes out the Amelia Bedelia *book and does her AR test on it, she will be able to take out the book on Kodiak bears at the same time.*

When Laura returns, the media specialist checks to see how she did on the AR test. Again this young girl surprises her: Laura performed poorly on the Amelia Bedelia *test, which is at her grade level, but has done remarkably well on books above her grade level. She seeks out Ms. Harris at lunch. Ms. Harris explains that Laura has difficulty with nonfactual reading material, especially if it uses figurative language (e.g., puns and idioms such as those used in* Amelia Bedelia*). Since Laura seems to be willing to participate in the two-for-one book deal, the media specialist decides to try to identify books that promote understanding of nonliteral language. Perhaps there is even a book with bears that can accomplish that purpose!*

Spelling

Learning to spell involves the ability to identify and form letter-sound relationships, which requires an intact phonological system for auditory and speech integration. Given these requirements, it is not surprising that students with ASD may have difficulty spelling words. As mentioned previously in regard to hyperlexia, some students with ASD demonstrate a remarkable aptitude for spelling. Others have difficulty understanding the sound-symbol relationships and the concept of spelling.

Students' spelling strategies should be evaluated to determine if the errors are rule based, predictable, developmental, or irregular (Attwood, 1998). Appropriate instructional approaches can then be identified for acquisition (e.g., DI, peer tutoring) or remediation (e.g., retest words in oral mode or in recognition format, similar to standardized tests where students choose the correct spelling out of an array of five) (Myles & Simpson, 1998). Some students may benefit from using compensatory strategies (e.g., talking word processor, electronic speller).

Time delay procedures (Touchette, 1971) have been found effective for teaching spelling and math to students with ASD (Ault, Wolery, Gast, Doyle, & Eizenstat, 1988; Doyle, Wolery, Ault, & Gast, 1988). **Time delay,** considered a near errorless learning strategy, systematically inserts more time between presentation of the stimulus and the prompt so that the stimulus begins to occasion the correct response. For example, a teacher may say, "Spell cat" and immediately provide the prompt "c-a-t." With progressive time delay, the amount of time inserted after students have answered correctly a specified number of times becomes longer and longer. With constant time delay, the same amount of time is inserted each time, usually three to five seconds. Time delay provides the correct response initially and then fades the prompt as students demonstrate proficiency with the skill. Incorrect responses or no responses are followed with correction procedures that are the same each time (Hughes, Fredrick, & Keel, 2002).

CAI can be used to improve students' ability to spell functional words (Baumgart & VanWalleghem, 1987). In addition to improving the ability to match words, complete word construction, and work anagrams, some students with developmental and hearing disabilities may show an improvement in writing after use of CAI (Stromer et al., 1996). Blischak and Schlosser (2003) found that students with ASD learned to spell using a computer (providing a mode for writing with visual feedback) and a speech-generating device (providing auditory feedback). The researchers concluded that visual and auditory feedback strengthened spelling performance. In a follow-up study with four students with ASD who did not have functional speech, Schlosser and Bliskchak (2004) found that the use of the print feedback was more effective for three of the students while one student performed better under the condition that combined speech and print. Differences in the students' characteristics might account for the mixed results, once again emphasizing the influence of student characteristics on treatment effectiveness.

Peer tutoring has also been suggested as an effective method for improving spelling in students with mild cognitive impairments (Peach & Moore, 1990). Peer tutors are trained and instructed to:

1. Call out the spelling word.
2. Wait for the other student to write the word.
3. Spell the word orally together.
4. Award points if the student writes the word correctly.
5. Spell the word aloud again if the student writes the word incorrectly. Have the student write the word correctly and spell it orally before scoring points.

As part of the original protocols for peer tutoring, reinforcement involves awarding points for correctly spelled words. The student can exchange these points during scheduled times for specific prizes (Peach & Moore, 1990). Providing prizes that are highly preferred for students with ASD naturally aids in improving spelling accuracy, engagement, and motivation.

Mathematics

Some individuals with ASD demonstrate remarkable mathematic skills, performing complicated computations in their heads (indeed, not knowing how to use a calculator) or using some unconscious integer arithmetic abilities to determine the name of the weekday for any date in time (Cowan, O'Connor, & Samella, 2003). These demonstrations are interesting but may not be associated with functional application of math concepts. There is a limited research base identifying effective and efficient instructional practices for improving math skills for students with ASD (NRC, 2001). The ability to adequately solve everyday mathematical problems can directly affect a student's success in community-based training programs, cooperative work programs, postsecondary education, and daily living. To be successful at math, students need to understand numerical symbols and processes, retrieve the operations from memory, and execute the operations (Berry, 2004).

Basic math skills involve an understanding of quantity (how many blocks are 5?) and numeral recognition. Most beginning curricula start with counting objects and teaching the student **one-to-one correspondence** (as the student touches each block, the count increases by one). Typically developing children often start counting one block at a time and then name a few additional numbers before touching the next block. They do not have the concept of one-to-one correspondence. Numeral identification can also be a difficult skill for some students to acquire. Constant time delay and the system of least prompts are two ways to teach students to name numerals (Ault et al., 1988). Whereas both of these instructional approaches improve students' effectiveness in naming numerals, the participants in this study were found to learn more quickly and make fewer errors using constant time delay.

As described with spelling, peer-tutoring approaches may also be effective in teaching functional math skills. Using reciprocal peer tutoring (students alternate roles), adolescents with moderate cognitive impairments were able to learn the next-dollar strategy and participate more fully in community life (Schloss & Kobza, 1997).

The use of visual and tactile cues can help students with ASD learn and understand math concepts (Griswold, Barnhill, Myles, Hagiwara, & Simpson, 2002). *TouchMath*™ (*www.touchmath.com*) is one math program that capitalizes on the visual and concrete characteristics of students with ASD. *TouchMath*™ uses a multisensory approach (Berry, 2004; Scott, 1993) that requires one-to-one correspondence touch cues to gain math skills that include computation, grouping, regrouping, time, money, and word problems. The sequence of instruction begins with concrete forms, moves to representational forms, and finally to abstract ideas to promote learning and generalization (Berry, 2004).

Initially, students learn the value for each number by pressing "touch-points" while counting aloud (requiring an understanding of one-to-one correspondence). Significant gains in grouping and regrouping addition and subtraction problems are reported in students with mild disabilities (Scott, 1993), as well as in fluency for elementary students with autism (Berry, 2004). Additionally, both groups demonstrated generalization when presented with new problems. Both *TouchMath*™ and the peer tutoring approach for teaching the next-dollar strategy have the added benefit of using tangible items (e.g., coins, dollar bills) that are readily available for practice and that are easily generalized across settings.

The rote memorization strengths demonstrated by some students with ASD may be beneficial when learning addition, subtraction, multiplication, and division facts. An understanding of the operations behind the calculations may be more difficult to acquire. Many schools use timed tests to determine accuracy and increase the speed of fluency in math calculations. Some students with ASD may have processing speed difficulties that interfere with their performance on timed tasks. As an alternative to paper-and-pencil tasks for increasing fluency, CAI can be used to increase student rates on completing addition and subtraction problems (Podell et al., 1992). Even though results indicate that students with mild cognitive impairments require additional trials to reach criterion, CAI was still found to be more effective than paper and pencil on rote math tasks.

Division can be problematic for students with ASD because of the necessity to perform actions in sequence. For long division, teachers may have to teach strategies such as mnemonics to help students remember the sequences to complete these tasks.

In the typical curriculum, student mastery of simple addition, subtraction, multiplication, and division is followed by introduction to word problems. These tend to be more difficult because they require the student to identify relevant and irrelevant details, a task many students with ASD find challenging. As with other academic skills, animated tutorial computer programs have been found to improve mathematical problem-solving skills on word problems (Scruggs & Mastropieri, 1997).

To compensate for difficulties when writing mathematical problems that require columns, students can be instructed to write individual numerals in separate boxes on graph paper. This helps them eliminate the chance of making errors in calculating digits, especially those with decimals (Moyes, 2002). An alternative is to turn a standard sheet of loose-leaf paper sideways so the students can write the numbers within the column width.

❖ LEARNING WITH MS. HARRIS: Collaborating for Success in General Education Settings

Ms. Harris has a number of ideas that may address the general educators' concerns about Craig's writing, Chan's attention, and Anthony's computation skills. First, she needs to talk to them to see what they have tried. No sense reinventing the wheel if the car is already rolling!

She drops by Craig's language arts teacher's classroom after school and, pleased to find the teacher alone, asks if it is a good time to talk. Ms. Harris finds out that the teacher is already providing written outlines of material for Craig with strategic words removed, so that he only needs to write a few words. Her main concern is Craig's journaling and narrative writing. Both teachers agree that it is important for Craig to improve his writing skills, but they don't want his struggles with writing to infringe on the development of his written expression. They agree that a graphic organizer could be used for the journaling. Craig can practice his handwriting while he writes several words and then use the computer (Craig loves the computer!) to create a full journal entry. Ms. Harris agrees to practice with Craig on the use of graphic organizers. Craig can also handwrite graphic organizers for his other compositions and then produce them on the computer. His keyboarding skills are adequate, and this will provide an opportunity for improving those important skills. He can also type the answers to questions from workbooks on the computer. The two teachers decide that getting Craig to complete assignments on the computer is better than having him sulk and whine about written assignments and not produce anything.

Seeing Chan's teacher at lunch, Ms. Harris confesses that she has been able to successfully capture Chan's attention by incorporating his favorite cartoon character, Pokemon, into many of her activities. Chan is more likely to complete a worksheet if there are Pokemon characters on the page, even if the characters aren't part of the lesson. If she can't figure out a way to work Pokemon in, she will tell him that he can look at a deck of Pokemon cards after he listens to the lesson or completes his assignment. This has motivated Chan to attend and complete assignments. The two teachers discuss Chan's difficulty with auditory-only information and talk about ways to incorporate more visual supports during instruction. Providing Chan with a duplicate book when the teacher is reading aloud may help him stay engaged. The teacher is enthusiastic about trying the ideas, particularly since most of her students like Pokemon.

Ms. Harris hears about an afterschool workshop on TouchMath™, *and invites Anthony's math teacher to go with her. The math teacher is enthralled with the concept of* TouchMath™ *and believes it may be useful for several of her students who have difficulty performing math computations without manipulatives (apparently Anthony wasn't the only one!). Ms. Harris knows that Anthony will benefit from the visual cues provided by* TouchMath™. *After the workshop, Ms. Harris also asks if the teacher has ever tried time delay to teach math facts. The teacher has not, and asks Ms. Harris to come to her classroom after school the next week and meet with her and the floating paraprofessional who comes in during math. Ms. Harris agrees to demonstrate time delay procedures so that the paraprofessional can use them with several of the struggling learners individually and in small groups.*

Ms. Harris is confident that the strategies she and the other teachers have collaborated to develop will be instrumental in increasing the participation and learning of the students with ASD. She knows that the solutions developed this week will need to be modified and added to over time as the task demands change and the students develop.

CONCLUSION

Some students with ASD will be making progress in the general education curriculum for their chronological grade level. Due to their unique skill profiles, other students with ASD may benefit from specialized instruction in skills that their peers have already mastered. Learning will be enhanced when students are in environments that support their sensory and instructional needs. Instructional strategies that are differentiated based on the general characteristics of students with ASD and tailored to the individual student may enhance learning and achievement. The use of a variety of concrete materials accompanied by visual cueing may be instrumental in teaching important concepts. The length and rotation of activities should allow for frequent responding and a sufficient number of opportunities to practice. Assistive Technology and computer-assisted instruction may be used effectively to support engagement and work production. Specific strategies can be incorporated to teach written expression, reading, spelling, and mathematics. Empirical studies provide support for the effectiveness of a variety of strategies for promoting the acquisition of skills that influence learning and achievement in academic content areas for students with disabilities. More research is needed that is specific to ASD. In addition to the suggestions provided in research literature, teachers make minor modifications based on their knowledge of the students. Teachers are encouraged to collaborate to share ideas found to be effective in promoting academic achievement for students with ASD.

DISCUSSION QUESTIONS AND ACTIVITIES

1. Identify five strategies that can be used to promote achievement for students with ASD in each of the following areas:

   a. Written expression

   b. Reading

   c. Spelling

   d. Mathematics

2. You are a special education teacher working with students on the autism spectrum. Ryan, a boy diagnosed with PDD-NOS, is in Ms. Aimes's second-grade class for math and science. After one month, Ms. Aimes comes to you and asks to have Ryan removed from her class. He is not attending to directions, getting out of his seat constantly, and withdrawing from the other students. Describe two strategies you would help Ms. Aimes implement in her classroom to facilitate Ryan's learning without causing a disruption in her class. Please be specific in your descriptions and create examples to support your answer. (Assigning a paraprofessional to Ryan as a support is *not* an option because of the long-term detrimental implications.)

3. Describe five ways that instruction can be differentiated for students with ASD. Consider variations that would be recommended for students in different age groups.

4. Go to a teacher resource center at a college/university or in a school system. Find several different software packages for CAI in reading (decoding and comprehension), math, and spelling. Evaluate the software programs based on how engaging they are and what skills students would need to have mastered prior to using them.

5. Go to either the DI or *TouchMath*™ websites and explore the utility of the programs with students of various ages and functioning levels. Conduct an Internet search to determine if there are other content area programs available that look promising for students with ASD.

REFERENCES

Attwood, T. (1998). *Asperger syndrome: A guide for parents and professionals.* London: Jessica Kingsley.

Ault, M. J., Wolery, M., Gast, D. L., Doyle, P. M., & Eizenstat, V. (1988). Comparison of response prompting procedures in teaching numeral identification to autistic subjects. *Journal of Autism and Developmental Disorders, 18,* 627–635.

Baird, B., Charman, T., Cox, A., Baron-Cohen, S., Swettenham, J., Wheelwright, S., et al. (2001). Screening and surveillance for autism and pervasive developmental disorders. *Archives of Diseases in Children, 84,* 468-475.

Baumgart, D., & VanWalleghem, J. (1987). Teaching sight words: A comparison between computer-assisted and teacher-taught methods. *Education and Training in Mental Retardation, 22,* 56-65.

Bedrosian, J., Lasker, J., Speidel, K., & Politsch, A. (2003). Enhancing the written narrative skill of an AAC student with autism: Evidence-based research issues. *Topics in Language Disorders, 23,* 305-324.

Bellini, S. (2004). Social skill deficits and anxiety in high-functioning adolescents with autism spectrum disorders. *Focus on Autism and Other Developmental Disabilities, 19,* 78-86.

Berry, D. (2004). *The effectiveness of the TouchMath™ curriculum to teach addition and subtraction to elementary aged students identified with autism.* Retrieved January 3, 2005, from the Innovative Learning Concepts website, *www.touchmath.com/* research.

Blischak, D. M., & Schlosser, R. W. (2003). Use of technology to support independent spelling by students with autism. *Topics in Language Disorders, 23,* 293-304.

Brown, L. T. (2004). Teaching students with autistic spectrum disorders to read: A visual approach. *Teaching Exceptional Children, 36*(4), 36-40.

Cavalier, A. R., & Ferretti, R. P. (1996). Talking instead of typing: Alternative access to computers via speech recognition technology. *Focus on Autism and Other Developmental Disabilities, 11,* 79-85.

Charlop-Christy, M. H., & Haymes, L. K. (1998). Using objects of obsession as token reinforcers for children with autism. *Journal of Autism and Developmental Disorders, 28,* 189-98.

Chen, S. H., & Bernard-Opitz, A. V. (1993). Comparison of personal and computer-assisted instruction for children with autism. *Mental Retardation, 31,* 368-376.

Church, C., Alisanski, S., & Amanullah, S. (2000). The social, behavioral, and academic experiences of children with Asperger syndrome. *Focus on Autism and Other Developmental Disabilities, 15,* 12-20.

Cowan, R., O'Connor, N., & Samella, K. (2003). The skills and methods of calendrical savants. *Intelligence, 31,* 51-65.

D'Ateno, P., Mangiapanello, K., & Taylor, B. A. (2003). Using video modeling to teach complex play sequences to a preschooler with autism. *Journal of Positive Behavior Interventions, 5,* 5-11.

De La Paz, S. (1999). Composing via dictation and speech recognition systems: Compensatory technology for students with learning disabilities. *Learning Disability Quarterly, 22,* 173-182.

Diehl, S. F. (2003). The SLP's role in collaborative assessment and intervention for children with ASD. *Topics in Language Disorders: Children and Young Adults with Autism Spectrum Disorder, 23,* 95-115.

Doyle, P. M., Wolery, M., Ault, M. J., & Gast, D. L. (1988). System of least prompts: A review of procedural parameters. *Journal of the Association for Persons with Severe Handicaps, 13,* 28-40.

Frank, A. R., Wacker, D. P., Berg, W. K., & McMahon, C. M. (1985). Teaching selected microcomputer skills to retarded students via picture prompts. *Journal of Applied Behavior Analysis, 18,* 179-185.

Fullerton, A., Stratton, J., Coyne, P., & Gray, C. (1996). *Higher functioning adolescents and young adults with autism.* Austin, TX: Pro-Ed.

Gaskins, I. W. (1998). There's more to teaching at-risk and delayed readers than good reading instruction (Distinguished educator series). *Reading Teacher, 51,* 534-547.

Ghaziuddin, M., Ghaziuddin, N., & Greden, J. (2002). Depression in persons with autism: Implications for research and clinical care. *Journal of Autism and Developmental Disorders, 32,* 299-306.

Ghaziuddin, M., Weidmer-Mikhail, E., & Ghaziuddin, N. (1998). Comorbidity of Asperger syndrome: A preliminary report. *Journal of Intellectual Disability Research, 42,* 279-283.

Graham, S., Harris, K. R., & Larsen, L. (2001). Prevention and intervention of writing difficulties for students with learning disabilities. *Learning Disabilities Research & Practice, 16,* 74-84.

Grigorenko, E. L., Klin, A., Pauls, D. L., Senft, R., Hooper, C., & Volkmar, F. (2002). A descriptive study of hyperlexia in a clinically referred sample of chidren with developmental delays. *Journal of Autism and Developmental Disorders, 32,* 3-13.

Griswold, D. E., Barnhill, G. P., Myles, B. S., Hagiwara, T., & Simpson, R. L. (2002). Asperger syndrome and academic achievement. *Focus on Autism and Other Developmental Disabilities, 17,* 94–102.

Hastings, D., Brecklein, K., Cermak, S., Reynolds, R., Rosen, H., & Wilson, J. (1997). *Notetaking for deaf and hard of hearing students: A report of the national task force on quality of services in the postsecondary education of deaf and hard of hearing students.* Retrieved January 5, 2005, from the Rochester Institute of Technology Northeast Technical Assistance Center website: *www.netac. rit.edu/downloads/* TFR_Notetaking.pdf.

Heimann, M., Nelson, K. E., Tjus, T., & Gillberg, C. (1995). Increasing reading and communication skills in children with autism through an interactive multimedia computer program. *Journal of Autism and Developmental Disorders, 25,* 459–480.

Hetzroni, O. E., & Schanin, M. (2002). Emergent literacy in children with severe disabilities using interactive multimedia stories. *Journal of Developmental and Physical Disabilities, 14,* 173–190.

Hetzroni, O., & Shalem, U. (in press). From logos to orthographic symbols: A multi-level fading computer program for teaching nonverbal children with autism. *Focus on Autism and Other Developmental Disorders, 20*(4).

Higgins, E. L., & Raskind, M. H. (2000). Speaking to read: The effects of continuous vs. discrete speech recognition systems on the reading and spelling of children with learning disabilities. *Journal of Special Education Technology, 15,* 19–30.

Howlin, P. (2003). Outcome in high-functioning adults with autism with and without early language delays: Implications for the differentiation between autism and Asperger syndrome. *Journal of Autism & Developmental Disorders, 33,* 3–13.

Hughes, T. A., Fredrick, L. D., & Keel, M. C. (2002). Learning to effectively implement constant time delay procedures to teach spelling. *Learning Disability Quarterly, 25,* 209–220.

Hunt-Berg, M., Rankin, J. L., & Beukelman, D. R. (1994). Ponder the possibilities: Computer-supported writing for struggling writers. *Learning Disabilities Research & Practice, 9,* 169–178.

Hutinger, P. (1996). Computer applications in programs for young children with disabilities: Recurring themes. *Focus on Autism & Other Developmental Disabilities, 11,* 105–115.

Isaacson, S., & Gleason, M. M. (1997). Mechanical obstacles to writing: What can teachers do to help students with learning problems? *Learning Disabilities Research & Practice, 12,* 188–194.

Kamps, D. M., Dugan, E. P., Leonard, B. R., & Daoust, P. M. (1994). Enhanced small group instruction using choral responding and student interaction for children with autism and developmental disabilities. *American Journal on Mental Retardation, 99,* 60–73.

Kamps, D. M., Leonard, B. R., Dugan, E. P., Boland, B., & Greenwood, C. R. (1991). The use of ecobehavioral assessment to identify naturally occurring effective procedures in classrooms serving students with autism and other developmental disabilities. *Journal of Behavioral Education, 1,* 367–397.

Kavale, K. A., & Forness, S. R. (1999). Effective intervention practices and special education. In G. N. Siperstein (Ed.), *Efficacy of Special Education and Related Services* (pp. 1–9). Washington, DC: American Association on Mental Retardation.

Kluth, P. (2004). Autism, autobiography, & adaptations. *Teaching Exceptional Children, 36*(4), 42–47.

Koegel, L. K., Koegel, R. L., Frea, W., & Green-Hopkins, I. (2003). Priming as a method of coordinating educational services for students with autism. *Language, Speech, and Hearing Services in Schools, 34,* 228–235.

Koppenhaver, D. A., & Erickson, K. A. (2003). Natural emergent literacy supports for preschoolers with autism and severe communication impairments. *Topics in Language Disorders, 23,* 283–292.

Kurzweil Educational Systems. (2004). *Kurzweil 3000.* Bedford, MA: Author.

Lamers, K., & Hall, L. J. (2003). The response of children with autism to preferred prosody during instruction. *Focus on Autism and Other Developmental Disabilities, 18,* 93–102.

Lancioni, G. E., VandenHof, E., Furniss, R., O'Reilly, M. F., & Cunha, B. (1999). Evaluation of a computer-aided system providing pictorial task instructions and prompts to people with severe intellectual disability. *Journal of Intellectual Disability Research, 43,* 61–66.

Lord, C., & Paul, R. (1997). Language and communication in autism. In D. Cohen & F. Volkmar (Eds.), *Handbook of autism and pervasive developmental disorders* (2nd ed., pp. 195–225). New York: Wiley.

Loveland, K. A., & Tunali-Kotoski, B. (1997). The school-age child with autism. In D. J. Cohen & F. R. Volkmar (Eds.), *Handbook of autism and pervasive developmental disorders* (2nd ed., pp. 283–308). New York: Wiley.

MacArthur, C. A. (2000). New tools for writing: Assistive technology for students with writing difficulties. *Topics in Language Disorders, 20,* 85–100.

Mastropieri, M. A., Scruggs, T., Mohler, L., Beranek, M., Spencer, V., Boon, R. T., et al. (2001). Can middle school students with serious reading difficulties help each other and learn anything? *Learning Disabilities Research & Practice, 16,* 18–27.

Mayes, S. D., & Calhoun, S. L. (1999). Symptoms of autism in young children and correspondence with the DSM. *Infants and Young Children, 12,* 90–97.

Mayes, S. D., & Calhoun, S. L. (2003). Ability profiles in children with autism: Influence of age and IQ. *Autism, 6,* 65–80.

Mayes, S. D., Calhoun, S. L., & Crites, D. L. (2001). Does *DSM-IV* Asperger's disorder exist? *Journal of Abnormal Child Psychology, 29,* 263–271.

Mechling, L. C., & Gast, D. L. (1997). Combination audio/visual self-prompting system for teaching chained tasks to students with intellectual disabilities. *Education and Training in Mental Retardation and Developmental Disabilities, 32,* 138–153.

Mirenda, P. (2003). "He's not really a reader . . ." Perspectives on supporting literacy development in individuals with autism. *Topics in Language Disorders, 23,* 271–282.

Moyes, R. A. (2002). *Addressing the challenging behavior of children with high-functioning autism/Asperger syndrome in the classroom.* London: Jessica Kingsley.

Myles, B. S., & Adreon, D. (2001). *Asperger syndrome and adolescence: Practical solutions for school success.* Shawnee Mission, KS: Autism Asperger.

Myles, B. S., Barnhill, G. P., Hagiwara, T., Griswold, D. E., & Simpson, R. L. (2001). A synthesis of studies on the intellectual, academic, social/emotional and sensory characteristics of children and youth with Asperger syndrome. *Education and Training in Mental Retardation and Development Disabilities, 36,* 304–311.

Myles, B. S., Cook, K., Miller, N. E., Rinner, L., & Robbins, L. A. (2000). *Asperger syndrome and sensory issues: Practical solutions for making sense of the world.* Shawnee Mission, KS: Autism Asperger.

Myles, B. S., Hilgenfeld, T. D., Barnhill, G. P., Griswold, D. E., Hagiwara, T., & Simpson, R. L. (2002). Analysis of reading skills in individuals with Asperger syndrome. *Focus on Autism and Other Developmental Disabilities, 17,* 44–47.

Myles, B. S., Huggins, B., Rome-Lake, M., Hagiwara, T., Barnhill, G. P., & Griswold, D. E. (2003). Written language profile of children and youth with Asperger syndrome: From research to practice. *Education & Training in Developmental Disabilities, 38,* 362–369.

Myles, B. S., & Simpson, R. L. (1998). *Asperger syndrome: A guide for educators and parents.* Austin, TX: Pro-Ed.

Myles, B. S., & Simpson, R. L. (2001). Understanding the hidden curriculum: An essential social skill for children and youth with Asperger syndrome. *Intervention in School & Clinic, 36,* 279–287.

National Research Council. (2001). *Educating children with autism.* Committee on Educational Interventions for Children with Autism. Division of Behavioral and Social Sciences and Education. Washington, DC: National Academy Press.

Needleman, R. M. (1982). A linguistic analysis of hyperlexia. In C. Johnson (Ed.), *Proceedings of the second international study of child language.* Washington, DC: University Press of America.

Olley, J. G. (1999). Curriculum for students with autism. *School Psychology Review, 28,* 595–606.

Olley, J. G., & Reeve, C. E. (1997). Issues of curriculum and classroom structure. In D. J. Cohen & F. R. Volkmar (Eds.), *Handbook of autism and pervasive developmental disorders* (2nd ed., pp. 484–508). New York: Wiley.

Peach, W. J., & Moore, L. (1990). Peer-tutoring to increase spelling scores of the mildly mentally handicapped. *Journal of Instructional Psychology, 17,* 43–46.

Podell, D. M., Tournaki-Rein, N., & Lin, A. (1992). Automatization of mathematics skills via computer-assisted instruction among students with mild mental handicaps. *Education and Training in Mental Retardation, 27,* 200–206.

Rubin, E., & Laurent, A. C. (2004). Implementing a curriculum-based assessment to prioritize learning objectives in Asperger syndrome and high-functioning autism. *Topics in Language Disorders, 24,* 298–315.

Safran, J. S., & Safran, S. P. (2001). School-based consultation for Asperger syndrome. *Journal of Educational and Psychological Consultation, 12,* 385–395.

Safran, S. P., Safran, J. S., & Ellis, K. (2003). Intervention ABCs for children with Asperger syndrome. *Topics in Language Disorders, 23,* 154–165.

Schloss, P. J., & Kobza, S. A. (1997). The use of peer tutoring for the acquisition of functional math skills among students with moderate retardation. *Education & Treatment of Children, 20,* 189–209.

Schlosser, R. W., & Blischak, D. M. (2001). Is there a role for speech output in interventions for persons with autism? A review. *Focus on Autism and Other Developmental Disabilities, 16,* 170–178.

Schlosser, R. W., & Blischak, D. M. (2004). Effects of speech and print feedback on spelling by children with autism. *Journal of Speech, Language & Hearing Research, 47,* 848–862.

Scoto, B. G., Koppenhaver, D. A., & Erickson, K. A. (2004). Parent reading behaviors and communication outcomes in girls with Rett syndrome. *Exceptional Children, 70,* 145–166.

Scott, K. S. (1993). Reflections on "multisensory mathematics for children with mild disabilities." *Exceptionality, 4,* 125–129.

Scruggs, T. E., & Mastropieri, M. A. (1997). Can computers teach problem-solving strategies to students with mild mental retardation? *Remedial & Special Education, 18,* 157–166.

Stein, M. T., Klin, A., & Miller, K. (2004). When Asperger syndrome and a nonverbal learning disability look alike. *Journal of Developmental & Behavioral Pediatrics, 25,* 190–193.

Stromer, R., Mackay, H. A., Howell, S. R., McVay, A. A., & Flusser, D. (1996). Teaching computer-based spelling to individuals with developmental and hearing disabilities: Transfer of stimulus control to writing tasks. *Journal of Applied Behavior Analysis, 29,* 25–42.

Touchette, P. E. (1971). Transfer of stimulus control: Measuring the moment of transfer. *Journal of the Experimental Analysis of Behavior, 15,* 347–354.

Tsatsanis, K. D. (2004). Heterogeneity in learning style in Asperger syndrome and high-functioning autism. *Topics in Language Disorders, 24*(4), 260–270.

Tsatsanis, K. D., Foley, C., & Donehower, C. (2004). Contemporary outcome research and programming guidelines for Asperger syndrome and high-functioning autism. *Topics in Language Disorders, 24,* 249–259.

Williams, D. (1992). *Nobody nowhere.* New York: Times Books.

Wilson, G. P., Martens, P., Arya, P., & Altwerger, B. (2004). Readers, instruction, and the NRP. *Phi Delta Kappan, 86,* 242–246.

Wing, L. (1997). Syndromes of autism and atypical development. In D. J. Cohen & F. R. Volkmar (Eds.) *Handbook of Autism and Pervasive Developmental Disorders* (2nd ed., pp. 148–170). New York: Wiley.

Wong, V., & Wong, S. N. (1991). Brainstem auditory evoked potential study in children with autistic disorder, *Journal of Autism and Developmental Disorders, 21,* 329–340.

CHAPTER 11

Organizing Instructional Opportunities in Nonacademic Environments

KEY TERMS

Adapted Physical Education (APE)

Cooperative Learning

Cross-Age Peer Tutoring

Delivery Options

Engagement

Extracurricular

Opportunities to Respond (OTR)

Paraprofessionals

Peer-Assisted Learning Strategies (PALS)

Peer Tutoring

Reverse-Role Tutoring

Self-Management

Self-Graphing

Self-Recording

Supplemental Learning

❖ LEARNING WITH MS. HARRIS: Kinta's Version of Jumping Jacks

Pausing during her task of putting dots on all the numerals on Anthony's math paper, Ms. Harris looked out the window to see who had PE warm-up duty that day. Ms. Reilly was leading four of the first-grade classes out to the asphalt between the buildings. It would be her task to guide the students through about five minutes of calisthenics before the PE teacher came. Since several of Ms. Harris's students were in the group, she continued to watch as Ms. Reilly waited until all the students were evenly distributed on the four lines of a huge square that had been painted on the asphalt. "Great visual cuing," she thinks. "And they did that long before any students with ASD were attending here."

Ms. Reilly instructed the students to do jumping jacks and counted out loud to keep the students going. Ms. Harris noticed that Craig was about half a beat behind the counting, but he certainly wasn't the only one. Suddenly, Kinta (tiring of jumping jacks?) began to twirl across the asphalt, straight toward Ms. Reilly. He had his arms out and his head back and was oblivious to where he was going, but he was obviously enjoying himself. To her credit, Ms. Reilly continued to count as she sidestepped Kinta and watched him twirl by her and off the edge of the pavement. "I think we just identified something else to work on with Kinta!" thinks Ms. Harris.

Students with ASD may perform well in structured environments with consistent expectations and routines. However, some instructional opportunities and activities that occur during and outside of school are less predictable and more flexible by nature. This chapter discusses challenges many students with ASD face in nonacademic learning environments. Instructional considerations will be described that may be useful in promoting participation in those environments. Finally, the unique challenges presented by homework and summer school will be considered.

CONSIDERATIONS FOR SUCCESS IN NONACADEMIC ENVIRONMENTS

Social, behavioral, and sensory characteristics of students with ASD affect their performance during nonacademic classes and activities (Cumine, Leach, & Stevenson, 1998), including art, physical education (PE), music, assemblies, lunch, recess, bus rides, afterschool programs, and extracurricular activities (e.g., swimming, karate, dance). Often, the lack of structure, increasingly complex social demands, ambiguity regarding acceptable behavior, increased intensity of noise levels, and physical proximity with others make these activities difficult for students with ASD (Adreon & Stella, 2001; Safran & Safran, 2001). Moreover, once their level of anxiety rises and their sensory systems become overaroused, students may continue to have difficulty functioning when they return to structured settings (Safran, 2002).

Fine motor deficits, competing channels of sensory input, and visual-motor deficits have a negative effect on the ability of students with ASD to complete art projects and participate in musical activities. Students may be unwilling to participate in these activities because of tactile demands related to such things as touching glue and different textures (Moyes, 2002). During assemblies, pep rallies, and concerts, teachers of students with ASD need to prepare and plan for outbursts related to frustration and sensory overarousal. Students can also be taught to prepare themselves for the possibility of increased demands on their sensory systems (Safran & Safran, 2001). Remedies include issuing earplugs or headphones to reduce the noise for the student, designating a support person, or allowing the student to leave if requested (Safran, 2002).

Physical Education

Most people expect students and youth to participate in and enjoy team sports. However, students functioning on the higher end of the autism spectrum tend to be clumsy and awkward, which creates problems during PE and in extracurricular programs (Groft & Block, 2003). Students functioning at the lower end of the spectrum may not understand the expectations in sports and social activities. Due to the motor issues, as many as 33% of students with ASD receive physical therapy to target movements requiring balance and coordination (Church, Alisanski, & Amanullah, 2000). Students with ASD may have trouble catching a ball because of visual motor deficits (Moyes, 2002). Therefore, during PE and recess times, students with ASD avoid participating by retreating or acting out. If they grudgingly agree to join, but begin losing points for their teams, peers may begin to exclude, tease, or bully them (Adreon & Stella, 2001). Although it is important for students to engage in physical exercise, teachers can avoid placing students with ASD in competitive situations requiring motor skills or an understanding of sports rules. One alternative is to assign the student with an ASD a specific role (e.g., timer or equipment manager). Providing explicit instructions for the game being played and using priming can facilitate participation.

The services of an **adapted physical education (APE)** teacher may be written into students' IEPs. Just like other physical educators, APE teachers are trained to evaluate and promote development in fundamental motor skills and patterns as well as skills for individual and group games in order to improve students' physical fitness and stamina. However, APE teachers receive specialized training in identifying and addressing problems that interfere with motor skill and pattern development (Auxter, Pyfer, & Huettig, 2005). With input from the APE teacher, the IEP determines the types of services and modifications that could be beneficial. Services may range from consultation with the general physical education teacher to one-on-one instruction (Etzel-Wise & Mears, 2004). APE teachers typically meet with small groups of students and facilitate participation in a variety of activities that develop competence in movement and participation.

One aspect of PE that can be particularly challenging for students with ASD is the requirement that students change clothes (i.e., "dressing out"). Most elementary PE programs require only that the students change into sneakers. Teachers can request that parents make sure their children wear sneakers on PE days or provide sneakers with Velcro. For older students who may prefer to wear their favorite shoes and frequently forget to pack their sneakers on PE days, parents may provide an extra pair to leave at school.

For students with ASD in middle and high school, physical education class usually requires a full change of all outerwear. Fine motor difficulties among students with ASD can affect their ability to perform tasks required for dressing and undressing (e.g., buttoning, zippering, or tying). In addition, students with weak proprioceptive and vestibular sensory systems may lose their balance or not be aware of where they are in space and may bump and hit peers accidentally while trying to change. There are options for students who have difficulty changing because of fine motor deficits, slowness, or embarrassment. One solution is to have the student wear PE clothes under the day's outfit. For example, basketball breakaway pants allow students to wear shorts underneath and then just pull the snaps apart on the sides of the pants to remove them. If students cannot manage to resnap the pants afterward, they can wear them open or ask for assistance at a less conspicuous time.

Part of dressing out involves the use of gym lockers for storing clothes and personal belongings during class. Students with ASD may struggle with manipulating combination locks because of their fine motor deficits. Using a different type of lock may be helpful. Although locks with keys are readily available, they often require better fine motor skills than the student has, or the student may lose the key. Some types of locks open with a remote control device that is big enough not to become lost, and they are available in an array of colors so that students can choose their favorite color. The color may also help students find their locker more easily.

To minimize the chance that the student with an ASD will be teased while changing (and for the boys, not understanding that the banter back and forth is typical in that situation), a smaller PE class with familiar peers may be preferable. Of course, priority scheduling is an optimal solution. If the student with an ASD is required to participate in PE only for the amount of time mandated by the state of residence, and is assigned to another nonacademic class the rest of the time (e.g., the computer or media centers), he or she is less likely to develop behavior problems related to PE. These problems can be serious and may include an aversion to school that becomes generalized, victimization, and disintegration of peer relationships. Alternative experiences for developing physical skills and stamina may be necessary for students who do not participate in school-based physical education beyond that required by state law.

Lunch

Students with ASD frequently attempt to avoid lunch period in the school cafeteria (Adreon & Stella, 2001). Whereas typically developing peers enjoy the hustle and bustle of large, noisy groups eating and interacting with one another, the sensory input may cause increased tension for students with ASD. Additionally, peers may tease students with ASD because they are messy eaters due to sensory and motor problems (Moyes, 2002).

A double standard exists between the behavior expected of students who are developing typically and those who have disabilities. It is usually acceptable when a typically developing student decides she wants to withdraw from her peers. However, students with ASD who try to withdraw during lunchtime or recess are usually directed back toward the group. Perhaps students with ASD can be allowed the same opportunities as their typically developing peers during lunch, which may include being able to leave the lunch area once they have finished eating (Adreon & Stella, 2001).

Or students may be able to sit at the end of a table or in alternative lunch locations. Students with ASD may be allowed to leave the cafeteria after they have finished eating to join a small group in an environment more conducive to supporting their social development.

Driver's Education

Although students functioning on the higher end of the spectrum may easily pass the coursework required in driver's education, their ability to successfully learn to drive may be impeded by deficits in visual-motor coordination, sensory perception, and inferential reasoning skills (Myles, Barnhill, Hagiwara, Griswold, & Simpson, 2001). As a result, students may not have the appropriate reaction time to meet the demands of driving. Students functioning on the higher end of the spectrum also tend to insist on an unfailing adherence to rules and may become emotionally charged when other drivers do not follow the rules (Church et al., 2000), which could result in dangerous situations. For these students, instruction in using public transportation as well as taxis may be beneficial.

Extracurricular Activities

Students with ASD may enjoy and benefit from participation in **extracurricular** activities, both at school (e.g., Science Olympiads, chess club) and in the community (e.g., Boy Scouts of America, karate). Students functioning on the higher end of the spectrum are more likely to be interested in participating in extracurricular activities. Several factors influence successful involvement. First, the focus of the activity must match the interests and skills of the student. Students with ASD may do well in clubs that focus on specific skills like chess and those that are related to specific interests like entomology. Second, the advisors and staff of the groups must be sensitive to the needs of all students and accepting of their differences. Teachers can support participation in extracurricular activities by students with ASD by informing prospective group leaders and members about the characteristics of students with ASD and offering to provide technical assistance if requested. Finally, teachers may need to meet with their students with ASD to identify and explain the unspoken social rules and expectations of the specific club (Safran & Safran, 2001).

OTHER INSTRUCTIONAL CONSIDERATIONS

Students learn throughout the day, whether they are in academic content classes, nonacademic classes, participating in assemblies, navigating the lunch line, or participating in extracurricular activities. During all of these activities, additional support may be useful for enhancing engagement and facilitating participation. These include opportunities to respond, grouping, peer tutoring, Peer-Assisted Learning Strategies (PALS), cooperative learning, use of paraprofessionals, and self-management.

❖ LEARNING WITH MS. HARRIS: Running Out of Time!

"So little time!" laments Ms. Harris to her general education colleague, Mr. Shael, as they wait for the students to be released from PE. "There is so much the students are capable of learning, but I just can't seem to find enough time to get to them all. After I spend 30 minutes with each of them individually, the morning is gone. Also, I'm pretty sure that working one-on-one with Andy was what taught him to answer questions only when I ask them and not to answer anyone else."

Mr. Shael looks at Ms. Harris with considerable surprise. "I'm going to infer that your students' opportunities to respond are fairly high when you are working one-on-one with them but pretty low when you aren't. I learned about that the hard way myself. Fortunately, during my first year of teaching I had a wonderful mentor who shared her experiences about maximizing engagement through the use of grouping and peer tutoring."

"I'm glad I whined to you! Please share what you have learned over your career about maximizing engagement!" Ms. Harris exclaims.

Opportunities to Respond

For both special and general education teachers, finding sufficient time to teach everything students need to learn is a tremendous challenge (Kamps, Walker, Locke, Delquadri, & Hall, 1990). Creating ways to maximize learning time in schools has been a dominant theme for all teachers over the last few years. With the goal of helping students learn more, some school systems have added time to the length of the school day and have gone to instructional arrangements such as block scheduling.

Researchers have attempted to identify how time can be best used to optimize student achievement. **Engagement,** the amount of time that students spend actively participating in learning activities, has consistently been identified as critical for achievement (Greenwood, 1991; Hollowood, Salisbury, Rainforth, & Palombaro, 1994; Logan, Bakeman, & Keefe, 1997). Active engagement in instruction for students with ASD may reduce levels of self-stimulatory and stereotypic behavior (Davenport & Berkson, 1963). Environmental variables (such as the use of certain materials) as well as procedural variables (such as method of presentation and prompting used) can have a substantial influence on engagement in students with ASD (Kamps, Leonard, Dugan, Boland, & Greenwood, 1991).

Student engagement in learning tasks is directly related to teachers' providing students with **opportunities to respond (OTR).** OTR is evident when teachers provide an antecedent that engages the student. Examples of antecedents leading to OTR include introducing interesting materials, providing a prompt, or asking a question. Research suggests the maximum OTRs are present when students are engaged in producing something (e.g., written product, project); the fewest OTRs occur during teacher lectures and group discussions.

The use of the strategies described in the differentiated instruction section of Chapter 10 and summarized in Figure 10.1 are helpful in encouraging OTR and engagement for students with ASD. These strategies include using a quick instructional pace with frequent OTR and allowing each student access to a set of materials. In addition, OTR is contingent upon the way the teacher organizes the students for learning activities.

Grouping

Teachers organize students based on a variety of interrelated variables. These include student ability, type of activity, amount of supervision required, and availability of adults and competent peers to facilitate instruction. Instructional activities can be provided to a whole class (referred to as a large group and usually consisting of 25–35 students in general education settings or 8–12 students in specialized settings), smaller groups, pairs, and individually (one-to-one instruction). In addition to variations in group size, a variety of people can provide instruction to the groups. In schools, instructors are usually teachers, paraprofessionals, volunteers, or competent students. Research on students with ASD has consistently shown that using individual and small group instruction produces the greatest achievement if led by an experienced staff member (Kamps et al., 1990). Lower student-to-teacher ratios permit immediate feedback, and ongoing assessment helps the teacher know when the material has been mastered (Gaustad, 1993).

Given that teachers are responsible for instructing all students on their caseloads, it is not feasible to provide instruction exclusively to small groups or on an individual basis without creating a situation that disengages the rest of the students. There are a variety of other instructional options that promote high levels of engagement and are positively correlated with achievement. Use of these well-researched options can allow the teacher to spend time in individual and small group instruction with students who need more intensive educational opportunities.

Peer Tutoring

Peer tutoring is one of the peer-mediated instruction and interventions (PMII) introduced in Chapter 9 and mentioned again in Chapter 10. In this chapter, peer tutoring will be described as it relates to increasing OTR.

Peer tutoring involves pairing trained typically developing peers with students with disabilities in natural contexts to promote (Newcomb & Bagwell, 1995) and reinforce (Hundert & Houghton, 1992; Odom & Strain, 1984) academic skills (Kamps et al., 1998; McDonnell, Mathot-Buckner, & Thorson, 2001). Students of the same age (peer tutoring) and those of different ages **(cross-age peer tutoring)** may be paired. Reciprocal peer tutoring occurs when the students take turns being the tutor and tutee (Gaustad, 1993; Mastropieri et al., 2001). In **reverse-role tutoring,** students with mild disabilities tutor younger students with and without disabilities (Utley & Mortweet, 1997).

Teachers need to deliberately select pairs of students who will work well together. The more similar the peers are (e.g., age, ethnicity, or social class) the greater the influence of tutor modeling on the tutee (Gaustad, 1993). With cross-age tutoring, greater age discrepancies generally provide more exposure to appropriate modeling (Mastropieri et al., 2001). Prior to actual peer tutoring sessions, teachers train tutors and prepare tutoring folders to include necessary materials and instructions (Mastropieri et al., 2001). During peer tutoring, the teacher's role alternates between delivering instruction, monitoring the pairs, and supporting and improving peer-teaching activities (Utley & Mortweet, 1997).

Peer tutoring has been shown to be an effective strategy for promoting engagement and achievement for both the tutor and tutee (Kavale & Forness, 1999). In addition to assisting students who are at-risk in reading (Goldstein, Kaczmarek, Pennington, & Shafer, 1992; Peck & Sasso, 1997; Utley & Mortweet, 1997), peer tutoring can be effective for increasing the tutees' skills in social studies (Kamps, et al., 2002), math (Baker, Gersten, Dimino, & Griffiths, 2004), and vocabulary (Kamps et al., 1998). Tutors also show gains in academic performance due to opportunities to review and practice the material (Gaustad, 1993). Nonacademic benefits include positive changes in behavior and attitudes (Kavale & Forness, 1999).

Peer tutoring requires considerable planning in order to be effective. Teachers must anticipate and address problems. Table 11.1 lists common challenges and possible solutions.

The use of peer tutoring increases OTR for students with moderate and severe disabilities (McDonnell et al., 2001), which can enhance skill acquisition. Peer tutoring may also facilitate skill generalization for students with ASD (Goldstein, et al., 1992).

Peer-Assisted Learning Strategies (PALS)

Peer-Assisted Learning Strategies (PALS) is one specific peer tutoring approach that divides students into reciprocal pairs of stronger and weaker abilities; the stronger student begins the sessions as the "coach" and the other student as the "player." These roles can be reversed during the sessions (Utley & Mortweet, 1997) or remain static. Although PALS is effective across content areas, it is used most for math and reading instruction. Table 11.2 shows the sequence of instruction used in PALS. The teacher's role throughout the sequence is to monitor the process and assess learning.

PALS has been demonstrated to be more effective than traditional instruction for increasing student engagement. Additionally, the strategies embedded in PALS (e.g., paragraph shrinking) offer opportunities for repetition and practice, which fosters achievement (Mastropieri et al., 2001). PALS was designed for students with learning disabilities and may be more applicable for students who are functioning on the high end of the autism spectrum.

TABLE 11.1
Making It Work: Solutions to Peer Tutoring Challenges

Challenges	Solutions
utors et rustrate it t e tutees an ave communication rea o ns e usin sarcasm or name callin	rain tutors in e ective communication s ills an a s to eal it rustration
utors are not as com etent as e ecte in t e content t e are tutorin	Assess t e tutor e ore an an consi er cross a e tutorin
utees o ten al at ein tutore someone t e same a e	Alternate roles et een tutor an tutee an consi er cross a e tutorin
utors ma not e consistent in i enti in an correctin t eir artner s errors	n oin trainin eit er in small rou s or ole la et een tutors se vi eos or re res er trainin sessions
Sc e ulin es eciall it cross a e tutorin	Colla orate it teac ers in ot er sc ools or communit a encies
Stu ent a sences	eac ers nee to ave a contin enc lan it su lementar materials availa le tions inclu e ma in eer rou s o t ree it res ective roles o tutor tutee an o server or error i enti ication an correction avin an assistant su stitute or t e a sent eer or avin t e eer o is resent or in ivi uall

Source: Adapted from Gaustad (1993); Mastropieri et al. (2001); McDonnell, Mathot-Buckner, & Thorson (2001).

TABLE 11.2
Sequence for Peer-Assisted Learning Strategy (PALS)

Sequences	Coach (Stronger skills)	Player (Skill improvement needed)
artner ea in Sessions e in it t e coac minutes total	ea s alou or minutes	ollo s t e coac an rea s alou or t e ne t minutes
Stor etell minutes total		Se uences t e ma or events o t e stor or minutes
ara ra S rin in minutes total	ea s alou ne material or minutes sto in a ter eac ara ra to summarize it rovi e it visual cues to ans er com re ension uestions in or s or less	ollo s t e coac an rea s alou or minutes sto in a ter eac ara ra to summarize it rovi e it visual cues to ans er com re ension uestions in or s or less
re iction ela minutes total	Coac an la er continue aire rea in summarizin an re ictin at ill a en ne t or minutes	Coac an la er continue aire rea in summarizin an re ictin at ill a en ne t or minutes

Source: Adapted from Utley & Mortweet (1997).

Cooperative Learning

Whereas peer tutoring and PALS focus on one of the students proving correct responses while the other student checks accuracy, **cooperative learning** requires that the students work together to create mutually beneficial outcomes. Cooperative learning groups increase school performance (NRC, 2001) and enhance OTR while simultaneously providing opportunities for students to learn how to cooperate and interact with each other.

Groups used for cooperative learning are small, usually consisting of three to five typical students in addition to the student with an ASD (Kamps et al., 2002). Members should have diverse abilities so that the group is heterogeneous. Membership is not static but may change at the teacher's discretion as the requirements of the task vary. Tasks used with cooperative learning are set up so that they cannot be accomplished unless everyone contributes (positive interdependence). Contributions are also evaluated individually (individual responsibility). Students are specifically taught the skills necessary to cooperate. Group members are assigned different tasks that promote the overall functioning of the group. The roles assigned change frequently so that each student is given the opportunity to gain expertise in all roles. Cooperative learning has been shown to produce measurable outcomes and generalization of skills among students with ASD (Dugan et al., 1995; Kamps et al., 2002).

For students with ASD whose core characteristics include social, communication, and behavior deficits, interacting and cooperating with others in a group setting can be frustrating. Students with ASD may need specific instruction for the behaviors that are necessary for group functioning (Safran & Safran, 2001). Using visual supports such as simple written directions may be helpful. For students with ASD who tend to dominate group discussions, visual reminders such as a timer can provide concrete cues. While students with ASD are learning essential prosocial skills and the students without disabilities are learning how to model, promote, and reinforce appropriate social and communication skills, it may be necessary for teachers to increase the structure of the academic cooperative learning groups. The teacher may assign students with ASD particular roles in the group, based on their abilities and interests (Myles & Southwick, 1999). For example, the teacher would not assign the role of recorder to the student with an ASD since she would probably react negatively to any writing task. On the other hand, the student may be assigned as timekeeper since she enjoys watching the clock and setting the alarm on her watch.

Although peer tutoring and cooperative learning groups improve academic performance for students with ASD, teachers need to continue arranging multiple **delivery options** (e.g., small group, whole group, one-on-one) and planning frequent and varied trials for student responses. Additionally, the peers need to be trained so that they do not complete the work for the student. Mathes et al. (2003) compared PALS, teacher-directed small group, and traditional delivery of instruction to struggling first-grade readers. Results indicate that teacher-directed small group instruction results in the greatest student performance, followed by peer-assisted learning groups, and finally, traditional delivery models. Similar results were found for students with ASD (Kamps et al., 1990).

Use of Paraprofessionals

Use of peers as tutors or cooperative group members requires that students with ASD have access to typical learning environments. Frequently, an adult is assigned to go with the student with an ASD into the general education classroom in order to promote participation and engagement in academic as well as social activities. The adult who provides this assistance is called a **paraprofessional,** paraeducator, teacher's aide, or instructional assistant (Giangreco, Edelman, & Broer, 2003). The term *paraprofessional* will be used here. Paraprofessionals also work with students in special education classrooms.

The paraprofessional offers social support in inclusive settings and helps the student with an ASD problem solve situations. Concurrently, the teacher helps the typically developing peers understand the abilities of the student with an ASD and value his special skills (e.g., computer graphics, math) (Safran & Safran, 2001).

Although paraprofessionals provide important instructional support in general education classrooms, they should be used with caution and faded as quickly as possible. A paraprofessional accompanying a student with an ASD into a general education classroom may have a number of negative effects. Most of these relate to the fact that the paraprofessional is viewed as having the primary responsibility for the student in the inclusive classroom. This minimizes interactions with, and subsequently the role of, the general education teacher (Marks, Schrader, & Levine, 1999). General education teachers report that when paraprofessionals remain in their classrooms, it is easier for them to avoid assuming responsibility for the students with disabilities (Robertson, Chamberlain, & Kasari, 2003). The presence of paraprofessionals has also been shown to interfere with the other students' acceptance of the student with disabilities (Giangreco, Edelman, Luiselli, & MacFarland, 1997).

One concern regarding the roles, responsibilities, and effectiveness of paraprofessionals has been and continues to be the inadequate or lack of training in addressing the needs of students with ASD across the spectrum (Giangreco et al., 2003; Tsatsanis, Foley, & Donehower, 2004). A related concern is that an individual with little training and no background in education is teaching the student. Giangreco and Broer (2005) cite this fact as untenable and imply that there would be an uprising if paraprofessionals provided the majority of the instruction to students in general education.

Students with ASD tend to become dependent on paraprofessionals, relying on them to prompt participation rather than responding directly to the directions given by the teacher. This may exacerbate a propensity for learned helplessness (Myles et al., 2001). Paraprofessionals may do the work for the student in an attempt to keep up with the rest of the class. Other strategies (e.g., peer tutoring) should be considered prior to assigning a paraprofessional to accompany a student into general education classrooms.

Facilitating Engagement Through Self-Management

Perhaps one of the more important skills for students with ASD to acquire during their educational career is the ability to self-monitor their (1) social responses to peers and the peers' reactions (Myles et al., 2001), and (2) academic behaviors (Moyes, 2002), such as remaining on task during instruction and being able to complete assigned problems independently. The recognition and evaluation of personal behavior with the intent to perform at a specified level is known as **self-management.**

❖ LEARNING WITH MS. HARRIS: An Expansion of Self-Management

During a team meeting, Ms. Harris and the general education teachers express concerns about students who are still having difficulty paying attention during instruction and staying on task during small group or independent activities. Ms. Harris assures her colleagues that she has been working on these skills in her room, and she has data that show the students are either using or readily accepting teacher direction on the skills of engaging, complying, staying on task, and completing appropriate academic tasks independently.

The general education teachers eagerly ask Ms. Harris to explain what she's doing. Ms. Harris briefly explains how she structures her activities, materials, and settings to promote engagement and how she is using students' interests to motivate their participation. She also mentions that she has started teaching the students to manage their own behavior. The ultimate goal of self-management is for students to have responsibility for measuring their own behaviors, decide whether they're on track or not, and then change their behavior if necessary. Ms. Harris runs to her room and brings back the sheet Craig uses to self-manage his behavior. The teachers listen raptly as Ms. Harris explains how the system works. Several of the teachers ask if they can have blank copies of the form to use with some of their other students. Ms. Harris goes home smiling about the fact that some of the strategies that are so useful for the students in her class may also be helpful for other students.

Teaching students to manage their own behavior can promote highly successful long-term outcomes. The use of self-management is based on the recognition that students can and should be responsible for their own behavior. Systematically teaching self-management increases the likelihood that students will acquire the skill, transferring control from an external agent to themselves. One component of self-management is **self-recording,** which requires the students to monitor their own behavior.

Self-Recording.   When students are just learning to self-monitor their behaviors, using techniques that provide visual cues may be most effective. For example, cards imprinted with happy faces and sad faces (or boxes with "yes" and "no") can be used to record behavior. A graphic of the students' favorite topic can be created and divided into segments for recording behavior. Figure 11.1 contains a self-recording sheet used with a student who was interested in battleships.

The self-monitoring card can be adhered to the desk or laminated so that it is more durable and can be carried across tasks and classrooms. Based on the abilities of the student, the teacher decides how long each measurement interval will last. For example, students with low rates of engagement may need frequent short intervals at the beginning of the instruction to increase the likelihood of success. A timer or alarm can signal the end of an interval. When the alarm sounds, the student makes a decision about how well he performed a target behavior (e.g., Did he keep his hands to himself? Was he working at the moment he was asked to record his behavior?). At that time, he marks the appropriate face or box or one of the picture segments (Moyes, 2002). A mark on the happy face or a segment would indicate

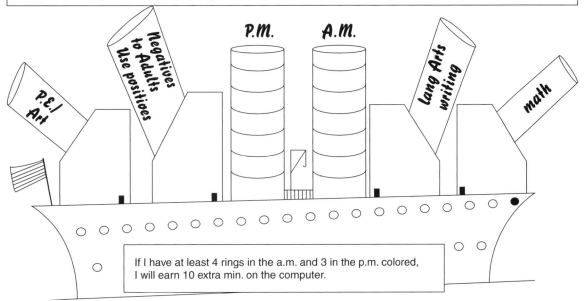

———— is **BATTLING FOR BETTER BEHAVIOR** this week. ———— will also improve his ability to self-monitor and refrain from negative comments toward the adults in his environment for 3/4 class periods. instead, ———— will jot down his negative comment on a sticky and either refrain from any comment or change it into a positive comment. Each time someone indicates to "Check yourself," think about if you are meeting the objectives listed on each gun turret. If you are, color in one of the rungs on the smokestack. If not, leave it blank, put an "X" on it, or write "No."

If I have at least 4 rings in the a.m. and 3 in the p.m. colored, I will earn 10 extra min. on the computer.

FIGURE 11.1
Battleship for Self-Monitoring

a positive evaluation, while a mark on the sad face or leaving a segment blank would indicate a negative response to the question about the target behavior.

During the learning process, teachers make sure that students appropriately mark (or leave blank) the spaces on the recording form. Eventually, external support will be faded, allowing students to record their own behavior with little supervision (Olley & Reeve, 1997). To fade the supervision by the adult, two cards may be used for a period of time. The student keeps one card and an adult keeps the other card. When the alarm sounds, each independently marks the appropriate space on the card. Later, the two cards are compared to determine agreement. Students should be reinforced for marking their cards accurately, even if the answers were negative (Cumine, et al., 1998). Eventually, the comparison process is used less frequently.

Other devices are available to fade the use of an audible alarm. Students can wear wristwatches or belt timers with a vibrating alert (Mitchem, Young, West, & Benyo, 2001; Shabani et al., 2002) to remind them when to record an evaluation of behavior.

Teachers and students together determine the criteria for expected behavior and the reinforcement that follows accomplishment of criteria. Criteria will be based on expectations in the learning environment and the student's ability. For example, although fewer than 10 call-outs per class period is still a lot, it is much better than the 24 interruptions the student originally demonstrated. Some students need frequent opportunities to access reinforcement for their behavior. A student who completes three work baskets and indicates his progress by putting the icons for each basket on a work strip may be allowed an opportunity to choose a preferred activity immediately after completing the work. Other students may need to record their behavior for several hours, days, or even weeks prior to accessing reinforcement.

Some self-recording cards serve as a permanent product of student behavior and can also operate as a communication system between school and home (Moyes, 2002). When families and schools support one another, results are more likely to be consistent, thereby increasing the prevalence of appropriate behavior.

Self-Graphing. In **self-graphing,** students use data recorded on self-monitoring cards to generate a graph, either manually or by typing the data into a computer program that automatically displays a graph depicting behavioral changes, which may increase the ability to self-manage behavior (Gunter, Miller, & Venn, 2003; Gunter, Miller, Venn, Thomas, & House, 2002). The use of computerized data management systems for self-recording and graphing reduces demands on teacher time. Graphing allows students to visually inspect and review data to determine if progress is being made. Graphing can also provide opportunities for the teacher and student to set goals for reinforcement. And teachers can use the graphs to determine if changes need to be made in the student's program.

SUPPLEMENTAL LEARNING

In addition to the instructional activities that occur during the school day, students may engage in activities designed to practice and extend their skills. These are known as **supplemental learning.** Assigning homework is a commonly used strategy for all students, including those with disabilities. IEP teams may decide that summer school is necessary for students to retain the skills they have learned during the school year.

❖ LEARNING WITH MS. HARRIS: Homework Woes

Ms. Harris is concerned because Laura has been coming to school with less and less of her homework completed. She remembers discussing homework at an IEP meeting and recalls that Laura's father did not want the amount of homework reduced. However, Ms. Harris feels that she needs to meet with Laura's father again to discuss what may be happening.

At the meeting, Laura's father explains the difficulty of managing time as a single father. By the time he picks her up from afterschool care, runs errands, and arrives home, Laura is so cranky that it is a constant struggle to get her to do the homework. Her father reports that lately Laura seems just overwhelmed and does not appear to know what she is expected to do. He thinks it is counterproductive to nag her to do her homework.

Ms. Harris thinks that there are probably some ways to help Laura get back to her previous productivity. Ms. Harris asks Laura's father about the old homework routines and what types of things now interfere with homework completion. They discuss whether Laura should be expected to complete all her homework once she starts, or whether she should be able to take some breaks. They also talk about how much help Laura should be given and who is the best person to provide the help (based on Laura's preferences). Given the time constraints of the family (she has siblings), they decide together that Laura should not have to do more than 30 minutes of homework a night. Ms. Harris accepts the responsibility of going through Laura's homework folder at the end of the day, identifying the priority activities, and making sure that the expectations for completion are clearly written on the top.

Together they decide that after Laura has had her bath, she will be asked to choose the activities she would most like to do. Her father will monitor her to make sure that she chooses activities that will total about 30 minutes. She'll be told that if she can complete the activities in 30 minutes, she will get to watch 15 minutes of her animal documentaries before going to bed (an activity that she is not usually allowed to do because the rest of the family is watching TV). If Laura decides that she needs help, she can ask any of her siblings, who have indicated in the past that they would help her with homework. If she doesn't finish her homework or demonstrates inappropriate behavior during homework time, she will go directly to bed and not be allowed to watch her videos. Ms. Harris and

Laura's father agree that the plan has potential and commit to working together to modify it as needed.

Homework

The use of homework as an effective mechanism for enhancing learning is hotly debated in the professional literature, with some suggesting it to be very beneficial and others claiming the opposite (Callahan, Rademacher, & Hildreth, 1998). As the school day progresses, students with ASD may become increasingly agitated due to fatigue resulting from irregular sleep patterns (Patzold, Richdale, & Tonge, 1998; Safran & Safran, 2001) and possibly sensory overload (Attwood, 1998). Sleeping problems may result from the anxiety experienced by some individuals on the autism spectrum (Tani et al., 2004). Students with ASD who experience severe and frequent sleep disruption demonstrate greater daytime behavior problems (Hoffman, Sweeney, Apodaca, Lopez-Wagner, & Castillo, in press). These behavior problems may create more stress on the family (Patzold et al., 1998).

When the family gathers at the end of the day, the student with an ASD and the other members of the family are tired. This can create an unpleasant situation when members of the family prompt the student to complete his homework, which he probably doesn't want to do. To further exacerbate the situation, the student may not remember what was assigned as homework. It is not unusual for students functioning on the higher end of the spectrum to write down only a partial description of the assignment or fail to record anything. When they get home, they may not have packed the necessary materials (Myles & Adreon, 2001). Distractibility, organization difficulties, and laborious handwriting can make the homework process a traumatic event in families' everyday lives (Myles & Southwick, 1999). Teachers and families need to discuss whether homework is necessary for enhancing learning or if it is not worth the emotional stress that it generates. If teachers and families decide that homework is an important component of the educational process, then proactive measures need to be developed to support the completion of homework with minimal stress on the family.

Homework Strategies

Teachers need to ensure that students can do the work assigned as homework. Homework should not introduce new concepts nor require the use of new skills. The teacher should also ensure that students know what is expected with the homework assignment. Reviewing the assignments before the student leaves for the day and adding visual prompts that will help the student remember what to do is helpful. Students should be taught routines for ensuring they have everything they need to complete the homework. Using self-recording, evaluation, and self-graphing has led to the completion of more homework assignments for students with learning disabilities (Trammel, Schloss & Alper, 1994) and may be useful for students with ASD.

The teacher can provide more detailed instructions or an example of the finished product for family members to refer to as a guide. Parents prefer written notes and the availability of a hotline with a recorded message for verifying homework requirements (Epstein, Munk, Bursuck, Polloway, & Jayanthi, 1999). Some school systems provide information about homework on a school website, where teachers list current and future assignments, tests, projects, links to examples, or notes on the subject. Teachers and parents can also communicated through an assignment notebook or homework agenda in which the student records assignments and due dates (Myles & Simpson, 1998).

Parents need to establish a routine at home that includes a set time and place for completing homework. Parents should determine whether their child works best with an adult present (Myles & Southwick, 1999) or if left alone with a self-monitoring strategy in place, such as a timer and checklist. To compensate for handwriting difficulties, children can use word processors, dictate, or record their responses (Myles & Southwick, 1999). The level of involvement of a family member has been shown to be related to homework completion and accuracy as well as correlated with greater gains in learning for students who are at-risk for school failure (Callahan et al., 1998).

For many students with disabilities, modifications are made to the amount and type of homework. Specific modifications for individual students should be determined early in the school year. Parents and teachers can use the *Homework Checklist* (Myles & Adreon, 2001) provided in Figure 11.2 when deciding what types of modifications could be beneficial.

Homework Procedures

Remembering, understanding, and completing homework does not always solve the problem of whether the student submits the assignments. In elementary schools, teachers usually check homework while circulating in the classroom or they collect the assignment and review it later. If a student does not submit homework, elementary teachers usually remind the student. In middle and high school the responsibility for turning homework in at a specified time and possibly even in a designated area belongs to the students. If a student does not submit the assignment, middle and high school teachers may enter a zero and may not notify the student. Students with ASD may end up failing a class because they have not turned in their homework (Myles & Adreon, 2001).

After teachers decide whether they are going to grade homework for completion or accuracy, procedures for how students submit assignments need to be established and practiced. This process should be reviewed until all students are successful, and it should be reviewed throughout the year if changes are made in the routine. The task of teaching students to hand in homework must be assumed not only by the teacher(s), but by family members as well. Family members can verify that completed homework is put in

eci e   et er to *(check one)*
☐ assi n ome or
☐ rovi e a ome or time urin t e a

Select ome or   lanner t at as *(check all that apply)*
☐ enou s ace or t e stu ent to   rite
☐ a s eci ic lace to rite assi nments or eac class

eci e   et er *(check one)*
☐ teac ers ill rovi e stu ent it   ritten ome or assi nment rat er
t an ave stu ent rite o n ome or
☐ teac ers ill rom t t e stu ent to rite o n assi nments in lanner

I t e stu ent   rites o n t e assi nment *(check all that apply)*
☐ teac er s ill ill in t e missin   etails stu ent as omitte
☐ s eci ic as ects o   ome or assi nments not ritten   t e stu ent
ill e i enti ie   an a s stem ill e tau t or t at ortion i e
ue ate
☐ teac er s ill rein orce stu ent s e orts to rite o n ome or

ome or assi nments *(check all that apply)*
☐ are resente in ritten orm in t e same manner an same lace
ever   a
☐ are s eci ic enou   so t at arents un erstan t e re uirements o
t e assi nment solel   rom t e ritten in ormation rovi e
☐ inclu e mo els o assi nments   enever ossi le

e ome routine or ome or com letion inclu es *(check all that apply)*
☐ a esi nate location ree rom istractions
☐ a s eci ic time   en ome or is com lete
☐ s ecial consi erations or t e stu ent   lease s eci
☐ use o te t oo s t at are e t at ome or eas re erence

A met o   or clari in   ome or is in lace t at inclu es *(check all that apply)*
☐ a sc ool ome or   otline
☐ assi nments a e or e maile to arents at ome
☐ a eer u   o can e calle to clari assi nments i nee e

e lan to monitor com letion o an turnin in ome or inclu es *(check all that apply)*
☐ avin a arent si n t e ome or   lanner ni tl
☐ arent assiste or anization o   ome or assi nments in ac ac
☐ teac er rom t to turn in ome or
☐ noti in   arents ee l o an assi nments t at ave not een
turne in

FIGURE 11.2
Homework Checklist
Source: Myles, B. S., & Adreon, D. (2001). *Asperger syndrome and adolescence: Practical solutions for school success.* Shawnee Mission, KS: Autism Asperger Publishing (p. 75). Reprinted with permission of Autism Asperger Publishing.

the correct place in the book bag and can even provide a visual prompt to cue the student to submit it appropriately (Myles & Adreon, 2001).

Teachers should be commended for attempting to set routines and expectations that assure that when the student is given an assignment, it is not only completed, but submitted. For the future success of students with ASD, it is imperative that they learn and practice the skill of documenting a finished product. Whether they elect to enter the workforce or enroll in college after high school, they will be assigned tasks, projects, and other work that needs to be completed.

Summer School

Students with ASD appear to be more susceptible to losing skills that they do not practice frequently. It is recommended that students with ASD receive structured instruction or structured opportunities to practice key skills throughout the year (NRC, 2001) with only brief breaks. How long those breaks should be before they have a negative effect must be determined on an individual basis. The fact that a summer program may be beneficial does not necessarily mean that it must be provided (Heflin & Simpson, 1998b).

The IEP team needs to consider several factors when discussing the types of summer activities that would be appropriate for students with ASD. If socialization is a priority, public schools may not be able to provide many opportunities because most typically developing students will be on vacation. Activities provided through community programs may provide more opportunities for students to extend their skill repertoires and practice the skills they learned during the school year. For students who have been gaining vocational skills during the year, the opportunity to do an apprenticeship or shadow a variety of workers could promote skill maintenance and enhance motivation to continue to learn.

One of the most important factors to consider for students functioning on the high end of the spectrum is their willingness to be involved in a summer program. It is not uncommon for an IEP team to work diligently to put together an extended-year program for students in middle school and high school, only to be told by a student that she is not interested in participating. If the family's culture dictates that the student should be engaged in structured activities during the summer, then the student should be involved in deciding what those activities will be.

CONCLUSION

For many students with ASD, the most challenging school environments are those involving nonacademic subjects, extracurricular activities, and unstructured time such as lunch. Many of the strategies described in Chapters 4 and 10 can be instrumental in supporting students' participation in nonacademic environments. With thought and a good awareness of the characteristics of students with ASD, teachers can work together to support the student's participation in all aspects of the school ecology.

Teachers have control over many variables that exert considerable influence on rates of student learning. Teachers can modify lesson presentation and performance expectations, get creative with grouping, and promote peer-to-peer interactions with the goal of maximizing opportunities to respond to heighten student engagement. Self-management has been shown to facilitate engagement and may be considered when addressing issues presented by supplemental learning activities like homework and summer school. The benefit of homework may depend on the level of involvement of parents and other family members. Some students with ASD benefit from attending structured summer school programs, while others may benefit from having the opportunity to engage in social or vocational activities. As students get older, they should assume increasing levels of responsibility for monitoring their own behavior and being involved in decisions that affect them.

DISCUSSION QUESTIONS AND ACTIVITIES

1. Summer school is a major social issue for adolescents. Interview several adolescents with ASD who are functioning on the high end of the spectrum and ask them to describe what they would like summer school to be like. Also interview teachers of adolescents with ASD who are functioning on the low end of the spectrum and find out what types of instruction typically occur during summer school (also called "extended-year services").

2. With a friend, practice the steps involved in Peer-Assisted Learning Strategies.

3. Identify one of your own behaviors you would like to change and design a self-monitoring program that will effectively modify your behavior.

4. Talk to family support groups for parents of students with disabilities and identify types of extracurricular activities that are available in the community for their children.

5. Develop a flowchart of decisions that need to be made related to assigning, reviewing, and grading homework. List times when homework may be more detrimental than beneficial and identify times when homework may be very effective for promoting generalized skill use and maintenance for students with ASD.

REFERENCES

Adreon, D., & Stella, J. (2001). Transition to middle and high school: Increasing the success of students with Asperger syndrome. *Intervention in School and Clinic, 36,* 266–271.

Attwood, T. (1998). *Asperger syndrome: A guide for parents and professionals.* London: Jessica Kingsley.

Auxter, D., Pyfer, J., & Heuttig, C. I. (2005). *Principles and methods of adapted physical education and recreation.* New York: McGraw-Hill.

Baker, S., Gersten, R., Dimino, J. A., & Griffiths, R. (2004). The sustained use of research-based instructional practice. *Remedial and Special Education, 25,* 5–24.

Callahan, K., Rademacher, J. A., & Hildreth, B. L. (1998). The effect of parent participation in strategies to improve the homework performance of students who are at risk. *Remedial & Special Education, 19,* 131–141.

Church, C., Alisanski, S., & Amanullah, S. (2000). The social, behavioral, and academic experiences of children with Asperger syndrome. *Focus on Autism and Other Developmental Disabilities, 15,* 12–20.

Cumine, V., Leach, J., & Stevenson, G. (1998). *Asperger syndrome: A practical guide for teachers.* London: David Fulton.

Davenport, R. K., & Berkson, G. (1963). Stereotyped movements of mental defectives: Effects of novel objects. *American Journal of Mental Deficiency, 67,* 879–882.

Dugan, E., Kamps, D., Leonard, B., Watkins, N., Rehinberger, A., & Stackhaus, J. (1995). Effects of cooperative learning groups during social studies for students with autism and fourth-grade peers. *Journal of Applied Behavior Analysis, 28,* 175–188.

Epstein, M. H., Munk, D. D., Bursuck, W. D., Polloway, E. A., & Jayanthi, M. (1999). Strategies for improving home-school communication about homework for students with disabilities. *The Journal of Special Education, 33,* 166–176.

Etzel-Wise, D., & Mears, B. (2004). Adapted physical education and therapeutic recreation in schools. *Intervention in School and Clinic, 39,* 223–232.

Gaustad, J. (1993). Peer and cross-age tutoring. *Emergency Librarian, 21,* 34–36.

Giangreco, M. F., & Broer, S. M. (2005). Questionable utilization of paraprofessionals in inclusive schools: Are we addressing symptoms or root causes? *Focus on Autism and other Developmental Disabilities, 20,* 10–26.

Giangreco, M. F., Edelman, S. W., & Broer, S. M. (2003). Schoolwide planning to improve paraeducator supports. *Exceptional Children, 70,* 63–79.

Giangreco, M. F., Edelman, S. W., Luiselli, T. E., & MacFarland, S. Z. (1997). Helping or hovering? Effects of instructional assistant proximity on students with disabilities. *Exceptional Children, 64,* 7–18.

Goldstein, H., Kaczmarek, L., Pennington, R., & Shafer, K. (1992). Peer-mediated intervention: Attending to, commenting on, and acknowledging the behavior of preschoolers

with autism. *Journal of Applied Behavior Analysis, 25,* 289–305.

Greenwood, C. R. (1991). A longitudinal analysis of time, engagement, and academic achievement in at-risk vs. non-risk students. *Exceptional Children, 57,* 521–535.

Groft, M., & Block, M. E. (2003). Children with Asperger syndrome: Implications for general physical education and youth sports. *The Journal of Physical Education, Recreation, and Dance, 74,* 38–43.

Gunter, P. L., Miller, K. A., & Venn, M. L. (2003). A case study of the effects of self-graphing reading performance data for a girl identified with emotional/behavioral disorders. *Preventing School Failure, 48,* 28–31.

Gunter, P. L., Miller, K. A., Venn, M. L., Thomas, K., & House, S. (2002). Self-graphing to success: Computerized data management. *Teaching Exceptional Children, 35*(2), 30–34.

Heflin, L. J., & Simpson, R. (1998). Interventions for children and youth with autism: Prudent choices in a world of exaggerated claims and empty promises. Part II: Legal/policy analysis and recommendations for selecting interventions and treatments. *Focus on Autism and Other Developmental Disorders, 13,* 212–220.

Hoffman, C. D., Sweeney, D. P., Apodaca, D. D., Lopez-Wagner, M., & Castillo, M. M. (in press). Sleep problems and symptomology in children with autism. *Focus on Autism and Other Developmental Disabilities, 20*(4).

Hollowood, T. A., Salisbury, C. L., Rainforth, B., & Palombaro, M. M. (1994). Use of instructional time in classrooms serving students with and without severe disabilities. *Exceptional Children, 61,* 242–253.

Hundert, J., & Houghton, A. (1992). Promoting social interaction of children with disabilities in integrated preschools: A failure to generalize. *Exceptional Children, 58,* 311–320.

Kamps, D. M., Kravits, T., Gonzalez-Lopez, A., Kemmerer, K., Potucek, J., & Harrell, L. G. (1998). What do the peers think? Social validity of peer-mediated programs. *Education and Treatment of Children, 21,* 107–135.

Kamps, D. M., Leonard, B. R., Dugan, E. P., Boland, B., & Greenwood, C. R. (1991). The use of ecobehavioral assessment to identify naturally occurring effective procedures in classrooms serving students with autism and other developmental disabilities. *Journal of Behavioral Education, 1,* 367–397.

Kamps, D., Royer, J., Dugan, E., Kravits, T., Gonzalez-Lopez, A., Garcia, J., et al. (2002). Peer training to facilitate social interaction for elementary students with autism and their peers. *Exceptional Children, 69,* 173–187.

Kamps, D., Walker, D., Locke, P., Delquadri, J., & Hall, R. V. (1990). A comparison of instructional arrangements for children with autism served in a public school setting. *Education and Treatment of Children, 13,* 197–215.

Kavale, K. A., & Forness, S. R. (1999). Effective intervention practices and special education. In G. N. Siperstein (Ed.), *Efficacy of Special Education and Related Services* (pp. 1–9). Washington, DC: American Association on Mental Retardation.

Logan, K. R., Bakeman, R., & Keefe, E. G. (1997). Effects of instructional variables of engaged behavior of students with disabilities in general education classrooms. *Exceptional Children, 63,* 481–497.

Marks, S. U., Schrader, C., & Levine, M. (1999). Paraeducator experiences in inclusive settings: Helping, hovering, or holding their own? *Exceptional Children, 65,* 315–328.

Mastropieri, M. A. (2001). Can middle school students with serious reading difficulties help each other and learn anything? *Learning Disabilities Research & Practice, 16,* 18–27.

Mastropieri, M. A., Scruggs, T., Mohler, L., Beranek, M., Spencer, V., Boon, R. T., et al. (2001). Can middle school students with serious reading difficulties help each other and learn anything? *Learning Disabilities Research & Practice, 16,* 18–27.

Mathes, P. G., Torgesen, J. K., Clancy-Menchetti, J., Santi, K., Nicholas, K., Robinson, C., et al. (2003). A comparison of teacher-directed versus peer-assisted instruction to struggling first-grade readers. *The Elementary School Journal, 103,* 459–479.

McDonnell, J., Mathot-Buckner, C., & Thorson, N. (2001). Supporting the inclusion of students with moderate and severe disabilities in junior high school general education classes: The effects of classwide peer tutoring, multi-element curriculum, and accommodations. *Education & Treatment of Children, 24,* 141–161.

Mitchem, K. J., Young, K. R., West, R. P., & Benyo, J. (2001). CWPASM: A classwide peer-assisted self-management program for general education classrooms. *Education and Treatment of Children, 24,* 111–140.

Moyes, R. A. (2002). *Addressing the challenging behavior of children with high-functioning autism/Asperger syndrome in the classroom.* London: Jessica Kingsley.

Myles, B. S., & Adreon, D. (2001). *Asperger syndrome and adolescence: Practical solutions for school success.* Shawnee Mission, KS: Autism Asperger.

Myles, B. S., Barnhill, G. P., Hagiwara, T., Griswold, D. E., & Simpson, R. L. (2001). A synthesis of studies on the intellectual, academic, social/emotional and sensory characteristics of children and youth with Asperger syndrome. *Education and Training in Mental Retardation and Development Disabilities, 36,* 304–311.

Myles, B. S., & Simpson, R. L. (1998). *Asperger syndrome: A guide for educators and parents.* Austin, TX: Pro-Ed.

Myles, B. S., & Southwick, J. (1999). *Asperger syndrome and difficult moments: Practical solutions for tantrums, rage, and meltdowns.* Shawnee Mission, KS: Autism Asperger.

National Research Council. (2001). *Educating children with autism.* Committee on Educational Interventions for Children with Autism. Division of Behavioral and Social Sciences and Education. Washington, DC: National Academy Press.

Newcomb, A. F., & Bagwell, C. L. (1995). Children's friendship relations: A meta-analytic review. *Psychological Bulletin, 117,* 306–347.

Odom, S. L., & Strain, P. S. (1984). Peer-mediated approaches to promoting children's social interaction: A review. *The American Journal of Orthopsychiatry, 54,* 544–557.

Olley, J. G., & Reeve, C. E. (1997). Issues of curriculum and classroom structure. In D. J. Cohen & F. R. Volkmar (Eds.), *Handbook of autism and pervasive developmental disorders* (2nd ed., pp. 484–508). New York: Wiley.

Patzold, L. M., Richdale, A. L., & Tonge, B. J. (1998). An investigation into sleep characteristics of children with autism and Asperger disorder. *Journal of Paediatric Child Health, 34,* 528–533.

Peck, J., & Sasso, G. M. (1997). Use of the structural analysis hypothesis testing model to improve social interactions via peer-mediated intervention. *Focus on Autism and Other Developmental Disabilities, 12,* 219-231.

Robertson, K., Chamberlain, B., & Kasari, C. (2003). General education teachers' relationships with included students with autism. *Journal of Autism and Developmental Disorders, 33,* 123-130.

Safran, J. S. (2002). Supporting students with Asperger syndrome in general education. *TEACHING Exceptional Children, 34*(5), 60-66.

Safran, J. S., & Safran, S. P. (2001). School-based consultation for Asperger syndrome. *Journal of Educational and Psychological Consultation, 12,* 385-395.

Safran, S. P. (2001). Asperger syndrome: The emerging challenge to special education. *Exceptional Children, 67,* 151-160.

Shabani, D. B., Katz, R. C., Wilder, D. A., Beauchamp, K., Taylor, C. R., & Fischer, K. J.

(2002). Increasing social initiations in children with autism: Effects of a tactile prompt. *Journal of Applied Behavior Analysis, 35,* 79-83.

Tani, P., Lindberg, N., Nieminen-von Wendt, T., von Wendt, L., Virkkala, J., Appelberg, B., et al. (2004). Sleep in young adults with Asperger syndrome. *Neuropsychobiology, 50,* 147-152.

Trammel, D. L., Schloss, P. J., & Alper, S. (1994). Using self-recording, evaluation, and graphing to increase completion of homework assignments. *Journal of Learning Disabilities, 27,* 75-81.

Tsatsanis, K. D., Foley, C., & Donehower, C. (2004). Contemporary outcome research and programming guidelines for Asperger syndrome and high-functioning autism. *Topics in Language Disorders, 24,* 249-259.

Utley, C. A., & Mortweet, S. L. (1997). Peer-mediated instruction and interventions. *Focus on Exceptional Children, 29*(5), 1-24.

Epilogue
What Ms. Harris Learned

What a year! Just when Ms. Harris thought she had completed her education, she quickly discovered that she had much more to learn. The courses she completed in the college program for her cross-categorical certificate in special education certainly provided a solid foundation in human development and basic pedagogy. Although she was confident she could be a great teacher after she completed the program, she soon realized that teaching was going to be a lifelong learning opportunity, particularly with students with Autism Spectrum Disorders. Every day that year had been as unique as the students she taught.

Ms. Harris learned that characteristics demonstrated by individuals with ASD are also demonstrated by everyone else. She was now more keenly aware of her own stimming behaviors and got tickled whenever people repeated phrases. Just recently, several of her friends had a wonderful time repeating lines from *Monty Python and the Holy Grail*. Ms. Harris had an easy time determining the function of that echolalia and wondered if they would like to hear the phrases from *Toy Story* that she had picked up from Chan. Ms. Harris also became aware of her own idiosyncratic sensory issues (she can't stand it when people grind their teeth!) and found the awareness allowed her to be more sensitive to her students' preferences. The demonstration of behaviors associated with ASD by the general population has led to refinement in the classification frameworks for the subtypes of Pervasive Developmental Disorders in the *DSM-IV-TR*. Ms. Harris learned from the parents of her students, as well as from other parents she met who had children with ASD, that securing an accurate diagnosis can be a frustrating experience, and one that has a significant impact on the family.

Ms. Harris learned the history of the recognition of ASD, and was fascinated that Kanner and Asperger were working separately but describing similar populations. How exciting it must have been to begin to recognize that the children and youth they observed shared common features, and how disappointing not to know what caused the differences. Modern technology has certainly provided dramatic insights into the underlying neurology of ASD and the genetic contributions that set in motion the development of the disorders. Future discoveries regarding the genetic and biological components of ASD carry the possibility of substantial implications for diagnostic procedures and implementation of interventions. As the spectrum has become more broad, identification of distinct subtypes, possibly based on etiology or neurological differences, has become more important. Meanwhile, Ms. Harris knows that she can make accommodations to support the behaviors resulting from inferred neurological differences in her students with ASD.

Ms. Harris learned that it can be very difficult for all advocates for the student to agree on what constitutes an effective program. She understands the differing perspectives that must come together and also recognizes the impact of individual personalities. She hopes she has learned to be a more active listener and better collaborator. She gets on the Internet periodically just to see what miraculous promises have emerged. The latest was that individuals with ASD would be cured if they drank raw cow milk and ate butter made from the raw cow milk. She knows it will be something different next week, and her heart goes out to all the parents who are grasping for any straw that provides hope. She also realizes that a lack of empirical validation does not indicate that an intervention is ineffective, just that the effectiveness has not been demonstrated.

Ms. Harris has become quite proficient at scanning an environment and predicting what might create the potential for difficulty for her students with ASD. She learned that her students with ASD performed much better with predictable structure and warning of upcoming transitions and changes. The first time she gave her students true "free choice" ("Go find something to do"), she discovered it was not a good idea. Structure, she realized, was important for providing the support the students needed to be available for instruction. Ms. Harris worked with other teachers to increase their use of visual supports and concrete language during instruction. It took her all year to convince one of Craig's teachers that he wasn't being rude or disobedient when he didn't follow a string of ambiguous instructions given verbally. Ms. Harris learned very early not to take the behaviors of her students personally but to analyze the behaviors for what they told her about the student. Dealing with behavior was probably the hardest issue for Ms. Harris. Putting into practice the understanding that all behavior has a function and should not be suppressed but shaped based on the function was invaluable. Self-stimulatory behaviors, stereotypies, and even self-injurious behaviors communicated something about the student's response to the environment, activities, and social interactions. Ms. Harris promptly learned that she needed to manage the environment rather than the student. She used a variety of antecedent modifications as a part of the Positive Behavior Support plans she developed and concentrated on teaching replacement behaviors that served the same function as the undesirable behaviors. She was very good at providing positive reinforcement for appropriate behavior but sometimes had a hard time using extinction when she was distracted or when the students did something that made her laugh.

Ms. Harris was delighted to be able to share the differences between ABA and DTT with Ms. Nelson as well as other parents and colleagues. She found that taking a step back to look at the science and principles of ABA allowed for more rational and open discussions about a variety of methodologies for promoting adaptive functioning in her students with ASD. Based on her knowledge of ABA, Ms. Harris implements a variety of techniques designed to promote generalization of the communication and social skills she is teaching her students. Ms. Harris continues to read the journals she receives from her professional organizations and looks for strategies with emerging empirical validation that may be useful for her students with ASD.

Ms. Harris enjoyed working with her colleagues, both general and special education, during the year. Her admiration grew for her general education colleagues who managed large numbers of students. She discovered that some of the strategies she used for her students were not easily implemented in their classes. However, together she and the other teachers were always able to derive a strategy for supporting the learning needs of their students with ASD. Ms. Harris found that TouchMath™ was an effective strategy for her to use when computing by hand. She learned to use a variety of grouping strategies very effectively and provided copious opportunities to respond so that her students with ASD were engaged the majority of the time. Self-management worked so well for her students with ASD that she even had herself on a self-management program to talk to her friends about a variety of topics, not just ASD.

In addition to the lessons she learned, Ms. Harris had a great deal of fun. She enjoyed each of her students' personalities and appreciated their uninhibited responses to the world. She got so tickled the day she walked in and the music teacher had all the students holding sticks like microphones while they were singing. The look of incredulous disbelief on the faces of her students was priceless. They were all holding their sticks, mostly by their sides or stiffly in front, but looking at everyone else as if they had lost their minds.

As she had heard from Ms. Owens, her students were not prone to deceit, which made it fairly easy to catch them when they did something they weren't supposed to do. Laura's math teacher barreled into Ms. Harris's room one day after school laughing so hard she could hardly talk. In class that day, some of the students sitting around Laura realized that she always got the answers on the worksheets correct. They started whispering to her, asking for answers to specific problems. Laura, not realizing that this was not an acceptable way to complete a math task, did not whisper back to give them the answers, but spoke in her regular voice. The teacher said she kept hearing sporadic numbers like "467" and "329," finally tracking them down to Laura, whose peers were trying earnestly to get her to whisper.

Ms. Harris learned how proud she could feel when her students with ASD mastered a skill. She also learned that sometimes progress in skill attainment was followed by regression. However, all of her students had made progress on their IEP goals. Ms. Harris was almost as thrilled as Gabe's parents when he received an award in his homeroom class. Gabe had looked so handsome for the award ceremony, wearing his tie (which he took off immediately afterwards, as did his father). Probably the greatest lesson Ms. Harris learned was that she could make a difference in helping the students with ASD develop skills to enable them to take advantage of a variety of learning opportunities and function as independently as possible now and in the future. As she reflected on the year, Ms. Harris remembered a fascinating book the school social worker gave her that had been written by a man who had a brother and a son with ASD. She had copied this quote out of the book and kept it by her desk:

> Throughout his life, which will last as long as yours or mine, he will be confused and challenged by a world that he doesn't comprehend, a world of causes and effects, of words that don't always mean what he thinks, and of human interactions based on gestures too subtle for him to master. Unable to understand his own differences and incapable of expressing his human commonalities, his biggest challenge will be our ignorance and our willingness to judge him on the basis of his behavior. (Charles Hart, *Without reason: A family copes with two generations of autism* [1989], p. 269)

Although she knew she would enjoy the summer break, Ms. Harris was looking forward to seeing the students with ASD who would return to her class as well as meeting the students who would be joining her class. She had learned a great deal this year but knew that she had much to learn and was eager to continue the lessons. As research unravels the mysteries of the spectrum disorders and individuals with ASD share their unique talents and gifts, a mutual respect is emerging, which contributes to the quality of life for all.

Name Index

Subject Index

Page numbers followed by f indicate figure; those followed by t indicate table.